O. HENRY
A Study of the Short Fiction

Also available in Twayne's Studies in Short Fiction Series

Twayne's Studies in Short Fiction

Gordon Weaver, General Editor
Oklahoma State University

O. HENRY
Courtesy of the Greensboro Historical Museum

O. HENRY

A Study of the Short Fiction

Eugene Current-Garcia

Auburn University

TWAYNE PUBLISHERS · NEW YORK

Maxwell Macmillan Canada · Toronto

Maxwell Macmillan International · New York Oxford Singapore Sydney

Twayne's Studies in Short Fiction Series, No. 49

Copyright © 1993 by Twayne Publishers

Twayne Publishers
Macmillan Publishing Company
866 Third Avenue
New York, New York 10022

Maxwell Macmillan Canada, Inc.
1200 Eglinton Avenue East
Suite 200
Don Mills, Ontario M3C 3N1

Library of Congress Cataloging-in-Publication Data

Current-Garcia, Eugene.
    O. Henry : a study of the short fiction / Eugene Current-Garcia.
        p.   cm.—(Twayne's studies in short fiction series ; no. 49)
    Includes bibliographical references (p.) and index.
    ISBN 0-8057-0859-6
    1. Henry, O., 1862–1910—Criticism and interpretation. 2. Short story. I. Title. II. Series.
PS2649.P5Z644   1993
813'.52—dc20   93-776
                                                                         CIP

The paper used in this publication meets the minimum requirements of American National Standard for Information Sciences—Permanence of Paper for Printed Library Materials. ANSI Z3948-1984.⊚™

10 9 8 7 6 5 4 3 2 1

Printed in the United States of America

For Ruth and Calvert,
whose hospitality and civic virtues
inspired this second venture

Contents

Preface: The Matrix of O. Henry's Literary Art

As one of the world's most popular writers of short fiction, O. Henry still remains a literary enigma. Was he a genuine literary artist or a literary mountebank, a creative innovator of narrative prose fiction, or an artful dodger and con man? Like Edgar Allan Poe, O. Henry is one of those rare writers who, long after their brief candle has sputtered out, still fascinate millions of readers, defying scholars and critics alike to explain or evaluate unequivocally the source and quality of their literary achievement as well as its enduring popular appeal.

Eighty years after the death of William Sydney Porter, who was then virtually unknown to all but a few of the millions who admired his alias in 1910, the impact of O. Henry's nearly three hundred stories is still monumental. Having captured the fancy and touched the hearts of newspaper and magazine readers throughout the United States during the single decade in which they first appeared, most of them were soon republished in countless English and American collections and later translated into many foreign tongues. As a result, volumes of O. Henry's stories, in varied formats, can still be found in bookstores everywhere, from Athens, Moscow, and Madrid, to Buenos Aires, Paris, and Hong Kong. Moreover, since many of these same stories have also appeared consistently in radio, television, motion picture, and stage adaptations, the pseudonym O. Henry has become a symbol representing, especially to foreigners, a particular kind of "All-American" short story, as well as a touchstone for evaluating the art of short fiction writing in general.

During the decade immediately following his death, O. Henry's vogue escalated so rapidly that serious literary critics in the United States began rating his stories on a par with those of Hawthorne and Poe while other critics in England and France compared them favorably with the works of such contemporary craftsmen as Kipling, Conrad, Hardy, James, Maupassant, and Edith Wharton. The merits and limitations of his artistry, technique, style, and manner were analyzed, weighed, and debated; by 1919 O. Henry's image seemed to overshadow all others in the field of short fiction composition. Almost inevitably, his name was chosen that year to inaugurate the annual single-volume selection of "best" stories, still known as the *O. Henry Memorial Award Prize Stories*, because it signified preeminence in a specific form of literary art. His work then stood, at least for the moment, as the highest standard of what the short story was meant to be.

The same year a French essayist, Raoul Narcy, no doubt echoed the thoughts of most of his fellow critics when he upheld the short story as an art form worthy of respect because "its compactness cannot tolerate either disorder in the construction or weakness in the style. . . . [It] has its own law; which requires the exactness of measures and proportions." O. Henry's stories, he added, fulfilled these requirements admirably, for they revealed great skill in selecting detail as well as a sharp, amused observation, "abounding *verve*, [and] intelligence armed with irony; he dominates his characters rather than suffering them."[1] From this Frenchman's point of view, moreover, O. Henry also deserved high praise for avoiding moral preachments in his stories; for presenting life as he saw it, however sordid or degrading it might be occasionally; and for letting his readers form their own judgments.

Such unqualified admiration as this, however, was not long sustained, as O. Henry's reputation among leading critics in the United States declined almost as swiftly after 1920 as it had climbed initially. Although popular stage and screen adaptations of his favorite stories were still appearing regularly in the mid-1920s,[2] by 1930 the "new fiction" of Hemingway, Anderson, and Fitzgerald made O. Henry's stories seem passé, at least from the critics' viewpoint. Scholarly interest in their literary significance likewise evaporated during the following decades; O. Henry was virtually dismissed by prominent literary historians as unworthy of any further consideration. Since his reputation was dead, wrote the author of an elaborate study on the development of modern American short fiction published in 1961,[3] there was apparently no need to consider O. Henry's work at all. This has remained pretty much the prevailing critical attitude toward O. Henry, as can be seen in such recent publications as *The History of Southern Literature* (1985) and *Short Story Theory at a Crossroads* (1989).

But, despite this critical interment, O. Henry's massive popular appeal still keeps his image very much alive in bookstores and public libraries. Both at home and abroad his stories are enthusiastically received as authentic embodiments of recognizable American attitudes and characteristics, activities and biases, actions and speech. And although they quaintly depict an era long departed, like Degas' frolicking *belle epocque*, for the many who enjoy these stories there is present in the voices heard in them an indigenous "all-American" flavor, not merely in the language of Manhattan's millions, but in that of the deep South, the Southwest, and the Midwest as well. In Part 1, I show through representative examples of O. Henry's stories how a three-pronged cultural background in Porter's experience contributed matter and form to the makeup and quality, the distinctive artistry or narrative mix that sets the O. Henry story apart.

Notes

1. See Raoul Narcy, "O. Henry Through French Eyes," *Living Age*, 303 (11 October 1919), 86–88.
2. See, for example, Upton Sinclair's play *Bill Porter: A Drama of O. Henry in Prison*, 1925.
3. See Austin M. Wright, *The American Short Story in the Twenties* (Chicago, 1961), 6.

Acknowledgments

The aid and encouragements of many kind friends and associates have made the task of writing this book a sustaining challenge at every stage of its composition. I am indebted first to long time colleagues in the Department of English at Auburn University—notably Professors Bert Hitchcock, Taylor Littleton, Richard Amacher, Ruth and Norman Brittin, Madison Jones, Ward Allen, Sara Hudson, Bernard Breyer, Ruth and Thomas Wright, and Oxford Stroud—for lively discussions that helped to dispel a flagging self-esteem and emeritus malaise. Secondly, I owe a debt of gratitude to various staff members of the University library, particularly Glen Anderson, Eugene Geiger, and their young assistants in the Humanities Division, who helped me obtain and make Xerox copies of research materials housed at Auburn and elsewhere.

I am also indebted to many others who provided important source materials and suggested methods of dealing with them, which I feel sure have enriched this study of William Sydney Porter's contribution to the development of the modern American short story. Among these I most gratefully acknowledge the attention my book has received from Professor Gordon Weaver at Oklahoma State University, Liz Fowler, Melissa Solomon, and Eric Haralson at G. K. Hall, and Mr. J. Stephen Catlett, Archivist at the Greensboro Historical Museum.

Finally, there are many other loyal Greensboro citizens whose generous hospitality and welcome invitations enabled me to share in numerous festivities dedicated to the memory of their city's renowned native son, O. Henry, at the centennial of his birth in 1962 and again at the 75th anniversary of his death in 1985. Besides Mr. Samuel Hummel, Chairman of the Festival Committee, and assorted members of the Porter family, their numbers include my dear cousins, Mr. and Mrs. Calvert R. Hall, to whom I am pleased to dedicate my second full-length treatment of "the Master Trickster."

Part 1

THE SHORT FICTION

O. Henry's Southern Ties

In a recently published study of antebellum southern literature, Louis D. Rubin makes a strong case for the middle-class motives and ambitions of socially prominent white citizens of the Old South. Whether plantation slaveowners or not, he writes, these citizens aspired to the same materialistic goal as did their northern neighbors: "a highly characteristic goal of success, fulfillment, and the good life that took the form of the plantation *ideal*—the dream of the plantation . . . as a goal powerfully coveted and imagined, [it] is a middle-class affair, representing a normally acquisitive society's hopes."[1] As the son of Dr. Algernon Sidney and Mary Jane Porter, O. Henry sprang directly from just such a middle-class southern background; and the cultural tradition he inherited from early childhood and adolescence in his native Greensboro, North Carolina, exerted a profound influence upon his literary career. But his birth and upbringing in a defeated South, suffering impoverishment and a humiliating adjustment to the harsh realities of postwar Reconstruction, also made a lasting impression on O. Henry's consciousness, coloring to the end his attitude toward the world of his youth.

The fact that late in life he seriously proposed writing a series of stories intended to draw sharp contrasts between the Old and New South, and even worked out a sufficiently detailed outline for the series to secure a contract from *Collier's* magazine, clearly illuminates a life-long attachment to his native region. His plan, basically, was "to show up the professional Southerner who was still trying to blame all his troubles on the Civil War," as opposed to the new southerner who was too busy making money to worry about lost causes.[2] Although hints of this plan had appeared in several earlier stories, such as "The Emancipation of Billy" and "A Municipal Report," the series itself was never written. But had O. Henry lived to fulfill that plan, he might well have enhanced significantly both the annals of southern literature and his own literary career, for few writers of his generation were as well qualified as he to capture in fictional form the essence of southern life and character.

Between 1896, when he was writing sketches and anecdotes for the Houston *Post*, and his death in 1910, O. Henry published about thirty short stories either laid in an Old South setting (aside from Texas and the Southwest) or that deal with the activities and attitudes of antebellum southern characters. Numerically, these make up barely 10 percent of his total output but even a cursory survey of their varied contents and narrative methods quickly discloses how intimately O. Henry's artistry was tied to a southern cultural background.

Some of them, for instance, were written in the vein of the immensely popular antebellum tall-tale frontier humorists such as A. B. Longstreet, J. J. Hooper, and J. G. Baldwin; others were fashioned in the equally popular contemporary mode of local-color regional romance that remained strongly in vogue both North and South throughout O. Henry's lifetime. In both these types of his short fiction one finds unmistakable characteristics of southern attitudes, manners, and speech, for O. Henry was influenced by mainstream literary trends in American fiction that were also motivating and would reappear in, for example, the works of Mark Twain, Stephen Crane, and William Faulkner on the one hand, and those of G. W. Cable, Kate Chopin, and Eudora Welty on the other. Close study of O. Henry's southern stories, accordingly, will show that his narrative methods often achieved in them a subtle blend of the two basic strains—a blend that became, indeed, a dominant feature in nearly all his other stories, particularly those dealing with Texas outlaws, and with swindlers, embezzlers, and fugitives from justice. Though few in number, his southern stories offer an important key to the understanding of his work as a whole.

At the heart of the antebellum frontier tall-tale yarns such as Hooper's *Adventures of Captain Simon Suggs* lay the problem of the narrator's authenticity. Since most of the earlier frontier tales dealt with the ludicrous antics of rawhide, uninhibited rogues and adventurers, the comic appeal of their outrageous feats of daring, physical prowess, and rascality rested on the narrator's ability to make them convincing and funny at the same time. If, like Coleridge's Ancient Mariner, he could hold his audience spellbound with glittering eye and conjuring speech, even the most incredulous reader might be moved to laughter by an unbelievable story involving bizarre action of the wildest sort.

As a young journalist in Texas, O. Henry showed he had already caught the trick of successfully juxtaposing a fantastic medley of inharmonious elements and a seemingly sober-sided, straightforward narrator to produce in "Vereton Villa" one of the most hilarious spoofs of his entire career. And as his technique developed he worked the same trick repeatedly with greater finesse, preserving a spirit of rollicking gaiety, yet toning down its vulgar explosiveness, as in "Hostages to Momus" and "The Rose of Dixie," two of his more mature light satires of old-fashioned southern pretentiousness.

In "Vereton Villa" O. Henry produced at the outset of his professional career what might be called an actual case study of the artist in embryo because it reveals within a compact framework of fewer than nine pages ample evidence of the deft ironist and resourceful narrative craftsman he would soon become. With his subtitle, "A Tale of the South," he sets the disingenuous tone of his approach and proceeds to explain and verify in a brief opening passage both its origin and merit.

> The following story of Southern life and manners won a prize offered by a Boston newspaper, and was written by a young lady in Boston, a teacher in one of the advanced schools of that city. She has never visited the South, but the faithful local color and character drawing shows an intimate acquaintance with the works of Mrs. H. B. Stowe, Albion W. Tourgee and other well-known chroniclers of Southern life. Everyone living in the South will recognize the accurate portraits of Southern types of character and realistic description of life among the Southern planters.

The sly oxymoron embedded in O. Henry's tongue-in-cheek analogy between his narrator and two of the most heartily despised Yankee writers among southerners, both before and after the Civil War, warns the alert reader a satiric tall-tale is about to unfold. And so it does, echoing through a barrage of ludicrously violent scenes the ridicule and resentment of southerners toward both the author of *Uncle Tom's Cabin* and the notorious carpetbaggers of the Reconstruction era, Tourgee in particular for having dramatized in the novel *A Fool's Errand* his harrowing sojourn as one of them in Greensboro during O. Henry's boyhood.

At the heart of the humorous tall-tale, whether written by the old southern yarnspinners or later by O. Henry, there is a funny narrator plus incongruity—the juxtaposition of unexpected, inharmonious elements built into the structure of the story. Thus, "Vereton Villa," purportedly written by a Bostonian schoolmarm who has never seen the South, retells imaginatively in her own words the shocking experiences of Penelope Cook, who lived and taught for a short while on a southern plantation. As she approached the mansion in a rickety ambulance driven by a sobbing old black man, a mule burst out of the front door just a step ahead of the aristocratic, broom-wielding Mrs. De Vere, who graciously welcomed

5

and simultaneously offered her a chaw of tobacco. Within the magnificently furnished parlor Penelope quickly noted several examples of southern sloth: a wheelbarrow of dried mortar in one corner, a pair of trousers hanging from the chandelier, and several chickens roosting on the grand piano. Aubrey De Vere, the tall godlike young son, clothed in "a dress suit of the latest cut," greeted her with patrician courtesy "in a deep musical baritone"; but she saw too that he was shirtless and barefooted, his mouth streaked with tobacco juice. Upon asking her opinion of Jefferson Davis, whom Penelope denounced as a traitor, he flew into a passion, seized one of the chickens, wrung its neck, and flung its carcass on the Brussels carpet, its head into her face. Then, humbly begging her pardon on one knee, he remorsefully explained that "twenty-eight years ago today my father was killed at the battle of Shiloh."

And so the fantastic contretemps, steadily revealed in a dry, matter-of-fact tone, briskly move the story forward. At a typically southern feast consisting of everything imaginable from opossum and sweet potatoes to catfish and squash, Aubrey buries his carving knife to the hilt in the old Negro for spilling gravy on the tablecloth. Later he displays the accuracy of both his musical technique and his aim by showing Penelope, seated at the piano, that the *A* natural note she had struck in a run of diminished sevenths should have been *A* sharp; the neighboring black key he designates for her with a stream of tobacco juice from across the room. Later still he proves the depth of his jealous desire and immediate shame when, his ardent lovemaking repulsed, he pitches Penelope through the window and sets her afire, but then promptly rescues her and goes all the way to Boston to fetch her beloved Cyrus Potts. Finally, as the affianced pair bid good-bye to the South from their railroad car, Aubrey, seated nearby on a keg of dynamite, blows himself up, leaving Penelope a memento for her married life—his great toe, which she keeps in a bottle of alcohol on her writing desk. She vows never to return to the South, however, because Southerners are too impulsive.[3]

If one may grant a certain youthful exuberance that led to some crudities or offensive expressions in "Vereton Villa," O. Henry's boisterous spoofing in this early story was nevertheless squarely within the antebellum Southwest frontier tall-tale tradition. At least half of his later southern stories bear recognizable traits of the same tradition, although as his career moved forward in the direction of local color regionalism these stories acquired a variety of newer characteristics skillfully adapted from the popular fiction of other southern writers, who were also exploiting the picturesqueness of the post–Civil War South.

As a nationwide literary phenomenon, the local color movement was ideally suited to the basic aims of the Reconstruction era; while O. Henry matured during the 1880s and 1890s, it served as a means of restoring the South to respectable literary company on the national scene. Growing apace till the end of the century, it produced an avalanche of stories from such writers as George W. Cable, Joel Chandler Harris, Mary N. Murfree, Constance Fenimore Woolson, Thomas Nelson Page, Sherwood Bonner, Kate Chopin, Grace King, and many others. The parallels between their stories and many of O. Henry's are too numerous and obvious to leave the relationship between them in doubt.

Local colorists everywhere, particularly those in the South, were developing in their fiction a type of modified realism aimed to identify and also to draw favorable attention to distinctive characteristics in a given region of the nation. Whatever its subject matter, their stories were intended primarily to dramatize human attitudes and behavior recognizable as elements belonging to a peculiar cultural mystique: in short, a sense of "place," as Eudora Welty succinctly described a major tenet in her own fiction many years later. But in representing the life peculiar to their respective regions, the local colorists of the 1880s were also bound by the prevailing taste and taboos of the period; hence their fidelity to the actual scene is often more evident in their treatment of external data—the sight and sound effects of setting and dialogue—than in their efforts to draw logical cause-and-effect relationships between the background and behavior of their characters. Since genteel critics often condemned even the mild vulgarities of speech and the jarring impurities of grammar and idiom ascribed to these characters, most local colorists dared not venture beyond the more severe restraints set by Victorian standards, and O. Henry, along with the rest, willingly adhered to these restrictions. He not only resented being compared to de Maupassant, for example, but often boasted his stories contained nothing unclean.

Many local colorists also tended to focus on the past rather than on the present in order to idealize human behavior by casting over it a filmy, nostalgic glow, as Thomas Nelson Page did in glorifying the age of slavery in the South. Most of them likewise studiously avoided dealing with sordid manifestations of ordinary human life, but preferred to satisfy the popular demand for stories "that end well," even when a note of tragedy was involved—a practice prominently displayed in the majority of O. Henry's stories. And practically all of them ignored the problem of sexuality in either its psychological or physiological effects, regardless of the social levels and relationships presented in their stories. Accordingly, from the viewpoint of present-day literary critics and scholars, the local colorists strove "to make oddities seem picturesque, to make the primitive seem romantic; . . . they specialized in cultural islands where peculiarities had survived, or they depicted a past age during which local individuality had flourished. . . . Significantly, a large proportion of local-color fiction concerns itself with the poor, yet it must quickly be said that poverty is generally accepted as a fact of life, sometimes with a recognition of its hardships; the note of protest is exceptional."[4]

How well O. Henry's southern stories conform to these criteria may be determined by examining in some detail their dominant characteristics and the resulting sub-classes suggested by them. To simplify matters, the stories may be arbitrarily classified under four headings as follows: (a) tall tales; (b) local-color romances; (c) romantic adventure tales with incidental local-color touches; (d) blended local-color tall tales. The relevance of this classification to O. Henry's southern stories may be explained as follows: eight of them in group (a) are labeled tall tales because, though laid in the South, their major significance lies in the interplay of narrator and plot, a series of wildly improbable adventures that might have occurred anywhere; on the other hand, the six stories in group (b) are distinctively local-color romances because the close relationship between setting and character motivation in them is clearly designed to govern the development and outcome of the plot. Finally, groups (c) and (d) are distinguished by the presence of definite tall-tale characteristics in their stories, as all fourteen of them reveal at least some traces of local-color influence.

The Tall Tales

Six of the eight stories classified here as tall tales appear in a single volume, *The Gentle Grafter*, a collection of fourteen that deal with the activities of swindlers and con men, allegedly picked up by O. Henry from his cronies in the Ohio Penitentiary. *The Gentle Grafter* is of particular interest for several reasons: first, it is the only volume in the O. Henry canon that contains a majority of stories not previously published or later reprinted in magazines; they were written specifically for this collection during O. Henry's final spurt of productivity in 1908. Second, it is the only volume in which a central character dominates all but three of the stories in the collection. All fourteen stories are tall tales of the picaresque variety, but only six of them are laid in the South, and five of these six deal with the exploits of the narrator, Jeff Peters, who is O. Henry's most fully rounded character.[5] The three remaining titles of the eight southern tall tales referred to are "Hostages to Momus," (also in the *The Gentle Grafter*), "Phoebe" (in *Roads of Destiny*), and "The Ransom of Red Chief," one of the most popular of all O. Henry favorites (in *Whirligigs*).

Jeff Peters, the Gentle Grafter, is an amusing rogue whose doctrine— "a kind a mulct 'em in parvo" (3)—carries him back through the tradition of picaresque fiction to Robin Hood and Lazarillo de Tormes. But in a manner closer to that of G. W. Harris's Sut Lovingood, Jeff carries the narrative forward chiefly in dialogue form. Much of the humor bubbling in any of his yarns emerges from his laid-back colloquial speech, a cascade of outrageous puns and malapropisms, usually couched in a pseudo-erudite style. Correspondingly, the rest of the humor is lodged in the subject matter itself—the absurd predicaments and petty grafting schemes Jeff tells of having shared with his partner, Andy Tucker. All of these stories could have come straight off the pages of the antebellum sporting journal, *The Spirit of the Times*, yet most of them also bear the unmistakable trademark of O. Henry's surprise ending.

In the first tale, "Jeff Peters as a Personal Magnet," Jeff tells of his "earlier days" when he sold "linaments and cough cures on street corners" and got picked up (despite his five dollar bribe) by the constable of Fisherville, Arkansas, for selling "Resurrection Bitters" at fifty cents a bottle without a city license. Summoned to the mayor's office the next day, he there met his future partner, Andy, who was also broke and seeking some easy graft. They then managed, through a complicated series of moves undisclosed until the end, to outwit the authorities and skip town with $250, the capital with which they sustained their business partnership. Later, in "A Midsummer Masquerade," while resting from their swindling labors at a mountain resort in Tennessee (probably Gatlinburg), they posed as visiting dignitaries at the request of the proprietor of the Woodchuck Inn—also a swindler—who didn't want to disappoint a houseful of normal school teachers lured there with the promise of meeting the Duke of Marlborough and Admiral Perry, the polar explorer. Andy prepares the reader for this elaborate hoax at the outset with an appropriate misquotation: "'I want to loaf and indict my soul,' as Walt Whittier says" (89).

Quite often the wittiest part of an O. Henry story comes in the first page or so, as he warms up to his plot by dropping an ironic wisecrack with a topical allusion related to his main theme. In "Shearing the

Part 1

Wolfe," for example, Jeff starts off by philosophizing about the ethics of swindling and the difference between his standards and his partner's: "I didn't approve of all of Andy's schemes for levying contributions from the public, and he thought I allowed my conscience to interfere too often for the good of the firm. We had high arguments sometimes. Once one word led to another till he said I reminded him of Rockefeller." Jeff accepted the taunt but, turning the other cheek, reminded Andy that he had yet "to shake hands with a subpoena server" (99). This launches Jeff into another yarn about the time when he and Andy fleeced a hypocritical small-town Kentucky merchant who was planning to expose, for his own profit, a mail-order counterfeiting scheme. In "The Man Higher Up" O. Henry varied this opening technique by setting himself up as his own narrator; in the first page he tells the reader how much he enjoyed Jeff's visits to New York during the winter, his off-season, when his swindling activities ranged from Spokane to Tampa. Then he lets Jeff take over by classifying three kinds of graft, his own and two illegitimate sorts:

> "There are two kinds of grafts," said Jeff, "that ought to be wiped out by law. I mean Wall Street speculation and burglary."
> "Nearly everybody will agree with you as to one of them," said I with a laugh.
> "Well, burglary ought to be wiped out, too," said Jeff, and I wondered whether the laugh had been redundant. (138)

Again, in "The Ethics of Pig," Jeff relates "his latest Autolycan adventure" (22), which occurred a year earlier during his temporary association with a hog stealer, Rufe Tatum, whom he employed to act as decoy in a shell game he was operating at a county fair in Kentucky; instead the employee mulcted him to the tune of eight hundred dollars, thereby proving his original point about the difficulty of securing a reliable partner in graft.

Each of the Jeff Peters stories is mildly amusing, but none of them achieves as high a level of tall-tale effectiveness as several others in the collection O. Henry earlier published elsewhere. In "Hostages for Momus," for instance, he created an utterly fantastic tall tale based on an idea allegedly drawn from Mark Twain's *Adventures of Tom Sawyer*.[6] Parleyvous Pickens, the narrator, is another bumbling swindler who tells how he and his partner, Caligula Polk, "of Muscogee in the Creek Nation" (198), failed in their attempt to secure a ten thousand dollar ransom after they had kidnapped Colonel Jackson T. Rockingham, the town banker of Mountain Valley, Georgia, president of the defunct Sunrise and Edenville Tap Railroad. Their venture is a total fiasco, yet the absurdities strung out in its situation and mode of expression make it a typical example of the antebellum tall tale. Its pure fantasy, exaggerations, and wise-cracking satire, its contrast between poverty-stricken, eroded land and miserable diet, on one hand, and the pretension of social status and the appreciation of a gourmet's delicacies on the other—all evoke a tissue of incongruities straight out of the frontier humor tradition.

Perhaps the best example of all, however, is Booth Tarkington's favorite, "The Ransom of Red Chief," another kidnapping tale cut on a pattern similar to O. Henry's many other con-man yarns, but with no waste of words or cute posturings.[7] Sam, the narrator, begins it conversationally this way: "It looked like a good thing: but wait till I tell you. We were down south, in Alabama—Bill Driscoll and myself—when this kidnapping idea struck us. It was, as Bill afterward expressed it, during a moment of temporary mental Apparition; but we didn't find that out till later" (*Whirligigs*, 100).

The nearly homonymous "apparition" neatly sets the comic tone, which is upheld throughout this delightful tale by similar rhetorical blunders whenever Bill is quoted by his more erudite partner, whose own pretentious vocabulary includes such preciosities as "undeleterious" and "philoprogenetiveness." And O. Henry's technique of balancing malapropisms with amusing linguistic contrasts is in turn supported by a variety of other risibly contrasting elements woven into the plot structure. There is the absurd situation of two grown men reduced to exhaustion and desperation by their juvenile victim; the boy's audacity and exuberant high spirits in contrast to their weary discomfiture; the dryness of his father's "counter proposition," an offer to take Johnny off the kidnappers' hands for $250 in cash; and particularly the narrator's serious, dead-pan tone of voice from beginning to end. All these, together with its sparkling wordplay, are so harmoniously combined in the story that it has deservedly endured as a popular favorite among high school anthologists for nearly a century.

But whereas "The Ransom of Red Chief" displays O. Henry's tall-tale artistry at its best, "Phoebe," another done in the same mold and published the same year (1907), reveals his skill only in disarray. For even though this story calls to mind what may have been actual experiences shared during his brief sojourn in New Orleans, its tissue of misadventures tied to a filibustering expedition in Central America fails to arouse the sympathetic laughter O. Henry probably anticipated. Like several others he was painfully grinding out toward the end of his life, its structure betrays the strain of his efforts to keep up with the demand for his work.

The Local-Color Stories

Much the same unevenness is also apparent in the local-color stories that impart a strong southern flavor in both setting and characterization as well as action and theme. Yet among the half dozen cited here as models of O. Henry's mastery of this genre, each clearly shows by one means or another how skillfully he could combine and set forth in seemingly realistic dialogue the remembered activities from his Greensboro background, his own personal history, and his first-hand observations of the various individuals and classes of people he had known. Several of these stories, moreover, are generally upheld as his finest achievements. The six stories are "A Blackjack Bargainer," "The Duplicity of Hargraves," "The Guardian of the Accolade," "The Emancipation of Billy," "Blind Man's Holiday," and "A Municipal Report." All but the last of these were among O. Henry's earliest publications, most of them having been written during his prison days and published shortly thereafter in various magazines between 1901 and 1905.[8]

Along with a fine-tuned use of dialect, these stories all project a sensitive feeling for place—rightness of setting, of the characters who inhabit it, and of the relationships among them. O. Henry quickly establishes these linkages among them, so that however implausible the plot, the skeptical reader is disarmed and taken in by the illusion, at least temporarily. "A Blackjack Bargainer" offers up a specious plot based on hackneyed "Old South" characterization and themes such as family feuds and codes of honor, noble self-sacrifice, and so on. Thus, the problem of disreputable lawyer Yancey Goree, who drinks and gambles away his family estate and then sells even the rights to a long-standing feud between the Gorees and the Coltranes, is patently absurd. Yet O. Henry manages to modulate the reader's disbelief and arouse some interest in it by injecting into the story an equally dubious but amusing class conflict between aristocratic Gorees and some ignorant but nouveau riche hill folk, the Pike Garveys. Although the sentimental denouement of the story is pretty hard to swallow, the ironic motivation of its three leading characters is palpably shaped by their respective backgrounds.

Again, in "The Duplicity of Hargraves," the close relationship between character and background produces a satisfying example of local-color romance, but here the immediate setting is less significant than the reflected one. The story is laid in Washington, where impoverished "Major Pendleton Talbot, of Mobile, sir, and his daughter, Miss Lydia," have come to stay in a modest boardinghouse while he finishes writing his book, "Anecdotes and Reminiscences of the Alabama Army, Bench, and Bar,"[9] the anticipated sales of which are their only hope for survival. Published originally in 1902, this story is the first of several in which O. Henry cleverly developed a favorite theme by ironically juxtaposing the outworn values of the Old South's romantic past and the more substantial values of a realistic present. Thus, while the courtly, old-fashioned Major can dwell endlessly on "the splendid, almost royal days of the old planters" with their thousands of slaves and bales of cotton, the only one interested in his garrulous reminiscences is Lydia's young suitor, Hargraves, a character actor who listens to them by the hour as he studies the Major closely in order to reproduce in a stage play all the lost glory unaffectedly symbolized in his host's behavior.

Eventually, the Major is outraged to find himself caricatured, even to the slightest details of his mint-julep ritual, but the play, a great hit, enriches Hargraves and thereby enables him to end both the Major's ire and his poverty by duplicitously assuming another role: playing the part of a faithful ex-slave, Cindy's Mose, he reappears in Washington to settle an old debt. With a consummate light touch, especially in his handling of mixed black and white dialogue, O. Henry weaves together past and present, background and character motivation, maintaining throughout the story a tone of mingled irony and pathos.

O. Henry's gentle irony is among the most distinctive elements in his portrayal of "Old South" values. Suffused throughout the texture of his best stories, it not only reveals a combined admiration for and a critical reappraisal of a vanished era, but also offsets much of the bathetic sentimentality found in earlier local-color tales of the South. As an undercutting force, for example, it sharpens in different ways the effect of both "The Guardian of the Accolade" and "The Emancipation of Billy," two stories obviously drawn from O. Henry's boyhood recollections of Greensboro and of his bibulous father and other old-timers who frequented his Uncle Clark's drugstore. Despite their far-fetched plots, both stories recapture nostalgic glimpses of a less than idyllic past.

In the first there is the amusing counterpoint between a faithful black servant's laborious but misguided efforts to preserve the unsullied reputation of his old white boss and the latter's chagrin over the loss of a suitcase containing, "two quarts of the finest old silk-velvet Bourbon . . . you ever wet your lips with" (*Roads of Destiny*, 39). But in "The Emancipation of Billy" a different skein of the Old South–New South theme unfolds. Here, through the doddering daily progress of the aging Civil War hero, "Governor" Pemberton, along Lee Avenue from his musty mansion to the drugstore where Mr. Appleby sets up drinks for the Old Guard, O. Henry represents the pathetic, decadent Old South; the energetic New South is embodied in Pemberton's son, a successful young lawyer whose appearances before the United States Supreme Court have brought him national acclaim. Yet, ironically, among the elder citizens of Elmville he is still patronized and downgraded beneath the overshadowing local grandeur of his pompous father until a flamboyant event in the end sets him free. Typically, O. Henry's surprise twist once again produces an absurdly far-fetched climax and denouement in this story, but his control of dialogue and description nevertheless support its pretense of local-color realism.

Despite similar aesthetic limitations, O. Henry was equally successful when he shifted his focus from the village and small town toward the southern city in "Blind Man's Holiday" and "A Municipal Report." In the earlier story his use of a New Orleans setting gives us a preview of the New York scene. The Nashville he portrays in the later one reminds us of the 150 or more Bagdad tales O. Henry had published when he wrote it. Between these two stories there is a noticeable contrast in tone and technique, although as examples of his local-color writing, they are alike in one respect. In both the interest centers less on the problem of environmental effect on character than on psychological tension; that is, on conflicts of loyalty, honor, duty, and the like, which the leading characters must resolve for themselves regardless of background influences. O. Henry did not attempt to probe very far beneath the surface in either of these stories; he simply resorted to trickery of one sort or another to resolve his crises—to an offstage murder in "A Municipal Report," and a deus ex machina in the person of a kindly priest in "Blind Man's Holiday." Nevertheless, he successfully evoked the local scene in both stories.

"Blind Man's Holiday" is a hopelessly idealized mélange based on the hackneyed theme of noble self-sacrifice and strung out woodenly to a moralistic harangue quite untypical of O. Henry's later work. For serious

14

students of his career its main interest may reside in his treatment of guilt feelings suffered over a shadowed past—an obvious parallel with his own painful history. But today's average reader can only view the story quizzically as a period piece, a study in outmoded taste as well as in its author's groping experimentation with fictional autobiography. In "A Municipal Report," however, authorial self-assurance is brashly evident from beginning to end. This may be why the story is still regarded as one of O. Henry's finest, although it scarcely deserves the extravagant critical acclaim it received in the 1920s. Several glaring excrescences mar its unity and thus weaken its impact. Economy is sacrificed, for example, in O. Henry's overuse of posturing tricks to build up his narrator's character as an ironic foil for the three other participants in the action: old Caesar, the faithful black coachman and hero; Major Caswell, the villainous white leech; and the starving, genteel author, Azalea Adair. After opening with quoted passages from Kipling and Norris, the narrator interposes two wisecracking paragraphs about cities as a basis for his thematic idea that it is rash to deny the possibility of romance in any given one, large or small. He follows these with a Rand-McNally thumbnail sketch of Nashville and more wisecracks about its limitations as he checks in at a hotel, dines, steps out to look over the somnolent little city where nothing ever happens after sundown, and finally encounters Caswell, the southern bore. In this leisurely way the story drifts on a few more pages—one-third its full length—with more chamber-of-commerce tidbits dropped in now and again before the narrator reveals his primary mission in Nashville as the agent of a northern literary magazine with a contract for Miss Adair. From this point on it does fulfill O. Henry's stated purpose, moving swiftly toward his climax and muted denouement to refute Norris's reckless supposition. But here as elsewhere O. Henry's mastery of picturesque dialect and sharp descriptive detail is clearly superior to his analysis of complex character in action.

Romantic Adventures with Incidental Local Color

Structurally, the stories in the foregoing group differ only slightly from eight others here in which a regional or local background plays a less significant role as a molder of character and action. They are all alike in requiring happenstance and/or sleight-of-hand contrivances, rather than a logical sequence of cause-and-effect events, to unravel their plots

15

and spring their preordained surprise endings. All of them likewise feature a variety of romantic adventures among a cast of idealized, two-dimensional characters who might easily be shuffled into any of the other stories with no great loss of identity. Accordingly, in reading these stories one's curiosity is aroused primarily by their plot manipulation, which does reveal O. Henry's famed inventiveness, even as early as the 1890s. In the order of their original publication dates, these eight stories are "Whistling Dick's Christmas Stocking" (1899), the first story published in a national magazine under his pen name; "Bulger's Friend" (1901); "The Renaissance at Charleroi" (1902); "A Retrieved Reformation" (1903); "October and June" (1903); "The Church with the Overshot Wheel" (1904); "The Door of Unrest" (1904); and "Thimble, Thimble" (1908).[10] There is a slight use of localized background to initiate and conclude the action in "Whistling Dick's Christmas Stocking," which opens in the midtown, riverfront district of New Orleans and moves forward along the levee past the French Market toward the sugar plantations of Chalmette. But with the hero established at one particular spot, where he can save a planter's family from armed robbery, setting has become much less important than his musical accomplishment.

And the same is true of "The Renaissance of Charleroi," a bizarre romance involving fierce Creole passions reminiscent of G. W. Cable's *The Grandissimes*, but woven into the hackneyed plot of a vanished brother's miraculous return just in time to reunite two loving hearts. The story is amply supplied with specific details of place names, furnishings, dress, mannerisms, and speech—all helpfully evoking a typical south Louisiana ambience, but its basic theme could be just as effectively dramatized with any other Arabian Nights decor.

As opposed to these two stories, however, the others in the group achieve their effects with even slighter focus on localized details. The personae in "Bulger's Friend" and "A Retrieved Reformation," for example, could have played out their equally romanticized roles virtually anywhere else in the United States besides the imaginary southern towns where O. Henry placed them. And yet, although the former languishes forgotten, justifiably enough, among his poorest stories, the other possesses two sure-fire dramatic qualities that have virtually immortalized it: namely, O. Henry's vividly realistic representation of a professional burglar's equipment, methods, attitudes, and milieu, and a breathless climactic scene that brings all of these together.

When the reformed Jimmy Valentine's sensitive fingers crack open the bank vault in time to rescue the trapped child within, he not only secures an immediate reprieve from the Fed tailing him, but a hero's universal acclaim as well. To the millions of readers, theater buffs, and video fans who have taken Jimmy and his creator into their hearts, it matters not that no detective in his right mind would behave as Ben Price does in this story. And again, in "The Church with the Overshot Wheel," everything important rests solely upon the miraculous reunion of a kindly old miller and his long lost Aglaia. The location of the church itself—a converted mill in the Cumberland Mountains—and the fact that Aglaia grew up in a village near Atlanta—have only a tenuous bearing on the outcome of her story.

Setting is still less relevant to the development of the three remaining stories in this group, although each rests on recognizable southern literary traditions while pursuing a different path toward the goal of its intended effect. "The Door of Unrest," for example, is almost unique among O. Henry's many tales; as a variation of the ancient Wandering Jew theme, its tension develops through a succession of strange encounters between a small-town southern newspaper editor and a disheveled old vagabond known as Michob Ader, whose wildly garbled memories, narrated in a rich Irish brogue, lead to the disclosure that he is only the town's tipsy shoemaker, Mike O'Bader. Thus, interest has been aroused and furthered by the combined devices of dialectal wordplay and mistaken identity. Similarly, but slighter in substance, "October and June" is another expanded anecdotal variation on the foolproof but hackneyed theme of marriage between youth and age. It functions solely to produce a surprising sexual mismatch in the last sentence; instead of the lady expected, the youthful bride turns out to be a nineteen-year-old captain of the Chattanooga cadets.

Trickery of this sort in wordplay and the manipulation of partially concealed details quickly became O. Henry's major stock-in-trade, and his clever use of such devices in these two early stories led the way toward the more elaborate legerdemain he performed in later ones like "Thimble, Thimble," a frankly acknowledged borrowing from Frank Stockton's sensational plot in "The Lady or the Tiger?" Though clearly overshadowed by its more famous model, O. Henry's imitation created a minor sensation of its own when the publishers of *Hampton's* magazine staged a contest and awarded prizes for the best solutions to the central mystery raised but left undisclosed in the story. Moreover, "Thimble, Thimble," like the stories of Jimmy Valentine and Hargraves, was readily adaptable for the stage and thus reappeared with nine of his other stories in a collection of one-act plays published in 1934.[11] But the story merits attention for more reasons than that. In its ironical treatment of "a Southerner's idea of a Northerner's idea of the South," it is analogous to—and nearly as effective as—"The Rose of Dixie," the funniest of all O. Henry's literary satires.

As a striking example of O. Henry's versatility, although his setting for "Thimble, Thimble" is a business office in New York, the substance and flavor of the story primarily convey a delicately balanced dichotomy of contrasting attitudes toward his native region. Both were derived from his "New South" philosophy, which respected the established ideals and traditions of the South but also sought to merge them with the broader, more comprehensive ideals and traditions of the nation as a whole. To dramatize the implied ambiguity in this effort, his story challenges the reader's curiosity with another well-worn old puzzle: given two young Americans of common ancestry, equal abilities, opportunities, and personal qualities, but reared in Virginia on the one hand, in Massachusetts on the other, how can one distinguish between them? Ever the hoaxer, O. Henry stands chuckling in the wings while preparing to baffle his reader as poor black Uncle Jake cannot tell the difference between his "young Marster," Blandford Carteret, and Blandford's Yankee cousin, John Carteret. The underlying idea supporting the comic scene played out on his little stage, however, is a serious one. Without the intimate feeling for the South O. Henry subtly reveals in this story, much of its effectiveness would be lost. (Clarkson, 99).

Local-Color Tall Tales

The last six stories that reflect O. Henry's close observation of picturesque southern customs and manners differ slightly from those discussed above, chiefly in two technical respects: they present a heavier concentration of local-color features, yet in pursuing their intended effect, each relies primarily upon tall-tale elements, either farcical or satiric. Actually, they are neither tall tales per se nor local-color stories exclusively but rather, at their best, a nice blend of the two types. And they are at their best in their latest form when O. Henry, seasoned through the production of more than two hundred stories, could mix his ingredients far more adroitly than he could at the outset of his career.

Yet three of these six were among the earliest he wrote, possibly while still in prison or shortly thereafter, for all three were first published in 1903. Their titles are "Cherchez La Femme," "The Whirligig of Life," and "Out of Nazareth." The later group, written and published during

O. Henry's last two years, are "The Rose of Dixie" (1908), "Best Seller" (1909), and "Let Me Feel Your Pulse" (1910). Geographically, the southern settings for the six range from Louisiana to Virginia and are functionally significant in each.

"Cherchez La Femme" is another good example of O. Henry's chameleonlike adaptability. Written in the local-color vein of *Old Creole Days*, it recaptures much the same Gallic flavor of the antebellum *Vieux Carré*'s setting, characterization, dialogue, and tone that one finds in George Washington Cable's exotic depiction of New Orleans life. The story opens with two newspaper reporters (Robins of the *Picayune* and Dumas of *L'Abeille*) drinking absinthe together "in the little Creole-haunted cafe of Madame Tibault, in Dumaine Street" (*Roads of Destiny*, 144). Catching note of a forthcoming auction in the morning's newspaper, they recall the mysterious disappearance two years ago of the Madame's twenty thousand dollar fortune, entrusted for safekeeping to a certain M'sieur Morin, now deceased. From here on the action develops into a wild goose chase as the two men strive to recover the hidden treasure because Dumas insists the old adage *cherchez la femme* would explain both its original loss and present whereabouts.

Eventually they discover it in the form of some glittering United States gold bonds that Madame Tibault, ignorantly assuming them to be pretty commercial calendars given her by Morin, used to paper over a crack in her own back parlor. But aside from the Madame's colorful Franco-English ("M'sieur Morin, he leave those li'l peezes papier in thos table, an say ver' much 'bout money thass hard for me to ond'stan. *Mais* I never see those money again"), the story is pretty far-fetched and unimpressive" (*Roads of Destiny*, 153). The other two stories are no better.

Except for O. Henry's sensitive control of the picturesque country speech in Georgia and Tennessee, both "The Whirligig of Life" and "Out of Nazareth" lack spontaneity and inventiveness. In the latter especially, both the characters and actions ascribed to them are so manifestly contrived and implausibly conventionalized that the story fails in its attempt to fuse the tall-tale fantasy of an elaborate real-estate swindle with the sentimental appeal of aged innocence requited. Accordingly, one may cheerfully turn for relief to "The Rose of Dixie" and its uproarious satire of "Old South" stuffiness unforgettably brought to life in the person of Colonel Acquila Telfair of Toombs City, Georgia.

Determined to edit a high-minded southern literary journal, the Colonel gathers together a staff of impeccably Confederate assistants—"a whole crate of Georgia peaches"—and adamantly refuses to sully his journal with any material produced above the Mason-Dixon line, because everything published in it must conform to his basic policy: "Of, For, and By the South."[12] He wavers a bit when a fast-talking New York salesman tries to persuade him to omit some of the southern deadwood scheduled for the next issue and replace it with more popular literary fare from elsewhere so that circulation can be boosted. But in the end the Colonel fills the space tentatively agreed upon with an essay entitled "Second Message to Congress/Written for/THE ROSE OF DIXIE/ BY/ A Member of the Well-known / BULLOCH FAMILY OF GEORGIA / T. Roosevelt."

Although "The Rose of Dixie" lacks O. Henry's customary romantic appeal of virtue rewarded, love requited, or innocence preserved, it clearly compensates for the omission in several ways. Besides the expected surprise ending, there is also the delightful spoofing that leads up to it throughout the interview between Colonel Telfair and the salesman, T. T. Thacker, both of whom are brilliantly characterized, the one with his stiff, self-righteous Southern intransigence, the other with his brash Yankee practicality. Thus, the story is not only a clever takeoff of antebellum southern periodicals, but is all the funnier for being partially truthful and yet kindly at the same time. And since the buildup of Thacker is equally barbed, its double-edged satire cuts both ways: against overprincipled southern states-rightsism, poor but proud, and against unprincipled northern commercialism, indifferent toward any ideal but that of making a "fast buck."

Light literary satire of this sort also embellishes "Best Seller," a story cavalierly dismissed by one critic because it "champions the 'Prisoner of Zenda' type tale with a commonplace parallel of its seeming improbabilities."[13] Actually, thanks to a subtle ironic tone maintained throughout the colloquy between the narrator and the protagonist, O. Henry parodies both the overdone best-selling "romance" of the period with its contrived escapades involving American businessmen and European princesses, and his own brand of more commonplace realistic romance. Though not wholly successful in developing his narrator's dual role—as author's mouthpiece for ridiculing badly written fiction and as independent spokesman for the ideals of ordinary middle-class Americans—O. Henry conveys fairly well through him the underlying idea that both imagination and finesse are required to give a valid fictional form to human actions on any social level whatever.

But of all the stories he ever wrote, O. Henry probably came closest to total success in the art of fusing comedy, pathos, and the human predicament, fittingly enough, in the last one he completed before he died: "Let Me Feel Your Pulse."[14] "So I went to a doctor," his narrator begins. And for the next fifteen pages O. Henry's jocularity bubbles through the narrator's account of ordeals he suffered at doctors' hands as he was being bumped, probed, peered into, and prescribed for until, finally, in the Blue Ridge Mountains of North Carolina he found the coveted response from old Doctor Tatum: "Somewhere in these mountains . . . there's a plant growing—a flowering plant that'll cure you, and it's about the only thing that will. It's of a kind that's as old as the world; but of late it's powerful scarce and hard to find. You and I will have to hunt it up" (170). Almost imperceptibly O. Henry takes the reader into the realm of fantasy to show him that the only cure he knew for human ills lies in the imagination; the magic plant they sought was amaryllis, symbol of love and poetic release since the days of Theocritus.

Even if O. Henry had never seen the South, he might well have produced as many stories and become as famous as he did become. But it is very doubtful his works would have possessed the same qualities that have distinguished them from all others of his period and made his name a byword in the field of short fiction. For the most prominent of those qualities—his playfulness and fondness for the exotic, the exaggerated, the fanciful, and the picturesque; his awareness of distinctive differences between northern and southern ideals; and especially his sympathetic feeling for agonies implicit in the changing attitudes of defeated southerners—are all products of a southern literary heritage. Even without his frank avowal of loyalty to southern ideals, as in "A Municipal Report," the debt he owed to this heritage would be visible in both his tall tales and his local-color romances.

O. Henry's Western Apprenticeship

If the Old South furnished the seedbed of O. Henry's art, the Southwest furnished the nutrients that stimulated its growth and embellished its forms. When he headed westward from Greensboro at age twenty, Texas was already a storied land of frontier romance, and during the next fourteen years there his varied experiences—on the ranch, as a Land Office draftsman and bank teller in Austin, and as a feature reporter on the Houston *Post*—were for him a storybook panoply that contributed valuable raw materials as well as daunting challenges to his literary apprenticeship. A self-imposed conditioning regimen, not unlike those of such eminent predecessors as Washington Irving, Edgar Allan Poe, and Stephen Crane, O. Henry's Texas years were also a period of trial and error during which his genius worked toward the forms best suited to his talents and his interests and, inevitably, his surroundings played an important role in this shaping process.

His love of books and his fascination for the chameleonlike qualities of words had been awakened first under his Aunt Evelina's tutelage; next, the technical knowledge and social contacts acquired in his Uncle Clark's drugstore stimulated his eagerness to study the flow of life around him, to notice its unity in variety, and, whenever possible, to capture its color and flavor. And now a whole new lifestyle in the West would give him both additional raw materials and incentives with which to develop an individual art form and a style of his own. From the blossoming of this apprenticeship there would come nearly a third of his total output; between eighty and a hundred stories and sketches based on his western experiences, most of them written and published before his pseudonym became an established fixture in the New York *Sunday World* in December 1903.

The shaping process began in the 1880s with the letters O. Henry was writing to friends back in Greensboro, describing his new surroundings and sensations, contrasting these responses with remembered conditions at home. His few surviving letters from this period reveal three qualities that foreshadow the budding professional writer-to-be: an eye for specific detail, a feeling for the suggestive power of words, and a sense of the effect, chiefly risible, that an appropriate combination of words can produce on the reader. In November 1883, for example, he informs his family's friends, Dr. and Mrs. James K. Hall, that the breeze vainly sought for the previous summer "is with us now, as cold as Callum Bros. suppose their soda water to be," describes a certain ranch hand as one who "wears a red sash and swears so fluently that he has been mistaken often for a member of the Texas legislature."[15] By this time O. Henry had grown accustomed to the rigors of life on a lonesome cattle ranch, remote from even such primitive centers of civilization as Fort Ewell and the ramshackle villages of Friotown and Cotulla. During the nearly two years spent in this new environment to which the Halls had introduced him, he quickly mastered the rudiments and the flavor of the cowboys' profession, though oftener as a leisured observer than as a participant in their roping and branding activities.

But he could talk their language and assume the blasé pose of one who knew himself to be a creature of "Wild West" legendary lore, as in his warning another friend in Greensboro to dissuade others from coming to live in Texas because the ranch country was "a silent but eloquent refutation of Bob Ingersoll's theory; a man here gets prematurely insane, melancholy and unreliable and finally dies of lead poisoning."[16] He knew that the double entendre, slipped in quietly here, would be appreciated, along with other effects, by an alert audience of one.

The Halls, in fact, had already contributed significantly to O. Henry's developing creative talents, even before they took him along as a guest in 1882 to meet their four sons, who were then managing extensive cattle and sheep ranches in La Salle County. Lee Hall, eldest of the Greensboro doctor's sons, had long since acquired a nationwide reputation as a fearless leader of the Texas Rangers, the symbolic scourge of desperadoes and outlaws. Together with his brothers, he was now triumphantly engaged in the fierce warfare between cattle ranchers and fence-cutting thieves and sheepmen, so Lee Hall himself readily gained heroic stature in O. Henry's imagination and reappeared in later stories as a bold champion of law and order.[17] And then, after the elder Halls returned to Greensboro, O. Henry stayed on as a welcome guest in the small household of Richard Hall, who with his wife, Betty, their little girl, and an assortment of ranch hands, was managing one of his brother Lee's sheep ranches (Langford, 21–30).

O. Henry's experiences at the Richard Hall ranch resembled those of his romanticized troubador, Sam Galloway, a privileged, footloose guest who pays his way at lonely ranches by singing and playing his guitar.[18] Apparently, the only duties he performed regularly were riding fourteen miles each week to fetch the mail at Fort Ewell, babysitting the Halls' child during their infrequent absences, and serving as a substitute cook in the intervals between the departure of one cook and the hiring of another. For a young man of twenty it was a lonely life in the wide-open spaces, yet his letters to friends back in Greensboro show little evidence of nostalgia or homesickness. On the contrary, they do show he filled long stretches of his time with a broad program of reading, absorbing in short order not only the Halls' slender stock of books, but also new arrivals in the mail, plus others in a large private library belonging to a lawyer friend in Cotulla (Langford, 27–30).

His literary fare during those two years included not only the standard English poets, novelists, and historians, but, more notably, Webster's dictionary, which he reputedly carried about with him and studied zealously by the hour. Thus, it was this breezy facility with words, often expressed in witty, sometimes bizarre or caustic and epigrammatic turns of phrase, that endeared him to his associates, who likewise admired the ease with which he picked up Spanish, French, and German locutions and, in a Chekhovian sense, scattered them like small coins across the canvas of his narrative. To amuse an Austin friend who had gone to Colorado, for example, O. Henry parodied the style of the local newspaper by describing the horrendous effects of a river flood, then built up the description to a ludicrous climax with an anecdote about a New York banker at the scene whose efforts to take up a collection for the forlorn victims produced "one dollar and five horn buttons. The dollar he had given himself. He learned on inquiry that . . . all they had lost by the flood was a few fishing poles." And in another letter to the same friend he contrived a mock-serious paragraph on the problem of suicide by leaping into the Colorado River chiefly to conclude his speculations with a triple pun: "sue a side-partner," "sewer sighed," "pursue a side issue."[19]

Many such examples from O. Henry's earliest writings betoken the artist in embryo. An impish spirit, eagerly seeking out the ludicrous incongruities and unexpected occurrences awaiting an observant eye and ear everywhere, fulfilled itself in these youthful jeux d'esprit through the medium of his shaping talent. Everything became grist for his mill. When he took up *The Rolling Stone* in 1894 and later served as the Houston "Postman," quips and squibs and little yarns, comic verses, parodies, burlesques, and touching tales on "life's little ironies" poured forth in profusion, but they were only a step from the more finished pieces he would soon be writing in prison as he turned to account his memories of Texas, New Orleans, and Central America. Of the nearly one hundred stories based on these experiences, well over two-thirds were published before 1904.

Early Short Fiction—*The Rolling Stone*

O. Henry's pathway to the earliest of his published literary effusions was a decade embracing some of the liveliest and most varied experiences of his young life as a Texan. Shortly after the Hall brothers liquidated their land holdings in March 1884, Richard Hall moved with his family to Austin, taking O. Henry along with them and introducing him to another Greensboro family, the Joe Harrellses, who had become prominent citizens in the thriving state capital. The Harrells welcomed him warmly into their capacious household, where he remained comfortably ensconced during the next three years as a virtual family member.

His engaging personal charm brightened the troubadour image he had created, especially among the younger Harrells boys, who took great delight in his cultural versatility—his witty repartee, his sketching, verse writing, mimesis—and above all, in his self-assurance as a manipulator of esoteric diction. Years later, one of them affectionately recalled that O. Henry had been "just like a brother to me"; he could never be baffled by the spelling or meaning of words chosen at random in Webster's unabridged dictionary.[20] Not surprisingly, they, too, were happy to introduce him to their friends, so that fairly soon his career among Austin's socially elite was launched. A young buck of twenty-two, he quickly assumed the role of desirable bachelor about town, dazzling the young ladies with his varied skills, serenading them with music and song, joining them in a succession of church choirs, writing and performing in a number of skits with them, and eventually courting and capturing one of them—the "dimity sweetheart"—for his bride.[21]

O. Henry's marriage on 1 July 1887, to vivacious but fragile Athol Estes, stepdaughter of a prosperous merchant named P. G. Roach, marked a significant turning point in his career, intensifying his ambition to gain renown as a literary artist but also strengthening his resolve to become a successful husband, father, and family breadwinner. Whereas he had seemed content during the preceding three years to hold down routine clerical jobs in a pharmacy, cigar store, and real estate office, shortly after their marriage he found a more congenial post as draftsman in the Texas Land Office.

It was an almost ideal spot, in fact, since the job itself, though paying only a modest hundred dollars a month, promised security and reasonable comfort, as well as ample time to continue his sketching and writing under the benign supervision of his former host, Richard Hall, the new land commissioner. Surely, the next four years during which O. Henry held this job must have been the happiest of his entire life. For Athol, his witty and spirited wife, was a young woman who both stimulated and encouraged him in his efforts to become a successful writer, and who delightedly shared his joys on receiving the first small checks his published skits occasionally brought in. Moreover, he obviously enjoyed and profited by the contacts and expanded horizons his regular work provided; the Land Office teemed with life and with new problems incident to the settling of new territory in the West, as evidenced in a number of stories he would write years later, such as "Bexar Scrip No. 2692" and "Georgia's Ruling."[22]

Thus, with steady employment in an atmosphere that favored his creative efforts, and a domestic anchorage that bolstered their marriage, O. Henry and his young bride apparently had every reason to anticipate a successful future. He liked and was liked by his fellow workers, and together he and Athol enjoyed the confidence and support of her parents, as well as the good will of a wide circle of prominent friends. From 1887 till the early 1890s, they evidently shared many bright, carefree moments in Austin society despite the woes and misfortunes that began piling up (Langford, 55–62).

But ill luck, when it came, proliferated. In 1888 Athol lost her first child, a son, in childbirth, and barely survived the birth of her second child, Margaret, the following year. Then, in January 1891, the Land Office job folded shortly after Richard Hall's failure to win a nomination for governor also cost him his job as land commissioner. Through friendly influence, O. Henry soon obtained other employment as a teller in the First National Bank, a job fated to bring him both disaster and fame (Langford, 62).

He had had very little experience as a bookkeeper, yet during his three years' service he apparently filled its requirements satisfactorily, if not very diligently, meanwhile blithely carrying on his inveterate sketching and skit writing both during banking hours and on his own time. Even so, he might have prospered indefinitely had not the slipshod banking practices in Austin and the lackadaisical mismanagement of his private affairs brought him to grief. The irregular banking methods prevalent at the time are amusingly dramatized in O. Henry's story "Friends in San Rosario," which tells how the president of one bank temporarily embarrassed for funds circumvents a federal bank examiner by making an unethical appeal to his friend, the president of another bank, for a short-term loan.[23] Such practices alone would probably not have ruined O. Henry, had not other problems, personal and domestic, resulting from his determination to conduct an unprofitable news-sheet enmeshed him toward the end of 1894 within an inescapable web of ruinous circumstances.

In March of that year he had realized a long-felt dream of publishing his own humor paper by purchasing a cheap printing press and the ownership rights of a monthly scandal sheet called *The Iconoclast*. O. Henry and his partner in the venture, James P. Crane, renamed their paper *The Rolling Stone*, changed it to a weekly, and began issuing it the following month. It was never a commercial success, surviving only a single year with an alleged circulation peak of fifteen hundred, but the fact that O. Henry managed to keep it going at all—at times virtually single-handedly—was a remarkable feat in itself. Each week he filled its eight pages with humorous squibs and satirical barbs on persons and events of local interest, not only producing most of the contents, which included some surprisingly well-finished fiction, but also taking over such mechanical tasks as typesetting and printing. Before long Crane left Austin and went to Chicago, yet O. Henry carried on, futilely striving to keep *The Rolling Stone* alive, pursuing a will-o'-the-wisp toward eventual degradation.

In his efforts to shore up its sagging prospects, he borrowed heavily from his father-in-law and other friends, apparently with too little concern as to how their money would be repaid if the paper failed. And sometime during the year he evidently began taking funds he needed from the bank and altering his accounts with the idea of readjusting them later upon replacing the money. Toward year's end, however, the shortages in his books stood revealed, and he was obliged to give up his job in December.

The worst was still ahead, although Mr. Roach and the others agreed to make up most of the shortage, while even the bank officials were apparently satisfied to let the matter drop. But Federal Bank examiner F. B. Gray, on the contrary, insisted upon prosecuting the case at a grand jury hearing scheduled for the following July.[24] During the ensuing six months prior to the trial, O. Henry remained out of work, living by the generosity of his father-in-law, earning only occasional small sums from random publications, but striving desperately to keep *The Rolling Stone* alive with infusions of cash sought from varied sources—all to no avail. The poor little humor sheet quietly rolled off its last issue on 30 March 1895, and was soon forgotten until its creator's worldwide fame a few decades later made of it a collector's item worthy of Sotheby's. For in his ephemeral little news-sheet—O. Henry's first published body of work— lay the foundation stones of his unique short fiction edifice: his themes, plots, methods, and style.[25]

A complete file of *The Rolling Stone* has never been republished, but enough of its contents are available in print to bear out the biographer Langford's assurance that during its brief career "its high-spirited gaiety camouflaged completely the editor's financial worries, as well as his difficulties at home and in the bank" (253). In the twelfth volume of O. Henry's collected works, published in 1912 under the title *Rolling Stones*, his friend Henry Steger gathered together a sizable number of representative pieces from the little weekly and prefaced them with an appreciative introduction explaining the nature and variety of its contents (ix–xv, 199–233).

Besides several short stories, these include O. Henry's amusing prospectus—a promise "to fill its pages with matter that will make a heart-rending appeal to every lover of good literature, and every person who has a taste for reading print; and a dollar and a half for a year's subscription"—as well as facsimile reproductions of cartoons and sample pages, especially of those containing "The Plunkville Patriot," the paper's most characteristic feature (x, 64, 80, 96, 128, 160, 176, 232–33, 242–43). Among the earliest critics to recognize the latent artistry in these youthful effusions was Professor Hyder E. Rollins of Harvard, who in 1914 published a series of critical essays assessing the author's artistic merits and shortcomings and tracing both to their origins in *The Rolling Stone*.

Though generally unimpressed by "The Plunkville Patriot," Rollins found O. Henry's burlesque interviews and satires "extremely funny." Because they represented, in his view, "the true O. Henry, both in method and in manner," he felt sure that if *The Rolling Stone* were still alive in 1914 under the same editor but someone else's sounder financial management, it would be rivaling *Life* and *Judge*. Moreover, he reiterated this view by pointing to the "delightful quality" of its short stories, wherein one could detect "the touches and mannerisms that made O. Henry great."[26] A later critic scoffed: "The mannerisms, yes, but hardly the touches. In that early work there were originality and promise, but at best it was the work of a talented prentice hand; and Porter had to go far and learn much before he began to master the mechanics of his craft, above all the art of compression" (*Caliph*, 77–78).

One needn't split hairs over "touches and mannerisms," however, as both are inescapably evident in both the short stories and the briefer thrusts and parries O. Henry kept up while poking fun at a varied gallery of targets—for example, a spoofing news reporter's interview with President Grover Cleveland; the Germanic citizens in Austin; the "new woman" with her freakish fashions and breezy manners—enough, at any rate, to support Langford's observation that "the spectacle of life in and around Austin . . . received most of Porter's attention, and although the quality of his humor varies considerably, the occasions for it seem to have been endless" (254). He might also have noted that although the short stories in *The Rolling Stone* do reveal a prentice hand rather than a master's, there is no lack of either compression or witty touches in such examples as "Aristocracy Versus Hash," a burlesque on genteel Austin boardinghouse keepers; "The Prisoner of Zembla," a parody of chivalric romance; "Fickle Fortune or How Gladys Hustled," another parody of the Hairbreadth-Harry type of adventure romance; or "Tictoq" and "Tracked to Doom," a pair of burlesque crime stories (*Rolling Stones*, ix–xv, 199–233).

The most impressive of all these early fictions, however, is "Bexar Scrip No. 2692," a chillingly tense story of mystery, chicanery, and revenge in which O. Henry cleverly combined the setting of the General Land Office he knew so well with "a well-known tradition in Austin and vicinity that there is a buried treasure of great value somewhere on the banks of Shoal Creek, about a mile west of the city" (*Rolling Stones*, 230; see also Langford, 78–80). The story depicts a brutal murder committed by a villainous land agent named Sharp who, while trying to remove from the Land Office files certain legal papers establishing a claim to some land, was discovered by the son of the claimant. Upon the disappearance of Harris, the young victim, and the papers, Sharp secured the land, but his guilty act was not revealed until after his own death twenty years later, when some young treasure seekers discovered Harris's remains with the buried evidence. In this story were fused the results of personal experience, observation, and imagination; the author himself had actually been one of the young men in search of buried treasure, which became a kind of compulsive theme in his later stories (Langford,

58–60). And if one could not detect in it the future O. Henry, he was not to be found at all.

Early Short Fiction—The Houston *Post*

Having decided at last the *The Rolling Stone* could not be resuscitated, O. Henry turned his attention to the quest for other employment, preferably something involving editing or journalism. He seemed not to be apprehensive about his upcoming session with the court, and when it opened, both his friends and the bank officials offered such strong testimony of his innocence that the grand jury nol-prossed the case, leaving him free, if somewhat shaken, to consider several other job possibilities away from Austin. Athol's physical breakdown at that point ruled out his first offer to edit a humorous paper in Washington, D.C., but upon her recovery later in the summer, he gratefully accepted another offer to serve as a fill-in writer for the Houston *Post*, even though his starting salary would be a mere fifteen dollars a week (Langford, 86).

When he left Austin to fill this job, O. Henry probably assumed his troubles with the bank case were safely buried; if so, he reckoned without the persistence of the bank examiners, whose determination to reopen the case brought orders from Washington to have it resubmitted at the next session of court in February. Undaunted by this setback, O. Henry quickly demonstrated in Houston his ability to win influential friends with his habitual geniality, courtesy, and dedication to his work (Langford, 82–84; 89–90). Within a very short time he captured favorable attention and salary advances from his publisher for an innovative new feature column called "Some Postscripts," which resembled the kind of anecdotal material he had written for *The Rolling Stone*.

At first, his special value to the *Post* lay in the satirical barbs and cartoons he turned out, but presently his major appeal to the public came from the longer sketches he began writing, many of them incorporating themes, plots, and situations destined to reappear later in the more polished and elaborate forms of his most famous stories.[27] Thus, for the first time in his life O. Henry was now drawing regular pay for doing the kind of work he was both inclined and best fitted to do. Even under favorable circumstances and with no cloud of recent unresolved court action hanging over him, the results of his efforts during the next six months would have been remarkable: a total of fifty-nine short stories and sketches, besides numerous other pieces of writing. All these remained entirely unknown to the public for over twenty years after his death, and a complete file of them is still not available in print.[28] Among the *Post* sketches definitely identified as O. Henry's work, one can trace his facility for ringing changes on the familiar themes of mistaken identity, false pretense, misplaced devotion, nobility in disguise, and the bitter irony of fate. They are here in embryo along with such sentimental types as the sensitive tramp, the ill-starred lovers, the starving artist, and the gentle grafter. Long before he reached New York to delight millions with such stories as "The Enchanted Kiss," "While the Auto Waits," "Roads of Destiny," "The Door of Unrest," "The Caliph and the Cad," and many others, both the basic structure and tone of his stories, as well as the attitudes responsible for them, were being shaped in these *Post* sketches by the harsh realities of his Texas experiences, from which there could be only vicarious escape.

Like the materials in *The Rolling Stone*, the *Post* stories and sketches were also based on personal experiences that he had either participated in, observed, or discovered in the writings of Longfellow, Mark Twain, Stephen Crane, Rudyard Kipling, and other authors.[29] Besides a daily column of anecdotes about prominent persons and events, other sketches described downtown shoppers, Christmas and New Year's scenes, horse-race and circus crowds, city nightlife, and miscellaneous odd characters about town. Equally varied in their appeal to popular tastes, the stories covered a range of topics from the farcical to the maudlin and sentimental: sick newsboys, heroic tramps, slick gamblers, disguised lovers, embarrassed husbands and wives, lonely artists, mirages, and buried treasure.

Finally, O. Henry also transformed the extracts of his readings into new forms intended to instruct or amuse, as in the example of his serious critical essay on "Newspaper Poets" or that of his burlesque mimicry of well-known fiction, such as "Vereton Villa," discussed in the preceding section (in *O. Henry Encore*, 119–29); "The Legend of San Jacinto" and "Binkley's Practical School of Journalism," which parody the kind of spoofing found in Twain's *Roughing It* (*O. Henry Encore*, 101–15, 221–26); and "The Blue Blotch of Cowardice," a takeoff of Crane's celebrated *Red Badge of Courage* (Watson, 319–20).

More significant than these parodies, however, are O. Henry's themes, situations, and methods in the various *Post* stories that embody original composition, for these show the artist at work experimenting with techniques and developing an individual style. As Mary S. Harrell indicates, "The word-usage, sentence-structure, mythological allusions, plot-manipulation, character types, and central ideas that characterize O. Henry's short stories generally, are also plainly recognizable in these selections" (*O. Henry Encore*, xv). In one story based on his favorite *Arabian Nights* legends, for example, the whole effect turns on the punning "too gross" and "two gross";[30] in another, on the fitting together of the two halves of a concert ticket;[31] and again and again, the outcome is a shocking discovery that upsets the complacency of the characters involved.[32]

To examine the technique of plot manipulation alone, perhaps the most interesting of these stories is "Simmons' Saturday Night," an elaborately worked out variation on the old theme of the "biter bitten," which introduces a harmless-looking Texas greenhorn to a snappily dressed Houston dandy posing as a railroad paymaster. Quickly sizing up the yokel as a soft touch, the dandy offers to show him the sights, takes him first to a nightclub to soften him up further, then to a gambling house. "The old story of the hawk and the pigeon has been told so often that the details are apt to weary" (*O. Henry Encore*, 73), says the narrator, and from here on the rising tension of the poker game is so neatly built up to the climax with slight touches evoking pity for the poor pigeon that, when the coup de grace falls in a reversal of roles, the unwary reader is astonished to find Simmons transformed into Diamond Joe, a sly New York gambler traveling incognito to earn his expenses en route. All the elements of the carefully plotted O. Henry yarn are in evidence here, along with the use of realistic dialogue for enhanced dramatic effect. The many swindling yarns to be told later by O. Henry's lovable Jeff Peters are plainly foreshadowed in this story.

Because many of these forgotten Houston *Post* sketches served as models for O. Henry's later stories, various instructive parallels can be drawn between them and the more famous stories written for his New York audience. The slight sketch entitled "A Houston Romance" (*O. Henry Encore*, 98–100), for example, is almost a verbatim replica of "The Robe of Peace," a far-fetched tale about a stylish American yuppie who disappears and is later discovered by friends in a Swiss monastery, thoroughly content to stay there forever with his friar's garb because it does not bag at the knees.[33] The earlier version is only three pages long and sketchily developed; the later, twice as long and with New York names substituted for Houston ones, reveals by comparison how O. Henry worked to strengthen his illusion and build up his climax.

Again, another four-page sketch called "An Unknown Romance," based on the theme of disparity between wealth and poverty and focused by the well-worn device of mistaken identity, reappears in varied forms in at least half a dozen later stories. In the original version two wealthy young Americans fall in love with each other while vactioning in the Alps; mistaking each other's peasant garb for the real thing, they subvert their feelings of mutual allegiance in favor of marriages of convenience arranged by their parents, only to find they were destined for each other after all (*O. Henry Encore*, 79–82). Variations of the identical situation are worked out in "A Night in New Arabia," (*Strictly Business*, 209–230), and "Lost on Dress Parade,"[34] and with roles reversed in "Transients in Arcadia,"[35] and "The Caliph and the Cad" (*Sixes and Sevens*, 258–64), and again with a double reversal in "While the Auto Waits," (*Voice of the City*, 58–66), one of O. Henry's most famous stories (Langford, 93).

Actually, the disguise or impostor motif is seldom absent from O. Henry's fiction. Often coupled with the assumption that destiny or fate imposes inescapable roles on the individual, it becomes a major theme, recurring in many forms throughout all his work and its treatment, both serious and comic, can be seen in most of his earliest stories. The fatalistic notion that "we are all marionettes that dance and cry, scarce at our own wills," expressed in one of the *Post* stories,[36] is implicit in most of the others regardless of the social levels of his characters or the kinds of situations he places them in. Like the helpless young lovers, the opium-eating bum who imagines himself to be a wealthy scholar;[37] the sodden tramp who responds to a kind word with kingly grace;[38] or the thoughtless mother who locks up her little children at home and then runs to tell her neighbor of a nightmare in which she as a child had destroyed herself with fire[39]—all these and others convey the fundamental idea that the individual, with or without a mask, must play the part cut out for him/her, and that no matter what choices are offered or what roads taken, the individual is inevitably destined for the same predetermined end.

Whether such rigidity bears out Langford's assertion that in 1896 O. Henry already "understood himself well enough to express in terms of fatalism his inadequacy in dealing with the actualities of life" (94) is, perhaps, open to debate. What is certain, however, is that he reworked these same themes and situations again and again in later stories, giving them a finer finish and a higher polish in order to make his illusory world of fiction a more enchanting one. Can this maturing artistry be blandly lumped in as further proof of his inadequacy?

The Western Stories

O. Henry's professional career as a successful writer of short fiction was remarkably short—barely fifteen years, in fact, from the flickering exit of *The Rolling Stone* in 1895 to his own death in 1910. But to obtain a just appraisal of his achievement during that brief period, it had best be examined in two stages of relatively equal duration: namely, from before and after his release from prison in 1901. For whatever ranking O. Henry's oeuvre may ultimately attain, whether high or low on the aesthetic scale of American fiction, there can be little dispute that the single most powerful force in its makeup was the trauma of his incarceration.

As noted above, when he began writing for the Houston *Post* in July 1895, O. Henry may have assumed the charge of embezzlement was invalid, the case against him closed. But he soon learned otherwise; early the next year he was arrested in Houston and taken back to Austin for arraignment, then was quickly released on a bond of two thousand dollars (signed by his father-in-law and another friend) and granted a continuance, enabling him to return to Houston to prepare a defense and help care for his prostrate wife. However, as July approached and the inevitable trial had to be faced, O. Henry could not face it. Notwithstanding the strong support of loyal friends in both cities, most of whom believed him to be innocent and thought the trial would be a mere formality, he had apparently prepared no defense nor made plans of any sort except on the spur of a final moment when, ostensibly entrained for Austin, he switched instead toward New Orleans and shortly thereafter sailed off to Honduras.

This bizarre act of desperate folly, marking the climax of his career in Texas, likewise opened the road of destiny he chose to follow. It was an act that initiated a series of experiences crowded within four "shadowed years" of exile and imprisonment and destined to remain shrouded in mystery, legend, controversy, and myth for the remainder of O. Henry's career and, indeed, for many more years after his death. For these were the crucial experiences that gave the ultimate substance, meaning, and form to his creative work.

Whether O. Henry's sudden flight was premeditated or impulsive as his apologists argue—the evidence is still ambiguous—when he reached New Orleans with the $260 loan raised by friends on the *Post* for his trial, he seems to have had no detailed plans for the future, except possibly to evade the law by remaining outside the United States until freed by the statute of limitations. Aside from rumor and conjecture, however, the record of his activities during his brief sojourn in New Orleans is largely inferential. Some casual acquaintances recalled later that he worked a short stint for one of the newspapers there and mingled convivially but unobtrusively with fellow reporters; others maintained he kept in touch with his wife and family by sending them notes and drawings through a third party (Langford, 101).

But perhaps the clearest evidence of both his state of mind and his activities at this point may be drawn from several of his stories about New Orleans, written and published many years later—particularly one called "Blind Man's Holiday," in which a fugitive gambler-embezzler paralleled his own case precisely.[40] More significantly, other stories in this group, such as "Cherchez la Femme," "The Renaissance at Charleroi," and "Whistling Dick's Christmas Stocking," show how accurately O. Henry could recapture in swift, flashing phrases the distinctive features of the locale: the lights and shadows, the flowered paths and local customs, the architecture and dim interiors of public buildings and little cafés, the speech rhythms of native Creoles—the very atmosphere of the Vieux Carré. Yet he had lived in New Orleans but a few weeks before sailing away to Central America, where he spent the remainder of the year 1896.

O. Henry's western stories, excluding those published in *The Rolling Stone* and the Houston *Post*, number about eighty in all; but for a closer look at distinctive individual features within such an unwieldy mass, that total may be more conveniently subdivided into three groups, the largest numbering thirty-nine stories with Texas settings. The smallest group, although similar in many important respects, consists of seventeen stories with settings in other western states; the third group of twenty-four stories are those with settings in Latin American countries. About half of these western stories were published in the three-year period prior to 1904, the others over the remaining six years of O. Henry's life. Thus, the figures show that the West, like the South, never faded from his consciousness (five of his western stories, in fact, were not published until shortly after he died). A closer look at individual titles also reveals that, notwithstanding their original publication dates, many of the western stories were written long before they first broke into print.

Texas

"In Texas you may travel a thousand miles in a straight line. If your course is a crooked one, it is likely that both the distance and your rate of

speed may be vastly increased." Typically, O. Henry begins one of his
Texas stories this way, slyly fixing, in two short sentences, the feeling of
spaciousness and the suggestion of fraud and violence to be dramatized
on this huge stage, where a large bundle of New Jerseys and Rhode
Islands "could have been stowed away and lost in its chaparral."[41] No
matter how far-fetched their plots or characters, the settings in many of
his western stories are often their most distinguishing feature—usually
sketched in with minimal detail yet so nicely done that both the atmosphere of the scene and its physical arrangements are brought sharply
into focus. This characteristic is vibrantly present in all but a few of the
nearly forty stories laid in Texas, most of which deal with the southwestern or chaparral region, a vast domain of sheep and cattle ranches
extending southward from San Antonio and the Frio River area to the
Nueces River and beyond, through the thinly populated no-man's-land
of outlaws lying between the Nueces and the Rio Grande.[42]

In this huge, open, rolling terrain, covered with mesquite and low-
lying evergreen oaks, the qualities O. Henry quickly evokes are, first, the
beauty of the natural scenery, enhanced even by its aridity and endless
vistas of unrelieved monotone; and, second, the simplicity and freedom
of movement that life in such a country inspires: thus—

> They swept out of the little town and down the level road toward
> the South. Soon the road dwindled and disappeared, and they struck
> across a world carpeted with an endless reach of curly mesquite grass.
> The wheels made no sound. The tireless ponies bounded ahead at an
> unbroken gallop. The temperate wind, made fragrant by thousands of
> acres of blue and yellow flowers, roared gloriously in their ears. The
> motion was aerial, ecstatic, with a thrilling sense of perpetuity in its
> effect.[43]

Again and again, O. Henry sends off a pair of horsemen, riding for
miles "in silence save for the soft drum of the ponies' hoofs on the
matted mesquite grass, and the rattle of the chaparral against their
wooden stirrups";[44] or in a buckboard, a couple speeding "upon velvet
wheels across an exhilarant savanna . . . and . . . the uncharted bil-
lows of the grass itself . . . [where] each tiny distant mott of trees was a
signboard, each convolution of the low hills a voucher of course and
distance."[45] These riders are usually on their way to a modest ranch-
house like the Rancho Cibolo, "composed of four large rooms, with
plastered adobe walls, and a two-room wooden ell . . . set in a grove of

immense live-oaks and water-elms near a lake";[46] or like Rush Kinney's two-room affair, resting "upon the summit of a lenient slope" amid a broad prairie, "diversified by aroyos and murky patches of brush and pear," in an atmosphere "heady with ozone and made memorably sweet by leagues of wild flowers," its silence disturbed only by the occasional drumming rush of frightened sheep in the corrals, the shrill yapping of coyotes in the distance, the twittering of whippoorwills, and "the clear torrent of the mockingbirds' notes that fell from a dozen neighboring shrubs and trees."[47]

The quiet orderliness and simplicity of living conditions in surroundings like these are heightened by the contrasts between them and the ramshackle little towns like Nopal, which "seemed to have been hastily constructed of undressed lumber and flapping canvas";[48] or like Paloma, where the Southern Pacific train stopped "at noon for the engine to drink and for the passengers both to drink and to dine. There was a new yellow-pine hotel, also a wood warehouse, and perhaps three dozen box residences. The rest was composed of tents, cow ponies, "Black-saxy mud, and mesquite-trees, all bound round by a horizon."[49] To such grim little settlements the ranch hands came with their chuck wagons to pick up supplies, patronize the saloons, gamble, and take part in other primitive forms of recreation. And some of them might even get on to attend the fairs and races at San Antonio, "the hub of the wheel of Fortune . . . [where] cattlemen played at crack-loo on the side-walks with double-eagles, and gentlemen backed their conception of the fortuitous card with stacks limited in height only by the interference of gravity."[50]

Whether at work or play, men who lived under these conditions were active, their lifestyles vigorous and rugged, if slow-moving at times, in the blistering summer heat along the Mexican border. In the branding season the *vaqueros* were awakened before dawn, mustered in gangs of up to twenty-five men, and made "ready to start for the San Carlos range, where the work was to begin. By six o'clock the horses were all saddled, the grub wagon ready, and the cow-punchers were swinging themselves upon their mounts."[51] When they were off duty, their behavior was equally rugged: for recreation, "they pounded one another hurtfully and affectionately; they heaped upon one another's heads friendly curses and obloquy";[52] and they played such boyish pranks with their six-shooters as pumping holes into the high silk hats of occasional dignitaries who came to their camps to solicit votes.[53]

But the same primitive society that evoked high jinks of this sort also tolerated widespread violence and ferocity, theft, and fraud in a land where "the law was mainly a letter"; outlaw bands roamed the open country along the border, from time to time running off "some very good companies of horses from the ranges, and a few bunches of fine cattle which they got safely across the Rio Grande and disposed of to fair advantage. Often the band would ride into the little villages and Mexican settlements, terrorizing the inhabitants and plundering for the provisions and ammunition they needed."[54]

At any moment the quiet of a sleepy town like Quicksand might be shattered by the exuberant sharpshooting of a drunken Calliope Catesby, so that "glass fell like hail; dogs vamosed; chickens flew, squawking; feminine voices shrieked concernedly to youngsters at large."[55] Oftener than that, however, the forces of law and order had to deal with the depredations of wild men, marauding like the Trimble gang—"ten of 'em—the worst outfit of desperadoes and horse-thieves in Texas, coming up the street shooting right and left . . . straight for the Gray Mule, a saloon which they proceeded to tear apart, drinking what they wanted and smashing what they didn't."[56] But no less often, perhaps, the authorities were called upon to settle bitter conflicts between evicted settlers and land sharks, a process that "entailed incalculable trouble, endless litigation, a period of riotous land-grabbing, and no little bloodshed."[57]

Such, briefly, was the colorful background for O. Henry's many romanticized tales about life in the Texas he knew. Whether writing about towns or open country, the few physical details he chose for each story usually bring the scene vividly to life by appealing strongly to one's senses of sight and sound, smell and taste, as in: the guitar's tinkling accompaniment to a señorita's sad ballad in "A Fog in Santone"; the acrid fumes rising from a sheep-dipping vat in "Law and Order"; the dull thumps of hobbled ponies moving about for fresh grass in "Jimmy Hayes and Muriel"; brown cottontails frolicking through a ranchyard while a covey of white-topknotted blue quail run past, in single file, twenty yards away in "The Last of the Troubadors"; a party of ranchers' wives and daughters gaily setting off for a ten-mile jaunt in a buckboard "with their Easter hats and frocks carefully wrapped and bundled against the dust";[58] the crash and whine of gold coins being rapidly counted by the nimble fingers of a bank examiner in "Friends in San Rosario"; the crowds of gaping cattlemen thronging the Capitol during a legislative session in "Art and the Bronco"; the little black heads of Mexican children peering at a neighbor's strawberry patch through "a crazy picket fence overgrown with morning glory and wild gourd vine."[59] The list could be extended on and on, for virtually every story flaunts its quota of vivid details.

In O. Henry's fiction, however, specific details of things visible or tangible in external nature far outnumber those that suggest or draw attention to inner states of thought or feeling; he appears to have been less interested in representing psychic conflicts within or among living individuals than in preparing a realistic stage or background for his puppets. Thus one can more readily visualize his western environment than accept as real individuals the characters who inhabit that environment, because the illusion of the one makes its presence appear to be there, alive, three-dimensional, as opposed to the flatness of the human creatures who move about, act, and speak their parts in the story. Most of them seem more like pawns, lacking the complexity of motives that governs the attitudes and behavior of even simple human beings, lacking inner conflicts and inconsistencies. Yet their actions do conform to O. Henry's own mechanistic view of the human predicament: like creatures managed by a master puppeteer jerking his cords, their lives are governed by chance much in the same manner as he believed to be the destiny of ordinary human beings of all classes. And so one's interest centers on the gyrations of the dance they dance rather than on the peculiarities of their makeup.

Critics now generally agree this sort of approach to nature and society weakens all of O. Henry's fiction because it leads to oversimplification and a consequent lack of subtlety, nuance, depth, or complexity of meaning. Noticeable especially in the western stories, the actions and interactions of his characters remain on the surface of things and are the result of a few basic passions such as love, hate, fear, greed, and anger. And the conflicts endured end in marriage or death, satisfaction or sorrow, which the reader must accept on faith, since little if any analysis of motives has been forthcoming. Too often stereotyped, the characters, most of them males, fall into recognizably conventionalized types— good guys and bad guys—but there is such an interesting variety of these types, and such clever variations are worked out among some of them, that all but the most fastidious readers can be easily beguiled into overlooking their lack of individuality.

For his Texas stories alone, O. Henry created more than 200 characters with speaking parts, representing more than forty distinct types drawn from towns, villages, and open range country (Howell, 112–37). In addition to cowboys and outlaws—the most colorful and numerous of all—these types include cattle kings and sheepmen, rangers, station agents, doctors, burglars, bankers, clerks, farmers, hoboes, cooks, and assorted wives and daughters of these and of still other types. From such a flavorful social potpourri O. Henry needed only to select a few types for each story, and by varying slightly the relationships among them he could mesmerize his readers with a succession of amusing plots that make up in varied entertainment for their failure to offer much insight into the mysteries of human nature.

The most frequent plot, of course, is a variant of the boy-meets-girl situation. This may involve either rivalry between two or more men for possession of a woman, or barriers between a man and a woman that, until removed in the story, preclude a satisfactory resolution of the problem. Nearly half of O. Henry's Texas stories deal with some aspect of this latter situation. The barrier may be a matter of pride, as in "Hearts and Crosses," "The Princess and the Puma," and "The Indian Summer of Dry Valley Johnson," or it may be one of misunderstanding caused by mistaken identity, as in "The Marquis and Miss Sally," or a mixture of both, as in "Madame Bo-Peep and the Ranches." The only difference between Santa McAllister, the proud cattle king's daughter in "Hearts and Crosses," and Panchita O'Brien, the Mexican heroine of "The Indian Summer," is a difference of wealth and social status; both are strong-willed women who know how to get their man by yielding at the right moment.

Again, in developing the male rivalry situation O. Henry usually worked out a predictable pattern in which the anticipated surprise ending of the story may well become less entertaining through repetition than do his methods for setting it up. The plot in "The Red Roses on Tonia," for example, hinges on a race to bring a new Easter bonnet with red roses on it to an impatient ranch girl; in "Buried Treasure," it is a matter of stumbling upon the girl hidden in the mountains by an obdurate father. In "The Pimiento Pancakes," a scorned sheepman outwits his rival by persuading the girl that the rival is a madman. Sometimes the contest is a draw, as in "A Poor Rule," wherein all four suitors are abandoned by the heroine for a career as a concert singer. In "The Sphinx Apple" the heroine falls asleep while listening to *her* four admirers' competitive efforts to tell a story. Or again, it may be coupled with a revenge motif, harmless, as in "The Moment of Victory," when the undersized but feisty little war-hero Willie Robbins tells off the girl who rejected him, or violent, as in "A Chaparral Christmas Gift," when the rejected suitor turns desperado, nearly murders his rival, and is later shot to death by another man. Whether grim or light-hearted, however, the denouement of these tales is usually less rewarding than the path leading up to it.

Another fruitful source for engaging plots in O. Henry's western stories is the idea of reformation or rehabilitation, and he was usually more successful in developing this theme than he was with that of the battle of the sexes. One of his best stories in this group, possibly because of a pronounced autobiographical element in it, is "Hygeia at the Solito." The story is about a spunky little New York hoodlum, "Cricket" McGuire, whose rehabilitation begins when Curtis Raidler, a gruff but kindly cattleman, discovers him sitting, sick and disconsolate, on the railroad platform in San Antonio. Raidler, like the Good Samaritan, takes "Cricket" off to his ranch, and from there on the story focuses on a fierce contest between the tough little pugilist and his equally tough but fatherly host, who is determined to make a man of him.

"The Higher Abdication" follows an almost identical formula, but in this story Curly, a broken-down tramp, is whipped into shape through hard knocks and ostracism so that in the end he can be transformed into the long lost prodigal son whose miraculous reappearance can unsnarl a frustrated love affair. And again, in "The Reformation of Calliope"—a story that bears an obvious kinship to Stephen Crane's "The Bride Comes to Yellow Sky"—the blustery, free-shooting Terror of Quicksand earns absolution and reprieve from the marshall he has wounded when Calliope's aged mother providentially appears on the scene.[60] As in Crane's famous tale, tall-tale elements provide the entertainment in this story, and the device of mistaken identity sets up the "snapper" at the end.

A useful comedic ploy since the ancient classic drama of Menander, mistaken identity is again the key to reformation in "A Double-Dyed Deceiver," one of the most tightly knit of O. Henry's badman plots, which develops the Llano Kid's transformation from murderous gunman to the adopted son of his last victim's wealthy South American parents through the device of a tattooed symbol. Here, the disguise motif is cleverly manipulated, as it is also in "The Passing of Black Eagle," but this latter story about a scavenging hobo temporarily elevated to leadership of an outlaw gang and organizer of an abortive train robbery is too far-fetched to be anything but a tall tale. Tall-tale elements, in fact, seldom failed to appear in O. Henry's best stories; he used them again in "Law and Order," another variation on the reformation theme published after his death.[61]

Third among his favorite plot situations is the ever-popular confrontation between criminals and the agents of law enforcement, usually engaged in mortal combat. This classic situation provided O. Henry one of his earliest opportunities to achieve a national audience with "The Miracle of Lava Canyon," published under his real name by the McClure Syndicate shortly after he entered prison in 1898. He evidently liked the story so much that, while in jail, he revised it completely and had it republished in 1902 under a new title, "An Afternoon Miracle."

Both versions are essentially identical—the handsome, powerful but inwardly fearful sheriff's encounter with a reckless desperado while under the scrutiny of a threatened woman afraid of nothing—but if placed side by side, the comparison reveals an illuminating study of O. Henry's maturing techniques: the "miracle" of the later version, involving the double switch between cowardice and courage, is given ironic overtones totally absent in the earlier one. The reader learns in the earlier version that the fearless girl, shortly after being rescued, screams with real fright on seeing a tiny lizard and that "the sheriff's strong arm reassured her. The miracle was complete. The soul of each had passed into the other."[62] But in the later version the heroine, Alvarita, only pretends to be frightened by a two-inch caterpillar in order to clinch her protector Buckley's solicitude.

Repeatedly in his western stories O. Henry shifted and rearranged the movers and shakers within his "cops-and-robbers" pattern. In "A Departmental Case," for example, the hero is an elderly government official, Luke Standifer (obviously based on O. Henry's former benefactor, Richard Hall), who avenges the mistreated daughter of his old-time ranger pal by gunning down her worthless husband, Benton Sharp—"one of the most noted 'bad' men in that part of the state—a man who had been a cattle thief, an outlaw, a desperado, and was not a gambler, a swaggering bully" (Roads of Destiny). In "One Dollar's Worth" revenge ignites the deadly duel between Mexico Sam and Littlefield, the young district attorney who sent Sam to jail four years before, but its outcome rests on Littlefield's fortuitous ownership of a counterfeit lead dollar, which serves as ammunition instead of the evidence it was intended to be. Here, by means of a neat twist in the action, O. Henry makes crime pay and not pay at the same time, while in "The Last of the Troubadors" he reverses the twist, causing his hero, singing Sam Galloway, to destroy the bullying badman, King James, just after James has reversed his own evil intentions.

Probably the most effective of all his badman plots, however, is worked out in "The Caballero's Way," which combines the revenge and infidelity motifs in a tale that packs a gruesome punch comparable to Conrad or Crane at their best. The story introduces the deadly Cisco Kid, O. Henry's fascinating but ambivalent hero-villain, who "killed for the love of it—because he was quick-tempered—to avoid arrest—for his own amusement—any reason that came to his mind would suffice" (*Options*, 54–55). His reason on this occasion is sufficient: he must avenge the insult done to his honor by his mistress, Tonia Perez, who has conspired to turn him in to her new lover, Sandridge, the Texas Ranger pursuing him. But to pay off her unfaithfulness, the Cisco Kid's modus operandi is the "caballero's way" of tricking Sandridge into performing the dirty work himself. Coldly told, and almost totally free of sticky sentimentality, "The Caballero's Way" is a brilliant performance. It is thus easy to see why the Cisco Kid has survived in countless versions of popular dramatic entertainment for stage, screen, radio, video, even music and song down to the present. Country music fans today can testify he lives again in Willie Nelson's rollicking "Pour Me Another Tequila, Sheila."

Even though O. Henry repeatedly overworked the same hackneyed situations based on primitive forms of conflict in these Texas stories, the plotting in most of them is often fresh and innovative, revealing a fecundity of invention in warming up and flavoring an old chestnut to make it palatable. The Damon-and-Pythias motif, for instance, is developed differently in "A Call Loan" and "Friends in San Rosario," both stories depicting the circumvention of banking laws through the collusion of friendly bankers. Similarly, the self-sacrifice or vindication theme is treated in two distinctive ways, yet with the familiar surprise ending both times, in "A Fog in Santone" and "Jimmie Hayes and Muriel": in the former a despondent young prostitute swallows the poisoned pills she has convinced a tuberculous youth to relinquish because there is so much to live for; in the latter the exhumed skeleton of a man despised as a cowardly deserter proves he had heroically tackled and destroyed a band of outlaws.

Another popular theme in nineteenth century idealistic fiction that strongly appealed to O. Henry was the idea of a young child's benevolent social influence, inspiring him to write both "A Chaparral Prince" and "Georgia's Ruling." The first is a variation on the Cinderella theme in which rampaging outlaws rescue little Lena Hildesmüller from the blight of child-labor exploitation; the second, equally sentimental, is a case of literal mortmain in which a child's dying wish saves an entire county's landless settlers from being evicted by a group of greedy land-sharks.

Among the long list of O. Henry's Texas plots three more should be noted because of the contrasting methods with which he developed them: they are "The Enchanted Kiss," in which a sequence of weird dreams vaguely reminiscent of de Maupassant dramatize the contrast between illusion and reality; "Art and the Bronco," in which liberal injections of tall-tale buffoonery and satire point up the incongruity between pretentious art and the primitive society of a frontier community; and "The Hiding of Black Bill," probably the most sophisticated performance of the three. It is a masterpiece of plot construction based on the theme of self-preservation as the first law of nature, set in motion by O. Henry's concealed narrator, who introduces two seedy hoboes, Ham and Snipy, one of whom then takes over to manage the progress of the story in a series of reported conversations that sound as natural as something overheard.

As they crouch below a railroad siding awaiting a freight train, Ham reports that while employed recently on a lonely sheep ranch in a region where sheriffs' posses were hunting a bank robber, he managed to throw suspicion on his employer, Ogden, and to collect a reward when Ogden was caught with the money on his person. Snipy's prompt reaction to this account is highly censorious: "I don't like your talk. You and me have been friends, off and on, for fifteen year; and I never yet knew or heard of you giving anybody up to the law—not no one. And here was a man whose saleratus you had et and at whose table you had played games of cards. . . . And yet you inform him to the law and take money for it. It never was like you, I say" (*Options*, 54–55). Ham simply explains that he himself was Black Bill and planted the stolen money on the sleeping Ogden when he saw the posse coming because he knew Ogden would surely be released later with an alibi.

Other Western Stories

Most of the remaining seventeen stories laid in other western states do not measure up in either color or quality to the ones about Texas, yet all but three of them were written long after he had left the state, possibly as a result of half-forgotten incidents recalled during his crowded New York years and easily fashioned into plots suitable for meeting the clamor of anguished editors. For the most part the settings of these stories, though laid in a broad area from Oklahoma to Montana and from Indiana to Arizona, are irrelevant: they could all be shuffled about like cards in a deck without altering either plot structure or meaning. Twelve of the stories qualify as tall tales, written purposely to draw laughter at the absurd antics described by their narrators; only five of them were reprinted in the early volume, *Heart of the West*, which contains those western stories O. Henry prized among his best. Four others were published only once, in *The Gentle Grafter*; the remaining eight reappeared only in the volumes containing his leftovers, published after his death.[63]

The most engaging of the twelve tall tales in this group are the four Jeff Peters stories in *The Gentle Grafter* and two others with the same narrator, written earlier and published in other volumes. The original Jeff Peters story, published in 1902 with the title "A Guthrie Wooing," and attributed to "Olivier Henry," reappeared in *Heart of the West* under a new title. As "Cupid a la Carte" its main distinction is that Jeff Peters, the loquacious narrator, for once does not speak about his swindling activities. Instead, he tells a ludicrous tale of rivalry between himself and another man for the hand of Mame Dugan, a hash-house owner's daughter who has grown so tired of dishing out food to hungry men that she vows to remain a spinster and "raise violets for the Eastern market."[64] But the best of all the Jeff Peters stories, O. Henry himself asserted, is "The Atavism of John Tom Little Bear," an uproarious farce involving Indian Medicine-show swindling, a brief love interest, a kidnapping, and a daring rescue, topped off with the foiled villain's scalp.[65] Here, laughter is evoked not only by Jeff's inimitable manner of telling a story, for O. Henry doubles the humor with his characterization of the educated Cherokee, John Tom, "a graduate of one of them Eastern football colleges that have been so successful in teaching the Indian to use the gridiron instead of burning his victims at the stake" (*Rolling Stones*, 35). Having savored the antics of these two characters, one finds the other tall tales in the group a bit tepid.

Each of the other five stories in this western category, however, offers some rewarding evidence of O. Henry's concern with life's darker aspects—specifically, his preoccupation with crime, violence, and death, as well as his varied narrative attempts to cope with such matters. Two of the stories that reveal contrasting methods of working up his western material are the early "Hearts and Hands," published in 1902, and "The Snow Man," which he was composing during his last illness but could not finish.[66] The first is little more than an expanded anecdote, yet within its single railway-coach scene a pathetic little drama with poignant autobiographical overtones is deftly set forth as young Easton, handcuffed to the marshall conducting him to Leavenworth, saves face while talking with a girl he knows by pretending that he himself is the police officer. "The Snow Man," however, is an elaborately fashioned treatment of boredom, frustration, and rivalry shared by four men stranded in a snowbound cabin in Montana. The arrival of a young woman raises a problem O. Henry might have solved more daringly had he lived to finish his own story; as he left it, his conventionalized surprise ending fails to uphold the ominous tone introduced at the beginning. But even so, a discomforting feeling of death lurks beneath the surface of this suggestive story.

Two other stories that recall the brutality of "The Caballero's Way," though constructed differently from it and from each other, are "A Technical Error" and "The Roads We Take." O. Henry's last completed story to appear in print before he died, "A Technical Error" is another treatment of infidelity avenged, coupled with the disguise motif, but here the narrator asserts he himself took part in pursuit of the fleeing couple, who were cornered in a hotel in Guthrie. But the avenger, Sam Durkee, we are told, withheld his fire at that point because it was contrary to the code to shoot a man in cold blood when he was with a woman (the victim had to be "cut out of the herd" and dealt with alone); yet at the next town Sam calmly pumped six bullets into his rival (who had exchanged clothes with the girl) when he found the couple sitting together.[67]

Equally brutal but quite differently worked up, "The Roads We Take" is also a story of betrayal that dramatizes, by means of a doubly contrasting device involving dream versus reality and East versus West, O. Henry's fatalistic theory that regardless of the path one follows in life the end is pre-determined by what one is. The story opens with a sensational train robbery in Arizona that reaches a climax when Dodson, the easterner, cold-bloodedly murders his partner because Bolivar, the one good horse they have left for their escape, "can't carry double" (*Whirligigs*, 163). Then we learn through a neatly turned transition that Dodson, a well-known New York broker, has dreamed the whole sequence of events while seated in his office chair. When his clerk comes to report that his old friend, Williams, has been caught short in the stock market and will be ruined unless Dodson agrees to settle a deal at the old price of ninety-eight, Dodson ruthlessly counters: "He will settle at one eighty-five . . . Bolivar cannot carry double" (*Whirligigs*, 165).

The initial paragraphs of this story offer a striking example of O.

Henry's technical virtuosity—notably his skillful use of terse yet vivid imagery. Within less than two pages the train robbers detach the engine, blow up the express-car safe, and escape with thirty thousand dollars by driving the engine two miles ahead to where they have tethered their horses. This portion of the narrative should be compared closely with a longer story, "Holding Up a Train," O. Henry published a few months earlier in 1904 and that probably served him as a model for the later one. For although "The Roads We Take" is tight, compact, and streamlined to fit the requirements of the New York *Sunday World's* feature page, the earlier story is discursive and rambling—deliberately so, however, because it was a collaborative effort between O. Henry and his prison-mate, Al Jennings.[68]

Actually, "Holding Up a Train" is unique among O. Henry's western stories in that it probably contains more fact than fiction, although there is no way to tell how much of it was written by either of its authors. Consequently, the story behind its composition is even more fascinating than the account itself, as Jennings, while still in prison, supplied O. Henry with original data in his own manuscript. And after analyzing it critically, O. Henry suggested at length how it might be expanded into a solid article of four to six thousand words that *Everybody's* would gladly accept; at the same time, however, he also promised to submit another of his own composition. Shortly afterward, he gleefully sent his "Dear Pard" the publisher's letter of acceptance along with this comment: "When you see your baby in print don't blame me if you find strange ear marks and brands on it. I slashed it and cut it and added lots of stuff that never happened, but I followed your facts and ideas, and that is what made it valuable."[69] By this time, O. Henry's western apprenticeship had served it purpose.

He had so fully mastered the art of mixing real-life adventures and pure fantasy through the medium of the tall tale that some literary critics in the East were unable to distinguish between the truth and the fiction in his stories. While they often praised what they considered to be authentic portrayals in his New York stories, they condemned his western stories for being grossly exaggerated. Yet the charge of exaggeration, though applicable enough to most of O. Henry's stories, is less applicable to his western tales than to any of his others, for it has been unmistakably shown that his Texas "badman" types are not only based on real-life outlaws who flourished in the *brasada* or chaparral region of the Rio Grande in the 1870s and 1880s, but that they are much less flamboyant in their behavior and speech than were their real-life counterparts—such men as John Wesley Hardin, King Fisher, Ben Thompson, and Ham White. These and other notorious desperadoes whom O. Henry encountered or heard of while living with the Halls were actually rendered with a greater degree of authenticity than New York critics could imagine in such stories as "The Last of the Troubadors," "The Passing of Black Eagle," and "The Caballero's Way." John Hardin, who had earned his distinction as "Texas' own greatest 'singlehanded terror' of all time" for having killed forty men before reaching his majority, thus offered a solid flesh-and-blood basis for O. Henry's Cisco Kid.[70] Moreover, the exaggerated characterizations, actions, and speech condemned in these western stories were, as we have seen, basic components in an indigenous American tall-tale humor tradition, which had flourished for many decades on the antebellum frontier.

Lotus Land—O. Henry's Hispanic Exposure

Many years ago, one of O. Henry's biographers observed that his stories generally followed chronologically "the background against which he lived his own adventurous life" (*Caliph*, 103). First came the Texas tales, then the New Orleans ones, then those about Central America, and finally the New York stories. Superficially, this assertion makes sense, but it does not tell us very much about the types and qualities of his stories; nor is it quite accurate, because O. Henry continued writing stories about Texas, the West, and the deep South long after he left his adventures in all those areas behind him. So too regarding his stories about Central America; for, while it is correct to say that "with *Cabbages and Kings* . . . he invaded the Arabian Nights for the first time" (*Caliph*, 103), it must be added quickly that O. Henry was still writing stories about Central America as late as 1908. But aside from its being a place of temporary refuge, the necessary questions to ask are: What did Central America represent in O. Henry's imagination? How did he depict it in his stories? Do they actually reflect his own life and environment—even if admittedly a bit overdone—during the fugitive months he spent in Honduras? When all of O. Henry's Latin American stories are carefully scrutinized, the answer to this last question can only be a firm "No"; they reflect rather what he himself referred to as the "far land of the lotus . . . land of perpetual afternoon . . . [where] life among this indolent, romantic people—a life full of music, flowers, and low laughter" could be perpetually enjoyed.[71] What these stories actually represent is wish fulfillment and romantic escape—and they were meant to do so.

They differ from O. Henry's other western tales in several important respects, but the problem of analyzing them carefully is complicated by a number of factors not generally known to casual readers. For example, there are in all twenty-six Latin American stories, eighteen of which are bound up together as "chapters" in the simulated novel, *Cabbages and Kings*, O. Henry's first full-length book; the other eight stories were published separately, for the most part, after the book appeared.

When *Cabbages and Kings* was published in 1904, some critics commented about its loose construction; one reviewer, comparing it to *The Golden Ass of Apuleius*, even called it "a series of Milesian tales which have no relation to each other" (*Caliph*, 105–106). But the book was nevertheless thought to be a single original piece of writing in which its various parts had been artfully designed to hang together. In a sense that assumption was correct, except for the fact that all but a few of its eighteen so-called chapters had been carved out of seven earlier stories published several years before in *Ainslee's, Everybody's, McClure's,* and *Smart Set*; also, some slight changes of chapter headings and the names of characters and places had been made to make the work conform to the requirements of a long single work of fiction. A thorough analysis of the makeup of *Cabbages and Kings* published in 1935 shows O. Henry based the "plot" on his long short story "Money Maze," which he had cut into segments and attached to other segments from other stories, combining these and newly written portions inserted at appropriate points of the developing story. Then he wrote an entirely new chapter, which he titled "Money Maze," and another for the conclusion, called "The Vitagraphoscope."[72]

By manipulating his earlier stories in this way, O. Henry doubled his profits from them; in place of the original, separate stories sold to the four magazines, he produced what appeared to be an entirely new work, an amusing light mystery novel about embezzlers and absconders in and around the fictive "banana" republic of Anchuria. Moreover, the book also extended his range, giving fictional shape to his Honduran interlude and raising his stature as a rival of Richard Harding Davis.

But to assert the characters and action in *Cabbages and Kings* "must have been drawn from life . . . [because] sheer invention was impossible" (*Caliph*, 104) is to pay greater tribute to O. Henry's narrative skill than to the perspicacity of the critic who said so. O. Henry worked diligently, together with Witter Bynner's capable aid, to conceal with seeming realism the unreality of his lotus land. When the book is read as a single entity, the illusion of reality projected in it is more seductive than it would be if each of the original stories composing it were read separately in its original context, for when this experiment is made, it can be plainly seen that most of these stories, like so many others O. Henry wrote, are tall tales. Virtually his entire collection of Latin American stories are tall tales; of the remaining eight that were not included in *Cabbages and Kings*, only "The World and the Door" does not obviously fall into the tall-tale genre.

Since none of the seven stories that make up the bulk of *Cabbages and Kings* has ever been reprinted, the experiment suggested above would not be easy to do, but if we recall what O. Henry told his "pard" Al Jennings about their joint authorship of "Holding Up a Train"—namely, that he had "added lots of stuff that never happened"—we need only compare *Cabbages and Kings* as it stands with the other stories about Latin America to draw the same conclusion. A good one to start with is "The Fourth in Salvador" (*Roads of Destiny*, 171–83), an uproarious tall tale about a drunken brawl in which four or five Americans, an Englishman, and "a buck coon from Georgia" shot up a town while celebrating the Fourth of July, thereby contributing to the success of a revolution that made them heroes in the euphoria of the new regime.

The whole story is utterly ridiculous but is told in such a bland, matter-of-fact way as a remembered episode that its integrated details can be easily accepted for historic fact. But it should also be read in the light of Al Jenning's reference to the same episode, which was allegedly what brought about the first meeting of these two famous fugitives from American justice: "Everyone who knows O. Henry knows how three loyal prodigals celebrated the nation's birth. He has made it memorable in his story, 'The Fourth in Salvador.' What he couldn't remember he fabricated, but many of the details . . . happened just as he had narrated them."[73] Well, maybe so, but the skeptical reader can only suspect that he also "added lots of stuff that never happened."

All the other Latin American stories are cut from the same colorful cloth, its texture so cunningly woven of a minimum of remembered fact and a maximum of fanciful invention that the illusion of truth is delightfully upheld. "On Behalf of the Management," for example, tells of a phony election campaign, cooked up and financed in New York but abortively conducted in an imaginary postage-stamp-sized country somewhere near Ecuador (*Roads of Destiny*, 243–57). "Two Renegades" likewise deals with the intervention of two crackpot Americans in a

Panamanian revolutionary escapade, one of whom, a Yankee named O'Keefe, is ransomed from a firing squad by the other, Doc Millikan, a dyed-in-the-wool Rebel. When O'Keefe reluctantly swears allegiance to the Confederacy, the ransom of twelve thousand dollars is paid in Confederate currency, of which Millikan has two full barrels back in Yazoo City (*Roads of Destiny*, 289–301).

An even more fantastic yarn, "Supply and Demand," tells about the exploitation of an innocent tribe of Central American Indians who, being totally ignorant of the exchange value of gold, supply it freely in quantity to a swindling Irishman, Patrick Shane, until another entrepreneur shows up with a cargo of mirrors, cheap jewelry, and safety razors to infect them with a knowledge of good and evil (*Options*, 89–103). Again, "He Also Serves" is another tale of Indian exploitation: located in the Aztec region of Mexico, it is accordingly flavored with pagan reincarnation rites and other high jinks that take place in an Aztec temple (*Options*, 134–49);[74] while still another, "A Ruler of Men," tells of a fake revolution an Irish giant named O'Connor is tricked into leading in an unnamed Latin American republic. Bilked of his funds, he is thrown into prison until rescued by his partner, Bowers, and then he winds up back in New York, ruling men happily by cramming them into overloaded subway trains (*Rolling Stones*, 8–33).

Finally, "The Day We Celebrate" wearily replays the bacchanalian motif of "The Fourth in Salvador," yet its dismally farcical account of a scrap between two drunken derelicts in Costa Rica probably comes closer to the actual conditions O. Henry experienced during his sojourn in Honduras than do all his other effervescent re-creations of lotus land, including its most elaborate presentation in *Cabbages and Kings*.

To assess O. Henry's Latin American stories properly one must not forget they are fiction, setting forth, as do his tales of the West and the South, a newly created world of fantasy, not the environment he actually lived in. His two worlds are, of course, related and made to appear convincingly identical through the narrative skill of the artist: his ability to convey realistically the surface details, the atmosphere of his setting, and the speech and action of his characters. But Lotus Land is exactly as Tennyson portrayed it—"a land in which it seemed always afternoon"—a world of dreams where one can "muse and brood and live again in memory."[75] In his Latin American stories O. Henry came closest to admitting the illusory nature of this realm in "The World and the Door," which during his last year of life he strove futilely to refashion into a stage play.

The story opens, jocularly, this way: "A favorite dodge to get your story read by the public is to assert that it is true, and then add that Truth is stranger than Fiction. I do not know if the yarn I am anxious for you to read is true; but the Spanish purser of the fruit steamer *El Carrero* swore to me by the shrine of Santa Guadalupe that he had the facts from the U.S. Vice-consul at La Paz" (*Whirligigs*, 3–21). The story tells of a romance between two affluent fugitives from justice: Ralph Merriam, a New York broker who has shot another man in a nightclub dispute, and Mrs. Florence Conant, who confesses to having poisoned her husband. So long as each knows of the other's guilt, both can be ecstatically happy in their shared company, but when Merriam's "victim," Hedges, unaccountably shows up alive and well and bearing no grudge, and when Mrs. Conant learns from an old newspaper that her husband did not die but got a divorce, both of them quietly make plans to escape and separate without ever seeing each other again.

Although this story ends with O. Henry's typical double reverse twist, there is a dash of bitters in the denouement that helps to offset some of his sentimentalized boy-meets-girl treacle, but a more welcome ironic note comes in O. Henry's own self-spoofing with his reader. He knows he is doing a parody of the "True Romance" pulp feature and that the reader knows it too; hence there is no point in pretending otherwise. But while the self-ridicule directed at his own "discourse in Bulwer-Lyttonese" smashes the illusion, it also reveals the deeper meaning of the theme that haunts him in the image of the world and the door—the realization that there is no lasting escape for anyone in lotus land.

Imprisonment and the Legacy of Professionalism

The third and perhaps most important contributing influence in the formation of O. Henry's art of short fiction was his relatively brief incarceration in the Ohio Federal Penitentiary. Although he had written and published a good deal of fictional material before his conviction in April 1898, most of it can be recognized and classified immediately as experimental and amateurish, whereas the stories he produced during and after his three years' stretch as Prisoner Number 30664 were obviously the work of a skilled professional. It was not simply the prison environment itself that wrought such a transformation, although enforced solitude and the constraints of ordinary prison life clearly played a part in the process. Rather, it was the total ambience of incarceration per se: what it represented psychologically, an inescapable trauma of guilt to be lived with daily and to be dealt with only by an equally powerful countervailing force, an iron-willed self-discipline imposed on O. Henry's creative consciousness.

The trauma was no simple feeling of remorse for misdeeds committed and punishment exacted, but more likely a deep-seated psychic wound, a stunned suffering of the soul for all the woe and deprivation that had befallen him during the interim between his return from Honduras and his arrival in the prison house—the shattered dreams, the death of Athol, the breakup of family life, and the forced abandonment of his child to the care of her grandparents. He may well have believed sincerely that in his case fate had done a grievous wrong to a completely innocent man.

How strongly the trauma must have motivated O. Henry's endeavor to exorcize it has been demonstrated in many ways. When he first entered prison, though still protesting his innocence, he seemed determined not only to blot out the past, avoid his fellow prisoners, and guard against mentioning his family to anyone, but also to immerse himself in writing letters and stories to and for them. His taciturnity and extreme gravity prompted Dr. John M. Thomas, the prison physician, to declare that he had "never known a man so deeply humiliated by his imprisonment."[76] By withdrawing into a two-sided realm of fiction, however, O. Henry gradually became reconciled to his plight. On one hand, he kept up an elaborate pretense of business travel in a long series of letters to his young daughter Margaret (Smith, 158–66); on the other hand, he also produced during the same period fourteen of the sentimentalized stories bearing the same stamp that would in time be widely acclaimed for their individual style.[77] In other letters to the Roaches, however, he occasionally depicted quite graphically the horrors of prison life as he found them, commenting sardonically that such "little things" as suicides, knifings, and other inhuman brutalities suffered by the prisoners as punishments "are our only amusements" (Smith, 157).

Bitter reactions like these, however, were strictly limited to private correspondence; notwithstanding O. Henry's stunned repugnance toward the worst prison conditions he witnessed or heard of, he was determined not to comment openly about them. When his fellow prisoners urged him to expose such atrocities in his writings, he refused, allegedly on the grounds that since he was not a newspaper reporter, the horrors of prison life were not his responsibility, and he would never describe crime and punishment as they were actually seen and felt. Nor would he ever try to cure "the diseased soul of society. I will forget that I ever breathed behind these walls."[78]

Thus, instead of attempting to become a muckraker like Upton Sinclair or Lincoln Steffens, O. Henry chose to blot out the memories of his actual prison experiences by concealing them within the cloak of fiction, and the transformation he performed succeeded so completely that regardless of where, when, or how his famous pseudonym originated, the art form it represented emerged from those prison walls (Smith, 113).

Beginning with "Georgia's Ruling" in 1900, the fourteen stories written and published before O. Henry left Ohio the following year were only part of the much larger number traceable to his prison experience; many others published in later years also grew out of yarns and anecdotes he picked up from his fellow prisoners. The Jeff Peters stories in *The Gentle Grafter*—as well as many of those involving the exploits of Texas outlaws and other types of banditry in *Heart of the West*, *Roads of Destiny*, *Options*, and still other volumes—came originally from the same sources. Among all of these, the most famous, of course, is "A Retrieved Reformation," the story of Jimmy Valentine, whose safe-cracking wizardry was later dramatized with smashing success on both stage and screen.[79]

Since so many of O. Henry's stories deal with outlawry, fraud, violence, and the problems of society's unruly misfits, literary scholars and critics have repeatedly tried to determine whether or how these may all be related to his own prison experience. Obviously, he drew a large volume of such fictional raw materials from both fellow prisoners and prison officials; despite his customary reticence about private affairs, he was not a solitary recluse. He won their friendship and respect with the same personal charm that attracted friends and supporters among prominent Texans. As Al Jennings recalled later, "They were all fond of the nimble-tongued, amiable dignity that was Bill Porter's. Everyone wanted to make him a present as he was leaving" (*Through the Shadows*, 252).

And the fact that O. Henry stored up and produced fourteen publishable stories between 1898 and 1901 also shows how diligently he was working at his craft throughout the long nights. A notebook he kept during this period reveals some of his most popular stories—for example, "The Enchanted Kiss," "A Fog in Santone," and "The Emancipation of Billy"—drew as many as ten or more rejection slips before finding a publisher, whereas several others gained immediate acceptance (Langford, 148).

But the most striking proof of O. Henry's professional growth is to be found in the prison stories themselves. For although the style of these fourteen stories is not noticeably different from that of either his earlier or later work, it has been clearly demonstrated that "they do testify to the results of a remarkably thorough self-discipline in a form that previously he had attempted only casually or spasmodically—the short story proper, or rather the short story as it was to flourish through his influence. The fourteen prison stories show almost the full range of O. Henry." Moreover, the same scholar finds in most of these stories a significantly prominent autobiographical element, as eight of them are concerned with the same basic idea: "the vindication of a character who has in some way forfeited his claim of respectability or even integrity . . . and the plot invariably turns on the regeneration of an admitted delinquent, not on the vindication of a character who is blameless" (Langford, 150).

Whether or not the forfeiture of integrity had become a compulsive idea O. Henry felt inexorably bidden to confess obliquely in these and many other stories, the mere fact that this autobiographical vein is discernible to the probing scholar but artfully concealed from the average reader shows how fully his art of the short story had developed. When he waved adieu to the Ohio Penitentiary, O. Henry was prepared to fulfill his destined role as Caliph of Bagdad on Broadway.

Fulfillment in Manhattan

Leaving Ohio, a free man at last in 1901, O. Henry faced a future that would bring him both public fame and private misery in nearly equal volume, although the world at large would remain unaware of this ironic ambivalence until after his death in 1910. His life in the few years granted him would abound in new sensations, adventures, and varied personal relationships, many of which he transformed into more than 140 new stories, and these in turn rapidly carried him to the peak of success as the self-anointed Caliph of Bagdad-on-the-Subway.

Yet during the same few years, the artist himself would suffer intensely from loneliness, insecurity, and guilt-ridden fear, while striving vainly to elude the shadow of his past and to overcome, through frenzied literary effort, his insatiable need for money. This lifestyle began taking shape in Pittsburgh, where O. Henry rejoined his family and spent nearly a year before moving on to New York in the spring of 1902. During this short interval, while becoming painfully reacquainted with Margaret, now twelve, he was working on and off for the *Dispatch* and also turning out stories rapidly to provide a substantial income for her support and his own.

By the year's end he had published ten stories in *Ainslee's* and *McClure's* and had about five or six others accepted and soon to be published; at the rate of seventy-five dollars per story he was being paid at first by *Ainslee's*, he could assure Jennings he was now averaging twice that sum each month.[80] Yet this amount was still insufficient for his needs, he complained, because once again he was spending money faster than he made it on expensive clothes, poker, and liquor.[81] The pattern for the remaining years of his life—furious writing activity coupled with spendthrift indulgence—would never change.

But at this point O. Henry's basic complaint was against life in Pittsburgh itself, which he condemned as "the low-downedest hole on the surface of the earth."[82] He wanted desperately to get on to New York and was even advised to do so by his employers at the *Dispatch*, who could not afford to pay the higher fees New York magazine editors were already paying for his stories. By the end of 1901, those already published in *Ainslee's*—"Money Maze," "Rouge et Noir," "Friends in San Rosario," and "The Passing of Black Eagle"—as well as others in several other magazines, had begun drawing attention to the fresh new talent still concealed behind a variety of pseudonyms. Moreover, O. Henry was also anxious to bury his identity among the nameless throngs of the metropolis, though even after being established there he would later disclose to Jennings "the horrible fear that some ex-con will come up and say to me " 'Hello, Bill, when did you get out of the O. P. P.?' " (*Jennings*, 297–98).

He joyfully accepted the invitation and the hundred-dollar advance sent him by Gilman Hall, associate editor of *Ainslee's*. Hall would presently become his best friend and benefactor in New York, where at last O. Henry found his natural habitat. For, as his first biographer firmly stated, "If ever in American literature the place and the man met, they met when O. Henry strolled for the first time along the streets of New York."[83]

Within a very short time he became an anonymous frequenter of hole-in-corner hangouts and glittering restaurants, secluding himself in out-of-the-way fleabag hotels, where even publishers' minions had trouble finding him. Before and after dark he prowled tirelessly through New York's streets, seeking like Poe's haunted "Man of the Crowd," to savor and absorb the varied color and texture of the city's life. But he was also churning out the stories that soon made everyone wonder who this new writer O. Henry really was.

Very soon after Witter Bynner, representing *McClure's*, flushed him out of a back-street rooming house to offer one hundred dollars for "Tobin's Palm," they were appearing frequently, often simultaneously, in nearly a dozen magazines; by the end of his first year in the city he had every reason to feel self-confident about his future.[84] To date he had published more than twenty-five stories, including such famous ones as "While the Auto Waits," "Roads of Destiny," and "A Retrieved Reformation," yet these were but a token of the resources New York had in store for him (Langford, 160–62). His big break came in the fall of 1903, when a contract with the *Sunday World*, America's largest newspaper, assured him of one hundred dollars for a single story each week throughout the coming year.

With its circulation of nearly half a million readers, the *World* would soon bring O. Henry the greatest audience he had ever enjoyed, as well as twice the income. At last he could begin to live, approximately, in the style he always coveted: moving to roomier quarters, first on East 24th

Street and later to 55 Irving Place, in the neighborhood of Gramercy Park, he found among the legendary haunts of Washington Irving both a fitting berth and just the right atmosphere needed "to establish himself in what he called 'the business of caliphing,' and to indulge in the vagaries and extravagances appropriate to the generous handed role" (*Caliph*, 260).

Bagdad: The New York Stories

When O. Henry first visited Irving Place—an old friend wrote long after his death—he stood reverently in front of Washington Irving's town house and softly observed: "A fellow kinda feels like wearing his hat in his hand when he stands here, doesn't he?"[85] If true, the image casts a sparkling light on both O. Henry's critical appreciation and his artistic desire to emulate the creator of Diedrich Knickerbocker, the native-born writer who first caught the flavor of New York and brought to the civilized world's attention a new form of fiction developing in America. Both Irving and O. Henry were innovators in a modern literary form; both approached and employed the materials they found appropriate to that form in much the same frame of mind. In the early 1800s, here is the way Irving described his attitude toward the shifting scenes surrounding him during his rambling about in search of literary subjects:

> I cannot say that I have studied them with the eye of a philosopher; but rather with the sauntering gaze with which humble lovers of the picturesque stroll from the window of one print-shop to another; caught sometimes by the delineations of beauty, sometimes by the distortions of caricature. . . . As it is the fashion for modern tourists to travel pencil in hand, and bring home their port-folios filled with sketches, I am disposed to get up a few for the entertainment of my friends.[86]

Except for the obvious changes that occurred during another century of development in Manhattan, O. Henry might well have echoed these same words at the outset of his career in New York, for he was soon to be the literary tourist of the early twentieth century whose roving eye and graceful pen captured the beauties and picturesqueness of the glamorous metropolis in story after story, sometimes rendering these qualities "by the distortions of caricature."

His residence within the confines of Irving Place was ideally situated for a peripatetic artist of O. Henry's temperament. At one extreme there were such respectable establishments as Scheffel Hall, known throughout the city as a fine restaurant; the Westminster Hotel, where Dickens had sojourned; and the Hotel America, frequented by Latin American exiles and delightfully caricatured in his stories as El Refugio.[87] At the other extreme there were such notorious dives and honky-tonks as McGlory's bawdy house, Tom Sharkey's saloon, and Tony Pastor's vaudeville theater (Langford, 169). During the eight years he spent in this area, O. Henry produced nearly 150 stories based on the life he shared in a constantly shifting backdrop suggestive of the city's colorful, never-ending variety. They began appearing in popular New York magazines shortly after he arrived, and their flow rose to a peak in the three years between 1904 and 1907, the period during which his biographers wrote: "O. Henry was Haroun in his golden prime" (*Caliph*, 260). But a trickle of the flow continued until a year after his death; more than a hundred were first published in the *Sunday World*, while the remainder were spread through the issues of practically every other well-known periodical competing for the mass audience of those days. And long before the last of them appeared in magazines the earlier ones were being reissued in the collected volumes that have borne O. Henry's fame far beyond the boundaries established by his magazine reputation.

Beginning with *The Four Million* in 1906, the majority of his New York stories (a total of 125) appear in this and five other volumes, two of which were published after his death,[88] and at least two or three of the New York stories, including some of his best ones, can be found in every other volume of his works.[89]

The panorama of New York spread across O. Henry's stories, like a mosaic carefully assembled from thousands of minute particles, is both real and unreal, authentic but distorted, recognizable yet elusive. The great city's essence is firmly embedded in hundreds of passages and may be felt, if not readily identified, even today, by any casual reader who seeks only momentary entertainment from a hackneyed story plot; the turbulent, indestructible spirit of the place that was demonstrated by a New York journalist of the 1960s is still there.[90] O. Henry struck the keynote of his love song to "the greatest of all cities" through the muted voice of Raggles, an itinerant tramp, who compares Manhattan's unfathomable charm to a jeweler's window display: "cold, glittering, serene, impossible as a four-carat diamond in a window to a lover outside fingering damply in his pocket his ribbon-counter salary."[91] This Circean allure of New York with its thousands of contrarieties, inducements, snares, and delusions, he would celebrate in story after story—

sometimes in maudlin outright praise, often in the subtler awareness in a casually dropped figure of speech, always with a clear understanding of the price exacted by such a mistress from the poet who lays siege to her heart.

Fully aware of the difficulties he faced, O. Henry's success in catching the essence of New York was due largely to his joyful eagerness to accept the challenge and bring into play all the blandishments his large stock of words and images could command. New York, he confessed, required the outlander to be either an enemy or a lover; O. Henry chose to be a lover, although never doubting that to possess the city's heart would be an unequal struggle: "Not only by blows does it seek to subdue you. It woos you to its heart with the subtlety of a siren. It is a combination of Delilah, green Chartreuse, Beethoven, chloral and John L. in his best days."[92] To record its voice would require "a mighty and far-reaching utterance," capable of mingling in one loud note "the chords of the day's traffic, the laughter and music of the night, . . . the rag-time, the weeping, the stealthy hum of cab-wheels, the shout of the press agent, the tinkle of fountains on the roof gardens, . . . the whispers of the lovers in the parks—all these sounds must go into your voice—not combined, but mixed, and of the mixture an essence made."[93] To penetrate its mystery, one would have to become a bold adventurer, a prowler by night and a part of (though apart from) the thronging "dreary march of the hopeless Army of Mediocrity" during the rush hours of the day, so as not to overlook the meaningful minutiae of signs visible everywhere.[94]

For "at every corner handkerchiefs drop, fingers beckon, eyes besiege, and the lost, the lonely, the rapturous, the mysterious, the perilous, changing clues of adventure are slipped into our fingers."[95] To appreciate the city's beauty would therefore demand both perspective and understanding, the ability to comprehend that it was "like a great river fed by a hundred alien streams. Each influx brings strange seeds on its flood, strange silt and weeds, and now and then a flower of rare promise. To construe this river requires a man who can build dykes against the overflow, who is a naturalist, a geologist, a humanitarian, a diver, and a strong swimmer."[96] And to know its worth would take insight and imagination enough to see beneath its "ridiculous sham palaces of trumpery and tinsel pleasures," as Blinker suddenly perceived at Coney Island, that "counterfeit and false though the garish joys of these spangled temples were, . . . deep under the gilt surface they offered saving and apposite balm and satisfaction to the restless human heart."[97]

As one New York critic noted not so long ago, O. Henry captured the essence of his beloved city with an abundance of images like these because he could "distil its true meaning from a welter of deceitful immediacies" (Millstein, 36). But neither did he blur or distort the immediacies: they are sharply registered on the sensitized film of his mental camera, the countless disparate sense impressions whose implications he could quickly synthesize and clarify.

Here, for example, are a few of "the copy-righted smells of spring" belonging to the city alone: "The smells of hot asphalt, the underground caverns, gasoline, patchouli, orange peel, sewer gas . . . Egyptian cigarettes, mortar and the undried ink on newspapers."[98] And then the fire-escapes, zigzagging down the front walls of dismal apartment houses—"laded with house-hold goods, drying clothes, and squalling children evicted by the midsummer heat."[99] And next, the melancholy prospect of a regiment of "dogmen," emerging daily at twilight from these dwellings with their leashed pets, each of them having been "either cajoled, bribed, or commanded by his own particular Circe to take the dear household pet out for an airing."[100] Again, there are always the idle curiosity seekers, swarming like flies "in a struggling, breathless circle about the scene of [any] unusual occurrence. . . . They gaze with equal interest and absorption at a chorus girl or at a man painting a liver pill sign. They will form as deep a cordon around a man with a club foot as they will around a balked automobile. . . . They are optical gluttons, feasting and fattening on the misfortunes of their fellow beings."[101]

O. Henry turned to account hundreds of concrete impressions like these in his continuous round of stocktaking. As an inveterate walker, he knew the city intimately from the Bowery to Harlem and from the Hudson River Ferry to Coney Island, and took note conscientiously of the manifold kinds of life that made its many neighborhoods distinctive. At one extreme he noted the jostling crowds thronging the downtown streets: the busy brokers and the trim shopgirls, the Broadway sports, the cops, con-men, and notions vendors; at the other extreme, the kids playing stickball on quieter side streets, idlers lolling on park benches while feeding or just watching the sparrows in Madison Square, and housewives exchanging gossip across front stoops or haggling with fruit peddlers over the price of strawberries. Such sharply observed details enrich the settings in most of his stories and thereby contribute to the authenticity of his characters' milieu. Theirs is the real New York of the four million of his day, we feel, because of the accuracy of his recorded sense impressions, because they square with the facts recorded by other contemporary media, such as newspaper advertisements, theater handbills, Sears Roebuck catalogs, and so on.

The authenticity of O. Henry's New York is further strengthened by the kinds of emphasis he placed on his varied social scene. Although his characters are generally flawed by the oversimplification in their attitudes and reactions toward whatever the problem confronting them, there is yet an air of truthfulness about the basic situations the author has prepared for them. Almost invariably these situations reflect the everyday life of the average man, woman, or child—at work, at home, or at play. Ikey Schoenstein behind his tall prescription desk, where his pills are "rolled out on its own pill-tile, divided with a spatula, rolled with the finger and thumb, dusted with caleined magnesia and delivered in little round pasteboard pill-boxes,"[102] is in his proper element. And so are the firemen in Company 99, arguing over the merits of the Russo-Japanese War;[103] and Gaines, slaving away in a downtown office during midsummer and pretending to like it so his wife and kids can enjoy an extra month's vacation in the mountains;[104] and Vesey with other newsmen on the *Enterprise* staff, trying to interpret their correspondent's coded dispatch from the Yalu River;[105] and so too, the cabby Jerry O'Donovan sitting "aloft like Jupiter on an unsharable seat, holding your fate between two thongs of inconstant leather."[106]

In scores of situations like these presented in O. Henry's stories, New Yorkers of the early 1900s could see themselves reflected, and even though nearly a full century has erased many a familiar landmark, implement, vehicle, and spectacle of that period, they still can.

To judge fairly the literary worth in O. Henry's treatment of this conglomeration of human activity, however, requires some sort of classification, although any effort to classify his New York would most likely prove futile. These stories simply do not conform so readily to the distinct patterns into which his western and his southern stories fall. Moreover, no two stories are exactly alike in form and content, despite the general sameness of tone that characterizes a great many of them. Still, one method for classifying them satisfactorily might be that of grouping together the types of activities their characters chiefly engage in, another, that of focusing attention upon the problems of adjustment the characters are obliged to face, still another, perhaps, a grouping together under the dominant themes developed in the stories.

But regardless of the classifying pattern imposed on the stories, careful study of their makeup quickly exposes the obvious lacunae in the lives of O. Henry's New Yorkers. At least sixty of the stories are concerned with the problems of men and women at work, but these problems seldom emerge from the nature or demands of their respective jobs. Another large group of thirty or so focus on the problems of the unemployed and underprivileged as contrasted with those of others whose superfluous wealth is burdensome, but even though most of these do throw some light on the pitiful consequences of such economic disparity, they offer little if any dramatic insight into the complex causes or possible alleviation of the social malaise. Just arrange a convenient meeting between the impoverished, underpaid shopgirl and a kind millionaire on the Coney Island ferryboat, or let the ubiquitous park-bench beggar draw a generous handout from a lavish Caliph—the standard role that O. Henry himself enjoyed playing when he had the funds to spare.

Another fairly large group of stories deals with the living conditions and/or domestic affairs of representative members of the "four million," but here too, the problems at issue in these households oftener seemed contrived rather than the result of normal family relationships, and so they lead to solutions that also seem equally implausible, if not downright bizarre. Finally, there is a fourth miscellany of stories in which the major activities of the characters are so diverse that no wholly satisfactory catch-all classification may be applicable for all of them; however, most of these may be lumped under the loose heading of "Bagdad on Parade," for the predominant trait shared among them in the exhibition of typical, dyed-in-the-wool New Yorkers' behavior in public. Let us now look a bit more closely into the substance of stories in each of the four categories.

O. Henry's Toilers—Men and Women at Work

There are at least two opposing ways to interpret O. Henry's fictional treatment of the working class New Yorkers in the early 1900s, and his Russian admirers, as well as many others, seem to have followed both at different times. From one viewpoint these stories may be regarded as an implied, if not an obvious criticism, of the gross inequalities in America's capitalist society; hence this withering jeremiad from the Soviet only thirty years ago: "He gave a general idea of the absurdity of the system under which dire poverty was the source of the amassing of fantastic wealth, and under which the rich became slaves of their millions and lost all human semblance. For O. Henry they were leeches who sucked their capital out of the poor, to whom they paid a pittance so that they might keep body and soul together and help the rich make their millions."[107] But from an opposite viewpoint—also Russian—the stories may be disdained for offering a complacent, if sometimes cynical, approval of the status quo, and their author condemned for his falseness, hypocrisy, and sentimentality—for being, indeed, "the great consoler," a slave to middle-class secular ideals, illusions, and false hopes.[108]

By arguing from a selected assortment of O. Henry's stories, one might have made out a plausible case for either view as recently as the 1960s, but neither would be likely to survive even casual scrutiny today. One might argue, for example, that two of his most popular tales, "The Gift of the Magi" and "The Furnished Room," convey a scathing indictment of the inequities that cause great suffering in America's materialistic society (*Voice*, 75–104; *Strictly Business*, 209–30), or one might turn instead to such stories as "The Shocks of Doom," "One Thousand Dollars," or "A Night in New Arabia" to find evidence of O. Henry's loyal support of the ultraconservative doctrine favoring the concentration of wealth in the right hands. But to evaluate his stories from this economic perspective is to endow him with socioeconomic or political philosophic biases he seldom, if ever, expressed. For although he was a sincere humanitarian in his sympathetic gestures toward the poor and downtrodden, as a writer of fiction his outlook was neither that of such realists as Twain and Crane nor that of naturalists such as Norris and Dreiser; his view of the human predicament as seen in the nation's greatest city was consistently that of the romanticist, not unlike Irving's. His most percipient biographer sums it up neatly in three sentences: "His half-dozen Jewish characters, for example, are superficial types, revealing no serious interest in the impact which New York had on the Jewish immigrant. Nor does he show an interest in one of the crucial issues of his day, the growing fight between capital and labor. Aside from his sentimental and somewhat ambivalent concern for the underpaid shopgirl, Porter's interest in New York was that of the perennial tourist" (Langford, 218–19).

This is a fair judgment of O. Henry's basic attitude toward the spectacle of America's working class society in general. His depiction of New York's toiling masses, like that of his more mobile western and southern folk, reveals the same artistic outlook and methods—the same romanticist's bag of tricks for capturing and recording the odd, the unexpected, and the picturesque antics he professed to observe among them. These were the desired effects he sought to achieve in his stories, and his popular success in achieving them underscored the validity of both his aims and his literary dexterity. To stir the reader's emotions lightly, either to laughter or tears (at times, preferably both), without upsetting one's equanimity unduly, was the key to success and a burgeoning, widespread appeal. Thus, again and again, whatever the problem posed in these stories, the reader may remain comfortably detached and entertained regardless of whether the characters and their predicament happen or do not happen to strike a sensitive personal psychic nerve.

Usually, the problem is somewhat remote, but even when it may be at least tangential to one's own anxieties or misgivings, O. Henry's sleight-of-hand mesmerism quickly converts it into an amusing farce, a naive sexual entanglement, or a ludicrous reversal of fortune. In "The Love-Philtre of Ikey Schoenstein," for example, the problem is that poor Ikey, a drug clerk, although too timid to approach his beloved Rosy Riddle directly, is fearful that his rival, Chuck McGowen, will get her. When Chuck applies to him for an aphrodisiac to spur Rosy's lust for an elopement, Ikey slyly gives him instead a sleeping potion intended to keep her immobilized until he can warn her father, but then Ikey learns on the morrow that the couple eloped on schedule while Mr. Riddle lay soundly drugged from the potion given him by mistake (*Four Million*, 119–27).

In "From the Cabby's Seat," problem and resolution are equally far-fetched: Jerry O'Donovan, feeling no pain, picks up a solitary fare near McGary's Family Cafe, drives her in and around Central Park for hours, and then, learning she has no money to pay him, angrily hauls her to a police station—only to discover there that she is the bride he had forgotten while getting drunk at his own wedding party (*Four Million*, 165–73). And again in "The Halberdier of the Little Rheinschloss," we learn of well-to-do young Mr. Deering's acute embarrassment when his fiancée finds him dressed in an iron suit while serving as part of the decor at a fashionable German restaurant—the only job he could secure as a means of gaining her father's consent to their marriage! (*Roads*, 278–88). This one fetches us even further than Banquo's ghost, yet it is included in the volume O. Henry allegedly named his favorite.

But synopsized in this niggardly way, these stories naturally lose all the piquancy with which O. Henry seasoned the meager substance of his hors d'oeuvres. His witty comparisons and turns of phrase, adroitly scattered among most of his stories, must be read in their context for one to appreciate their contribution to the overall effect. So too, his usually clever handling of point-of-view or angle of narration: "The

Halberdier," for instance, gains a good deal in comic effect by having it told entirely from the viewpoint of a sympathetic but uneducated observer, Waiter # 18, whose fractured phraseology contrasts ludicrously with the agonizing scenes he describes with dead-pan sincerity. Thus, a double irony is concealed in this one: "He give the millionaires a lovely roast in a sarcastic way, describing their automobiles and opera-boxes and diamonds; and then he got around to the working-classes and the kind of grub they eat and the long hours they work—and all that sort of stuff—bunkum, of course" (*Roads*, 286–87).

Almost invariably O. Henry's capacious bag of tricks yields up a new device or two to help him spice up an otherwise empty or banal plot. In "A Midsummer Knight's Dream" it is the contrast between Gaines's dream of his courtship days in a mountain resort and the letter he receives from his wife as he toils sweating in a hot office building (*Trimmed Lamp*, 189–97). In "The Diamond of Kali," it is a rapidly diminishing supply of whiskey a newspaper reporter consumes while noting down the hair-raising details in General Marcellus B. Ludlow's pompous narrative of his discovery and pilferage of a fabulous Indian jewel (*Sixes*, 265–74). And a suite of adjoining cubicles in which a divorce lawyer places three contestants in a lawsuit provides for the comic fiasco of mistaken identity in "The Hypothesis of Failure" (*Whirligigs*, 37–54), while miscalculations based on an eccentric editor's methods for obtaining critical evaluations of manuscripts from elevator operators and furnace tenders lead to the downfall of a writer's hopes for publication in "A Sacrifice Hit" (*Whirligigs*, 152–58).

From reading these and other stories like them, one might readily conclude that the more routine the occupation and setting O. Henry chose for his subject matter, the more likely he would be to embroider their fictional development. Consider two more examples, one concerning a stock brokerage, the other a neighborhood bakeshop. Marvey Maxwell is such a busy broker that, on arriving at his office one morning accompanied by his stenographer, Miss Leslie, he has already forgotten that he proposed to her the day before and that "they were married last evening at eight o'clock in the Little Church around the Corner."[109] Still more bizarre, in "Witches' Loaves" there is Martha Meacham's costly misjudgment of a regular customer's daily purchasing ritual: because each morning the seedy little German has been buying only two loaves of stale bread from her shop, she assumes he must be a starving artist who would appreciate her friendly effort to upgrade their palatability by placing some butter inside the loaves this time. But, alas, Martha soon learns from outraged Mr. Blumburger that she has "schpoilt" him. Instead of eating the bread, he had been using clumps of doughy crumbs to erase the penciled lines on his finished architectural drawings; and the buttered ones ruined in a stroke the produce of three months' labor on a prize competition (*Sixes*, 32–37).

Even in this far-fetched little tale, however, O. Henry's amused sympathy for his puppets shines through the irony of their shattered hopes, and so their predicament infects the reader. His treatment of the futile lives of striving but untalented artists, writers, stage folk, and teachers, in fact, covers another fairly extensive segment of the working population. He usually presents them in a well-balanced tone of mingled irony, pathos, and humor. Sometimes the predominant tone is lightly satiric, as in the tale of Miss Medora Martin, a headstrong Vermont damsel who has recently come to New York with easle and paints, determined to establish her career as a professional artist. Soon she is right at the heart of things in Bohemia's "Vortex," rapping and drinking with other artists, whose chatter about Henry James blends oddly with popping corks and silvery laughter—"champagne flashed in the pail, wit flashed in the pan."[110] And for just a moment the reader may fear Medora teeters on the brink of fulfilling her aim to become a conquering courtesan, until her old beau, Beriah Hopkins, appears in time to rescue and restore her unblemished to Harmony. Surely, Beriah is not just an accidental clone for Cyrus Potts in O. Henry's juvenile tall tale, "Vereton Villa."

But similar touches of whimsicality based on the contrast between rural naïveté and urban sophistication are also present in "The Rathskeller and the Rose," an amusing yarn about a new Broadway star, Posie Carrington (née Boggs), who has attained stardom since her arrival from a backwoods hamlet by working her way up through the ranks of burlesque shows, musical comedies, and bit parts (*Voice*, 179–87). Now at the peak of her career, she is scheduled for the lead in a new play, "Paresis by Gaslight," and an unknown but ambitious young actor named Hightower hopes to secure the leading male role in it, the part of "Haytosser," a rural rube. To persuade Posie of his fitness for the part, he does such a convincing act of posing as her fellow townsman that, overcome with nostalgia, she cancels all engagements and hastens back to Cranberry Corners. Light foolery with much the same sort of material also sparkles in "Strictly Business," which pretends to deal with the "real life" of a vaudeville team, but the punch line here is less successful (*Strictly Business*, 3–20).

Sometimes the laughter in these stories shades off into sighs of sadness and even despair, wherein a faint echo of O. Henry's own personal suffering may be felt. Two stories that illustrate this shift of tone are "The Last Leaf" and "A Service of Love," both of which pursue the sacrificial theme for their effect. The latter, like the better-known "Gift of the Magi," tells of an earnest young pair of art students, the Larrabees, who prop up each other's courage when their funds run out by pretending to have lucked into a steady income from their professional skills in painting and music, but it turns out Delia's service has been ironing shirts in a laundry while Joe has been firing the furnace in the same building (*Four Million*, 58–68). Far more touching than this, however, "The Last Leaf" has long been a very popular favorite despite its obvious implausibility, no doubt because it strikes a deep symbolic chord. The tale of a kindly old artist who gives up his life painting his one and only masterpiece—the last leaf on an outdoor vine—in his effort to restore a dying young girl's will to live, simply transcends the gimcrackery of its plot (*Trimmed Lamp*, 198–208).[111]

Closer to home than either of these, however, is "The Plutonian Fire," which deals directly with the problems of the aspiring neophyte from the hinterland who strives desperately to produce fiction to satisfy the demands of hard-boiled New York editors. They have rejected the writing of young Pettit from Alabama because his stories lack "living substance." But when he falls deeply in love and writes about that experience, his story is even more harshly condemned as "sentimental drivel, full of whimpering soft-heartedness and gushing egoism. . . . A perusal of its buttery phrases would have made a cynic of a sighing chamber-maid" (*Voice*, 111). As he survives the end of this affair with the aid of a strong drink and more disciplined writing, Pettit soon meets another girl whose unrequited love for him drives her toward attempted suicide, and when he transforms this sad case into fiction, his editor whoops joyfully because now "Just as though it lay there, red and bleeding, a woman's heart was written into the lines." Pettit, however, remains unimpressed: he has learned "You can't write with ink, and you can't write with your own heart's blood, but you can with the heart's blood of someone else. You have to be a cad before you can be an artist" (*Voice*, 113–14). Completely disillusioned, he plans to give up writing and return to Alabama to sell ploughs for his father. Although O. Henry clearly had no intention of abandoning his own profession at the peak of his career, there is yet more than a touch of flippancy in his ironic attitude toward Pettit's predicament; sharp critical acumen lurks beneath the bantering surface here.

Another story in the same vein, perhaps the bitterest in the group dealing with artists and entertainers, is "The Memento," which embalms all the gaudy notoriety of early twentieth-century vaudeville circuits along with an aroma of O. Henry's innate Puritanism (*Voice*, 230– 44).[112] The story is based on the scandalous feat of Rosalie Ray, whose pièce de résistance was that of swinging on a trapeze from the proscenium far out and above "bald-head row" and then kicking off one of her yellow garters, which all the lechers below scrambled to grasp. After two years of this she quit the stage, revolted by lascivious men pawing at her, and had gone to a village on Long Island, where she became engaged to a young clergyman. Before telling him about her own past, however, she learned he was the proud owner of a memento sent to him by a former "'ideal love far above him in a roundabout way—yet rather direct'" (*Voice*, 241). But instead of being either amused or flattered to discover one of her own yellow garters, Rosalie angrily returned to the playhouse, convinced all men were equally depraved.

In its treatment of the unmarried working girl adrift in the great city, "The Memento" resembles many other stories O. Henry wrote on the same theme, most of them equally as dated and sentimental. There are at least twenty in which the lonely, underpaid shopgirl, showgirl, clerk, model, or domestic servant presents a tearful spectacle of threatened innocence or unfulfilled hopes. Seldom does the reader encounter an aggressive young woman, capable of exploiting her physical resources successfully, and never a triumphant fallen one such as Dreiser's Sister Carrie, although there must have been a number of both types among O. Henry's extensive circle of acquaintances. Thus, his tendency to overdramatize in a cloying fashion the martyrdom of the agonized working girl may well draw snickers rather than tears from knowledgeable readers today.

In "The Trimmed Lamp," for example, two girlfriends named Lou and Nancy are striving determinedly to keep up a respectable appearance on meager salaries, although Lou, a laundry ironer, earns $18.50 a week, better than double Nancy's paltry $8.00 as a department store clerk. Moreover, besides her better-paying job, Lou also has Dan, a steady young electrician earning $30.00 a week and eager to marry her; she chides Nancy, not only for being satisfied with a poorer job, even though it does enable her to mingle with "swell" people and to imitate in home-made clothes the "posh" styles of her rich customers, but also for turning down offers of marriage from wealthy men. Meanwhile, Lou puts off Dan and ditches him eventually to become a rich man's mistress; Nancy, of course, gets him. And in the tear-stained finale Nancy can add to her trimmed lamp the unction of consolation for Lou, the foolish virgin, who on learning her fate collapses, "crouching down against the iron fence of the park, sobbing turbulently"—despite her "expensive fur coat and diamond-ringed hands" (*Trimmed Lamp*, 21).

The vulnerability of the unattached girl as a potential victim of varied predators is given similar development in three other stories that were great favorites among O. Henry's admirers a century ago: "Elsie in New York," "The Skylight Room," and "An Unfinished Story." Strongly implied in the first is the daring idea that society's agencies themselves, created specifically for the care and protection of the innocent and needy—including the police, the church, the law courts, and the welfare agencies—tend rather to thrust them into the clutches of predatory monsters. And so, poor Elsie, a little "peacherino" who might have had any number of safely respectable jobs but for her "protectors," becomes a model whose fate O. Henry assures us—in Dickens's words—will be numbered among the "Lost, your Excellency" (*Trimmed Lamp*, 280). For while she admires herself in Russian sables, her employer, Otter, gleefully reserves a private dining room for two, with "the usual brand and the '85 Johanissburger with the roast." Another Elsie, heroine of "The Skylight Room," escapes a less dismal fate, but not before the poor typist nearly starves to death (*Four Million*, 47–57).

Of all these victimized damsels, Dulcie in "The Unfinished Story" was the heroine of what Professor C. Alphonso Smith wrote was "probably the most admired of all O. Henry's stories" during the decade following his death.[113] What captured the public's admiration in that sentimental era was the grim picture drawn in the story of the joyless life of a shopgirl who, on a beggarly week's salary of six dollars, had to provide for room rent, food, clothes, and all her other needs. That Dulcie managed somehow to preserve her chastity, despite hunger and deprivation, by turning down a dinner date with Piggy Wiggins, gave balm to the troubled reader's soul. For Piggy was the sort who "could look at a shopgirl and tell you to an hour how long it had been since she had eaten anything more nourishing than marshmallows and tea" (*Four Million*, 180). Yet with a shuddering twist at the end that brings Poe to mind, the narrator observed ominously that on another day, while feeling lonelier than usual, Dulcie might not be so resolute. But lest today's blasé reader be tempted to smile superciliously at O. Henry's concern for poor

Dulcie, there is a double irony in the fact that on one occasion he allegedly confessed he himself in real life had played the role of the suave fat villain, Piggy (*Caliph*, 309). Not all of O. Henry's peacherinos teeter on the brink of starvation or rape. Some acquire comfort and security in the approved manner; others find such rewards freely offered, although sometimes their inability to distinguish the real from the spurious gift may rob them of the coveted prize. This is nearly the fate of Miss Archer, a dazzling model of Zizzbaum's wholesale clothing company, whose IQ—rather less impressive than her hourglass proportions, which exceeded "the required 38–25–42 standard"[114]—mistakes a visiting executive's fumbling marriage proposals for dishonorable advances. And the same fate does await both Claribel Colby in "The Ferry of Unfulfillment" and Maisie, the heroine of "A Lickpenny Lover." Poor Claribel, exhausted from a previous night of dancing plus a full day's labor behind a counter, misses a golden opportunity when, half-asleep, she gives the wrong answer to a rich prospector who wants to marry her (*Trimmed Lamp*, 233–39). Maisie, even with her eyes open, rejects her wealthy suitor because she thinks his promise to take her to faraway places only meant he "wanted me to marry him and go down to Coney Island for a wedding tour" (*Voice*, 30).

The strong appeal of these stories that dramatized such shocking contrasts between the lifestyles of the rich and famous and those of the indigent shopgirls is another reminder of the changing tastes in American society at the dawn of a new century, an awakening public concern about hardening class barriers within the social structure that threatened to destroy the basic ideals and values implicit in democracy and the American Dream. To lower, if not break down, these barriers by applying some variation of the Cinderella or Horatio Alger formula was still widely held as a valid approach to the problem, even though in actuality statistics could quickly show that a great many believers in such dreams were deluding themselves. Thanks to his close observation of the metropolitan scene, O. Henry was well aware of his public's wavering hopes and fears *and* the economic conditions that evoked them. In different stories he cannily shifted his focus of attention upon details of one economic extreme to its opposite. Nevertheless, his sympathetic portrayal of the working girl's hard lot drew an enthusiastic response chiefly because its minute details were palpable and appropriate.

His friend Anne Partlan, a journalist, testified to the accuracy of his data; he knew from close up, she affirmed, the kinds of rooms they lived in, the food they ate, the clothes they wore, the working conditions they

endured, and the simple pleasures and dreams they could afford with
which to make life bearable (Smith, 185–87). No matter how far-fetched
the Cinderella motif woven about the lives of these working girls in such
stories as "The Third Ingredient," "Springtime ala Carte," "The Purple Dress," and "The Enchanted Profile," there was an inescapable
basis of truth supporting his depiction of their predicament.[115] And the
reading public recognized and approved it. As his first biographer pointed
out long ago, the two types of New York society that interested O.
Henry the most were "those who were under a delusion. The first stirred his
sympathy; the second furnished him unending entertainment. Both are
abundantly represented in his stories" (Smith, 184). Since this division
probably includes as large a proportion of our citizens today as it did in
the early 1900s, it is not surprising that O. Henry's stories, though
quaintly dated, still enjoy such widespread popularity.

The Rich and the Poor

In 1962, the centennial anniversary of O. Henry's birth, the USSR's
leaders shrewdly achieved Brownie points for themselves and some
embarrassment for our American postal authorities by issuing a commemorative stamp in his honor. Taking note of the event, the New York
Herald Tribune sniffily observed that the Russians' tastes in American
literature were somewhat odd because they had made favorites of such
writers as Jack London and O. Henry, "both of whom are rather out of
fashion here nowadays," but a sharp dialectical riposte to that observation soon appeared in *Izvestia*.[116] Many good American writers who
criticized the "American way of life," the writer said, had gone out of
fashion in the United States, but they would nevertheless continue to be
honored as classics in Russia. The implication that O. Henry, as well as
Mark Twain, Dreiser, Hemingway, and Steinbeck, deserved to be honored primarily as critics of American capitalism could, of course, be
documented sufficiently to support the Marxist propaganda line of the
1960s. But that simplistic image of O. Henry would have been no nearer
the truth than its opposite. For, even though he was a true friend of the
friendless and the poor, both in actuality and in his fiction, he was
assuredly no publicly avowed antagonist of the wealthy.

In depicting the hardship and deprivation endured by his underpaid
shopgirls, O. Henry occasionally condemns with sweeping Dickensian
censure the tight-fisted employers who ignore their economic plight.
And now and then, using irony and understatement, he also chides the

idle rich for having so much to waste while others have so little to live on. Yet, more often than not his detailed characterizations of the rich themselves reflect a tolerant, even at times affectionate attitude toward them. Anthony Rockwell, for example, the blustery old retired soap tycoon in "Mammon and the Archer," is the epitome of O. Henry's concept of the self-made American C.E.O. He knows money talks, even in affairs of the heart, and he proves it to everyone's satisfaction by arranging a custom-made midtown traffic jam to provide his son with time enough to propose to the girl *he* wants to marry before she can slip away to Europe (*Four Million*, 128–39). Though Rockwell grouses boorishly about his snobbish, aristocratic neighbors—whom we never meet—he himself is both a lovable and generous character, no less so, indeed, than old Jacob Spraggins, the multi-millionaire Caliph in "A Night in New Arabia" (*Strictly Business*, 209–230). For years Spraggins eased his conscience by donating large sums annually to colleges and charitable organizations until he grew tired of trying to buy his way into heaven and decided to concentrate his attention and his wealth on his infant grandson. In the opening paragraphs of this story, O. Henry's satirical references to "the powerful genie Roc-Ef-El-Er who sent the Forty Thieves to soak up the oil plant of Ali Baba; . . . [and] the good Caliph Kar-Neg-Ghe, who gave away palaces;" are mildly critical of America's wealthiest capitalists but by no means hostile or scornful. His tone, in fact, rather jokingly implies that philanthropic multi-millionaires in New York compete vigorously with one another in their quest for the beggars they outnumber.

Thus, O. Henry romanticizes the well-to-do as blatantly as he does the poor, creating the impression through those whom he selects to represent the privileged class that money is a good thing to have so long as one knows how to enjoy spending it liberally, like a Caliph, in handouts to the underprivileged and the destitute.

Though well aware the possession of great wealth, like that of power, may weaken as well as strengthen one's character, O. Henry apparently did not wish to overemphasize such a dreary theme. So the miserly, the greedy, and the inhumane he condemns by indirection and in broad terms, but seldom gives them a name or a character role to play in the story. At most, they may be referred to by another character, as in the thinly veiled allusion to the notorious Hetty Green in "The Enchanted Profile" (*Roads*, 48–56); whereas the very rich men and women who figure prominently in his stories are almost always heroic individuals.

Open-handed, magnanimous, compassionate, they fulfill their role of noblesse oblige like knights and their ladies in the *Morte d'Arthur.* For example, like good King Wenceslaus, Carson Chalmers, the wealthy but troubled hero of "A Madison Square Arabian Night," sends his butler out on a frigid January evening to fetch him a dinner guest at random from those in a row of homeless men shivering in a bread line, requesting only that the one selected be reasonably clean. And when the contumelious guest, Sherrard Plumer, cynically presumes his host will want to hear his life story in exchange for the free meal ("Catch anybody in New York giving you something for nothing. They spell curiosity and charity with the same set of building blocks." [*Trimmed Lamp*, 26]), Chalmers graciously reassures Plumer he has no desire to pry into his guest's private life. Here again, although sharp criticism of the capitalistic system is implied in the butler's explanation of the bread line's purpose—which calls to mind Stephen Crane's powerful "Experiment in Misery"—and in Plumer's condemnation of New York's many cheap Haroun al Raschids, Chalmers himself is depicted as a quite charming and sensitive person, not as a malefactor of great wealth. This portrayal of Carson Chalmers, incidentally, also brings to mind echoes of Henry James's famous tale, "The Liar," because Plumer, his guest, turns out to be an impoverished portrait painter whose skills are identical to those of James's character, Oliver Lyon.

In all these romanticized accounts of philanthropic caliphs there is rarely a hint of the ascetic Christian doctrine that the love of money is the root of all evil, nor is there latent advocacy of the more modern liberal notion that the rich owe a debt to society payable through graduated income taxes. Young or old, O. Henry's opulent heroes, however blind or indifferent their wealth may have rendered them toward the plight of the homeless, underfed, or unemployable, miraculously see the light and respond at the touch of a magic wand, setting about promptly, if not too effectively, to rectify the situation. Bored young Alexander Blinker, for example, the heir to more downtown real estate than John Jacob Astor, but too annoyed to bother signing legal papers his family's lawyer thrusts at him, escapes for an outing at Coney Island. There he suddenly discovers, through the aid of lovely Florence, a milliner's helper, the concealed beauty underlying the vulgar pleasures of the masses. He is chagrined to learn not only that girls like Florence must meet their dates on the street or in the park, but also that he himself is the owner of Brickdust Row, the miserable slums they all live in; his angry outburst explodes: "Remodel it, burn it, raze it to the ground."[117]

Then there is another idealistic young chap, Dan Kinsolving, heir to an enormous fortune acquired by his late father, who had cornered the wheat market and raised the price of bread. Dan is anxious to restore his ill-gotten inheritance piecemeal to all the little people who suffered from that monopolistic crunch, but his socialist friend Kenwith, a watch-maker, convinces him that such restitution is now impossible, no matter how great his wealth. During the five years Dan was in college and abroad, Kenwith explains, the lives of various individuals were wrecked. Boyne's bakery had gone bankrupt and closed down; Boyne himself died in an insane asylum after setting fire to the building; his son turned criminal and was indicted for murder; and his pretty daughter, Mary, was slaving away in a shirt factory to pay off legal debts. A bit later, when he introduces Dan to her, she angrily dismisses them; yet within two more months Kenwith, on meeting her again in a neighborhood bakery, learns she is no longer Miss Boyne but Mrs. Kinsolving![118]

It can be argued that with Kenwith's catalogue of horrors in this story O. Henry does criticize—as harshly as he dared—a market system that permits such an unprincipled accumulation of wealth, but if so, his denouement obviously blows all implied criticism away. Yet the story as a whole is a good example of his skill in turning a current muckraking topic to fit his own agenda by producing an innocuously sentimental tale that evades the harsh realities at the same time that it makes its massive reading public feel warm and good. Again and again, this is the tactic he exploits in dealing with the rich.

For instance, there is Tom Crowley, the Caliph in "What You Want," worth forty-two million dollars but so bored with all his luxuries that he prowls about the city searching for something his money can't buy. He finds it in Jack Turner, a young hat-cleaner who scornfully rejects the older man's offer to set him up in business and subsidize his higher education. When Crowley calls him an impudent pup, he retaliates, and presently their scuffling lands them both in jail on a disorderly conduct charge, neither of them having the necessary bail in cash. Wondering whether the old fellow really was rich, Turner contentedly settles down on his cot to read, and his concluding response to the officer who announces presently that Crowley has arranged to have him bailed out, is: "Tell him I ain't in" (*Strictly Business*, 310). The story is utterly ludicrous, yet O. Henry's focus on the typical New Yorker's indepen-dence, although exaggerated, is a nice comic touch.

A more fundamental implication, however, in this and most of his other stories dealing with both the rich and the poor, is summed up in the romantic cliché: "Money isn't everything." He works this theme over thoroughly in virtually every story wherein money, as a symbol of desirability in life, is set up in the scales of human issues against other less tangible values. In "The Discounters of Money," kindness and thoughtfulness toward others reward the heart's desire of young millionaire Howard Pilkins, but only after his arrogant assumption that the elegant but impoverished Alice von der Ruysling would readily accept his proposal for the advantages of his money has almost killed his chances (*Roads*, 40–47). In "One Thousand Dollars," young Bob Gilliam gallantly foregoes his rigid uncle's fifty thousand dollar bequest by pretending to be a wastrel in order that his uncle's faithful secretary, Miss Hayden, may inherit the money (*Voice*, 75–84). And the same theme is given another implausible twist in "The Shocks of Doom," which opens with a park-bench discussion between two amiable cousins who have been victimized by their whimsical uncle. By reversing his decision to disinherit one in favor of the other, the uncle confers joyful relief on the disinherited cousin and pain on the other, who gets the money unexpectedly (*Voice*, 95–104). Still other variations are played on the same theme in "The Fool Killer," "From Each According to His Ability," and "The Marry Month of May," (*Voice*, 159–69, 219–29; *Whirligigs*, 116–24). The underlying idea at the heart of all these stories is that love, freedom, joy—the attainment of the heart's desire—are all preferable to wealth and that sensible people will relinquish any amount of it to obtain them. Is there any wonder O. Henry's popularity still endures?

If so, let us now consider the reverse side of that coin: the idea, namely, that poverty and deprivation have their compensations too, so long as one accepts his/her hard lot and tries to live joyously and honestly within his/her limitations. O. Henry also dramatizes just as skillfully this consoling, if unrealistic doctrine from numerous contrasting perspectives, most of which tend to accentuate the picturesqueness rather than the grimness inherent in the lives of the destitute and homeless. Nothing could be grimmer or more depressing in metropolitan society than the dope-infected derelicts that haunt the mean streets and darkened doorways of ghetto neighborhoods, yet in numerous stories O. Henry endows these poor wretches with rare spiritual attributes and insights—qualities such as grandeur, nobility, tenderness, even wisdom—all of them designed to evoke mingled tears and sympathetic smiles but not to awaken or disturb one's complacency with tragic realism.

In "The Caliph, Cupid, and the Clock," for example, we have Dopey Mike, an addict whose pipe dreams transform him into "Prince Michael of the Electorate of Valeluna," his sole mission in this guise created to re-stitch a raveling love affair. By urging a despondent young man to wait with him on a park bench just a half hour longer for the expected sign and by promising as wedding presents a check for one hundred thousand dollars and a palace on the Hudson River, Mike prevails but falls asleep; as the hour strikes, a scarf flutters from a window nearby, the young man rushes off to meet his girl, and the story ends with a bum asleep on the bench, clutching a fifty-dollar bill. (*Four Million*, 186– 96).

In "According to Their Lights," O. Henry doubles the pathos by setting up two derelicts, Murray and Captain Maroney, a dismissed policeman, starving together on a park bench. Although neither of them has been able to cadge a free meal, the Captain does get an opportunity to gain a large bribe for testifying against his former superior; when he refuses to accept it, Murray scoffs at his naïveté. Yet, as they shuffle off toward the breadline, Murray also refuses to compromise his principles. When an old acquaintance recognizes and informs him that his rich uncle will take him back into favor if he will agree to marry a certain heiress, he turns the offer down flat (*Trimmed Lamp*, 179–88). The innate dignity of the Bowery castaway is once again embellished with Christmas trimmings in "Compliments of the Season," a retread from one of O. Henry's earliest Texas sketches (*Strictly Business*, 194–208).[119] Here, Fuzzy's determination not merely to accept a token reward for returning a child's lost doll to a fashionable residence, but also to be permitted to offer the season's greetings personally to the mother herself, is much more richly repaid, of course. That the lady graciously receives her ragged guest, even serves him a drink and has her chauffeur drive him off in her Mercedes, is all in keeping with O. Henry's reassuring holiday gift to his reading public.

Common to all these and still other stories—"The Higher Pragmatism," "The Cop and the Anthem," and "Two Thanksgiving Day Gentlemen"—there is also the appearance versus reality motif: the underlying idea (or theme, if you will) that things are not as they seem, that they do not turn out as expected, even under the most convincing manifestations. The hard-featured bum lolling on a park bench has a worthy lesson of wisdom and courage to impart, but only if one is patient enough to listen to his story of conquered fear and to apply his experience to one's own problem of frustrated courtship.[120] Soapy, trying desperately to get himself arrested in ways not appropriate to his character, goes unobserved, but he achieves his aim to secure a comfortable cell on Blackwell's Island when a policeman nabs him for loitering outside a church.[121] And Stuffy Pete, a Union Square bum, although now bursting from one Thanksgiving Day meal, must consume another one so as not to disappoint an elderly benefactor who is actually suffering from malnutrition.[122] In each of these stories, irony is the key enabling O. Henry to switch from pathos to humor and back again to pathos within a single story; indeed, throughout a whole series of such stories, each of them designed to entertain his Sunday morning readers with the oddities he had encountered—or could visualize existing among the lowly. Now and then in writing about society's castoffs, O. Henry did inject a touch of real bitterness to stiffen the harshness of his irony, and there are hints in these few stories of what he might have achieved with more of his material had he chosen to reveal these people as the individuals he had actually seen and talked to, rather than as mere talking puppets. In "Vanity and Some Sables," for instance, we meet "Kid" Brady, member of a tough gang of hoodlums and pickpockets from Hell's Kitchen (*Trimmed Lamp*, 111–20). Heeding his girl Molly's plea, the "Kid" promises to go straight, works steadily for eight months, and then gives her an expensive set of furs, which he says were not stolen but bought with his own hard-earned wages. He and the girl are picked up anyway on suspicion of a theft of furs from his employer, but they escape a jail sentence when it turns out the furs are just cheap imitations worth only $21.50. Then Brady angrily confesses he would rather have spent six months in the pen than admit that he could only afford so small a sum for fake Russian sables. Although the plot here is as creaky a contrivance as any O. Henry cranked out, he did inject into the action a touch of the realism he usually concealed or evaded.

And the same sort of touch appears, a bit more prominently, in "The Assessor of Success," which opens with a brightly picaresque account of Hastings Beauchamp Morley, a fellow who lives entirely by his wits. Broke one day, flush the next from his gambling, picking pockets, and working a confidence game, Morley is nevertheless good-looking, well-groomed, charming, and witty. The only important thing in life is gulling others without being gulled, he assures a beggar to whom he gives a dollar shortly after having bilked another man out of $140. "The world is a rock to you, no doubt; but you must be an Aaron and smite it with your rod. Then things better than water will gush out of it for you" (*Trimmed Lamp*, 68). But then, out of the blue comes O. Henry's searing autobiographical thrust; as Morley goes jauntily on his way, he catches sight of a former schoolmate whom he can no longer face, and his last words are: "God! I wish I could die."

Stories like these that end on a sour or unrelieved melancholy note are rare in O. Henry's fiction, especially in his treatment of the dispossessed and the degraded. Had he chosen oftener to dramatize life in the raw as he doubtless saw and understood it, he probably would not have endeared himself to the public he was writing for. But neither would he have remained true to his own concept of life as an adventure to be confronted gaily. Whether rich or poor, one could scarcely avoid seeing life's drabness in Manhattan of the 1900s; for O. Henry, the point was to observe and transcend it.

New Yorkers at Home

On one occasion O. Henry was quoted as having avowed, quite seriously, that he "would like to live a lifetime in each street in New York. Every house has a drama in it" (Smith, 233). To grasp what he meant by "drama" in this context, it might be well to reconsider carefully two of the most frequently anthologized stories still heading the list of O. Henry favorites, "The Gift of the Magi" and "The Furnished Room." Representing the diametrically opposed visions of joy and sorrow with which his imagination repeatedly enlivened the domestic affairs of ordinary New Yorkers, they still flaunt a strong popular appeal that defies both the erosion of time and the literary critics' jeers. For despite their obviously dated props and gimmicks, their appeal is based on a universal yearning for an unattainable ideal. Actually, it is not surprising "The Gift of the Magi" still enjoys such widespread fame because this trite little drama of mutual self-sacrifice between husband and wife encapsulates what the world in all its stored-up wisdom knows to be indispensable in ordinary family life. Unselfish love shared, regardless of the attendant difficulties or distractions, is the idea implied again and again in O. Henry's fiction as a major criterion in his treatment of domestic affairs. If that love is present, life can be fun, however drab it might otherwise be; if it is absent, nothing else can take its place. And conversely, because it often *is* absent—or when present, existing only momentarily or in a fragile condition—the world had better note and take to heart the grim meaning of life without it. O. Henry wrote only a few stories of average family life that approach in tenderness and popular appeal the action and upbeat tone of "The Gift of the Magi," but he wrote fewer still that can match the bleakness of "The Furnished Room." Among the twenty or more in which he did attempt to portray family life among the four million, however, possibly seven or eight others deserve to be compared with them.

One reason for the scarcity may be simply that O. Henry knew too little at first hand about the life of middle-class New Yorkers and thus had to rely mainly on chance details picked up or observed externally. There are almost no children involved in any of these stories, for instance, and only two of the stories deal with the problems of childhood and child care. Except for singles or young married couples living transiently like himself in furnished rooms, the lives he knew were public lives, seen from their outward behavior rather than from within the family environment, and occupying predominantly lower economic and social strata. Thus, as against a paucity of stories that reflect ordinary family problems at home, there are the many that display New Yorkers of all shades and levels in restaurants, shops, offices, and parks, on the streets, and at summer resorts, bars, theatres, and bistros. Another reason for the disparity may be that O. Henry could not readily imagine a plethora of exciting situations taking place behind those private walls he seldom penetrated, despite his belief that every house has a drama in it. He began one of his more amusing fantasies of ordinary family life in New York with a typically proverbial gambit: "There is a saying that no man has tasted the full flavor of life until he has known poverty, love and war. . . . The three conditions embrace about all there is in life worth knowing.[123] And the three conditions he laid down as essential to the full life are indicative of the kinds of drama he sought. To find and fashion them so as to set forth the adventuresome qualities supposedly inherent in even a dreary existence, he conceived domestic situations that turn out to be pretty far-fetched, as well as somehow attached to the outside world rather than self-contained.

From O. Henry's imaginative perspective, what the average New Yorker's life too often provided may be observed in a pair of stories entitled "The Complete Life of John Hopkins" and "The Pendulum." The Hopkins's flat, he writes, was like a thousand others, as were its occupants and their flea-bitten terrier: he, a typical small-wage-earner holding down a nondescript job; his wife, a typical flat-dweller whose attributes included "the furor for department store marked-down sales, the feeling of superiority to the lady in the third-floor front . . . [and] the vigilant avoidance of the installment man" (*Voice*, 12). After their usual "compressed dinner" they usually sat staring at each other, and while she "discoursed droningly of the dinner smells from the flat across the hall," he would occasionally try to "inject a few raisins of conversation into the tasteless dough of existence" (*Voice*, 13). Because there was no concrete evidence of either poverty or love or war in such a barren routine, O. Henry would have to conjure up these essentials by sending Hopkins out for a cigar and then involving him in a series of wild adventures before bringing him safely back to the Naugahyde sofa in his flat and the resumption of his conversation with his wife. Hopkins's street brawl, his escape from the police, and his accidental intrusion into a private tiff between a pair of wealthy young lovers bring to mind a Buster Keaton routine, but O. Henry does not imply that Hopkins dreamed up all this excitement on his way to and from the cigar store.

In "The Pendulum" the portrayal of both the dull flat-dweller's routine and its occasional disruption carries out more successfully the hints dropped in its opening sentence: "There are no surprises awaiting a man who has been married two years and lives in a flat" (*Trimmed Lamp*, 42). So, as John Hopkins hops off the elevated at 81st Street and approaches his apartment, he can morosely foretell to the split second precisely what will occur at each stage of the evening's progress following his inevitable pot-roast dinner. First, his wife will show him her quilting; at 7:30 the ceiling plaster will start falling because of overhead thumping; then the drunken vaudeville troupe across the hall will start up their nightly ruckus; pretty soon there will be other nearby disturbances. At 8:15 Perkins will pick up his hat and, staring down Katy's reproaches, let her know he is going over to McCloskey's to shoot a few games of pool with his friends.

But this time things turn out differently: on entering, Perkins finds the apartment a bit upset, no Katy, but her hastily scrawled note explaining she rushed off to take care of her stricken mother. And as he goes about straightening up the rooms and preparing his solitary meal of cold mutton and coffee, Perkins gradually realizes how gratifying the old routine has always been compared to this new prospect. "The night was his. He might go forth unquestioned and thrum the strings of jollity as free as any gay bachelor there. He might carouse and wander and have his fling until dawn if he liked; and there would be no wrathful Katy waiting for him, bearing the chalice that held the dregs of his joy" (*Trimmed Lamp*, 46). Now, however, there is no joy for Perkins. With Katy gone, he remorsefully considers how lonely it must have been for her during all those long evenings he spent at McCloskey's, and he resolves, almost tearfully, to treat her more solicitously when she returns. Virtually on cue Katy opens the door, explaining the emergency call had been a false alarm, and the household machinery silently shifts back into its accustomed rhythm. At 8:15 sharply, John reaches for his hat and briskly repays a querilous inquiry with placid coin: "Thought I'd drop up to McCloskey's . . . and play a game or two of pool with the fellows" (*Trimmed Lamp*, 49).

For all his innovative skills, even O. Henry might have found it hard to work up many more variations on the theme of dull lives such as these. The only other one he attempted, evidently, is "Suite Homes and Their Romance," a somewhat cynical story about a typical lower-middle-class couple, the Turpins, whose income of two hundred dollars a month enables them to live high on the hog because they never pay their bills (*Whirligigs*, 135–42). After its sharply satirical opening exposé of the rootlessness and irresponsibility of such people, the story degenerates, however, into a fatuous sequence of improbable events that lead finally to a bookmaker's setup disguised as a Browning Society and serving as a front for an illicit ice-cream parlor. As a fictional mirror image of middle-class domestic life, "Suite Homes" is too far-fetched even for effective satire, despite its wisecracks and tomfoolery. Yet O. Henry could employ these same tactics more effectively—and achieve some variety as well—by applying his fictional brush to the lives of Irish laboring-class families, where his requisite conditions of poverty, love, and war were inescapably present and could be manipulated amusingly in at least half a dozen different ways.

Humor predominates in all but one of these Irish tales. In "Between Rounds," for example, the marital scuffling between John and Judy McCaskey regularly disturbs the peace at Mrs. Murphy's boardinghouse but they stop fighting when her little son disappears (*Four Million*, 36–46). Joining the search party to help look for him, they become reconciled while thinking of him as the child they might have had, but as soon as he turns up, the McCaskeys are at each other's throats again as vigorously as ever. In "A Harlem Tragedy" O. Henry gives the marital warfare plot a slightly different twist: Mrs. Cassidy brags to Mrs. Fink about all the bruises and black eyes her brutal spouse has inflicted on her because, she says, he always contritely rewards her forgiveness afterward with pretty gifts and dinner dates, whereas Mr. Fink, a dull, modest fellow who "reposed in the state of matrimony like a lump of unblended suet in a pudding," never does his wife any harm (*Trimmed Lamp*, 165–66). Mrs. Fink, humiliated and jealously enraged, tries to provoke his fury by publicly bawling out and even striking him, but instead of thrashing her in return, he humiliates her still further by giving in and doing her washing. Poorer than either of these, "The Harbinger" involves a trio of thirsty Union Square loafers, one of whom tries to wheedle his two-hundred-pound wife out of the dollar she earned washing clothes so they can buy some beer. Though deaf to his demands and excuses, the wife apparently yields only when he begins making ardent love to her; instead of the dollar, she brings him a dose of medicine and a spoon to counteract his springtime malady (*Voice*, 141–48).

Thus the most successful of these Irish dialect stories are the few that combine a more serious attitude toward family relationships with oddities of speech and mannerisms, which O. Henry invariably handles skillfully. Instead of pure slapstick farce, there is a touch of genuine mirth and winsomeness in two stories, "The Easter of the Soul" and "The Day Resurgent," both of which were written as special Easter feature stories for his *Sunday World* audience (*Voice*, 149–56; *Strictly Business*, 43–53). In the former, young "Tiger" McQuirk, idled because the stone-cutters are on strike, irritably nurses his restlessness at home; his little brother attributes his splenetic behavior to his girl, Annie Maria; his mother, simply to spring in his bones. "Tiger" denies everything, asserting there is no spring in sight; then he goes searching for signs on his own but finds no sure ones till he reaches Annie's house. And when she assures him spring is everywhere, he is at last happily convinced and reinvigorated. Virtually plotless, the story is suffused with charm and subtlety skillfully woven into the dialogue between McQuirk and those he meets casually during his progress.

In "The Day Resurgent" the same tricks are again used effectively. Danny McCree, the gruff young hero all dressed up and ready to join the Easter parade, is puzzled by his blind father's wistful desire to have Danny's mother finish reading to him about "the hippopotamus." As Danny meets others along the way to church with his girl, Katy Conlon, he keeps trying to work out the connection between Easter and hippos. Finally, during the sermon, he realizes his father's reference was to a book, *The History of Greece*, from which Danny had been reading aloud to him an account of the Peloponnesian War but had not finished it. So, much to the old man's delight, Danny picks up the reading again on his return and even brushes aside gruffly his father's hint that he might prefer being with Katy. Far-fetched and fatuously sentimentalized, the story nevertheless conveys O. Henry's aim to dramatize the strong family ties shared by laboring-class Irish, despite their apparent harshness toward one another.

Although superficial in content and theme, these Irish dialect stories

Part 1

are perhaps a cut above most of the others in O. Henry's wide-ranging gallery of Manhattan's family portraits. Still, he demonstrated in several of these both his versatility in manipulating other dialects and ethnic characteristics and in combining them with tall-tale elements and satirical overtones such as the ones frequently employed in his tales of the West and South. Two examples are "The Gold That Glittered" and "The City of Dreadful Night," both of them mildly amusing farces. The former will be recognized as another variation of one of his favorite situations—the fomenting of Latin American revolutions, hatched and subsidized by exiles huddling in an obscure downtown bistro called "El Refugio" (*Strictly Business*, 21–33). But in this yarn O. Henry seasoned the plot by tossing into it both an abortive swindle and a successful romance. General Perrico Ximenes Villablanca Falcon (O. Henry's orbicular Hispanic nomenclature!), who is about to be fleeced of his twenty-five thousand dollars by two Irish confidence men posing as United States government officials, falls in love with his buxom boardinghouse landlady, the widow O'Brien, and buys her establishment instead of squandering his funds on a fake order of Winchester rifles for the revolution.

A generous supply of hyperbole, puns, clownish metaphors, and unrestrained dialogue keeps the humor bubbling throughout both this story and "The City of Dreadful Night," which is a takeoff on the effects of a heat wave that had driven hundreds of suffocating tenement occupants to sleep in the public parks. Besides the obvious physical discomforts and multiracial irritations that give the story its distinctive hoi polloi flavor, O. Henry also undercut the absurdity of the whole situation by having his wealthy apartment house landlord decide to raise the rents by fifteen per cent because of the extra benefits of grass and trees his tenants were reaping in the park (*Voice*, 141–48).

Even ironic humor of the absurd such as this, however, fails to compensate for the hollow plotting and/or feeble characterization one finds in the ten or twelve remaining stories of this domestic category. Several, in fact, appear to be attempted reruns of earlier ones, as in "Memoirs of a Yellow Dog" and "Ulysses and the Dogman," which ridicule henpecked husbands obliged to take their family pets out for an airing each evening (*Four Million*, 110–18; *Sixes and Sevens*, 64–73). And another pair entitled "Girl" and "The Struggle of the Outliers" deals with the standard problem of the suburbanite—how to secure a household maid—in the same hackneyed way, by making it appear the hero is contending with a rival for the girl's affection (*Whirligigs*, 81–88; *O. Henryana*, 75–89).

In fact, the theme of frustrated love triumphing over self-imposed obstacles or the machinations of assorted rivals, also stretches the reader's credulity in at least five or six other stories.[124]

Finally, there are two more stories in this group that reveal O. Henry's light-fingered ability to transform into entertaining fiction his own critical attitudes toward literature and society. In "Tommy's Burglar," for example, he spoofs the typical juvenile *Youth's Companion* fiction of his day by having a burglar and the little boy who apprehends him critically discuss the appropriate methods and clichés to be used in writing a story involving a burglar and a little boy. And in "A Newspaper Story" he tells us how a single copy of a castoff newspaper can link together through several fortuitous events the disparate lives of various families unknown to one another (*Whirligigs*, 215–22, 209–214).

The combination of ephemeral laughter and light romance evoked in nearly all these stories, most of them hastily churned out under contract each week to fill a page of the *Sunday World*, is a testament to both O. Henry's artistic awareness and his craftsmanship—proof he had not only precisely gauged the taste of his mass audience, but had also achieved the appropriate means to satisfy it. This, it seems evident, was his major concern: the problem of producing a weekly diet of light entertainment rather than the more demanding one of rendering in the manner of a Henry James or Edith Wharton the dramatic depths of Manhattan society. If now and then he could manage to cast a penetrating shaft of light into the behavior of greedy landlords, miserly employers, crooked public officials, or the tortured souls of their victims along with his entertainment, so much the better. This is one reason why "A Municipal Report," for example, is still one of his most frequently anthologized favorites. But among his New York stories of domestic life the entertainment took precedence over everything else; the only other exception to his common practice aside from "The Gift of the Magi" and "The Furnished Room" is "The Guilty Party—An East Side Tragedy," a grim tale of parental neglect that "was made a full-page feature by the Sunday [*World*] Magazine editor, with a prize contest announced for the best letter regarding it" (Clarkson, 26; *Trimmed Lamp*, 169–78). Slightly resembling Stephen Crane's *Maggie*, "The Guilty Party" tells of twelve-year-old Liz, who grows up to become a drunkard, murderess, and suicide because of her father's unwillingness to play with her as a child. By means of his typical "envelope" technique, consisting of a brief opening scene and a swift transition to the main scene, couched in the form of a dream, O. Henry achieved in this story a respectable domestic drama that suggests more truthfully than many of his others some of the festering social problems underlying the picturesque surface of metropolitan life. Although it too, like most of the others, suffers from a heavy overlay of sentimentality in its conclusion, it still deserves parity rating along with "The Furnished Room."

Bagdad on Parade—Gothamites in Public

"O. Henry's favorite coign of vantage," wrote Professor C. Alphonso Smith, "was the restaurant. From his seat here . . . he gazed at his peep-show with a zest and interpretative insight that never flagged" (*O. Henry Biography*, 187). No subsequent biographer has found a more vivid metaphor than this to circumscribe the artistic mood and milieu of his lifelong friend. For no characteristic of O. Henry's fiction displays his individuality more lavishly than does his unflagging fascination with the passing show, which he could observe at greater leisure and perhaps with sharper insight while seated at a restaurant table, alone or with friends, than he could while ambling about the city's avenues and side streets. The many anecdotes his few intimate friends told later of his fondness for dining out in all manner of public eating places are both colorful and explicit, but his readers would not need to know any of them to sense the excitement he must have felt in the presence of Manhattan's kaleidoscopic scene. More clearly than any recollections at second hand, his own stories convey both the impressions and their effects upon him—an ebb and flow of faces arriving and departing, the hum of lively talk, the flashing colors of women's garments, the tinkle of silver and glassware, the popping of corks, and the savor of varied dishes served forth by hurrying waiters—as he lays bare the public image of New York in its scores of food and drink emporiums, from the most fashionable of dining halls to the obscurest of Bohemian rathskellers. These stories show, more convincingly than do his tales of family life, that the public spotlight was his special turf. The restaurant, not the furnished room, was where he found the real drama of New York life. And this, too, is an augury of his perennial appeal.

Of his thirty or more stories about New Yorkers at large, there is scarcely a single one in which a restaurant does not fill some role, either as the central scene of action or as a point of reference against which social activity elsewhere in the city can be adjudicated. Thus the dispensing and consumption of food and drink in public serve as important symbols—sometimes consciously, sometimes unintentionally employed—

in O. Henry's dramatization of what he took to be the significant conduct of his fellow citizens. The kinds of places they patronized, as well as their behavior in those places, were the basic source materials he relied on for classifying and evaluating the patrons and would-be patrons who served as models for his fictional characterizations. As Professor Smith pointed out long ago, O. Henry divided these people into two broad groups: "those who knew or thought they knew, the real thing and those who would be considered the real thing" (*O. Henry Biography*, 188). As seen from that vantage point of his restaurant table, O. Henry's passing throng of New Yorkers offers its most glittering configuration in this group of stories, each of which sets forth an idealized version of romantic adventure framed in an illusorily realistic setting.

The major themes dramatized in these stories, however, are much the same as those developed in all his other stories, neither simpler nor more complex in probing the mystery of human motives, though perhaps oftener dressed in a more attractive package. As commentary on the follies, frailties, ambitions, and attainments of human nature, they can hardly be called trenchant; but their exposure in such a variety of forms is another testament of O. Henry's artistry. The four themes that recur consistently in the stories about New Yorkers on parade are concerned with the following manifestations of motivation, endeavor, and behavior: (a) pretense and the reversal of fortune—"turning the tables on Haroun" (*O. Henry Biography*, 188); (b) initiation and discovery through adventure; (c) the city itself as a magic Arabian Nights' source and symbol for imaginative exploration; and (d) the universal human yearning for individual fulfillment. One or more of these themes may be clearly identified in virtually every story, even though the major theme itself in some stories may be coyly concealed beneath several layers of seemingly irrelevant chaff—as in the waving of a magician's kerchief.

Almost inescapably, the theme of pretense strikes the dominant chords of these stories—the pervasive desire to pose for what one is not, if only for a brief spell of time and regardless of the acknowledged risk involved—for it is the most persistent theme in O. Henry's total canon, shadowing forth, perhaps, a profound recognition of his own character, which could be readily exorcized through transference to the makeup of his fellow citizens. In any event, it crops up again and again in nearly all his stories from the earliest to the last few he left unfinished at his death.

It is the linchpin of "While the Auto Waits," one of the first stories that aroused the curiosity of magazine editors and literary critics about an unknown author who called himself James L. Bliss (*Voice*, 58–66). Still recognized as one of his best, the story dramatizes the pathos of false pretenses in the transparent claims to family grandeur with which a comely young woman tries to impress a young man who stops to chat with her in a park. Taking his cue from her pretentiousness, he too masks his real identity by pretending to be a humble restaurant cashier, which is actually the position she holds! Meanwhile, he is also the wealthy owner of the chauffeured sedan awaiting occupancy, which she has pointed to as her own. The loss to both individuals as a result of what O. Henry perceived to be a natural human urge toward one-upmanship is neatly driven home with quiet irony, unblemished by either sentimentality or gratuitous moralizing.

In "Lost on Dress Parade" O. Henry gave virtually the same situation a reversed plot development by portraying the man as victim of his own folly, but also heightening the poignance of lost hopes with several fresh touches of characterization. Towers Chandler, a likable, generous young hero, scrimps along on a meager salary, saving one dollar each week so that every tenth week he can splurge his wad at a fashionable Broadway restaurant. But on this icy winter evening Towers happens to witness on his way there a pretty young woman, not too well dressed, who has slipped on the sidewalk and sprained her ankle. Helping her up considerately, he introduces himself and promptly invites her to dine with him. Reluctantly, she accepts; then throughout the meal she has to listen to him brag about his life as an idle clubman and habitué of fine restaurants. But after thanking and bidding him good-bye, she returns sadly to her palatial home, convinced that although she might cheerfully marry a poor man so long as he had "some work to do in the world," she could never love a social butterfly, "even if his eyes were blue and he were so kind to poor girls whom he met in the street" (*Four Million*, 23). Once again, that double loss gives the story its special O. Henry sting.

But he could also work up other situations like these in which profit instead of loss comes to one or more of the persons involved without necessarily hurting anyone else. In "Transients in Arcadia," for example, the therapeutic effect of playing poseur occasionally is very amusingly developed from its initial mouth-watering description of the elegant but unobtrusive Hotel Lotus on Broadway: "an oasis in the July desert of Manhattan." Here can be found "brook trout better than the White Mountains ever served, sea food that would turn Old Point Comfort— 'by Gad, sah!'—green with envy, and Maine venison that would melt the official heart of a game warden" (*Voice*, 170). Enter next the lovely, soignée Madame Heloise D'Arcy Beaumont, whose graciousness dazzles bellboys and management alike: she stays a few days, seldom going out, and soon meets handsome young Harold Farrington, also well-groomed and manifestly a leisured man of the world. They congratulate each other for having found such a quiet retreat away from all the blatant foreign resorts, already overrun and cheapened by tourists.

But after three days of such pleasant persiflage, the lady owns up that she is actually Mamie Siviter, a hosiery clerk at Casey's Mammoth Store; that she has only a dollar left from the fund she saved up for a year to finance this one week's glorious holiday; and that last dollar must abate the installment now due on her dress. Unperturbed, Farrington scribbles a receipt and takes her dollar, disclosing meanwhile his real identity as Jimmy McManus, bill collector for O'Dowd and Levinsky, confessing that he too has saved pennies out of a paltry salary because, like Mamie, he "always wanted to put up at a swell hotel" (*Voice*, 177). Clearly, Jimmy and Mamie have both obtained more than their money's worth with the *lagniappe* of blossoming romance to boot; in parting at the elevator, they have also made a date to take in Coney Island the following Saturday. Their story is a brilliantly contrived idyll that combines all four of O. Henry's major themes within fewer than nine pages.

With somewhat more piquancy than he normally applied, O. Henry cooked up the same recipe in a later story, "A Ramble in Aphasia," which hints of neurosis and the split personality, although it is also a study in wish-fulfillment and the urge to cast aside social constraints in order to live a free, uncommitted life, if only for a short while.[125] Elwyn Bellford, the narrator, is a prominent lawyer from Denver who apparently cracks under the strain of hard work, forgets his past, and gets on a train for New York with three thousand dollars in his wallet but no baggage. Aboard the train are a number of western pharmacists en route to a convention; Bellford pretends to be a member of their group, adopts the alias Edward Pinkhammer, and registers at the same hotel with the others. At this point O. Henry casually drops a hint that the amnesia malady may be merely a hoax contrived by a smart fellow who wants to abscond, for Bellford quickly brushes off a traveling salesman acquaintance who greets him in the lobby and promptly moves to another hotel.

Safely anonymous again, Bellford proceeds to enjoy the sparkling glamor of Broadway as O. Henry describes in lyrical terms the gold and silver delights of Manhattan, available to all who possess imagination and intelligence enough to partake of them within the framework of the order of things: "the key to liberty is not in the hands of License, but Convention holds it. Comity has a toll-gate at which you must pay, or you may not enter the land of Freedom" (*Strictly Business*, 138). And now Bellford runs into another old friend in a quiet off-Broadway restaurant, a lovely lady in her mid-thirties who recognizes him at once as the lover she had fifteen years before. Bellford still insists he is Pinkhammer and has forgotten everything, despite her recollection of specific intimacies they shared, plus details she knows of his subsequent career. To his persistent denial of these things, she replies with a soft laugh of mingled bliss and misery, "You lie, Elwyn Bellford. . . . Oh, I know you lie!" Then she climbs into her carriage and disappears—unidentified. On returning to his hotel, Bellford is confronted by his family physician and his distraught wife and, while still trying to brazen out the Pinkhammer disguise, gradually cracks under the doctor's grilling, admitting he may have been a victim of aphasia during the two weeks spent in New York. "But, oh, Doc" he concludes, after confessing he is now rather tired of the whole experience, "good old Doc—it was glorious!" (*Strictly Business*, 142).

Among the many other stories in which O. Henry developed the pretense theme, few can match these in either technical virtuosity or popular appeal, yet it is interesting enough to consider how often he did attempt to vary his treatment of the theme effectively. In "The Social Triangle," for example, he applied it ironically to expose the pretentiousness of three different levels of New York society: showing how the impoverished Ikey Snigglefritz spends his hard-earned week's pay to set up drinks for his ward boss, Billy McMahon, who in turn sits and suffers with his wife later in a fashionable restaurant until he can figure out a way to become publicly greeted by Cortland Van Duyckink, a multimillionaire sitting nearby. Then, to resolve the improbable triangle, Van Duyckink, while looking over a slum-clearance project he is sponsoring, impulsively leaves his car to grasp "the hand of what seemed to him a living rebuke" and, sincerely wishing to be friendly and helpful, drives away contented but unaware that "he had shaken the hand of Ikey Snigglefritz" (*Trimmed Lamp*, 129).

O. Henry devised still other devices in "The Caliph and the Cad," "The Poet and the Peasant," "The Country of Elusion," and "From Each According to His Ability"[126] to juxtapose ironically the pretenses of different social levels and the effects of pretense among members of the same social class. Sometimes amusing, but also painful, these are achieved with varying success in four or five more stories.[127] In each of these, as usual, O. Henry's trademark surprise ending is carefully contrived to cut off all further consideration of the problem raised, but by that time, the theme and its implications have been set up.

O. Henry's two major themes of pretense and discovery through adventure are often combined, but are not always closely linked or mutually dependent upon each other in a single story. Quite the contrary, in fact, for the idea of eagerly probing the unknown, with or without the protective mantle of a disguise, seems to have been a dominant force in his own mind throughout his youth and mature years, and even more urgently toward the end. Seeing life itself constantly as a chancy adventure at best, O. Henry's eagerness to crowd in all possible chances exploded in his stories like a colorful display of fireworks. Thus, the characters he admired most would be seekers like his protagonist in "The Green Door," Ralph Steiner, who seemed to find the most interesting thing in life "to be what might lie just around the next corner" (*Four Million*, 153). A true adventurer, Steiner will gladly pay the toll collected for following up a lead, even though past experience has taught him the charge may be excessive. There are many others like him in O. Henry's stories, most of them obvious projections of their own author's self-image.

Nor are they always males. The adventurer in a loony but charming story, "A Philistine in Bohemia," is a winsome Irish girl, Katy Dempsey, who with her mother keeps one of the cheap rooming houses below Union Square. Ardently courted by one of their lodgers, the meticulous Mr. Brunelli, Katy is wary of him at first because he is Italian as well as, from her mother's viewpoint, perhaps a bit "too coolchured in his spache for a rale gintleman" (*Voice*, 213). But Katy accepts his invitation to dine at a noted Bohemian restaurant in the Village, patronized by poor artists and other sporty characters and managed by a chap named Tonio. After escorting her to a table, Brunelli excuses himself, and before he returns one of the waiters spreads before her a veritable Lucullian feast. Katy's fascination with the gay atmosphere of the place and the excellence of her food is overshadowed somewhat by Brunelli's odd disappearance; she begins to suspect him of being a titled patrician, "glorious of name but shy of rent money," and wonders why he left her to dine alone. Meanwhile, the other patrons are all clamoring for Tonio, who treats them like princes, and when the crowd thins out slightly, Brunelli reappears at Katy's table, disclosing himself as "the great Tonio" and once again professing his "loaf" for her. Sated with such a rich repast, she accepts him gratefully: "Sure I'll marry wid ye. But why didn't ye tell me ye was the cook? I was near turnin' ye down for bein' one of thim foreign counts!" (*Voice*, 218).

Neither does the adventure itself and its consequent reward have to be among the more sensational experiences the great city provides. It can be the merest departure from routine activity and still yield rich results—as Big Jim Daugherty discovers when he takes his wife out to dinner. A typical Broadway "sport," he has been married more than three years, yet has barely noticed his Delia except to swap trivia with her at breakfast; while escorting her along the street to their dinner engagement this time, he soon notes the admiring glances and murmurs his stunning spouse attracts and, altering his original plan to take her to an ordinary cafe, he steers her instead to swank Hoogley's—"the swellest slow-lunch warehouse on the line"—where she shines like a solitary star. Chatting joyously over their meal, she soon draws the attention of "the Honorable Patrick Corrigan, leader in Daugherty's district" who chides Big Jim, after the introductions, for concealing a treasure.[128] His eyes opened at last, Daugherty can only mutter remorsely to himself over the time he has lost with this dazzling creature, his own wife, as she goes on charming a tableful of his politician friends.

Although the story is blatantly overdone for comic effect, the fact that the situation is not too far-fetched to appeal to tastes more elevated than those of Daugherty's level offers another sign of O. Henry's firm hold on his public. Quite often the underlying moral of his story, though woven neatly into its dramatic texture as it is here, is so obvious and broadly applicable that sages and dunces alike must applaud it.

The best of O. Henry's stories that develop this theme stress the point that simplicity and alertness are no less needful than courage for pursuing an adventurous life. And even his less successful ones, such as "Psyche and the Pskyscraper," which strains rather feebly to produce a dramatic effect, usually manage to convey the message with a certain winsomeness. Thus, although Daisy, the shy young heroine of this story, is not very bright, she can quickly determine which of her two ardent suitors offers her the more promising future: down-to-earth Joe, who operates a humble newsstand, or his rival, Dabster, a self-assured pseudo-intellectual snob, who from the skyscraper's pinnacle bombards her with statistics about the smallness of human affairs in the broad vista laid out before them. Wholly dismayed by all those figures signifying the cold, heartless immensity of things in the universe, Daisy scurries back gratefully to Joe's newsstand, where it is "cozy and warm and homelike," and one must indeed admire her wisdom in offering herself to Joe whenever he wants to take her (*Strictly Business*, 173–82).

O. Henry's most ambitious effort on the theme of adventure and discovery, however, is the late story entitled "The Venturers," published only a few months before he died. Also among the most provocative and enigmatic, the story grew out of the following seminal idea pinpointed in his notebook: "Followers of chance—two 'Knights errant' one leaves girl and other marries her for what may be 'around-the-corner'" (Langford, 191; Smith, 214–15). On one level the story clearly expresses what Alfonso Smith referred to as O. Henry's "revolt against the calculable," a problem he grappled with from the beginning to the end of his career. But on a deeper level, perhaps reflecting the more immediate specific problem of his own second marriage, one can readily sense the tension and ambiguities of an inner conflict, for in the two knights errant of the story, Foster and Ives, are visible the unresolved halves of their creator himself, O. Henry, the adventurous literary artist, and Porter, the alter ego who had taken a second wife in what was turning out to be a sadly mistaken venture for him. This element of the divided self accounts for both the story's complexity and for what Smith construed as its misplaced center (Smith, 214–15).

The story opens with John Reginald Forster considering where to go for an exciting dinner as he leaves his exclusive Powhattan Club. He stops under the corner street light, fumbles through his pockets, and, though personally wealthy, discovers they are empty. Another well-groomed gentleman, Ives, noting his predicament, strikes up an acquaintance and, confessing that he too possesses only two pennies, proposes they dine together in style at the swank restaurant across the avenue and then match coins to see which of them will have to deal with the proprietor's outraged wrath. Forster delightedly agrees and the two men order a typical O. Henry meal, replete with rare French wines and exotic dishes, meanwhile entertaining each other with tales of their fondness for encountering unexpected but eagerly sought adventures in odd corners of the world. Ives has had more varied experiences than Forster, who although largely confined to New York, has always dreamed of doing things that would not lead to clearly predictable ends, such as their shared dinner. Still, as the dinner ends both men have to confess that even this adventurer's finale was predictable, since it turns out that Forster, on losing the toss, has only to sign a credit chit, and that Ives himself owns the place.

But, reluctant to break off their friendship, Forster now discloses that he is engaged to be married to a lovely woman within a month and cannot decide whether to go through with the marriage or cut out for Alaska, for, although he loves the lady, it is the dead certainty of all their future that makes him doubtful. The two men agree to meet again for another dinner on the following Thursday. Ives then trots off to meet a beautiful young woman, Mary Marsden, and their dialogue reveals they have known each other since childhood and that he could have married her three years before if he had not decided to take off on another of his periodic junkets around the globe; now it is too late—she is about to be married to another man. Observing her in her unpredictably unchanged surroundings, Ives thinks she will always be the same there; the certainty of it was what had driven him away before. On Thursday, Forster tells Ives their dinner will have to be postponed because he had decided to sail round the world and had already explained this need to his fiancée in a letter. Ives, of course, tells him not to bother, he has married the same girl himself, having discovered this was the real Venture for him. It was the one hazardous course a man might follow all his life without knowing, even to his dying day, whether it was destined to end in the highest heaven or the blackest pit.

Although it may be argued "The Venturers" is not a veiled commentary on O. Henry's misgivings about his own second marriage, the story nevertheless does reveal a deep-seated conviction, the result of painful personal experience, that one cannot escape one's destiny regardless of the road taken, and that accordingly it is better to accept willingly the chances that come than to try to manipulate one's fate. Neither withdrawal nor escape will serve, for both lead to unsatisfactory ends, as he shows in another strange story, "To Him Who Waits," about a man who became a hermit because the woman he desired chose a richer husband.[129] Then, when the same woman, divorced, contrite, and still desirable, offered him a second chance, he compounded his folly by rejecting her to pursue a younger woman who rejected him. In O. Henry's litany the essence of the adventurous life rests in confrontation and eager acceptance of the chances offered; even though these too may lead to sad ends, these ends themselves are unforeseen in any event. Satisfaction can only be derived from the kind of race one runs. These implications re-echo throughout his stories repeatedly.

Naturally, New York is the inevitable spot for pursuing the adventurous life, simply because its storehouse of chances is inexhaustible. And this idea marks another prominent motif in O. Henry's work. But unlike the foregoing themes, that of the great city as a spiritual reservoir for the imagination is a more pervasive idea, which appears in many scattered passages, hints, and overtones, as in "Voice of the City" and other tales already cited, rather than as the predominant motif of complete specific stories.[130] Still, its reappearance among the other themes can often be recognized in the presentation of contrasting viewpoints or attitudes O. Henry employs as a standard device in many stories. In "A Little Local Color," for example, his main purpose is to spoof with light satire both himself and other feature-writing journalists in New York because they are all desperately seeking the picturesque word, phrase, image, and metaphor with which to describe the city. Since their livelihood depends on giving the reading public what it demands, the writer-narrator badgers his friend, a "young-man-about-town and a New Yorker by birth, preference and incommutability" (*Whirligigs*, 231), to show him around where he can note down the real local color in people's polyglot speech, mannerisms, and idiosyncrasies. Wherever they go, however, the unexpected rather than the typical turns up—college professors talk Bowery slang, whereas a genuine, dyed-in-the-wool native Boweryite, speaking impeccable English, mercilessly ridicules the literary commercialization of alleged Bowery argot. In the end both are obliged to conclude that New York is too colorful and variegated to be easily stereotyped and classified. That the city does produce the unexpected where one is least prepared to find it is the real source of its charm, even though pulp feature writers thrive on their standardized but faked local-color portrayals.

O. Henry dramatizes this idea continuously, even when poking fun at New York's manifest discomforts in midsummer heat. In "Rus in Urbe" he spreads it as flavoring for an otherwise stale plot involving a rich versus poor man's pursuit of the same girl, and yet manages to make both men's patently deceitful praise of the city's summer delights sound quite authentic (*Options*, 227–39). And again, in "The Call of the Tame," he works up the same theme by relating it to another of his favorite situations, the contrast between a confirmed New Yorker's viewpoint and that of a bluff, hearty man of the West, who becomes a convert as soon as he gets the message (*Strictly Business*, 100–108). Greenbrier Nye, baffled and bored by the hubbub of Sixth Avenue, can hardly wait to return to his quiet home in Arizona, despite the luxury surrounding him in the exclusive café where his former partner, Longhorn Merritt, has taken him for luncheon. His scorns the effete drinks and dishes Merritt orders—dry Martinis, green Chartreuse, squab en casserole—and sticks to straight whiskey, saddened by the realization

that city life has softened and feminized his old cow-punching pal of
bygone days. Then his eye falls upon an elegantly dressed woman in
speckled silk at a table nearby; before long the comforts of city life thus
viewed from a new perspective have cast their spell upon him.

It didn't matter whether O. Henry found his magic symbol in a
woman's stylish garb, an absinthe frappé, or a restaurant table's glittering
array of silverware; his loyalty to the city's endless lure could be so
fervently expressed that one need not wonder why New Yorkers loved
his stories ninety years ago—and still do. But to appreciate his method of
singing hymns of praise to Manhattan one must often peer beneath the
insouciance and bravura of his approach. His most emphatic paean to the
enchantment of New York occurs in the last few pages of "The Duel," a
story resembling "The Venturers" by offering two contrasting views,
both of them his own, which are brilliantly synthesized in a concluding
passage of poetic prose. William and Jack, the two young westerners who
meet at luncheon after a four years' residence in the city, are both
projections of O. Henry's personality. William, the successful business-
man, defends the city in crude, slangy terms, and for the wrong reasons—he
is making money fast, meeting VIPs, and seeing the plays he doesn't
understand. Jack, the successful artist, condemns the city in more liter-
ate terms as "a monster to which the innocence, the genius, and the
beauty of the land must pay tribute." He hates it because it is crude,
base, materialistic—a city controlled by its lowest elements—and he
would return to the purer air of the West at once if he could, rather than
sell his soul to it as his friend has done. Then at midnight Jack throws up
his window and looks out across the city far below, catching his breath at
the massive beauty of a sight he has seen and felt hundreds of times. As
a westerner, he sees its irregular background shapes in the imagery of
canyons, cliffs, and gulches, but as an artist he responds to the implications of its myriads of glowing lights like a rapt devotee before an altar:

> . . . out of the violet and purple depths ascended like the city's soul
> sounds and odors and thrills that make up the civic body. There arose
> the breath of gaiety unrestrained, of love, of hate, of all the passions
> that man can know. There below him lay all things, good or bad, that
> can be brought from the four corners of the earth to instruct, please,
> thrill, enrich, despoil, elevate, cast down, nurture, or kill. Thus the
> flavor of it came to him and went into his blood. (*Strictly Business*,
> 300–301)

O. Henry leaves it up to the reader to decide whether either of the two
won the duel over the city, but after such a purple passage as this, the

reader has no trouble in discerning the effect of the city's "cup of mandragora" on O. Henry himself. It was the draught of vintage that enabled him in imagination to offset all leaden-eyed despairs.

Although New York became the chief stimulus for O. Henry's fertile imagination during his final decade, the city reflected as a microcosm in each of his 140 or more stories simply serves as his objective correlative to pin down the broadest of his themes—the idea of oneness at the heart of things in human society. A typically romantic or idealistic approach, this notion that a strong common bond unites all human beings sweeps aside or ignores as irrelevant superficialities the infinite gradations and distinctions that persist among rich and poor, strong and weak, intelligent and stupid, good and evil, in order to focus attention on an assumed centralizing principle or ideal toward which all humanity aspires. It is an approach abhorred by skeptics and realists, who insist on the importance of such distinctions in the world we know and inhabit, and who warn the literary artist not to ignore them in his fictional portrayal of the world we all live in. For whatever the tie between them may be, says the realist, saints and sinners are not the same; the differences between them are no less significant than the ties that bind them together.

Nevertheless, there is perhaps an indestructible appeal in the romanticist's creed which the world cherishes and clings to. It also helps to explain O. Henry's hold on the reading public, despite the critics' scorn. The reader knows well enough that things seldom work out in the world as they do in O. Henry's stories; but in reverie he would like to believe they might. He would like to believe not only that all brides are beautiful but also, beneath their beauty, sisters of the golden circle; that all bums and millionaires are alike redeemable; and that all lads and lasses, regardless of their hue, seek the blue flower of contentment together in the far fields of the human heart. O. Henry's stories about New Yorkers, westerners, southerners, and Hispanics are but part of a vast literature of romanticism that has always fed this basic human hunger—"the search for those common traits and common impulses which together form a sort of common denominator of our common humanity" (*O. Henry Biography*, 243). Their ultimate theme, as his first biographer aptly concludes, "is your nature and mine."

Notes to Part 1

1. Louis D. Rubin, *The Edge of the Swamp* (Baton Rouge and London: Louisiana State University Press, 1989), 47.

Part 1

2. See Langford, *Alias O. Henry*, 224–26, 231–32; hereafter cited as Langford.
3. See Harrell, *O. Henry Encore*, 119–29; hereafter cited as Harrell.
4. Critical purists and reviewers in the 1880s and 1890s often attacked local colorists because of alleged vulgarity in the dialect used in their stories. See Claude M. Simpson, *The Local Colorists* (New York, 1960), 12, 13, n. 7. See also Langford, 232.
5. The titles of these five are "Jeff Peters as a Personal Magnet," "A Midsummer Masquerade," "Shearing the Wolf," "The Man Higher Up," and "The Ethics of Pig."
6. See Davis and Maurice, *The Caliph of Bagdad*, 355–58; hereafter cited as *Caliph*.
7. See *Caliph*, 379. The story was first published in the *Saturday Evening Post* (6 July 1907) and collected in *Whirligigs*, 100–115. See Clarkson, 50.
8. These six were first published and later collected as follows: "A Blackjack Bargainer," in *Munsey's* (August 1901) as by "Sydney Porter" and in *Whirligigs*, 166–87; "The Duplicity of Hargraves," in *Junior Munsey* (February 1902) and in *Sixes and Sevens*, 133–53; "The Guardian of the Accolade," in *Brandur Magazine* (11 October 1902), and again in *Cosmopolitan* (May 1903), on both occasions under the title of "The Guardian of the Scutcheon," and as by "Olivier Henry," and in *Roads of Destiny*, 29–39; "The Emancipation of Billy," in *Everybody's* (May 1904) and in *Roads of Destiny*, 184–96; "Blind Man's Holiday," in *Ainslee's* (December 1905) and in *Whirligigs*, 259–87; "A Municipal Report," in *Hampton's* (November 1909) and in *Strictly Business*, 148–72. For further bibliographical data on all these, see Clarkson, 47–56.
9. Almost certainly O. Henry had in mind William Garret's book *Reminiscences of Public Men in Alabama for Thirty Years* (Atlanta: Plantation Publishing Company's Press, 1872).
10. In *McClure's* (December 1899). For further bibliographical information on these, see Clarkson, 39, 40, 43, 56, 57, 68.
11. See Clarkson, Appendix, 143–44, for O. Henry's letter awarding prizes for the best solutions of the problems set forth in this story. See also Clarkson, 99.
12. In *Options*, 7.
13. See Clarkson, 44.
14. In *Sixes and Sevens*, 154–73; see Clarkson, 52, 56.
15. Letter to Mrs. Hall, 31 November 1883. *Works*, 2:1071.
16. Letter to Dr. W. P. Beall, 27 February 1884. *Works*, 2:1075.
17. Dora Neill Raymond, *Captain Lee Hall of Texas* (Norman, Oklahoma, 1940), chapter 1. See also Edmund King, *The Great South* (Hartford, Connecticut, 1875), 178. See, e.g., "An Afternoon Miracle," a rewritten version of one of O. Henry's earliest stories, "The Miracle of Lava Canyon"; also "The Caballero's Way" and others in the volume *Heart of the West*, vol. 4.

18. "The Last of the Troubadors," in *Sixes and Sevens, Works*, 8:5; hereafter cited in the text.
19. Letters to Dave [David Scott?], 28 April 1885. *Works*, 2:1077, 1079–80.
20. Dan Hollis, "The Persecution of O. Henry," Austin *American-Statesman Magazine* (30 August 1925), 10. Quoted in Langford, 37–38.
21. The titillating tale of O. Henry's courtship and elopement has been told from many points of view. See, e.g., Frances G. Maltby, *The Dimity Sweetheart* (Richmond, Virginia: Dietz Printing Company, 1930); Leslie Cave Wilson, *Hard to Forget* (Los Angeles, California: Lymanhouse, 1939); Mary S. Harrell, "O. Henry's Texas Contacts," University of Texas Master's Thesis, 1935.
22. See *Rolling Stones*, in *Works*, vol. 12; hereafter cited in the text; see also Current-Garcia's *O. Henry*, 35, 85.
23. See *Roads of Destiny, Works*, 6: 155–70; hereafter cited in the text.
24. For a detailed discussion of these preliminaries, see Langford, 71–74.
25. For an excellent descriptive analysis of *The Rolling Stone*, see Langford, 75–81, and his Appendix, 251–58.
26. H. E. Rollins, "O. Henry," *Sewanee Review*, 22 (April 1914): 217; "O. Henry's Texas Days," *Bookman* 40 (October 1914): 164. See also by the same author, "O. Henry's Texas," *Texas Review* 4 (July 1919): 295–307.
27. For a brief but careful analytic summary of these, see Langford, 92–96; also Harrell, *O. Henry Encore*, for the entire collection; hereafter cited in the text.
28. Credit for the discovery of this treasure trove of O. Henryana belongs to two young graduate students at the University of Texas who, in the mid-1930s, established beyond question the authenticity of their findings. One of them subsequently published a book containing some, though not all, of O. Henry's *Post* stories; but since the companion volume promised in her introduction has never appeared, the only extant collection of all these stories, aside from the original newspaper files, is in the unpublished thesis of her fellow student, Grace M. Watson, *O. Henry On The Houston 'Post,'* Master's Thesis, University of Texas, 1934, hereafter cited as Watson; Mary S. Harrell, *O. Henry's Texas Contacts*, Master's Thesis, University of Texas, 1935. For Miss Harrell's findings, see *O. Henry Encore*, Preface and Introduction, vii–xvii. Harrell's claim to have "discovered" this material is debatable, however, as Watson's thesis antedates hers by a full year.
29. A misleading statement concerning these *Post* stories appears in the foreword of the latest so-called *Complete Works* published in 1953: "A number of unsigned stories taken from the files of the Houston *Post* and thought to have been written by O. Henry were published in 1936, but they are of indifferent quality and not positively identified as his" (vol. 1, vii). Watson's thesis shows that many of the stories were not only signed "W.S.P." and "The Postman," but also identical in theme, characterization, and style to later ones published by O. Henry.

30. "A Tragedy," *O. Henry Encore*, 35–36.
31. "In Mezzotint," *O. Henry Encore*, 11–14.
32. "The Bruised Reed," "Simmons' Saturday Night," "Nothing New Under the Sun," "How She Got in the Swim," "Barber Shop Adventure," *O. Henry Encore*, 60–78, 132–34, 149–51, 158–66.
33. In *Strictly Business*, 83–89; hereafter cited in the text.
34. In *The Four Million*, 221–31.
35. In *Voice of the City*, 170–78; hereafter cited in the text.
36. "Night Errant," *O. Henry Encore*, 1–10.
37. "An Odd Character," *O. Henry Encore*, 93–97.
38. "An Aquatint," Watson, 340–44.
39. "A Story for Men," *O. Henry Encore*, 145–48.
40. In *Whirligigs*, 13: 259–87; hereafter cited in the text.
41. "A Departmental Case," in *Roads of Destiny*, 213.
42. See Dana M. Howell, *Settings and Characters of O. Henry's Texas Stories*, Master's Thesis, George Peabody College, 1937; hereafter cited as Howell.
43. "Madame Bo-Peep of the Ranches," in *Whirligigs*, 288–314.
44. "Hearts and Crosses," in *Heart of the West*, 3–20.
45. "Hygeia at the Solito," *Heart of the West*, 93–113.
46. "The Higher Abdication," 132–61.
47. "The Missing Chord," 228–39.
48. "Madame Bo-Peep," *Whirligigs*, 293.
49. "A Poor Rule," *Options*, 240; *Options* is hereafter cited in the text.
50. "An Afternoon Miracle," *Heart of the West*, 120.
51. "Hygeia at the Solito," *Heart of the West*, 106.
52. "The Higher Abdication," 157.
53. "The Marquis and Miss Sally," *Rolling Stones*, 93–97.
54. "The Passing of Black Eagle," *Roads of Destiny*, 128.
55. "The Reformation of Calliope," *Heart of the West*, 303–4.
56. "The Lonesome Road," *Roads of Destiny*, 308–9.
57. "Georgia's Ruling," *Whirligigs*, 246.
58. "The Red Roses on Tonia," *Waifs and Strays*, 4.
59. "The Indian Summer of Dry Valley Johnson," *Heart of the West*, 260.
60. See Clarkson, 30, for data on the reprint history of this story.
61. In *Everybody's* (September 1910); see Clarkson, 57.
62. See Clarkson, 134–40, for helpful editorial comment and a complete reprint of the earlier story.
63. The five titles in *Heart of the West* are "Christmas by Injunction," "The Ransome of Mack," "Telemachus, Friend," "The Handbook of Hymen," and "Cupid a la Carte." The five in *The Gentle Grafter* are "The Octopus Marooned," "Modern Rural Sports," "The Chair of Philanthromathematics," "The Exact Science of Matrimony," and "Conscience in Art"; the

two other tall tales are "New York by Campfire Light" (in *Sixes and Sevens*, 197–203) and "The Friendly Call" (in *Rolling Stones*, 112–26).

64. *Heart of the West*, 168; also see Clarkson, 29.
65. In *Rolling Stones*, 34–52; see also Clarkson, 60.
66. Both in *Waifs and Strays*, 72–75, 102–26; see Clarkson, 64–65.
67. In *Whirligigs*, 125–34; see Clarkson, 50.
68. In *Sixes and Sevens*, 46–63; see Clarkson, 55.
69. See "The Story of 'Holding Up a Train,'" *Rolling Stones*, 288–92.
70. See J. S. Gallegly, "Backgrounds and Patterns of O. Henry's Texas Bad-man Stories," *Rice Institute Pamphlet*, 13 (October 1955), cited in Langford, 212–14.
71. In *Cabbages and Kings*, 32. Citing this passage, Langford notes that in chatting years later with his friend Anne Partlan in New York, O. Henry "'spoke of Honduras as Mecca' where he had found 'freedom . . . infinite peace,'" and that he would even urge that they go there together. Surely, he was idealizing his memories even then.
72. P. S. Clarkson, "A Decomposition of Cabbages and Kings," *American Literature* 7 (May 1935): 195–202. See also Langford, 280–81 for a detailed summary of Clarkson's analysis.
73. *Through the Shadows*, 75.
74. This story obviously served as the basis for the musical comedy *Lo!*, jointly composed by O. Henry and Franklin P. Adams in 1909. Most of O. Henry's biographers have mistakenly asserted that *Lo!* was based on his story "To Him Who Waits," published in *Collier's*, 23 January 1909, whereas the actual source, "He Also Serves," was an earlier story on an entirely different theme, but also published in the same magazine on 31 October 1908. The chain of errors responsible for this confusion of titles is fully explained in a master's thesis by Eleen Mitchell, *The Dramatization of O. Henry's Short Stories*, Auburn University, 1964, 20–26. For an account of how the story itself was transformed by O. Henry and Adams, see Langford, 226–28. Adam's fuller discussion, including songs from the play, appears in the essay "The Misadventures in Musical Comedy of O. Henry and Franklin P. Adams," *Waifs and Strays*, 205–21.
75. Alfred Tennyson, "The Lotos-Eaters," in *Poems by Alfred Tennyson* (London: The Scolar Press, 1976), 141–43.
76. Letter quoted in Smith, 148.
77. The titles of these fourteen stories are: "Whistling Dick's Christmas Stocking," "Georgia's Ruling," "An Afternoon Miracle" (rewritten version of "The Miracle of Lava Canyon"), "A Medley of Moods" (first published as "Blind Man's Holiday"), "Money Maze," "No Story," "A Fog in Santone," "A Blackjack Bargainer," "The Enchanted Kiss," "Hygeia at the Solito," "Rouge et Noir," "The Duplicity of Hargraves," "The Marionettes," and "A Chaparral Christmas Gift."

78. See Al Jennings, *Through The Shadows With O. Henry* (London: Duckworth & Co., 1923), 222; quoted also in Langford, 145–46.

79. In *Roads of Destiny*, 134–43; but first published in the *Cosmopolitan*, April 1903. Cf. Langford, 147.

80. The titles of these are listed in Langford, 276; but Langford overlooks one story, "Bulger's Friend," which is listed in Paul S. Clarkson, *A Bibliography of William Sydney Porter* (68, 111) as published in *The Youth's Companion*, December 1901.

81. The complete letter is reprinted in *Complete Works* (1953) 2:1092–93.

82. Quoted in Jennings, 257.

83. Smith, 173.

84. Clarkson lists publication in ten different periodicals for the year 1902: 103–111.

85. Williams, *The Quiet Lodger of Irving Place*, 121: quoted also in Langford, 169.

86. "The Author's Account of Himself," *The Sketchbook*, in *The Complete Works of Washington Irving* (Boston: Twayne Publishers, 1977), vol. 1.

87. See "The Gold That Glittered," in *Strictly Business*, 21–23.

88. In chronological order, the titles of these volumes are *The Trimmed Lamp*, *The Voice of the City*, *Strictly Business*, *Whirligigs*, and *Sixes and Sevens*.

89. The numbers of New York stories in other volumes are as follows: *The Gentle Grafter*, 2; *Roads of Destiny*, 3; *Options*, 7; *Rolling Stones*, 4; *Waifs and Strays*, 6; and *O. Henryana*, 3.

90. Gilbert Millstein, "O. Henry's New Yorkers and Today's," *New York Times Magazine* (9 September 1962), 36–38, 132–38; hereafter cited in the text.

91. "The Making of a New Yorker," *The Trimmed Lamp*, 104–106.

92. "The Duel," *Strictly Business*, 295.

93. "The Voice of the City," *The Voice of the City*, 8.

94. "Extradited from Bohemia," *The Voice of the City*, 200.

95. "The Green Door," *The Four Million*, 153.

96. "A Little Local Color," *Whirligigs*, 238.

97. "Brickdust Row," *The Trimmed Lamp*, 95.

98. "The Marry Month of May," *Whirligigs*, 117–18.

99. "Girl," *Whirligigs*, 83.

100. "Ulysses and the Dogman," *Sixes and Sevens*, 64.

101. "A Comedy in Rubber," *Voice of the City*, 67–68.

102. "The Love-Philtre of Ikey Schoenstein," *Four Million*, 119.

103. "The Foreign Policy of Company 99," *Trimmed Lamp*, 139–49.

104. "A Midsummer Knight's Dream," *Trimmed Lamp*, 189–97.

105. "Calloway's Code," *Whirligigs*, 55–65.

106. "From the Cabby's Seat," *Four Million*, 165.

107. Roman Samarin, "O. Henry—'A Really Remarkable Writer,'" *The Soviet Review* (December 1962), 57.

108. Deming Brown, "O. Henry in Russia," *The Russian Review*, 12 (1953); 253–58.
109. "The Romance of a Busy Broker," *Four Million*, 214.
110. "Extradited from Bohemia," *Voice of the City*, 204.
111. See also *Caliph*, 323ff. for location of the house on Grove Street allegedly the exact site.
112. See Clarkson's *Bibliography*, 34 for a reference to the particular vaudeville act serving as background for this story.
113. *O. Henry Biography*, 221.
114. In "The Buyer from Cactus City," *The Trimmed Lamp*, 73.
115. These four stories are in the following volumes: *Options*, 20–37; *The Four Million*, 140–50; *The Trimmed Lamp*, 130–38; *Roads of Destiny*, 45–56.
116. Quoted in Greensboro *Daily News*, 30 September 1962, Ai9.
117. "Brickdust Row," *The Trimmed Lamp*, 89–101.
118. "The Unknown Quantity," in *Strictly Business*, 109–17.
119. The earlier title was "An Aquatint."
120. "The Higher Pragmatism," *Options*, 199–209.
121. "The Cop and the Anthem," *The Four Million*, 90–100.
122. "Two Thanksgiving Day Gentlemen," *The Trimmed Lamp*, 50–58.
123. "The Complete Life of John Hopkins," *Voice of the City*, 11.
124. See "The Count and the Wedding Guest," *The Trimmed Lamp*, 209–18; "Schools and Schools," *Options*, 56–71; "The Marry Month of May," *Whirligigs*, 116–24; "Nemesis and the Candy Man," *Voice of the City*, 115–24; "Mammon and the Archer," *The Four Million*, 128–39; "The Defeat of the City," *Voice of the City*, 85–94; and "The Rubber Plant's Story," in *Waifs and Strays*, 25–31.
125. In *Strictly Business*, 130–47. The term "aphasia," derived from the Greek, is now defined as a "total loss of power to use or understand words, usually caused by brain disease or injury"; it is not defined as loss of memory. O. Henry may have deliberately misused the term for "Amnesia."
126. In *Sixes and Sevens*, 258–64; *Strictly Business*, 73–82; *The Trimmed Lamp*, 219–32; *Voice of the City*, 219–29.
127. See "A Bird in Bagdad," in *Strictly Business*, 182–93; "The Coming Out of Maggie," *The Four Million*, 69–81; "Past One at Rooney's," *Strictly Business*, 255–75; and "The Rubaiyat of a Scotch High Ball," *The Trimmed Lamp*, 32–41.
128. "Dougherty's Eye-Opener," *Voice of the City*, 213.
129. For background and sources on how this story allegedly transformed into the musical comedy *Lo!* by O. Henry and Franklin P. Adams, see note 74.
130. Other variations on the same theme, but less skillfully managed, may be found in "Roses, Ruses, and Romance," *Voice of the City*, 132–40; "The Badge of Policeman O'Roon," *The Trimmed Lamp*, 81–88; and "The Enchanted Kiss," *Roads of Destiny*, 197–212.

Part 2

THE WRITER

Emergence from the Shadows

Very soon after O. Henry's unheralded funeral services at Trinity (the Little Church Around the Corner) on 7 June 1910, the movement to recreate his alter ego, Bill Porter, as a real-life historic figure got under way. Although Porter's identity had been made public at least seven years before he died, aside from the few journalists and publishing folk who attended that service, the man behind the pseudonym, which was already being idolized by millions of American readers, had died virtually unknown, unrecognized, and unmourned; as Bill Porter he would still remain a somewhat mysterious, shadowy presence for another decade or so.[1] He had, of course, deliberately fostered such a shadowy role from the moment he left the Ohio Penitentiary; even the few editors and publishers who soon came to know him familiarly and to enjoy his conviviality and repartee often noted later on that his witty table-talk seldom yielded specific details about either his family background or his career before he came to New York.

Upon his arrival there in April 1902, Porter received a warm welcome from the coeditors of *Ainslee's* magazine, Richard Duffy and Gilman Hall. Having only recently learned his right name, they were eager to meet the author of four stories previously published in *Ainslee's* whom they knew only through correspondence as O. Henry. And as Duffy recalled years later, "whatever mind picture Gilman Hall or I had formed of him from his letters, his handwriting, his stories, vanished before the impression of the actual. . . . To meet him for the first time you felt his most notable quality to be reticence, not a reticence of social timidity, but a reticence of deliberateness."[2]

This idiosyncrasy, detected by Duffy and Hall at a first impression, remained with Porter throughout the rest of his life despite the extraordinary fame and fortune his prolific writings achieved. And it affected in a like manner others in the publishing world who also came to know him well. Thus, Robert H. Davis, who came from the *Sunday World* to offer him a contract in 1903, remarked later that "Porter fled from publicity like mist before the gale . . . shrank from the extended hands of strangers . . . and avoided conversations about himself."[3] Until the mystery of Porter's imprisonment became public knowledge in 1916 few, if any, of his associates in New York were aware (as, of course, Jennings was) that his furtive behavior could be attributed to "the horrible fear that some ex-con" might accost him in any public place to inquire when he had got out of prison, and that before leaving Pittsburgh he had urged Jennings to "please keep my *nom de plume* strictly to yourself. I don't want anyone to know just yet."[4] Determined to bury his recent past, or at least keep it concealed behind a convenient alias, Porter launched himself—as O. Henry—upon a phenomenal career, publishing seventeen stories in 1902 and a dozen more in the early months of 1903. This successful breakthrough led in turn to the lucrative arrangement with the *Sunday World* and the 113 syndicated weekly stories that began appearing in that newspaper in December and continued almost without a break well into 1906. Moreover, during the same two-year period twenty-five more of his longer stories were also published in such popular monthly magazines as *Everybody's*, *McClure's*, and *Munsey's*: it was the period in which Porter established the fixture of his legendary namesake, "the O. Henry whose stories suggested to his friends the role in which he is familiarly pictured—that of the Caliph of Bagdad-on-the-Subway" (Langford, 169).

Another major accomplishment of the same period, possibly Porter's most significant, was his serious commitment to the task of assembling his burgeoning output of tales into collections for book publication. The idea got under way early in 1904 when Witter Bynner of *McClure's* suggested Porter's Central American stories might be rearranged and strung together by means of a single narrative thread to produce a simulated novel. Working together, chiefly with scissors and paste pot, in a few months they thus turned out Porter's first book, *Cabbages and Kings*, published by McClure, Phillips and Company in November 1904.[5] Although the book was no smashing success, it drew some favorable reviews and apparently sold well enough outside the United States to spearhead Porter's new career. When his second book, *The Four Million*, appeared in April 1906, his worldwide fame was assured. This collection of twenty-five stories—most of them culled from the files of the *Sunday World*, including such favorites as "The Gift of the Magi," "The Furnished Room," "The Cop and the Anthem," and "An Unfinished Story"—broadcast to the far corners of the earth Porter's noble panegyric to Manhattan's nameless "little people." Like its predecessor, *The Four Million* did not draw an immediate chorus of hosannas, though its appeal remained steady and long-lasting. Moreover, this collection also received some favorable notice from serious literary critics, who began comparing Porter to de Maupassant and other pre-eminent writers of fiction; although he shrugged off his newly won fame derisively, he could be sure that future collections of his stories would be promptly noticed (Langford, 204–205).

Following publication of *The Four Million*, seven more collections of O. Henry's stories, most of them rather haphazardly assembled, appeared before his death in 1910: these were *The Trimmed Lamp* (1907), *Heart Of The West* (1907), *The Voice Of The City* (1908), *The Gentle Grafter* (1908), *Roads Of Destiny* (1909), *Options* (1910), and *Strictly Business* (1910). And there would still be more to come later—thanks to the initiative of Harry Peyton Steger, "Porter's taskmaster and paymaster at Doubleday-Page" (Langford, 228). But notwithstanding the widespread acclaim these volumes added year by year to their author's renown, Porter still faced his world ambiguously, his approach to others scarcely less furtive than it had been in 1902. A lonely, harried individual, determined "to put the past behind him, to transform himself from W. S. Porter to O. Henry," he lived in a "self-imposed exile from which he never succeeded in escaping" (Langford, 184–85). And yet, as early as 1904 Porter must have been striving to break through this psychic barrier, to face up to his past and join the mainstream by openly disclosing to his editor friends how he had found in prison "enough spare time to take up fiction seriously" (Langford, 171). But such disclosure, though promised, was more than he could manage at that point. Meanwhile, Porter had also begun reaching out tentatively for companionship among a succession of young professional women, whose curiosity about his past had likewise to be satisfied with evasive, if whimsical or humorous accounts of his cowboy exploits in Texas. With one notable exception, however, these were chiefly platonic relationships that involved some mutually pleasurable exchanges of sprightly dialogue and correspondence between Porter and Anne Partlan, Mabel Wagnalls, Ethel Patterson, and others. The exception led to Porter's disastrous second marriage in November 1907, to a childhood girlfriend, Sara Lindsay Coleman— essentially a bleak denouement to his painful, frenzied, overburdened last two years.

The movement to explore the arcanum of developments that lay athwart Porter's ante-Manhattan career quickly gathered momentum after his death, adding substantially to the republication of materials by and about O. Henry in six more posthumous single-volume collections published by Doubleday, Page and Company as late as 1939. In order, these six were entitled *Whirligigs* (1910); *Sixes and Sevens* (1911); *Rolling Stones* (1912); *Waifs and Strays* (1917); *O. Henryana* (1920); and *Letters To Lithopolis* (1922). Two more later volumes were entitled *Postscripts*, published by Harper and Brothers in 1923, and *O. Henry Encore*, published by Doubleday and Company in 1939.

Influence of Harry Peyton Steger

The driving force behind this publishing venture was Steger himself, who was now Doubleday's official literary adviser as well as Porter's literary executor and official biographer. He had begun assisting and promoting the ailing writer for several years before Porter died, and promptly thereafter he began systematically rounding up every scrap of memorabilia about him to be found. During the following year he traveled extensively in Texas, seeking personal interviews, letters, and copies of Porter's earliest publication, *The Rolling Stone*. Steger's first brief account of his findings appeared in an essay entitled "Some O. Henry Letters and the Plunkville Patriot," published in the weekly magazine *The Independent* on 5 September 1912. His essay featured a pair of attractive photographs, another pair of jovial early letters, and a number of amusing spoofs Porter inserted in a typical issue of his little "newspaper," such as one he called "the delightful literary item that Mark Twain and Charles Egbert Craddock are spending the summer together in their Adirondacks camp," together with a facsimile reproduction of a complete page from *The Rolling Stone*.[6] Thoroughly fascinated by his discovery of *The Rolling Stone*, particularly its own uniquely featured "news" sheet, Steger described the origin and makeup of "The Plunkville Patriot" in detail and assured his readers he had discovered in Texas "a lot of interesting material, cartoons, verse, early stories, and many, many letters, a representative collection of which" he would be publishing shortly in the "last volume" of the author's work, "Rolling Stones" (547).[7]

True to his word, Steger followed up this essay with another illustrated one, published in the popular monthly magazine, the *Cosmopolitan*, in October; before the year's end a revised condensation of the two essays became the introduction of Doubleday's twelfth (and mistakenly assumed to be the final) volume of O. Henry's work, *Rolling Stones*. Titled simply "O. Henry," the second essay was obviously designed to present more "new facts about the Great Author," which Steger had unearthed during his sojourn in Texas, but also to publicize "a hitherto Unpublished Story by O. Henry Himself" (63 [October 1912], 655).

Steger did not know exactly when O. Henry had written this story, "A Fog in Santone"—perhaps as early as 1904, he surmised—but he was happy to see it published at last in the same magazine where O. Henry's last completed story, "Adventures in Neurasthenia" (later retitled "Let Me Feel Your Pulse") and his unfinished one, "The Dream," had also appeared. Thus, elated over the treasure trove of original materials turned up in Texas and elsewhere, Steger concluded he had barely scraped the surface, and that now was the time to undertake a full-length "biographical record of a great man who has gone and whose work stays on. Unknown in 1900, dead in 1910, his life began but yesterday" (657). The bizarre "array of perfectly confused type" and other farcical mis-cues were all a deliberate expression of the basic satire.

But alas for Steger's noble plans; although he succeeded in sending forth *Rolling Stones* with his introductory blessing in 1912, thinking it would be "the final volume of O. Henry's work," Steger himself would not survive another year. The massive quantity of biographical data he gathered would now fall into other willing hands to be organized and assimilated, and on that solid foundation others would prepare and publish the "authorized" biography and supervise the publication of five more volumes in the O. Henry canon, as well as several collected editions under the Doubleday aegis. During the interval between 1912 and 1916, while Professor Alphonso Smith was writing the biography, numerous articles written by journalists who had known Porter person-ally were published in such literary magazines as *Ainslee's*, the *Bookman*, *Everybody's*, *Hampton's*, and the *North American Review*. And following the example set by Steger in *Rolling Stones*, selections from among the most authoritative of these essays filled more than half the space in the next volume of stories entitled *Waifs and Strays*, published in 1917.

The sheer bulk of these essays played a significant role, not only in stimulating further public interest in Porter's life and literary career and thereby augmenting the popular demand for his stories, but also in adding stature and luster to the image of a folk hero, providing at last an appropriate body of allegedly authentic detail with which to immortalize him. The essays likewise served as prelude for at least some of their authors to the production of full-length books in the 1920s and 1930s, notably Al Jennings's *Through The Shadows With O. Henry* (1923), *The Caliph of Bagdad* (1931) by Robert Davis and Arthur Maurice, and *The Quiet Lodger of Irving Place* (1936) by William Wash Williams. These writers and others like them, however, owed much of their specific data to the pioneering genius of Harry Peyton Steger.

Among the original single-volume collections of O. Henry's works, *Rolling Stones* is perhaps the most imaginative assemblage of materials in the entire canon. In it Steger attempted to sum up in a nutshell, so to speak, a prefatory glimpse of the extraordinary career of the famous writer who was still largely unknown to the public at the time of his death. The attempt was notably successful; within fewer than three hundred pages Steger brought together many comparative samples of short fiction anecdotes and sketches published in *The Rolling Stone* in 1894, as well as still earlier unpublished fiction written in the form of letters from Texas in the 1880s and from prison in the late 1890s. The importance of these early efforts Steger emphasized by setting them off against several other stories, such as "A Ruler of Men," "Helping the Other Fellow," and "The Friendly Call," written at the peak of O. Henry's career and published in leading monthlies up to and even after his death. To provide additional impact to his profile of the writer, Steger also included in the volume several impressive photographs from early and late in O. Henry's career, plus numerous poems salvaged from his manuscripts, and facsimile reproductions of both his own comic drawings and full-page reprints of *The Rolling Stone*. For its purpose the volume was a skillfully conceived backward glance.

Following an imposing "last photograph" and a dedicatory poem to O. Henry by James Whitcomb Riley, Steger's brief introduction stresses in particular the importance of an "extant mass of O. Henry's correspondence that has not been included in this collection": namely, letters "he wrote constantly to editors, and in many instances intimately," during his Manhattan years (xv). But the few letters he did include in the volume had been carefully chosen to serve as an "exhibit," another manifestation of the writer's versatility and artistic integrity, and thus unimpeachable evidence of his life-long dedication to the task of enlightening the public through the medium of fiction. Even more convincingly than the stories themselves, Steger seems to have felt, these letters written to relatives, close friends, and associates revealed the true character of the man behind the pseudonym, Bill Porter himself.

Steger's arrangement of the other materials in *Rolling Stones* reflects this primary intention. His first item in the text, "The Dream," is a slight four-page fragment of an unfinished manuscript which, he explains, was actually being written when "in the very middle of a sentence the hand of Death interrupted the telling of O. Henry's last story" (6).[8] Ironically, this story, Steger continues, was to have begun a new series "in a style he had not previously attempted. 'I want to show the public,' he said, 'that

I can write something new—new for me, I mean—a story without slang, a straightforward dramatic plot treated in a way that will come nearer my idea of real story-writing' " (6). Yet the concluding paragraph, outlining the writer's plans for developing "The Dream" fully, suggests whatever innovative techniques the story might have displayed, its denouement very likely would have offered the familiar O. Henry surprise reversal—with perhaps a Biercean acridity.

Steger's arrangement lists the remaining items in the volume under thirty-five headings in the table of contents, and as a whole they constitute a fascinating potpourri of literary endeavor in both fragmentary and finished forms of prose and verse. Following "The Dream," for example, there are seven finished stories that had been published in leading magazines such as *Ainslee's* and *Everybody's* between 1902 and 1912; then there are a dozen or so shorter pieces dating from the files of *The Rolling Stone*, plus another dozen poems of the same vintage; and finally, about nineteen or twenty letters ranging in time from 1883 to 1909. Moreover, interspersed among this total of 292 pages are numerous facsimile reproductions of scenes, cartoon drawings, and more printed pages from Porter's typo-infested little journal. Clearly, each of these illustrative selections was intended to verify and enhance the image of the author's artistic capability, his broad range, versatility, and seriousness of purpose; their range of effect extends from the parodic and broadly farcical to hyperbolic whimsy, waggish satire, and ultimately to serious introspective analysis. Thus, it is no accident to find Steger pairing off a double-full-page reproduction of "The Plunkville Patriot" and a facsimile handwritten as well as a printed copy of Porter's letter to his daughter Margaret, or funny letters to his old "pard" Al Jennings, along with serious ones to both Jennings and Steger himself on the basic theme of fiction-writing methodology. From beginning to end, each item in the collection augments, assertively and suggestively, the stature of the writer.[9]

Thus, the twenty letters reproduced in the last forty pages of *Rolling Stones* provide an appropriate climax to the dominant theme set forth in Steger's introduction concerning the protean character of their author. Juxtaposed as they are, the variety of their content and style reveals a writer whose fertile imagination enabled him to play many roles with gusto and aplomb, and who played them seriously from youth onward. The clownish satire and egregious syntax of the opening letter written to Gilman Hall, the associate editor of *Ainslee's*, contrast sharply with the milder, more conventional impish humor of the next half-dozen letters, written twenty years earlier from Texas to friends in North Carolina; yet the basic aim in all of them is much the same. Signing himself "W.S.P.," young Porter was no less impelled to entertain them with hyperbole and waggish anecdotes than was his self-confident older self in addressing his friend as "Mr. Hall, part editor, of everybody's [*sic*]" over the signature "O. Henry" (252).

Steger's Legacy: The Letters

The example set by Steger in *Rolling Stones* inspired other journalists to carry forward the task he had begun, to establish an authentic full-length portrait of the writer whom they had known as Bill Porter. During the four-year period 1912–1916, while Professor Smith was preparing his *O. Henry Biography*, authorized by Doubleday, Page and Company, Arthur W. Page himself wrote a series of biographical essays entitled "Little Pictures of O. Henry," which appeared in the *Bookman* magazine from June to October 1913. The following year Hyder E. Rollins, a native Texan and future renowned professor of English at Harvard University, wrote a pair of essays, one of which, entitled "O. Henry's Texas Days," also appeared in the *Bookman*, the other, in the *Sewanee Review*. The *Bookman* also published in 1914 a third essay, "O. Henry and New Orleans," written by Caroline F. Richardson, while still more essays by Rollins and others continued appearing in the *Texas Review* before 1920.[10]

Just as Steger had refined and condensed this sort of material for his introduction to the *Rolling Stone*, the anonymous editor of the next volume of O. Henry material, *Waifs and Strays* (1917), transformed the bulk of these newer essays into an elaborate critical and biographical commentary occupying nearly two-thirds of the contents. This editor may well have been Arthur W. Page himself, but in any case, Steger's influence is apparent in both the arrangement and the variety of individual items in its makeup. A two-part collection, *Waifs and Strays* contains twelve more O. Henry stories in part 1 and an odd miscellany of thirteen separate pieces of reminiscent lore in prose and verse in part 2, plus an extraordinary concluding item of twenty-five pages called "O. Henry Index," which lists in alphabetical order the titles of each of the thirteen volumes of O. Henry's stories published so far *and* the titles of every single story and other separate item contained in each of the volumes. A remarkable achievement, the index alone must have been worth the price of the book, since it provides invaluable editorial assistance toward an understanding of important minutiae in the locale, characterization, and language differences among O. Henry's nearly three hundred stories. The twelve stories in part 1 of this volume are not an impressive lot, though some of them appeared in magazines as early as 1902; all but the last one had been passed over in the selection of stories to be included in each of the preceding collections from *Cabbages And Kings* (1904) to *Rolling Stones* (1912). They were thus appropriately labeled as waifs and strays now returned at last to the fold.

That twelfth story, "The Snow Man," however, is another matter. Its inclusion in the volume at this point required that it be introduced with the following editorial comments, written in italics:

> Before the fatal illness of William Sydney Porter (known through his literary work as 'O. Henry') this American master of short-story writing had begun for Hampton's Magazine the story printed below. Illness crept upon him rapidly and he was compelled to give up writing about at the point where the girl enters the story.
>
> When he realized that he could do no more (it was his life-long habit to write with a pencil, never dictating to a stenographer), O. Henry told in detail the remainder of The Snow Man to Harris Merton Lyon, whom he had often spoken of as one of the most effective short-story writers of the present time. Mr. Porter had delineated all the characters, leaving only the rounding out of the plot in the final pages to Mr. Lyon. (*Waifs and Strays*, 102)

As it stands, the story raises some curious possibilities. Somewhat analogous to works by both Bret Harte and Stephen Crane, it seems at first to be merely an elaborately designed treatment of boredom, frustration, and rivalry shared by four men stranded in a snowbound cabin in Montana. The arrival of a young woman raises a problem that O. Henry might have solved in a more daring manner had he lived to finish his own story, but, as he left it, the conventionalized surprise ending fails to support the ominous tone introduced in the opening pages. But even so, the feel of death lurks just beneath the surface of this suggestive story, beckoning persuasively toward the nonfiction commentary bringing up the rear in its wake.

The longer second part of *Waifs and Strays* opens with a skillfully crafted reproduction of Arthur W. Page's biographical essay, "Little Pictures of O. Henry," which had appeared originally as a series of summer installments in the *Bookman* in 1913. For any O. Henry enthusiasts not as yet familiar with Alphonso Smith's authorized biography, Page's essay was strategically placed because, in bringing Will Porter sharply into focus at the outset, it clarified to a large extent the still

mysterious relationship between the popular literary idol and his alter
ego, the writer himself.

Securely based on factual data and quoted reminiscences drawn from
Steger's researches and other random interviews, Page's "Little Pictures" provide a colorful vignette of the Will Porter who was fondly
remembered by old friends from his childhood and youth in Greensboro,
North Carolina, and Austin, Texas, until his death in New York at the
peak of his fame. The essay faithfully follows the development of his
career, stressing repeatedly the talents and skills that made him from the
outset "the delight and pride of men two and three times his age," as
well as a favorite among young ladies during his long residence in Texas,
and a boon drinking companion among prominent magazine editors and
newsmen in New York. Here, for example, are two typical recollections
of Porter's effect upon close associates, the first attributed to a Dr.
Daniels, who helped him put together the *Rolling Stone* in 1894; the
other, to Richard Duffy, coeditor of *Ainslee's Magazine*, in 1904.

> Porter was one of the most versatile men I had ever met. He was a
> fine singer, could write remarkably clever stuff under all circum-
> stances, and was a good hand at sketching. And he was the best mimic
> I ever saw in my life. He was one of the genuine democrats that you
> hear about more often than you meet. . . . I've seen the most ragged
> specimen of a bum hold up Porter, who would always do anything he
> could for the man. His one great failing was his inability to say "No"
> to a man. (146–47)

> To meet him for the first time you felt his most notable quality to be
> reticence, not a reticence of social timidity, but a reticence of delib-
> erateness. If you also were observing, you would soon understand that
> his reticence proceeded from the fact that civilly yet masterfully he
> was taking in every item of the "you" being presented to him to the
> accompaniment of convention's phrases and ideas, together with the
> "you" behind his presentation. It was because he was able thus to
> assemble and sift all the multifarious elements of a personality with
> sleight-of-hand swiftness that you find him characterizing a person or
> a neighborhood in a sentence or two; and once I heard him character-
> ize a list of editors he knew each in a phrase. (151–52)

Forthright praise of this sort runs throughout Duffy's "narrative," which
fills part 3 of Page's essay, but it is even more prominently displayed in
part 4, a climactic ten-page characterization of Porter "As He Showed

Himself in His Letters" (158–68). Here Page asserts that among the mass of revelatory material Steger assembled from Porter's estate "the most revealing things are his own letters." Because they are almost always filled with "quaint conceits" and good cheer, even during his harassed declining years, "they are the kind of letters that give the most pleasure to an average person." To prove his point, Page then offers verbatim copies of nearly a dozen of them, written as early as 1883 from Texas to old friends in Greensboro and as late as 1909 to Steger, other publishers and editors, and to his "Dear Pard," Al Jennings, "ex-train robber, lawyer, author, and reformer" (161). Porter's jaunty tone in the following brief examples firmly supports the assertion. Virtually at death's door in Asheville, he could still be as breezy and brash referring to his poor health in 1910 as he had been in greeting Jennings at the outset of his New York career eight years before.

Page noted the letter to Griffiths was written at a time when Porter's stories were in such demand that he could have sold more than he could write and at higher prices than a mere one hundred dollars apiece; yet ten years earlier, when he began selling them to *Everybody's*, "he was un-known to the magazine field of literature." His correspondence with Jennings had begun at about the same time, Page continued, quoting a portion of the initial letter, wherein the idea for their collaboration on "the now famous story Holding Up A Train" was broached, and a very small fragment of "a second letter [included in the letters already published in 'Rolling Stones']" (161–62).[11]

Page felt, however, these recent letters were no sprightlier than earlier, but longer ones Porter had written from Texas to friends in Greensboro in the 1880s. But even more interesting than those "in showing the spirit of the man," he added, "are the letters that he wrote from time to time to his daughter, Margaret, especially those written when she was a little girl. In them he speaks quite often of Uncle Remus, which they evidently read together, and they are all filled with the quaint conceits that enliven the two following" (165–66).

It is curious that Page reprinted only two of these letters to little Margaret, omitting any reference to how many of them had been sal-vaged by Steger and how or where they came to be written from in the first place—that is, from the Ohio Penitentiary. Nor did he indicate that Steger himself published another pair of them in *Rolling Stones*, one in handwritten facsimile with date attached—then reprinted in type but dateless, as a follow-up to the other, which is dated 1 October 1900 from Toledo (242-A, 276–78).

Part 2

From these letters alone, one can see why the few women who knew Porter well responded so favorably to his appeal, and why Margaret herself, who perhaps knew him best of all, cherished the memories of her brief association with him. In a touching memorial entitled "My O. Henry," published in 1923, she avowed that from her infancy until their last good-bye in Asheville the relationship they shared "was never that of father and daughter; rather that of two good friends, for never did he give a command, and never did I fail to follow his advice or to try to fulfill his expressed wish." During her early childhood, Margaret recalled, "We were inseparable playmates and companions until my eighth year and the death of my mother. . . . 'Uncle Remus' was a strong bond between us. These stories were read and read until he would find himself prompted for the slightest deviation from the text." And despite a mutual reserve that developed between them as she grew older and went off to school and college, they remained "friends of few words and great understanding." Thus, from first to last the theme of friendship predominates, filling her mind with "priceless etchings of memory: gentle, generous, gallant; a wonderful playmate, a rare companion, and a friend. The perfect friend."[12]

As we shall see presently, several other women who also exchanged letters with Porter corroborated with their own evidence the merits of his daughter's accolades. But before getting to them, we must return briefly to some of the remaining efforts to explore the magic of his appeal crowded into the last hundred pages of *Waifs and Strays*. Here in a dozen different ways the writers strove with only moderate success to distinguish between the living writer they remembered from the persona he created, but the nom de plume had already become too firmly embossed on the public consciousness to be cast aside. Accordingly, Stephen Leacock, distressed "that any writer could deliberately christen himself 'O. Henry'," least of all one whose own "works abound in ingenious nomenclature," nevertheless admits that "there is no use in calling him anything else."[13] So his adulatory tribute to Porter's artistry glitters with repetitive use of the "hopelessly tame and colorless" nom de plume. And only slightly less so do the remaining essays in this group, written by such prominent New Yorkers of that era as Franklin P. Adams, George Jean Nathan, William Lyon Phelps, and Arthur B. Maurice (205–62). Although each of their pieces is focused on a distinctive pattern of remembered activity involving its author and the real-life Bill Porter, the pseudonym rather than his actual name appears in its title and then reverberates throughout the essay. An adaptation of Adam's original account of their collaboration, for example, is entitled "The Misadventures in Musical Comedy of O. Henry And Franklin P. Adams"; similarly, George Jean Nathan's little vignette, "O. Henry In His Own Bagdad," introduces both "William Sydney Porter" and his "alias 'O. Henry'" together in its opening sentence but carries on thereafter with the alias alone. And so with the other titles in the collection.

Collectively, however, the basic value of these contributions was substantive: each was engaged in the process of bringing back to life and action a real individual who had been until yesterday, so to speak, only a shadowy, legendary figure. Each was recalling innate characteristics along with physical attributes—attitudes, habits, expressions, preferences, observed or reflected through speech, laughter, or taciturnity; each was attempting to show, as Margaret would also a few years later, why the living man had been a rare companion as well as a consummate craftsman, and each was bent on showing how and where he found his material and transformed it into such enjoyable fiction. This fact is manifest in the longest essay, "About New York With O. Henry," by Arthur B. Maurice (233–62). Divided into six parts, Maurice's essay abounds in factual details, identifying in part 1, "The Heart of O'Henryland," Porter's residential surroundings at Irving Place; analyzing in part 2, "The O. Henry Appeal," some of his most enjoyable stories; and showing in part 3 through 6 where and how specific sites and establishments there and elsewhere in Manhattan also contributed characters, settings, and dramatic action to many of those stories.

As a whole, the essay provides significant explanatory data about Porter's workmanship: how he approached his craft, where and how he sought and found his raw material, and how he transformed it into fiction that delighted millions of readers. But for readers of the late twentieth century, perhaps the most interesting segment of this information is the author's discussion in part 2: actually the result of Maurice's ingenious experiment, it sought by polling a symposium of ten experts (including himself) to find out which ten of O. Henry's 250-plus tales had the widest appeal. Thus the taste of that era, represented by such leading lights as Booth Tarkington, George Barr McCutcheon, Robert H. Davis, Gilman Hall, Arthur Page, Maurice himself, and several others, is spread abroad in "ten lists of ten tales apiece, and sixty-two different titles, most of them appearing on but one list" (245). Oddly enough, Booth Tarkington's number-one favorite "The Ransom of Red Chief," was one of those. But the star among these experts was no less a figure than Mrs. William Sydney Porter herself, and Maurice's account of the "very

Part 2

beautiful letter" in which she told of her preferences deserves quoting
verbatim:

> To her the stories *were* Mr. Porter. She found it hard to name them
> in a list in order. But immediately one story came to her mind. That
> was A Municipal Report.
> "'After all,' she wrote, 'I am not sure that it is the story—good as
> is—for O. Henry's own face lifts from a Nashville "roast" that was
> given that story and I see his puzzled, 'Why did it offend? Do you see
> anything in it that should offend?' The Fifth Wheel—and we stand
> together on Madison Square in the deep snow, or the biting wind,
> looking at the line waiting for beds. When we turn away ten men have
> found shelter. The recording angel must have seen us there some of
> the snowy nights of 1908. He must have known that when we turned
> homeward there were times when O. Henry had not a dollar fifty left
> in his pocket." One story in Mrs. Porter's list likely to surprise readers
> is madame Bo-Peep of the Ranches. But Mrs. Porter said that that
> story figured largely in her own life. In the spring of 1905 her mother
> came home from Greensboro and said to her: 'Your old friend Will
> Porter is a writer. He lives in New York and writes under the name of
> O. Henry.' 'O. Henry! In my desk lay Madame Bo-Peep and I loved
> her. I wrote O. Henry a note. 'If you are not Will Porter don't bother to
> answer,' I said. He bothered to answer. The letter came as fast as
> Uncle Sam could bring it. 'Some day when you are not real busy,' he
> wrote, 'won't you sit down at your desk where you keep those
> antiquated stories and write to me? I'd be so pleased to hear some-
> thing about what the years have done for you, and what you think
> about when the tree frogs begin to holler in the evening.' Thus after
> many years a boy and girl friendship was renewed. Last in my list, but
> first in my heart, is Adventures in Neurasthenia, the new title, Let Me
> Feel Your Pulse, the publishers gave. It brings back the little office in
> Asheville, the pad, empty except for the title and the words: 'So I went
> to a doctor.' So often at the last the pad was empty. The sharp pencil
> points in their waiting seemed to me to mock the empty pencil, the
> weary brain. The picture is too vivid." (240–42)

To appreciate the full import of this widow's wistful reminiscence,
one would need to recognize what its tone and imagery encompass. Her
reference to the empty pad and pencil, the weary brain, deep snow and
biting wind, the line of homeless men, the recording angel and nearly
emptied pocket, plus the four story titles, cumulatively evoke a sweeping recollection of the twilight of Porter's fabulous New York career from

the point where she reentered his life in 1905 until his death five years later. An aspiring writer herself, Sara Lindsay Coleman was an aging spinster of thirty-seven when a million-to-one chance discovery enabled her to reawaken a brief adolescent relationship in North Carolina that would presently become transformed through correspondence into an ardent courtship and—two years later—marriage ties predestined to a raveling insecurity.[14] With romanticized fictional trimmings, Sara would eventually describe the courtship itself—but not her subsequent wifely role—in a novella entitled *Wind Of Destiny*, which contrasts sharply with the sad ironies implicit in her "too vivid picture" of her husband's ambivalent career and its roller-coaster sequence of motivation and achievement, prosperity and adversity.[15]

Sara's reentry into Porter's consciousness came at a moment when he had reached the zenith of his inordinate productivity. By 1905 his stories were not only bringing in four or five times the one hundred dollar fee for "Madam Bo-Peep" that paid his railway fare to New York in 1902; their market demand had also swelled beyond his capacity to satisfy all the editors competing for them. And his self-indulgence had likewise pro-liferated, enabling him to fulfill the Caliph role he had adopted. For as Robert Davis noted later, "in the vagaries and extravagance appropriate to the generous handed role . . . he was in a position to toss about his 'purses of gold.' In the years from 1904 to 1907, O. Henry was Haroun in his golden prime. (*Caliph*, 260; Langford, 169). Despite such lavish expenditures, however—gourmet dining in favorite restaurants, heavy drinking and partying, huge tips to waiters and bartenders, excessive handouts to homeless beggars and social castaways, as dramatized in "The Fifth Wheel"—Porter remained to the end a lonely, reclusive individual.

His efforts to overcome such malaise are reflected in further corre-spondence with several other articulate ladies whose published reminis-cences of their acquaintance with him add significant depth to the portraits drawn by his wife and daughter. The most colorful of all these commemorative tributes, if not also the most incisive, appeared in a small book entitled *Letters To Lithopolis // From O. Henry To Mabel Wagnalls*, published by Doubleday, Page in 1922. Loosely resembling in form Sara Coleman's *Wind of Destiny*, but without any romanticized fictional pretentiousness, this work is a carefully developed, straightfor-ward account of a brief platonic relationship based on a series of seven letters written to Miss Wagnalls between June and December of 1903, plus an eighth letter dated 28 October 1907.

One may wonder how much influence, if any, the composition of this book owed to Sara's, which was published six years earlier by the same publisher. For there are intriguing similarities and differences in the makeup of both books: the basic purpose of both authors is virtually identical—to reveal and verify for all lovers of O. Henry's fiction the warmth and greatness of its real-life creator, Sydney Porter, whom both women knew closely and genuinely admired, notwithstanding certain psychic weaknesses they both recognized in his character. Oddly enough, both women also came to know him through his joyful response to their initial inquiries, but Mabel Wagnalls, the talented young daughter of a prominent New York publisher, got to him first and eventually strove to recapture for "every reader of [her] little book . . . the thrill of astonishment" her first meeting with O. Henry produced. Carefully setting the stage for the moment of this "delightful experience," she explains how the impact of the story "Roads of Destiny" and the originality of its unknown author's name led to her "few lines to his publisher . . . [begging] to know whether O. Henry was a man, woman, or wraith."[16] Then, following an extensive description of Lithopolis itself, a tiny hamlet of 350 inhabitants in Ohio, she tells how months later during her annual spring visit to her grandmother's home there, came the sensational arrival of "the jolliest, breeziest, most unusual letter that had ever come my way" (xvii). After several rereadings aloud entertained the entire family, she met the problem of answering "this post-impressionist-epistle" by setting down in her next letter "all that seemed needful about the cosmopolis Lithopolis" and was again, shortly thereafter, liberally rewarded when "eight pages of uproarious manuscript from my mysterious, ink-slinging, Texas cowboy correspondent sojourning in New York were read aloud to my mother and grandmother, the hired girl and the cat . . . [and] as I read those rollicking pages, I realized that Lithopolis had occasioned them. . . . A great mind and spirit, speeding on to fame, found time once to note and give heed in his letters to the side-tracked tiny town" (xviii–xix).

From here on Miss Wagnalls's preface summarizes the remaining years of her acquaintance with the "timid stranger" who, "as an occasional caller in our New York home, leaves the memory of a quiet, serious, hard-working author; one whom I felt was predestined to fame though he had slight regard for the author-craft." (xxiii). Though delighted with the humor in Porter's succeeding letters, she was also deeply moved by both his sincerity and concern in dealing with serious subjects such as poverty during a conversation shared over cakes and tea, when "his voice became almost tragic." Recalling that shortly after that occasion she went to Europe with her mother, she then noted cryptically that they never again saw O. Henry (xxiv–xv). From his plight as a lonely "timid stranger," unheralded as yet in New York in 1903, Porter's fame soon skyrocketed, however, and despite no more meetings they evidently kept in touch, exchanging compliments for each others' publications along with bantering chaff inscribed in the gifts of their own, as shown in his last letter in the book dated 28 October 1907 (57–58).

But Wagnalls's preface likewise closes on a somber note as she describes Porter's muddled funeral service (which she had attended with her mother) and picks up his own self-imposed "timid stranger" image as an apt one: "So it seemed with O. Henry. Never quite at home—just a little out of place—and even in death. . . . Out of place, it would seem, to the last, was O. Henry; with hardly time in the church to bury him. But his work, his books—there is place for them in four million homes of those who speak his tongue; more than four million copies of his books have been sold" (xxv–xxviii).

As one biographer has noted, Porter's letters to Mabel Wagnalls reveal a good deal about his ambivalent attitudes and self-image during the course of what she described as her "lively but brief correspondence with O. Henry" (Langford 162; *Lithopolis*, 18). His hearty reaction to her first two letters does suggest that, although Porter's self-confidence was evidently on the upswing after a year's residence in New York, he was also beginning to find the strain of a lonely underground existence irksome. He was obviously delighted with her praise for his stories—yet over-modestly pretending to disparage them—as well as with her queries about his career and his interest in music and other arts besides literature. For in the same letter he promised to send her a few of his recent stories "that you may not have noticed, as being afflicted with 'O. H.' stuff. I'll send you the July 'McClure's' in a day or two (if I may) which contains another. I don't think that anybody but you reads them, and I don't want my audience to get away" (*Lithopolis*, 10).

In closing his second letter, Porter urged Miss Wagnalls to tell him more about herself and Lithopolis in her next one and was evidently so well pleased with her response that he took special pains to enliven his third letter, dated 23 July 1903. She had described not only some curious citizens and their activities in the little community, but also an absent-minded magazine editor and family friend in New York named Dr. E. J. Wheeler, the man who advised her to seek the unknown author of "Roads of Destiny" by sending an inquiry to his publisher. Moreover, since she had now found him, she thought it might be nice to have the two men meet each other and accordingly had "sent my new friend a letter of introduction to the old one, and expressed a hope that he would present the letter before Dr. Wheeler forgot he was coming. (I was mailing at the same time a note to the Doctor explaining his prospective caller.) These precautions on my part are what stirred up O. Henry's artistic instinct to the point of picturing my absentminded editor friend" (15). She stirred it up even further by raising the tantalizing but as yet taboo question of his curious name: "just asked point-blank what the 'O.' stood for, and told him the only names I could think of were Oliver, Otto, and Obadiah. His reply was delightfully disconcerting. . . . I was left in the air—with a subconscious feeling that someone had told me his front name was his own and would I kindly stay put in my grandmother's yard and not try to play in Madison Square" (16).

Porter's light-hearted reply shows he may have been more amused than nettled by Miss Wagnalls's prying into his personal nomenclature, as well as rather touched by her efforts to extend his acquaintanceship among magazine editors. He thanked her for the card of introduction to Mr. Wheeler, but instead of promising to use it at any time soon, he drew an imaginary sketch dramatizing a "reluctance to beard editors" by giving "Mr. Wheeler a perfectly straight face" (25–26). Then, to make it clear the "O." in his name was not an exclamation, he drew sketches of the three men named in her letter (Otto, Oliver, and Obadiah) and suggested she might have added " 'Orlando' and 'Oscar' and 'Orville' and 'Osric' and heaps more" (27–28). Almost inevitably, the two sketches called forth a third—of the village itself with Alta Jungkurth, the "tombstone lady," in the foreground, as Wagnalls had depicted her. For in closing, with thanks once again "for the nice things you said about my little old stories," Porter rated them beneath the products of his pictorial skill and assured her of his inability "to take things solemnly. The whole business—life, literature, operas, philosophy & shirt waists—is a kind of joke, isn't it? . . . When the illusions go the best thing to do is take it good-humoredly" (29–30).

Porter's next four letters to Miss Wagnalls, written once each month between September and December 1903, bore a perceptibly but subtly altered tone. As he soon discovered shortly before she returned to New York, she was not just "a simple Manhattan maiden in Lithopolis," but a seasoned concert artist with publications and kudos of her own attesting to her professional status. He had been showering her with magazine copies of recent stories showing how speedy a pace he was setting "on the road to fame, and," she explains, "I could not resist the impulse to send something myself to show that I, in my own poor way, was snailing along that same deep-rutted, long long road. I mailed him a copy of my book 'Miserere,' and deftly, sort of careless-like, slipped in among the pages a circular of press notices about my concert work" (32–33). She also explains she felt obliged to confess sheepishly to Porter how her prideful bragging to a Lithopolis shopkeeper about her correspondence with O. Henry led to her flustered prevarication that the writer was a distant cousin of her great grandmother, whose name really was Hannah Henry. Porter's response to all this gratuitous information was predictable: he was both visibly impressed with Miss Wagnalls's accomplishments and highly amused by the predicament she stepped into in her conversation with the storekeeper. Having read with great interest both her book and "the little collection of press notices" she enclosed, he congratulated her "most heartily" but jokingly accused her of duplicity by making him "feel quite small and unimportant. Oh, what an exquisite, rippling allegro, staccato little 'jolly' you have been giving me!" he added. "Telling me nice things about my poor little stories, when all the time you were getting bouquets in Berlin and 'bravas' in Binghamton and curtain calls in Conewago and—well, I'm real mad—so, there!" (37–38).

In jest, Porter also ribbed Miss Wagnalls for inquiring "so demurely and offhandishly" if he was interested in music, as well as for extravagantly overpraising his stories. But to show he seriously admired her writing and professional status in a field remote from his own, while enjoying at the same time the game of laudatory praise they were playing with each other, he enclosed a self-photograph to be used as proof of her veracity if in any future hazardous conversation with the local storekeeper she might be "called upon to give him a description of your grandmother's vague & mysterious, not to say suspicious relative" (38–42). Saying nothing further about his real identity, however, Porter concluded this letter with a gallant flourish ("Very glad you wrote again. I enjoy your letters very much, only they are too brief. Sincerely yours//O. Henry" [43]) Disclosure and defence of the nom de plume would be deferred for yet a little while.

Whether any further meetings occurred between this visit and Miss Wagnalls's departure for Europe is not recorded, but her book indicates that Porter's sixth letter, dated 11 November, grew out of a discussion they had about books, authors, and their pseudonyms. Shortly after that she had run across a story by Rex Beach—"a new name in those days"—and recalling that O. Henry admitted he sometimes wrote stories under other names, she assumed this also was another one of them. But the day after mailing him a copy of the story with his name superimposed over Beach's name, Porter's tart reply, addressed "To Her Majesty // The Queen of Bad Guessers," haughtily straightened out her misapprehension, yet closed with a humble request for more tea and little cakes (50–51). His seventh letter, dated nearly a month later on 8 December, shows the two were still on close, friendly terms, regardless of whether or not Porter ever called on Miss Wagnalls again for tea and cakes. For it was another jocular response to a second embarrassing confession she had hurriedly written him about a recent encounter she endured with "a terrible person from Texas" who brusquely demanded to know the origin of her acquaintance with the famous writer, O. Henry. Thoughtlessly, however, she had again answered the question of her having met him "with a commendable regard for the half-truth: 'Oh, through an editor friend.'" Then she was horrified to learn from the Texan that he, too, planned to look up O. Henry at once. Porter was, of course, delighted to welcome her, "as an honorary Member, into the noble army of Prevaricators"; he therefore promised to protect her faithfully so that "if the 'terrible person from Texas' dares to propound any of his impertinent interrogations, I shall swear to him by the eyetooth of Ananias in the sacred Lodge Room of the Prevaricators that Mr. Wheeler was so kind as to introduce me to you at a tea party at half past five under an oleander tree in the prairie during a snowstorm in July while you wore a pink chiffon overcoat and an organdie muff just after a cattle round-up in Madison Avenue" (53–54).

Keeping up this jocular strain for several more paragraphs, Porter ribbed Miss Wagnalls a bit more about her ongoing enjoyment of operas, inquired about further news from Lithopolis, if any, and recalled some of the exciting persons and events she described months before. Hence, in closing, his wistful pretense of fear that she had become fickle, "and you now prefer Rex E. Beach and Marietta Holly, or you would keep me posted about these matters in which we were once mutually interested. Aha! Do I see you turn pale? You are discovered! Once your Cousin but now forgotten! 'O HENRY'" (53–56). If Wagnalls acknowledged this one, she doesn't say, nor does she indicate that they corresponded at all between this seventh letter and Porter's eighth, dated nearly four years later, at a time when plans for his marriage to Sara Coleman were under way.

It is possible no further correspondence did occur between them after

Miss Wagnalls's departure for Europe with her mother in 1903, for she states unequivocally in her preface that they never again saw him alive. Her next sentence, however vaguely recalls that "some time later he sent, through my father's office, his most recent book with an inscription highly typical and dashed off in his best freehand style":

> *To Miss Mabel Wagnalls—*
> *with pleasant recollections of a certain*
> *little tea party where there were such*
> *nice little cakes and kind hospitality*
> *to a timid stranger.*
>   *O. HENRY* (xxv)

Depending on the date she received Porter's gift, his "most recent book" might have been either *The Four Million* (1906) or *The Trimmed Lamp*, which appeared early in 1907. It was not likely to have been *Heart Of The West*, also published later in 1907, because that is probably the one referred to in his eighth letter, dated 28 October 1907, a friendly but somewhat more formal response than any of his others in the Lithopolis group. Though equally witty, Porter's restraint in acknowledging this final gift from Miss Wagnalls matches the terseness of her own comments about both the book and his reaction to it. "This letter," she begins, "is almost self-explanatory. The book, sent through my publisher, is dedicated:

> 'To those who love music but have no
> opportunity of familiarizing themselves
> with Grand Opera.'

O. Henry, with his characteristic cleverness in juggling phrases, wittily inverts my dedication."

But signing himself Sydney Porter for the first time, his acknowledgment is a masterpiece of one-upmanship that brings a fitting close to the amusing little book:

> My Dear Miss Wagnalls:
>   Your publishers sent me your latest book some days ago, and your card accompanying it leads me to suspect that you instigated the deed.
>   I am sure proud to get it; and have waited a few days before writing in order to send with my acknowledgment my latest volume of poor,

insignificant, tiresome, unworthy, dull, pusillanimous, insufferable stories.

(Of course, you understand that the adjectives are hypocritical.)

I am going to read "Stars of the Opera" carefully, and use the information in my conversation to gain a "rep" as a musical critic without having to go through the work of listening to the music.

I feel that I am one of the dedicatees of your book, and that the printer has been in error, and that it should read "To those who love musicians but have no opportunity to familiarize themselves with writers on grand opera."

Oh, those proof-readers!

Sincerely yours
SYDNEY PORTER. (57–58)

During the period between Porter's seventh and eighth letters to Mabel Wagnalls, his astonishing production of short fiction fulfilled her prophecy of meteoric progress toward enduring fame. Throughout the two full years of 1904 and 1905, for example, he turned out weekly stories consistently for the *Sunday World* besides publishing numerous longer ones in the monthly magazines—a total of 120 stores, which his biographer interprets as "a measure of his determination to put the past behind him, to transform himself from W. S. Porter to O. Henry"; so that he "became for millions of readers the familiar and eagerly applauded spokesman of the decade. . . . It is an incredible output, not so much from the standpoint of bulk as from the standpoint of inventiveness" (Langford, 185–86). This week-to-week routine was nevertheless a grueling experience for both Porter and his various editors, one or another of whom would be badgering him repeatedly for stories he had promised and been paid advances for but had not yet delivered, an experience that likewise reflected what has been called his "paradoxical personality"—a shying away from social commitments with his equals, yet prowling about the city's nightspots furtively because of his "inability to face the truth of his past, to take off his mask and show himself to the world as he was" (Langford, 180–93). Thus his conduct during these two crucial years was also a reflection of his poignant loneliness, dramatized once again in two groups of correspondence which, beginning perhaps in the same month, eventually appeared in print before *Letters to Lithopolis*.

The shorter of these, "a correspondence which most appropriately of all illustrates the underground aspect of Porter's life," began with a personal-column advertisement he placed in the New York *Herald* on 10 September 1905:

> Two neighborly literary fellows, 35 and 30, seek social acquaintance of two intelligent, attractive and unconventional young ladies interested in artistic ideas, with a view to mutual improvement and entertainment. Omar. 116 Herald.

And the full story of the abortive little romance that might have been was ruefully told in *Everybody's* eight years later by the lonely young woman, Ethel Lloyd Patterson, who promptly answered that "Personal" with misgivings (Langford, 197).[17] To show she was lonesome enough to be talking to elevator boys and car conductors and yet prudent enough not to risk giving away her name and address right off, Miss Patterson carefully screened her impulsive response with appropriate references to the "Rubaiyat" of Omar Khayam: "Who are you? Out of space you have spoken a name I love. Out of space I am answering you. Will you come within signaling distance you ships that, perhaps shall not pass in the night?" And begging pardon for withholding her own name and address, she signed it, "I am just—'A Woman.'" Within a week she received Porter's enthusiastic reply addressed to "Mysterious 'A Woman,'" reassuring her no evil snare was involved in the 'Personal' he and his "brother 'Omar'" had launched except "the hope of winging some wild, free creature of the aerial regions above who might prove congenial company in our quiet excursions in search of the (genuinely) romantic and the (reasonably) adventuresome." Typically evasive, Porter then drew his fanciful distinction between himself and the imaginary "Omar No. 1":

> I came from the saddle of a Texas bronco four years ago to New York. The conventionalities and the routine of the little circle I have been revolving in have about caused me to stampede. The more 'people' I meet the . . . 'lonesomer' I get. I can well sympathize with a woman who is lonely in the Big City
> 'Omar' No. 1 is a New Yorker and a charming and bright fellow. I recommend him—so there!
> Please ma'am will you try a chat with us instead of the car conductors and elevator boys? I am sure my brother 'Omar' will recommend me, too.

And, enclosing both a photo of himself and his card with name and address, he challenged her "to come within speaking distance and give

us a hope that we may gather 'underneath the bough' with you . . .
Yours to the bottom of the jug, 'THE TWO OMARS'" (206–208).

Miss Patterson was sufficiently encouraged by this letter to reply
"almost at once," thanking Porter for his card and address but doubting
whether she could as yet show her appreciation by being equally frank
before at least seeing him. Yet the problem was, she felt, that of achieving mutual recognition at a suitable meeting place: "how in the name of
Heaven am I to know you when I get there?" she queried, closing
resignedly, "for a while I remain to you a little longer just "'A Woman'"
(206–208). Having begun this letter by revealing that she, too, had come
"from the saddle of a Texas bronco" even before Porter and thus
had suffered "two more years of pent-up homesickness" than he, she
gave Porter all the stimulus he needed to repay her promptly with a
blockbuster response, a letter of double-barreled self-characterization,
achievement, and aspiration that fills nearly two full magazine pages of
single-spaced type. (209–210).

If she was really from Texas, he began, then she could safely approach
"the campfire of a Texan" to hear her own language spoken. Nevertheless, he was glad she had not yet revealed herself and given him "permission to 'call.' Why spoil these wireless signals by a 'call'?" And from
here on, rehearsing in memory both his visit with Mabel Wagnalls and
the themes he had discussed in his letters to her, Porter rehashed all of
them with cowpunchers' campfire detail and imagery:

> Why should I add to the tedium of your life by sitting on a slippery
> couch in your 'parlor,' hitching up my trousers an inch at the knees to
> preserve the crease (when you weren't looking), and drinking a cup of
> English breakfast tea (which is no good—always get uncolored Ja-
> pan), and asking you whether you like 'Man and Superman' or the
> hippodrome the better.
> Not for Old Bill Omar, the Texas Scout.
> My Dear 'A Woman,' I can do these things sometimes. I can be a
> perfect gent when I want to. They used to round me up a year or two
> ago and drive me to 'functions.' Once I was corralled with a bunch of
> poets and poetesses up-town. The poets sat in semi-circles and read
> 'things of their own.' . . .
> Truth is, I'm tired of the New York bluff, I want a 'pal' who hates
> this sort or conventionality, who will be a 'good fellow'— in the best
> sense of the term—and would like to go about and enjoy the Arabian
> Nights that can be found here by the true followers of the Com-

mander of the Faithful. *Unconspicuous unconventionality*—these two large words seem to hit off the idea.

Carrying on in this vein for three more columns, Porter rehearsed all of the things he would really enjoy doing on successive nights—dining in style at Moquin's one evening among "well-known artists and hungry writers," attending the theater the next evening and afterwards a dance-hall, where someone could be inveigled into telling him "THINGS! . . . that make literature if only the editors would let us write 'em"; reading or writing letters to relatives, etc.—but often feeling bored, angry, and dissatisfied because he lacked a steady 'pal' to help him enjoy them. These observations led in turn to his offering further reassuring descriptions of "the tent-makers"—his accomplice, Omar No. 1, a magazine editor, and himself. To bolster the latter Porter even included a newspaper clipping carrying a favorable review of his "first novel" (*Cabbages and Kings*) and a brief summary of his "varied life," which, however, required further emendation and modification. Then, coming finally to the question of how their meeting could best be managed, Porter could not resist adding one more touch of cowpoke foolery ("This is all new to me. I'm accustomed to lasso ladies to whom I take a fancy, throw them across my saddle, and gallop away, firing my trusty revolver as the horse's hoofs strike fire from the asphalt pavement on the prairie") before seriously proposing she might agree to come by subway to the station at Lenox Avenue and 125th Street any evening of the week at her convenience, and that he would be there "with my friend Omar (or alone if you prefer it)." Thus his closing appeal, a model of circumspect formality, expressed the hope that she might feel confident enough on meeting to accept their invitation to dine but also the reassurance that her lightest wish would "rule all the procedure after we meet"; and finally, the request that, if satisfied, she would return a favorable answer shortly, "naming the day and time and something by which we can recognize you" (209–210).

Ironically, however, for whatever reason, unknown even to herself, Ethel Patterson decided not to answer this letter; so that when later by chance they were introduced to each other, she concludes, mournfully striking the same Proustian chord of *les temps perdues* that marked her opening: "As it was I missed two whole years in which I might have known O. Henry. Too much to lose. For it was all of that before I finally did meet him in a friend's home and place him in my mind as the man of the 'Personal Letters.' Then it was quite a long while, too, before I summoned courage to tell him I was the 'Personal Girl.' After he knew, he used, as I say, to call me 'The Miss Terry.' And he plagued me insufferably about it all." Since by then Porter was a married man, the two-years' loss she mourns of the "Royal Friend" she might have known perhaps suggests another, subtler irony.

At any rate, Porter's plea for a "pal" surfaced again in a third series of letters between him and Sara Coleman, the lady from Asheville who became his second wife, a series that may have begun during the same month in which he was corresponding with Ethel Patterson, September 1905. One must say "may have" because of a discrepancy in the dating of two identical sources for the ascribed date of Sara's initial letter in this new series.[18] But a persuasive case can be built on the theory that Sara, in composing *Wind Of Destiny*, one of the sources, had Ethel Patterson's story, "O. Henry and Me," in the forefront of her mind.

According to information cited above, Sara got the idea of writing to Porter originally from gossip her mother picked up during a visit to Greensboro in the spring of 1905, and this is confirmed by the other source, a letter and newspaper clipping in the Greensboro archives stating Porter's response to Sara's first letter was dated 15 July. In *Wind of Destiny*, however, the narrator becomes Caroline Howard, while Porter's alias becomes Robert Haralson. And Caroline receives the news about him, not from her mother, but from a young friend in New York, Henrietta Dickerson, a very lonesome, hungry young thing, who has been corresponding with Haralson as the result of a "Personal" she encountered in the *Herald*: "'The 'ad' I answered says the man is lonely; that he wants an attractive woman friend. The 'ad' was signed Telemacus.' His letter fairly scintillated. I answered. He wrote again. Now he asks for a meeting. But the letter is oh, so chivalrous, so witty, so wonderful, Caroline. And there's a reticence, an impersonal note in it that piques a woman's fancy, stirs her imagination—"[19] From this point forward Sara's fictional narrative develops along a path that re-echoes the progress of Patterson's correspondence with Porter. Dicky, the nineteen-year-old Miss Dickinson, proceeds to reassure Caroline that she did not meet "Telemacus" after all because, instead of showing up at their prearranged meeting place, he sent a messenger boy with a note nobly explaining the reason for "'going against my desire . . . It isn't fair to you that I meet you. It is not fair to the nice little girl homesick for her southland who has never as yet spoken to a man to whom she has not been introduced. The 'ad' was just a wager between a man and me. My name will mean nothing to you, but I sign it.' The name was Robert Haralson, Caroline" (14).

The name did ring a faint bell in Dicky's memory. Where had she known a Robert Haralson? The mystery is cleared up presently as she returns to her room to find her troubling question fortuitously answered in another letter from a good friend from Roseboro (i.e. Greensboro), Mary Tate, "who is coming to New York for her first visit" and whose letter throbs with hometown excitement where "everybody is talking about Robert Haralson, known at home still at Bobby. Everybody is saying that he was the cleverest and most popular lad that the town ever raised. A brilliant future was prophesied for him, but he got a wanderlust and went trailing off to the ends of the earth. . . . Roseboro, of course, is shaking congratulatory hands with itself that its prophecy has come true. Now he seems permanently to have settled in New York and to have found himself. Mary asks me if I have read 'Heart of the World.' It came out anonymously, as did no end of brilliant stories. . . . Gossip says further that shy Bobby Haralson loved one girl like mad. That girl was Caroline Howard" (14–15).

So although Dicky, too, has "fallen in love with Bobby's fascinating letter [and] with his chivalrous protection of me," and although "this minute his card, name, and address lie on my table—and I am lonesomer than I was before I answered the 'ad'—I won't do what it is in my mind to do. It is your Bobby Haralson'" (15–16).

Returning to her narrative, Caroline tells of the newspaper clipping Dicky enclosed: It described Haralson as being "at present one of the most interesting men in American literature"; the news has stirred her effort to recall events of her adolescent relationship with Bobby, whom she had not even thought about in many years. And these vague ruminations, she confesses, have evoked other disturbing reflections—her long-felt distaste for the thought of marriage as opposed to more recent fears of loneliness, dull monotony, and lost youth at forty—so that in a mood of "frantic haste" she dashed off a bootless inquiry to him. Could he remember anything about "the little girl who lived next door? She'll never get to New York, never! . . . But if ever you come to Marsville [Asheville] whistle across the fence. The little girl's got one of your stories treasured in her desk without knowing until some one's letter gave away the secret of its authorship. Big congratulations, Bobby!" (25–26). Certain her letter would have been tossed unanswered into a wastebasket, Caroline was astonished to have Bobby's exuberant reply within less than a week.[20]

Bobby's first letter to Caroline fills more than two full pages of her autobiographical story and bears a fascinating comparison in content and style to Porter's original letters to Mabel Wagnalls and Ethel Patterson. The Porter-Coleman epistolary duet, as played out between Bobby Haralson and Caroline Howard in *Wind of Destiny*, re-echoes with many of the familiar strains heard in *Letters to Lithopolis*—embellished now by a nostalgic tone reminiscent of youthful pleasures shared in Greensboro long ago. Porter's gift of his picture and a copy of *Cabbages and Kings* had been promptly but prudently acknowledged with thanks; within a week his second letter appears, longer and move effusive than his first, to reassure and captivate Sara with sage appeals to her sense of propriety, self-interest, and literary aspiration:

> Was it cheeky of you to write to me? My dear Miss Carrie [Sally], I don't know exactly what the unpardonable sin is, but if you hadn't written, I'd feel awfully anxious about your future. . . .
> Don't chain up your impulses, friend; let 'em skallyhoot around. We don't live more than nine times; and bottles and chains weren't made for people to confine and tie up their good impulses with. (30–34)

Stringing out at length this complimentary vein, Porter vows he has long remembered Sara as an ideal; congratulates her "heartily" for a "very sweet and tender" story of hers published recently in *Leslies*; and advises her "to come to New York, where you will be *in medias res*. There's nothing like being on the ground. You get artistic ideas and associations here that would be invaluable to you. Writing is a bully game. You want to know the dealers. . . . Today I get five times more per word than when I came. Sister of the pen and stamped-envelope-for-return, I speak wisdom to you." Thus abandoning his normal modesty for a moment, Porter can't help bragging a little about his recent success, but without overdoing such boastfulness he concludes with a genuinely ardent plea for the picture Sara had mentioned. A week later, as the game of complimentary memory-swapping continued, his response to her evasiveness in writing about carefully preserved memories while ignoring the request was a single blunt paragraph, 4 October:

> DEAR LADY OF THE UNLAVENDER SCENTED MEMORIES:
> Please send that picture. You have moved to the very last seat in the car and I have picked up my traps and followed you. Will you send it, or are you going to move into the Pullman?
> Yours as ever,
> B.H. (36)[21]

Shortly afterward Sara relented momentarily, sending Porter an attractive portrait in her next letter, but then hastily demanding its return in another. In a delayed response to both letters he explained in December that a severely injured hand had kept him from thanking her for the photo, which, he emphasized: "I appreciate highly, and shall not return as you suggest in your P. M. (particularly Mean) letter. What's the matter with it? It looks all right to me. I can't suggest any improvement in it." Porter at this point was just warming up for another of his strung-out, chatty missives, page after page sparkling with trivia, with metaphors, sly innuendoes, and colorful compliments, enjoying himself immensely as he turns over references and reminiscences picked up in Sara's letters and transforms them into freshly crafted imagery. Thus the concluding portion of this particular letter (which he begged her at least to condone if she did not like it) exemplifies the "delightful toil" he admitted while writing to her: "it's like lifting the lightest feather from the breast of an eider duck and watching it float through the circumamblent atmosphere."

As their correspondence progressed well into the new year, its tone deepening slightly with each exchange of letters, Sara and Sydney both had evidently begun taking the relationship quite seriously. If his early letters were indeed, "clearly . . . those of a man playing a role that he imagined was expected of him" (Langford, 204), Sara had reason enough to wonder whether he was falling in love after reading his next ardent appeal, dated 1 April, begging her to visit him in New York: "Say— please come, won't you? I do so long to see a human—a Heaven-sent, home-bred, ideal-owning, scrumptious, sweet, wholesome human with a heart such as I know you are" (60–61). Entreaties like these, coupled with assurances that Sara would find her life in the great city vastly more desirable than it could be in North Carolina, continued throughout the ensuing months. By the summer of 1907 she was convinced. Not only would her career as a writer flourish, but so, surely, would her prospects for a successful marriage.

Second Marriage, Intensive Literary Activity, and Final Illness

With funds in hand from the sale of one of her stories, Sara was at last ready for that long-discussed visit—first with some old friends in Boston and then briefly with Porter on her way back home. For the first time since her childhood they met again, and Sydney played his part as the ardent suitor so convincingly that his proposal was accepted, possibly even more promptly than he anticipated. For now, the problem of his shadowed past, so often side-stepped before, he could no longer evade. He would have to confess—and did so, frantically, the night she left— that he had concealed from her something about his past that would make their marriage impossible. He promised to write her the full details after she returned home; evidently assuming this would end their engagement, he set forth both the facts of his trial and imprisonment as well as his unshakable feeling of innocence. Since neither the written confession nor Sara's reply has survived, the precise wording in them remains speculative, but there is no doubt whatever that Sara chose not to break the engagement, because she obviously brushed aside Porter's caveat, urging her in a follow-up letter to reconsider the proposition carefully from all sides before making a definite commitment. From her standpoint it was enough to have his reassurance once again that he loved and needed her; for then and thenceforward to the close of a long-widowed life she believed implicitly—as did many others—that he was completely innocent.[22] So the wedding was scheduled to take place in Asheville on 27 November 1907.

Although their wedding had been as eagerly planned for as the mating of any ardent young couple, the brief married life they shared for barely thirty months would prove to be, at best, a bittersweet experience that sorely tested the innate good will and decency of both Sara Coleman, the spinster bride of thirty-seven, and Will Porter, the blasé Caliph of forty-six. Even before their month-long honeymoon ended in the North Carolina mountains, weariness and sickness pointed ominously toward the physical breakdown that would diminish Porter's creative energy in the months ahead, besides altering the sunny personality he displayed as a lover. And shortly after they returned to New York Sara quickly learned how ill-prepared she was to take over in a family hotel like the Chelsea her dual role as housewife for a temperamental writer and, shortly afterward, as stepmother to his headstrong teen-aged daughter, Margaret. But Porter, too, was likewise unprepared: for his "marriage was a futile attempt to re-establish himself as a member of respectable society, to re-activate the roots from which he had tried to cut himself off when he left North Carolina to find a new life in Texas. From the very beginning—and for both of them almost equally—the marriage was a strain and little more than that" (Langford, 214)[23]

The strain for Porter was intensified by the need to produce now more regularly than before in order to support a family residence and a second establishment where he spent the day writing while Sara brooded morbidly and idle at home. And although he drove himself relentlessly, publishing twenty-nine new stories in 1908, as compared with only eleven in 1907 and even fewer in 1909, the income of roughly fourteen thousand dollars they brought him was still not enough to offset his casual, thriftless lifestyle. Moreover, this was his only income, since he had sold for a pittance the rights for his collected volumes issued up to that point.[24]

Despite the further signs of Porter's declining health in the spring and summer of 1908, and despite the familial tensions and distractions that must have exacerbated his condition, he made significant progress as a published author. Besides the twenty-nine separate stories he turned out, two more volumes were added to the four which the McClure Company issued between 1904 and the close of 1907. These were *The Voice of the City* (May 1908), which completed the trilogy of New York stories, and *The Gentle Grafter* (November 1908), which extended the list of his western tales. Moreover, since both of these collections were more favorably received by the New York reviewers than the earlier volumes, they not only added gratifying stature to the O. Henry reputation, but also encouraged Porter to carry forward the task of assembling three more collections, which would appear during the last full year of his life, thanks largely to the initiative and untiring assistance of Harry Peyton Steger. And, during those final months there was still more activity, productions both noteworthy and abortive, along with grandiose plans for future achievement, which he would not survive to fulfill.

There is abundant evidence that the expanding chorus of praise for O. Henry's stories during this twilight period of his life was offset by

Porter's own growing dissatisfaction with the quality of his achievement. "My stories?" he exclaimed irritably in 1909. "No, they don't satisfy me . . . It depresses me to have people point me out or introduce me as 'a celebrated author.' It seems such a big label for such picayune goods."[25] Such an outburst reflected both the frustration caused by a sharply diminished creative output and the deteriorating physical condition that fed his depressed sense of failure. For even as he struggled with the strange malady that was killing him, Porter had been planning an elaborate series of stories (as well as a novel) that would seriously develop a major contemporary theme of contrast between the old, pre–Civil War South and the new, emerging South of the twentieth century. None of this projected fiction ever got written, although Porter allegedly drew some sizable cash advances for writing it from both *Collier's* magazine and Doubleday, Page & Company.

Had Porter devoted more time and the remainder of his flagging energy to the writing of high-quality fiction in 1908–1909, he might well have produced something more substantial than just a few fine stories, such as "Thimble, Thimble," "The Rose of Dixie," and "A Municipal Report." But instead of tackling either the novel or the planned series of short stories already contracted for, he pursued an ignis fatuus, squandering more than six months of that year on a collaborative venture with Franklin P. Adams to produce a musical comedy based on one of his stories, "To Him Who Waits," which had appeared in *Collier's* in January. The play, *Lo!*, that emerged from their combined talents, opened in Aurora, Illinois, in August, but expired in December after road performances of fourteen weeks in several other midwestern towns. Long before then, however, Porter's health had deteriorated so badly that by September he accepted Steger's advice to abandon New York and rejoin Sara for an extended rest cure in the North Carolina mountains. And with his characteristic hyperbolic flair, by November he could joyfully reassure Steger that "on the whole I'm improving vastly. I've a doctor here who says I have absolutely no physical trouble except neurasthenia, and that out door exercise & air will find me as good as new. As for the diagnosis of the N.Y. doctors—they are absolutely without foundation. I am 20 pounds lighter, & can climb mountains like a goat."[26]

Mercifully, although such optimism was totally misleading, the self-confidence reflected in it fueled Porter's determination to carry on his literary activity. But once again his arbitrary choice of a suitable medium played him false; even though he chose this time to continue dramatizing another of his stories for the theatre, instead of working on "A

Retrieved Reformation," which he had apparently agreed to undertake for the theatrical producer George Tyler, he preferred to work on a dramatization of "The World and the Door," despite Tyler's indifference to it. Tyler's plans however, were not to be circumvented by such dalliance. He offered Porter a mere five hundred dollars for the dramatic rights to "A Retrieved Reformation," and, with the deal closed, promptly hired another playwright, Paul Armstrong, to transform the story into the stage play *Alias Jimmy Valentine*, which became one of the smash hits throughout America, England, France, and Spain during the next decade. Armstrong's royalties alone quickly topped eight hundred dollars weekly; by the end of the play's run he had earned more than one hundred thousand dollars for a week's work that Porter in his prime might have surpassed in a day or two.[27]

Sometime between his last sojourn with Sara and Margaret in Asheville and his return to New York, Porter managed to complete his final story, "Let Me Feel Your Pulse," which Sara fittingly declared to be the first in her heart. Facing certain death and fully aware that no medicines, nostrums, or panaceas were likely to cure his shattered health, Porter brought to bear all his talents to fashion a delightfully ironic little allegory based on his own painful search for relief—his futile interviews with doctors in New York and his extended rest cure in Asheville—but embracing in its sensitive grasp broader implications touching all human endeavor. The story ends with a question that delicately implies all that Porter had discovered about himself and the world, and about his relationship to the world as an artist: "What rest more remedial than to sit with Amaryllis in the shade, and, with a sixth sense, read the wordless Theocritan idyll of the gold-bannered blue mountains marching orderly into the dormitories of the night?" Those who remember Milton's *Lycidas* can never forget that the next few lines following that familiar allusion speak of fame as the "spur that the clear spirit doth raise . . . To scorn delights, and live laborious days," as well as of "the blind Fury with abhorred shears [that comes] and slits the thin-spun life."[28] Death and fame were much on Porter's mind at this juncture, but his swan song uttered a clear, pure note.

Notes to Part 2

1. See the announcement published in the *Critic*, February 1904, and quoted in Langford's *Alias O. Henry*, 170. The most carefully documented discussion

of Porter's meteoric career in New York may be found in the last five chapters of this biography, 152–247.

2. See "Little Pictures of O. Henry," *Waifs and Strays*, 151–52.
3. *Caliph*, 206; quoted also in Langford, 159.
4. See *Shadows*, 297.
5. See "A Decomposition of *Cabbages and Kings*," by Paul A. Clarkson, in *American Literature* 7 (May 1935): 195–202; the article offers a close analysis of how the process was carried out.
6. Most of his readers in Austin in 1894, would have recognized at once that Craddock was the pen name for the popular local colorist of the 1890s, Mary Noailles Murfree. See Steger's essay, 543–47.
7. A detailed analysis of Porter's *Rolling Stone* appears in Langford, 251–58.
8. The fragment appeared posthumously in the *Cosmopolitan* in September 1910.
9. See, e.g., Steger, 31, 47, 64, 80, 96, 112, 128, 160, 176, 232–33, and 242–43.
10. See Current-Garcia, 84–87.
11. The complete story behind their joint production of "Holding Up A Train" had appeared at the end of Steger's prior volume, *Rolling Stones*, pp. 288–92, and the story itself, published originally by *Everybody's*, reappeared in the collection *Sixes And Sevens*, issued in 1911. Oddly enough, neither Steger nor Page called attention to the fact that in this communication of 1902 Porter's desire to remain anonymous was still so strong that he urged Jennings not to publicize his identity: "By the way, please keep my *nom de plume* strictly to yourself. I don't want any one to know just yet." [*Rolling Stones*, p. 292.] Both men must have known about Porter's imprisonment long before 1910.
12. *Mentor*, February 1923, 17–20.
13. See "The Amazing Genius of O. Henry," 175.
14. For details of these developments, see Langford, 202, 204; 207– 209.
15. The significant value of *Wind Of Destiny*, published by Doubleday, Page & Company in 1916, lies in the fact that the letters in it, except for the changing of names, are avowedly the actual letters that Porter wrote to Sara after she had shyly initiated the exchange. As set forth bluntly in her Foreword, "The letters in this story are real letters. I know this because they were written to me by the man the world knows as O. Henry, author, and only as the author. Not half a dozen people know the real Sydney Porter, and the man was greater than the author. . . . The background of the letters is pure fiction. Maybe I have let more of myself creep into this tale than I had planned. If this be true, the reason is that my whole thought centered upon revealing Sydney Porter to the lovers of O. HENRY. SARA LINDSAY COLEMAN."
16. Preface, *Lithopolis*, viii–ix; hereafter cited in the text.
17. Langford succinctly summarizes the story "O. Henry and Me" and the letters in it, but omits mention of some important details such as the

illustrations and Miss Patterson's concluding paragraph. See *Everybody's*, February 1914, 205–210; hereafter cited in the text.

18. See Langford, 202-204 and notes 12 and 13 on 282 for an explanation of the discrepancy.

19. *Wind Of Destiny*, 5.

20. As noted above the story referred to in Caroline's letter was "Madam Bo-Peep of the Ranches," which Sara Coleman named as a favorite among O. Henry's earliest stories that she had kept in her desk; it appeared in the magazine *Smart Set* in 1902, and thus evoked Porter's concluding reference to "those antiquated stories" in his response to Sara's initial inquiry. His original letter, housed in the Greensboro papers is dated 15 July rather than 25 September, as in *Wind Of Destiny*, but except for changed names of persons and places, the text of the two letters is virtually identical. See Langford, 202 and 282.

21. In the narrative Caroline confesses that she had fibbed about her old memories laid away in lavender-scented sheets, and that instead of addressing the problem of spinsterhood at thirty plus, she had written about a drummer who had tried to flirt with her on a train.

22. A copy of Sara's letter confirming this is located in the Smith papers: see Langford, 208–209 and 282, notes 24, 25, and 26. Sara's novella, *Wind Of Destiny*, makes no direct reference to this matter, but it does end on a very strong upbeat note with an impassioned declaration from Bobby Haralson to Caroline ("I want you, my honey. I need you"), which may have been Porter's actual words. Further confirmation of her life-long loyalty appears in an interview published many years later when she was eighty-four years old. See Walter Carroll, "An Afternoon With O. Henry's Widow," *The Prairie Schooner*, Summer 1852, 138–43.

23. Numerous specific details of their marital difficulties, as summed up in Sara's widowed reference to "our poor, tragic little life together," are cited by Langford in the following pages of this chapter and the next one.

24. Langford points out that Porter received no royalties from his books until Doubleday, Page and Company "became his publisher and took over the earlier copyrights in 1909" (215).

25. *Mentor*, February, 1923, 45; also quoted in Langford, 224.

26. *South Atlantic Quarterly*, January 1939, 38; also quoted in Langford, 233.

27. Alexander Woollcott, "O. Henry Playwright," *Bookman*, October 1922, 155–57; details of the transaction between Porter and Tyler are discussed in Langford, 234–40.

28. John Milton, "Lycidas," *Complete Poetical Works*, Cambridge Edition (Boston: Houghton Mufflin, 1965), 117–18.

Part 3

THE CRITICS

Introduction

The elements of his art were not many. . . . He knew precisely how much of the sugar of sentimentality the great average reading public must have, and how much of the pepper of sensation, and the salt of facts, and the salad dressing of romance. . . . But brilliant as were the possibility of his powers, and distinctive as was his technique, his final place can never be high even among the writers of short stories. He did not take literature seriously: he was a victim of Momus and the swift ephemeral press. His undoubted powers were completely debauched by it. He became exclusively an entertainer, with no thought but of the moment, and no art save that which brought instant effect upon his reader. To accomplish that he would sacrifice everything, even the truth.[1]

Had Bill Porter survived just another dozen or so of his allotted six score and ten years, he would have witnessed in this harsh rebuke from F. L. Pattee the wisdom of Milton's dictum that "Fame is not plant that grows on mortal soil, / Nor in the glistering foil / Set off to th' world." The severe tone of Pattee's contemptuous dismissal of O. Henry's preeminence in the annals of American literature shows how strong a reaction against his popularity and influence had set in during the debunking period of World War I, after the first wave of critical enthusiasm for O. Henry was spent. Critics such as Pattee, Alexander Woolcott, N. Bryllion Fagin, and several others repudiated his stories on the grounds of superficiality and sham; they could not excuse O. Henry's failure, as they saw it, to take himself and his art seriously because they felt that the very brilliance of his technical skill, so misapplied, wrought great mischief upon the corpus of American short fiction as a whole. At its best, Fagin declared, O. Henry's work "discloses an occasional brave peep at life, hasty, superficial and dazzlingly flippant. . . . At its worst, his work is not more than a series of cheap jokes renovated and expanded. But over all there is the unmistakable charm of a master trickster, of a facile player with incidents and words."[2]

Thus began, shortly after Porter's death, a critical controversy regarding the ultimate value of his massive literary output, a prolonged contest among critics and literary historians to determine how high a ranking he deserved as an heir of Irving, Hawthorne, and Poe. Between 1916 and the mid-1920s Pattee, Fagin, and several other hostile critics voiced strong disagreement with the mounting praise of the O. Henry stories that had been initiated by Steger, whose crusade to elevate Porter's literary stature gained momentum after his own untimely death in 1912. The barrage of enthusiastic information presented in his edition of the volume *Rolling Stones* broadened the publicity about Porter, and its impact stimulated various other critics whose views gained further support from Alphonso Smith's *O. Henry Biography* (1916), which sought to establish Porter's claim to rank as a coequal among America's major writers of fiction. Smith's high praise for Porter's work quickly evoked a strong negative response from some of the more fastidious academic critics of the period, notably Katherine Fullerton Gerrould, who in July 1916 deplored the "pernicious influence" of his stories and condemned them as superficial "expanded anecdotes," lacking serious intellectual content; and a few months earlier Pattee himself had also dismissed them as "specious journalization," the work of a "harlequin Poe," in a detailed essay that may have inspired Gerrould's attack.[3] These attacks promptly drew forth spirited counterattacks, first by Stephen Leacock, a Canadian humorist who brushed aside all such animad versions as sheer nonsense, unworthy of a serious reply. If O. Henry's stories were only anecdotes, he chuckled, "let's have another barrelful," and then concluded with another extremely adulatory prediction that soon "the whole English-speaking world will recognize in O. Henry one of the great masters of modern literature."[4]

Forty years ago Van Wyck Brooks's even-tempered acknowledgment that O. Henry was "occasionally an artist" probably marked a turning point in the plunging descent of his literary reputation, although it may not have seemed so to his fellow critics. For by the 1950s they had virtually dismissed Porter's contribution to American fiction as unworthy of further serious consideration. "The World of O. Henry is an intellectual Sahara," wrote George F. Whicher in one of the two major literary histories published at the same time; while the other scarcely bothered to mention Porter's name at all in its revised edition.[5] And at the threshold of a new decade the author of an elaborate treatise on the development of the American short story could thus bluntly assert that Porter's reputation was already dead and ignored his work altogether, even though, ironically, the most thoroughly researched analysis of Porter's achievement was already in print to cast doubt on such premature dismissal.[6] By the 1960s it was a moot question whether such harsh judgments would long endure; because just as the original adulation lavished upon Porter had proved to be thoughtlessly overdone, so might the more recent disparagement of his work turn out to be both imperceptive and unjustified. Its uniqueness and popular appeal—however dead and dated its mannerisms and contrivances—were still vigorously resisting interment. Many of those quaint, old-fashioned yarns, such as "The Ransom of Red Chief," could still draw hearty enjoyment from intelligent readers. And if Porter's latest biographer, Gerald Langford, may have seemed overly optimistic for sensing in 1957 that "at long last the time has come when O. Henry can be given his rightful place in American literature," the decades since then have supported his prophetic verdict. He was correct in asserting that Porter, as a *minor* classic who is here to stay, deserves his permanent niche by virtue of the unique flavor that, in so many of his stories, is compounded of humor, enchantment, and compassion for all who suffer from a sense of isolation and frustration.

Has Porter been granted his permanent niche, now that a full century has elapsed since he first stepped across the threshold of Gilman Hall's office at *Ainslee's Magazine* in New York? Depending upon the authoritative evidence available since the 1960s, it seems that his rating among both the reading public at large and the literary critics and scholars has suffered little if any further decline. His reputation as an important contributor to the development of American short fiction may, indeed, have risen a notch or two during recent decades, although that would be difficult to demonstrate, perhaps, on a quantitative basis. Now that all of his published writings are in the public domain, for example, the Doubleday Company no longer keeps inventories of editions reprinted or of adaptation rights to individual stories sold. There are no longer any accurate statistics to show just how wide and deep the popular appeal of Porter's stories still may be.

Aside from their popular appeal, however, there is another important criterion to be considered: namely, the steady accumulation of biographical and critical studies that are being published yearly, each of them sifting the data, measuring the man and his work, analyzing, comparing, and evaluating the merits and shortcomings of both. The variety and scope of these studies are impressive, for they range considerably in the depth and selectivity of materials dealt with in each of them. During the 1960s and 1970s at least half a dozen full-length studies were published, and a number of shorter ones appeared in collections of critical essays dealing with short fiction. The titles of all these, together with thumbnail judgments of their value, are recorded in Richard C. Harris's *William Sydney Porter (O. Henry): A Reference Guide*, published by G. K. Hall in 1980. Still more such studies, both long and short, appeared in the 1980s in such collections as the monumental *Dictionary of American Literary Biography* series and the less ambitious one, *Fifty Southern Writers after 1900*. And the trend shows few signs of coming to a halt shortly, as the 1990s have already added substantially to the stockpile: a colorful biography published by the Scarborough Press in 1990, shorter critical essays published by the St. James Press in 1991, plus several more of them scheduled also for 1994. Then, there is this one. . . .

The durability of Porter's fame and wide appeal seems reasonably secure. It was demonstrated by the citizens of Greensboro in April 1985, when a fair number of them gathered to pay homage to the memory of their native son. They came to witness an impressive ceremony: to hear plaudits at the unveiling of a life-sized bronze statue erected in his honor in the heart of the city's commercial center. It was a ceremony carefully planned to initiate a week-long O. Henry Festival, a foretaste, no doubt, of others like it to come. Surely, one felt, if the ghost of Will Porter's alter ego were hovering nearby on this seventy-fifth anniversary of his demise, he must have felt securely established in his proper niche.

Some of Porter's earliest and most perceptive critics recognized that at the heart of the O. Henry afflatus there lies an element of surprise or wonder, as though almost everything his senses recorded were a potential source of awakened pleasure. This is a keynote struck in the very brief essay with which we begin our series of representative extracts from critical reactions to the bulk of Porter's oeuvre: written by Henry James Forman and published originally in the venerable New England journal, the *North American Review*; in 1908, it was the first and only serious critique that appeared during Porter's lifetime. It was also republished a decade later in *Waifs and Strays*, along with a dozen other essays of reminiscent nostalgia referred to above.[7]

Forman's brief tribute to Porter's artistry did not have long to wait for enthusiastic support. By the time Steger's final volume of O. Henry's "complete" works appeared in 1912, several other critics were prepared to explain why his stories had so swiftly raised the stature of their still unknown author to place him at the head of American short-fiction writers. Leading the group was a young scholar at the University of Texas, Hyder E. Rollins, whose 1914 essay in the *Sewanee Review* set the pattern for such critical analysis by skimming rapidly through each collection, synopsizing action, situation, and/or personae in a succession of stories to support the judgment that in all twelve volumes of his short stories "O. Henry has not a single dull or dragging subject. To this modern Caliph Haroun-al-Raschid the most trivial incident in the life of the proletarian is teeming with romance, and touched by his facile pen it becomes a story of at least passing interest to every reader."[8]

Henry James Forman

Mr. Sydney Porter, the gentleman who, in the language of some of his characters, is "denounced" by the euphonious pen name of O. Henry, has breathed new life into the short story. Gifted as he is with a flashing wit, abundant humour, and quick observation, no subject has terrors for him. If it be too much to say, in the old phrase, that nothing human is alien to him, at least the larger part of humanity is his domain. The very title of one of his books, "The Four Million," is a protest against those who believe that New York contains only four hundred people worth while. O. Henry backs the census-taker against the social arbiter. The rich and the fashionable are, in his tales, conceived much in the spirit of similar characters in melodrama, except that the ingredient of humour is put in to mitigate them. Indeed, they figure but seldom. But the poor and the lowly, the homeless lodger of the city park, the vagabond of the "bread line," the waitress, the shop and factory girl, the ward politician, the city policeman, the whole "ruck and rabble" of life, so meaningless to the comfortable, unobservant bourgeois, are set forth always with keen knowledge, with a laughing humour, and not infrequently with a tender, smiling pathos. As this panorama of the undenoted faces of the great city passes before the reader, he becomes his own Caliph Haroun-al-Raschid, and New York a teeming Bagdad, full of romance and mystery.

The facility, the light touch of O. Henry, his mastery of the vernacular, his insight into the life of the disinherited, make it needless for him to resort to such inventions as Stevenson's learned Arabian, imaginary author of the "New Arabian Nights." The piquant and picturesque phrasing, the dash of slang, the genial and winning fancy seem to carry off the most fantastic situations. The Touchstone, the jester, the merry-maker has always enjoyed a certain license if he had but the wit not to abuse it. O. Henry's fun is never of the slapstick variety and his pathos never bathos. We are shaken with sad laughter at the many and divers

From "O. Henry's Short Stories," *North American Review* 187 (May 1908). The essay was reprinted verbatim in *Waifs and Strays* (1917), 277–80.

attempts of the park-bench vagabond, Soapy,* to be arrested and sent to the workhouse for the winter months. He eats a meal and does not pay, he steals an umbrella, he accosts unescorted women, but all to no purpose. The police seem to regard him "as a king who could do no wrong." But as he passes by a church the organ music of an anthem vividly recalls his boyhood, stirs the tramp to his depths, and he resolves to turn over a new leaf. He will seek work and be a man. Then the policeman lays a hand upon him, hales him before a magistrate as a vagrant, and the city's swirling machinery of the law sends Soapy to "the Island" after all. And the author smiles with tender compassion over this poor shuttlecock of fate.

With no less humorous kindness does he deal with 'Tildy, "the unwooed drudge," the plain little waitress in an Eighth Avenue chop-house.* All the hurrying *clientèle* of that eating-house admired Aileen, who "was tall, beautiful, lively, gracious, and learned in persiflage." But no one had a word for 'Tildy of the freckles and the hay-coloured hair, until one day a tipsy laundry clerk put his arm round 'Tildy's waist and kissed her. For a brief space that transformed her life. 'Tildy the unnoticed began to bind ribbons in her hair, to prink and to preen after the fashion of daughters of Eve. "A gentleman insulted me today," she modestly informed all her customers. "He put his arm around my waist and kissed me." And as the diners turned upon her the stream of badinage hitherto directed at Aileen alone, 'Tildy's heart swelled in her bosom, "for she saw at last the towers of Romance rise above the horizon of the gray plain in which she had for so long travelled." 'Tildy had a thrilling sensation of fear lest Seeders, the laundry clerk, in a mood of jealous love-madness, rush in and shoot her with a pistol. This she deplored, for no one had shot Aileen for love, and she did not wish to overshadow her friend. When Seeders does come in it is only to apologize, with the plea that he was tipsy. 'Tildy's towers of romance crumbled to earth. The glory fades suddenly, for it was not love at all that actuated Seeders. But Aileen the staunch-hearted comforts 'Tildy in her sorrow, for if Seeders "were any kind of gentleman," she tells her, "he wouldn't of apologized."

"The Trimmed Lamp" is of a piece with "The Four Million," filled with the tragi-comedy of life much as it appeared to Dickens and to

---

*The Cop and the Anthem, in "The Four Million."

*The Brief Début of Tildy, in "The Four Million."

François Villon. In "Heart of the West" the author exploits a vein many have attempted in a short story as well as in the novel—the so-called "wild West." But no one, it is safe to say, has brought so much fun and humour to the Western story. Cattle-king, cowboy, miner, the plains and the chaparral—material of the "dime novel," but all treated with the skill of Maupassant, and a humour Maupassant never dreamed of. The merest sketch of them has a certain substance to it. Yet it is idle to compare O. Henry with anybody. No talent could be more original or more delightful. The combination of technical excellence with whimsical, sparkling wit, abundant humour, and a fertile invention is so rare that the reader is content without comparisons.

Hyder E. Rollins

There is little skirmishing in the body of his stories: it progresses rapidly, and shows a rigid economy of words. O. Henry's mania for suppression of detail comes nearer to equalling that of "Guy de Mopassong" (as he calls him) and of other French writers than does that of any other American writer, not excepting Poe. He had a distinct aim, and he wrote every word with this aim in view. His stories are customarily short: not many run over three thousand words, and the majority contain about two thousand. In a story called "Tommy's Burglar" he satirizes the two-thousand-word story. "The burglar got into the house without much difficulty," he wrote; "because we must have action and not too much description in a two-thousand-word story." And finally the burglar says to Tommy: "Now hurry and let me out, kid. Our two thousand words must be nearly up."

Yet, paradoxical as it may seem, nearly every one of his stories contains one or more digressions, which always seem necessary, and which remind one forcibly of Thackeray. . . . They add the humor for which O. Henry always sought.

His conclusions—they are O. Henry's and no one else's. Children play "crack-the-whip," not for the fun of the long preliminary run, but for the excitement of the final sharp twist that throws them off their feet. So adults read O. Henry, impatiently glancing at the swiftly moving details in pleased expectancy of a surprising ending. The conclusion is an enigma: the author has your nerves all a-quiver until the last sentence. There are few explanations, the surprise comes quickly, and the story is finished. O. Henry is as much a master of the unexpected ending as Frank Stockton was of the insolvable ending, and one must admire his skill. For although these endings are unexpected, the author never makes any statement in the body that can be held against him. On the contrary, the body is a careful preparation for the dénouement, even if the most searching reader can seldom detect it. . . . In "Thimble, Thimble" and several other stories he has adopted the conclusion made

From "O. Henry," *Sewanee Review* 22 (April 1914): 213–32.

famous by "The Lady or the Tiger?" In all the others, the unexpected dénouement occurs, and in many of them are two distinct surprises that will shock the most phlegmatic reader to laughter. The most popular of the double-surprise stories is "The Gift of the Magi." But the continued use of the unexpected ending grows tiresome, and when one sits down and reads all or the greater part of the two hundred and forty-eight short stories, he feels that the biggest surprise O. Henry could have given him would have been a natural, expected ending. But it should be added that his surprise endings have none of the brutal cynicism which distinguishes de Maupassant's "Necklace" and Mérimée's "Mateo Falcone"; his endings, on the other hand, are genuinely humorous, genuinely sympathetic, and genuinely human.

For the sake of vividness the majority of the short stories are told in the first person. Either a character who participated in the action is the narrator; or an outsider tells the story as a participant told it to him; or the story is told apparently in the third person until the author intrudes with his own comments and makes it a first-person narrative. At other times the strict third-person narrative is used; but in whatever way the stories are told, O. Henry is always talking, always explaining his views.

Stages of plot as definite as those in the Shakespearean drama may be located in most of his stories, and they are well adapted for dramatization, as the recent success of *Alias Jimmy Valentine, A Double-Dyed Deceiver*, and others show. This goes to prove that even though O. Henry pokes fun at all rules, he obeys them in the fundamental particulars. He is a clever architectonist in spite of himself. While he prided himself upon his disregard of conventional rules and upon his originality, his technique (if one ignores his manneristic digressions) conforms closely to the very rules that he affected to despise. . . .

The author portrays, in the main, the common people, since he rightly believed that "the four million" are more representative than "the four hundred" of whom contemporary novelists tell us. Into every nook and corner of their lives he takes us, showing us the capitalist, the broker, the underpaid clerk, the underpaid shop-girl, the dweller in flat and tenement, the actor, the 'con' man, the masher, and the rest. His portraits are convincing and realistic, but the characters themselves lack individuality. One feels that O. Henry regarded them as mere types of life, that each acts as the other 3,999,999 would if placed in similar situations, and that he was more interested in life in general than in the study of individualized characters. Out of his attitude to life he formulated this philosophy: "My purpose is to show that in every human heart there is an innate tendency towards a respectable life; that even those who have fallen to the lowest depths in the social scale would, if they could, get back to the higher life; that the innate propensity of human nature is to choose the good instead of the bad."

Life is a mixture of smiles and sniffles and sobs, with the sniffles predominating, declared O. Henry in "The Gift of the Magi." The petty joys, the petty pretentions, the petty worries of his people confirm the statement; but he also has the idea that life is one constant surprise, that the unexpected continually happens. He is, then, a pure romanticist who strives earnestly for realistic effects. Furthermore, he is a broad-minded democrat. . . .

He shows that the shopgirl is human, that she is not all pompadour and chewing gum. He chronicles the meagre, dreary facts of her existence, but he neither patronizes, ridicules, nor preaches. In the powerful "Unfinished Story," . . . he quietly shows the public the cruelty and danger of her social life.

Likewise he condemns the city's pitfalls for innocence, showing that parents, because of indifference, are to blame for their children's missteps; or the wealthy landlord, who provides no parlors for his ill-smelling tenements, thus forcing young girls to entertain in the streets; or the vile pandar, the most depraved of beasts, who preys on half-paid, starving women.

In shams he sees only humor. Shop-girls and workingmen may masquerade as great ladies and great gentlemen and derive pleasure from it, he thinks, without injuring anyone. He understands, too, the code of ethics of the lower classes, and makes us understand it. . . . For the world is not a philanthropic institution. It is a place where the fittest survive, and where the silly goose is picked. The dregs of humanity are treated with a sympathy that pierces to the core of the trouble and sees its solution. And if we accept O. Henry's point of view, never again will we scoff at the flimsy pleasures of the poor: we will try to give them more pleasures.

We see motion pictures of these people. A glimpse, and the fate-driven actors are gone on their unchanging way, not suspecting how near by the wings of romance have swept. They are described by their actions, or by brief, trenchant sentences that are hurled at our heads, as "He wore heliotrope socks, but he looked like Napoleon." . . . Where many writers would waste three hundred words in a vain attempt to catalogue features so as to put an image of a character in one's mind, O. Henry can in twenty-five words paint a clear, unforgettable picture. No other writer has excelled him in the use of suggestive description. Sometimes his characters are described by their unusual surroundings. But since he seldom assumes complete omniscience, it is rare that he attempts any psychological analysis.

Subjectivity of delineation makes our author's characters interesting chiefly as they reveal his views of life, and interest in characters is overshadowed by interest in plots. But for briskness, sympathy, and humor of characterization, O. Henry has few peers.

Just as his plots and his characters are humorous in conception and in treatment, so the most striking trait of O. Henry as a stylist is humor. . . . Humor lightens even the brief descriptions that are scattered through his stories. There is little more tendency to adjectivity in his descriptions of objects than there is in his descriptions of persons. The force and vividness of his descriptions are due rather to unusual words, to an abundance of verbs that suggest sound and movement, to numerous and striking similes and metaphors. . . . Rarely indeed does he write a description that is not redolent of slang.

About O. Henry's diction let me explain in the apt words of one of his characters: "That man had a vocabulary of about 10,000 words and synonyms, which arrayed themselves into contraband sophistries and parables when they came out." His vocabulary, which is really very large, is a servant, not a master. He had absolutely no respect for conventional usage. Words must be coined to express his thought, or the usual meaning of words must be distorted; O. Henry did both without compunction. In addition to this maltreatment of words (and in the mouths of his low characters it becomes mere punning), his vocabulary was stretched by an appalling number of slang words and slang phrases. There can be little doubt that it is the presence of slang that makes O. Henry appeal so strongly to the general reading public to-day; for the public is drawn to a writer who scorns academic niceties of speech and strikes out on a new path, untrammelled by convention. There is no doubt, further, that in his unexcelled mastery of slang our author was quite effective. But taste changes and, what is more pertinent, slang itself changes, so that his constant use of slang will some day count heavily against him. . . .

That O. Henry's piquant audacities of style are attractive is indisputable, but they are certain to lose their piquancy and to lower his rank in literature.

On the other hand, his stories have the absolute harmony of tone so essential to the short-story writer. Harmony is felt even in "Let Me Feel Your Pulse," a short story that opens with broad burlesque and ends in the subtly allegorical. There is, also, a nice proportion, an artistic condensation of details, and a vividness of style that call to mind Poe in America, Mr. Kipling in England, and de Maupassant in France.

Many of his stories are marred by local and contemporaneous allusions that in a few years will be pointless and vague. . . . The slanginess of his style, too, is certain to render him distasteful, perhaps unintelligible, to future readers, just as it has already hindered the translation of his stories into foreign languages. Slang is ephemeral. It will make one a writer for the hour, not a writer for all time. Realizing this, O. Henry had planned a series of new stories. "I want to show the public," he said, "that I can write something new—new for me, I mean—a story without slang, a straightforward dramatic plot treated in a way that will come nearer my ideal of real story-writing." "The Dream," which was to be the first of the new series, was broken off in the middle of a sentence by his death. In its incomplete form it appeared in the September, 1910, *Cosmopolitan,*—a more pathetic "unfinished story" than that of Dulcie.

If necessary, O. Henry's claim to permanence in American literature could be based, like Poe's, on his mastery of the short-story form, for in this respect no other American writer has excelled him. But he has other admirable traits: his frank individuality, his genuine democracy, his whole-souled optimism, his perennial humor, his sympathetic treatment of characteristic American life are irresistible.

For several years O. Henry has been the most popular short-story writer in America, and the "four million" have cried for more stories. It would be absurd to say that the inherent value of his work was not primarily the cause of his popularity, for although slangy mannerisms might attract readers, the latter will not be held if there is not something worth while in the stories themselves; and it seems improbable that the public will soon change from an enthusiastic to a Laodicean temper. To judge O. Henry as if he were a novelist is unfair. He wrote only short stories. He should be judged only by the short-story standard. And although I cannot consider O. Henry great, because of the limitations previously mentioned, yet I do believe that he will always be counted as one of the best American writers of the short story.

Anonymous

Every reader of current American newspapers and magazines is familiar with the name "O. Henry." It is a pen name, concealing the identity of Mr. Sydney Porter, the author of sundry books of short stories. For some time now his reputation has been steadily growing. Throughout the country are people of all sorts and conditions who agree enthusiastically on one point—that no one else can write short stories like O. Henry's. The critics were at first slow to accept his work. The suggestion that he was "a Yankee Maupassant,"* came from his publishers, and did not, for a while, impress the writing fraternity. But now the tables are completely turned. We find William Marion Reedy, of the St. Louis *Mirror*, affirming that, to his thinking, Mr. Porter deserves the very flattering designation conferred upon him; and Henry James Forman, of the editorial staff of the *North American Review*, declares: "He writes with the skill of a Maupassant, and a humour Maupassant never dreamed of." The *Bookman* says, editorially:

"While we are inclined to be conservative in the matter of estimating a contemporary writer, and find exceedingly exasperating these impulsive and extravagant recognitions of 'new Stevensons' and 'new Kiplings,' and 'new de Maupassants' and 'American Dickenses,' the time is past for any restraint in the frank appreciation of the work of the author who signs himself 'O. Henry.' The man is in many respects an extraordinary workman and a consummate artist."

The distinguishing characteristics of O. Henry's work are his journalistic style and his democratic instinct. The two combine, as Francis Hackett, the literary editor of the Chicago *Evening Post* points out, in what is distinctly "an original revelation of life." Mr. Hackett says:

"O. Henry writes with a glitter that is characteristic half of the New

From "A Yankee Maupassant: A Summary of the Criticism of Ten Years Ago. *Waifs and Strays* (1917): 271–276.
*This appellation is an unconscious tribute to the broad Americanism of a man who lived most of his life in North Carolina and Texas.

York *Sun*, half of the *Smart Set.* . . . His scope is restricted. His manner is not discursive. He gets sensational contrasts and assertive colouring into each short story. Allowing for this, he gives us a humorous yet profound understanding of a phase that has not yet been treated before in American art, gives us intimacy with an order of metropolitan characters and circumstances not likely to be better focused or illumined in our generation.

"O. Henry accepts, with a mixture of irony, wit, and sympathy, the distressing fact that a human being can be a clerk, the remarkable fact that a clerk can be a human being. He knows the clerk, knows him in his works and pomps. But there is a peculiarity in O. Henry's attitude toward the clerk. . . . Most literary men are intrenched in culture, obfuscated by it. They take the uncultured morosely or pityingly or mordantly. They discuss those who are not 'élite' as a physician would discuss a case—scientifically, often humanly, interested, but always with a strong sense of the case's defects and deficiencies.

"To O. Henry, on the contrary, the clerk is neither abnormal nor subnormal. He writes of him without patronizing him. He realizes the essential and stupendous truth that to himself the clerk is not pitiable. He takes into account, in other words, the adjustments that every man makes to constitute himself the apex of this sphere—for, after all, there are 800,000,000 apices on this sphere, if we dare to assume that fowl and fishes are not also self-conscious and self-centred.

"When one says 'clerk' one means $15-a-week humanity. O. Henry has specialized in this humanity with loving care, with a Kiplingesque attention to detail. But his is far from the humourless method of Gissing and Merrick, who were no more happy in a boarding-house than Thoreau would have been in the Waldorf-Astoria. O. Henry never forgets the inherent, the unconscious humour in the paradoxes and contrasts of mixed civilization, the crudities of which serve only to exasperate the misplaced and morbid. He is no moral paradoxist, like Shaw, no soured idealist, like Zola, no disgruntled esthete, like Gissing. It is the comedy of the paradoxes and contrasts that he searches and displays—a comedy in which he miraculously keeps the balance, often by the adventitious aid of irony and satire, not sacrificing the clerk to the man of culture, nor, on the other hand, losing perspective in magnifying the clerk."

But O. Henry does not confine himself to the clerk. As Mr. Hackett tells us:

"In one sense Broadway is the spinal column of his art, and the nerve branches cover all Manhattan. He knows the side streets where Mamie boards. He knows Harlem. He knows the narrow-chested flat. He knows the Bowery, Irish and Yiddish. He knows the Tenderloin, cop, panhandler, man about town, sport, bartender, and waiter. He knows Shanley's and Childs's, the lemon-odoured buffet and the French table d'hôte. He knows the sham Bohemia, the real Bohemia. And his stories are starred with little vignettes of the town, paragraphs of unostentatious art that let us see Madison Square, or the White Way, or the Park (over and over again the Park), or the side street in spring-time—all clear as the vision in the crystal.

"O. Henry's triumphs are often triumphs of fancy. He has the sense of the marvellous which belongs to tellers of the short story since the nights of Arabia. And O. Henry can discover in Manhattan the wonder of fable and adventure, the eternal symbols of imagination, the beauty of the jewel in the toad."

To this should be added the tribute of William Marion Reedy:

"As a depicter of the life of New York's four million—club men, fighters, thieves, policemen, touts, shop-girls, lady cashiers, hoboes, actors, stenographers, and what not—O. Henry has no equal for keen insight into the beauties and meannesses of character or motive. Mordant though he be at times his heart is with innocence and right, but he sees the fun that underlies sophistication and selfishness. Not only does he see life, but he sees its problems and in a certain shy-sly way suggests his solutions therefor. His gifts of description are of a surprising variety in method. His pictures, mostly small, intimate greater scopes and deeper vistas. Afraid of pathos, his very promptness to avoid it upon its slightest hint of imminence gives poignancy to the note he thus strikes as by suggestion. He loves the picaroon and the vagabond, and dowers them with vocabularies rich and strange and fanciful. . . . He always has a story. The style or the mood may lure you away from it momentarily, but the tale always asserts its primacy, and its end comes always in just the whimsical way you didn't expect. O. Henry is inexhaustible in quip, in imagery, in quick, sharp, spontaneous invention. In his apparent carelessness we suspect a carefulness, but this is just wherein he is sib to the French short-story writers, chief among them de Maupassant. Della Cruscan critics may disapprove of him for his slang, but until you know his slang, you never know what a powerful vehicle slang can be in the hands of one who can mate it with the echoes from and essences of true literary expression. It is not the slang of George Ade, or Henry M. Blossom, or George V. Hobart. Henry's slang has some of the savour that we find in the archaic vocabulary invented for himself by Chatterton. Its content transcends the capacity of the mere argot of the street. In the American short story to-day O. Henry has demonstrated himself a delightful master, one absolutely unapproachable in swift visualization and penetrative interpretation of life, as any and all of the books now to his credit will show to any one capable of understanding."

Carl Van Doren

"If I could have a thousand years—just one little thousand years—more of life, I might, in that time, draw near enough to true Romance to touch the hem of her robe." These words illuminate the mood and substance of O. Henry. The object of his vision was not history or morals, as with Hawthorne, or the world of dreams, as with Poe, but what he called adventure. "The true adventurer," he said in *The Green Door*, "goes forth aimless and uncalculating to meet and greet unknown fate." One need not be a hero or a philosopher to adventure thus. It is enough to keep an open and hopeful mind, a vigilant eye, and an unfading gusto for the prizes one takes on such a hunt. Like a scientist, the adventurer desires to find his facts in reality, but he wants to meet them at a time when the meeting will seem to have the significance of art. O. Henry was an adventurer of this type and a connoisseur of adventure whose restless avidity in exploring his field of romance appears in the astounding riches of his invention and illustration.

The first impression, indeed, which one is likely to take from a volume of his stories is of his high-spirited profusion. Images, turns, strange conceits, fantastic foolishness pour in upon him like a flood. He is gay, irresponsible, impudent, hoaxing; no writer in the language seems clever immediately after one has been reading O. Henry. Much of his ingenuity is verbal, but it seems almost exhaustless. A single word will set him running in a riot of language, as when, for instance, in *Sisters of the Golden Circle*, he has spoken of a "Bride." "Capitalize it, friend typo—that last word—word of words in the epiphany of life and love. The scent of the flowers, the booty of the bee, the primal drip of spring waters, the overture of the lark, the twist of lemon peel on the cocktail of creation— such is the bride. Holy is the wife; revered the mother; galliptious is the summer girl—but the bride is the certified check among the wedding presents that the gods send in when man is married to mortality." In the midst of slang he can rise, as in *Hearts and Crosses*, to an image of sudden splendid pomp: "And the days, with Sundays at their head, formed into

*From "O. Henry," *Texas Review 2* (April 1917): 248–59.

hebdomadal squads; and the weeks, captained by the full moon, closed ranks into menstrual companies carrying 'Tempus fugit' on their banners; and the months marched on toward the vast camp-ground of the years." Or again he commits one of those swift exaggerations by which wit takes the breath as poetry does: "My two Kentucky bays went for the horizon until it came sailing in so fast you wanted to dodge it like a clothes-line." (*Cupid à la Carte.*)

The same irresponsible opulence shows in his plots. Not ignorance of the austere bounds of probability but chuckling unconcern for the timid conventions of realism lies behind his romancing. Some have found in O. Henry's capricious plots the defect of the recluse who writes about a world of other men. There is no reason, however, to think that he regarded his strange tales as normal. He wrote to please himself and the magazines that paid him.

A Night in New Arabia thoroughly illustrates the point. Old Jacob Spraggins, a retired malefactor with a conscience which impels him to charity, has a daughter Celia, who loves the grocer's boy. This, of course, is only a new version of the case in *The Squire of Low Degree*. And O. Henry, like the nameless medieval poet, takes the wish of his readers for a guide. After a period of suspense much briefer than the Squire's seven years in Lombardy, the grocer's boy, having suddenly been made rich and worthy by certain expiatory thousands from his sweetheart's father, is made richer by the girl herself. Such an outcome is quite in the popular tradition: so is Celia's stooping to a parlor maid's cap and apron to conquer the modesty which she knew would never aspire to an heiress. Moreover, as the title of the story makes clear, O. Henry was deliberately parodying, with the sympathy of knowledge, *The Arabian Nights*. Indeed, that great fountain head of romance comes to one's mind again and again in a reading of O. Henry. Not only verbal reminiscences, which abound, and the atmosphere of the swarming city suggest it, but a certain popular quality in the plots, as if not a man but a generation had invented them. They seem too varied to have come from one head, and their bewildering conclusions, no matter by what breathless route arrived at, generally fulfill the desires of a whole populace.

This quality of fulfillment, of course, lies at the very heart of popular romance. It is the supernatural providence of the world of fiction, and the changes which have come over the fashions in heroes and manners have not essentially altered it. Heracles, happening by, wrests Alcestis from the death that has been decreed; St. George appears just at the moment of despair and defends the English against the horrible Saracens; exactly at the right instant, in *The Church with an Overshot Wheel*, the stream of flour sifts down through the gallery floor and reveals the lost Aglaia to her father. Deity, saint, coincidence,—something must furnish the element of wonder and the desired miracle. One should not be misled by the fact that new names have been given to the mysterious agent. Named or nameless, it has existed and exists to accomplish in art the defeated aspirations of reality. It is O. Henry's most powerful aid, brilliant in his endings, everywhere pervasive. His strong virtue was the genius to select from the apparent plane of fact whatever might bear testimony to the presence in life of this fiery spirit of romance. By this he spoke to the public with something of the authority of a priest of their well-trusted providence. . . .

Thus in language, as in plots, it appears that he was close to the general audience which took his art for its amusement. And the evidences of that kinship have led many persons into cant about his universal humanity. As a matter of fact, it was his curious search for romance, quite as much as his humanity, which took him into every hole and cranny of the world he worked in. He was no indiscriminate lover of the human race, swollen to quick tears and tenderness at the mere proximity of a crowd. He was not even a hail fellow, back-clapping and vociferous, but shy, chary of intimates, too much an ironist for general embraces. His whole life was a spectatorship. He was often obliged to deny what was said of him as soon as he took the public fancy, that he had been engaged in every calling he wrote about. Nor should critics who thus complimented him on his experience at the expense of his insight, have needed the facts of his career to obviate such a judgment. His work alone carries the proof that he was a spectator. Few workers could have mastered the details of so many crafts as he learned how to use, in fiction, by his observant loafing. Moreover, when one comes to think of it, almost all his stories have at least one end in the street or some public place, where he might have seen it and deduced the rest. And, finally, there was in his temper a certain balance arising out of a philosophy which, whether natural or deliberate, is invariably a detached philosophy, a spectator's reading of life.

N. Bryllion Fagin

Is it not a propitious time to attempt a revaluation of our short-story dogmas? What is the contribution of O. Henryism to our national letters and to the short story as a form of literary expression? How great an artist really was William Sidney Porter, the founder of the Cult? Is it sacrilege to attempt to answer these questions?

O. Henry left us more than two hundred and fifty stories. In the decade before his death he turned out an average of twenty-five stories a year. Mr. William Johnston, an editor of the New York *World*, relates the struggles of O. Henry in trying to live up to a three-year contract he had with that paper calling for a story a week. There were weeks when O. Henry would haunt the hotels and cafés of New York in a frantic search for material, and there were times when the stories could not be produced on time and O. Henry would sit down and write the most ingenious excuses. Needless to state that O. Henry's stories bear all the marks of this haste and anxiety. Nearly all of them are sketchy, reportorial, superficial, his gift of felicitous expression "camouflaging" the poverty of theme and character. The best of them lack depth and roundness, often disclosing a glint of a sharp idea unworked, untransmuted by thought and emotion.

Of his many volumes of stories, "The Four Million" is without doubt the one which is most widely known. It was his bold challenge to the world that he was the discoverer—even though he gave the census taker due credit—of four million people instead of four hundred in America's metropolis that first attracted attention and admiration. The implication was that he was imbued with the purpose of unbaring the lives of these four million and especially of the neglected lower classes. A truly admirable and ambitious self-assignment. And so we have "The Four Million." But to what extent was he successful in carrying out his assignment. How much of the surging, shifting, pale, rich, orderly, chaotic, and wholly incongruous life of New York is actually pulsating in the twenty-five little stories collected in the volume?

From O. Henryism," *Short Story-Writing: An Art or a Trade?* (New York: Thomas Seltzer, Inc, 1923).

What is the first one, "Tobin's Palm," if not a mere long-drawn-out jest? Is it anything more than an anecdote exploiting palmistry as a "trait"—to use another technical term—or point? It isn't New York, nor Tobin, nor any other character, that makes this story interesting. It is O. Henry's trick at the end. The prophecy is fulfilled, after all, in such an unexpected way, and we are such satisfied children!

What is the second story, the famous "Gift of the Magi"? We have discussed it and analyzed it in our texts and lauded it everywhere. How much of the life of the four million does it hold up to us? It is better than the first story; yes, much better. But why is it a masterpiece? Not because it tries to take us into the home of a married couple attempting to exist in our largest city on the husband's income of $20 per week. No, that wouldn't make it famous. Much better stories of poverty have been written, much more faithful and poignant, and the great appreciative public does not even remember them. It is the wizard's mechanics, his stunning invention—that's the thing! Della sells her hair and buys a fob for hubby's watch; while at the same time hubby sells his watch and buys her a comb. But you don't know all this until they get together for the presentation of the gifts, and then you gasp. We call this working criss-cross, a plot of cross purposes. In this story we usually overlook entirely one little thing—the last paragraph. It really is superfluous and therefore constitutes a breech of technique. We preach against preaching. Tell your story, we say, and stop. "Story" is synonymous with *action*. O. Henry didn't stop—so that even he was sometimes a breaker of laws. But this uncomfortable thought doesn't really have to be noted! . . .

Thus an examination of O. Henry's work by any one not blinded by hero-worship and popular esteem, discloses at best an occasional brave peep at life, hasty, superficial and dazzlingly flippant; an idea, raw, unassimilated, timidly works its way to the surface only to be promptly suppressed by a hand skilled in producing sensational effects. At its worst, his work is no more than a series of cheap jokes renovated and expanded. But over all there is the unmistakable charm of a master trickster, of a facile player with incidents and words. . . .

Just how long O. Henry's stories will live and his influence predominate is a prediction no one can safely undertake to venture at this time. It depends upon how long we will permit his influence to predominate. The great mass of our reading public will continue to venerate any writer as long as our official censors continue to write panegyrics of him, and our colleges to hold him up as a model. The literary aspirants coming to us for instruction are recruited largely from among this indiscriminating public. Sooner or later, however, we must realize that the American Maupassant has not yet come and that those who foisted the misnomer upon William Sidney Porter have done the American short story a great injury. Before this most popular of our literary forms can come into its own the O. Henry cult must be demolished. O. Henry himself must be assigned his rightful position—among the tragic figures of America's potential artists whose genius was distorted and stifled by our prevailing commercial and infantile conception of literary values. Our short story itself must be cleansed; its paint and powder removed; its fluffy curls shorn—so that our complacent reader may be left to contemplate its "rag and a bone and a hank of hair."

When the great American short-story master finally does come, no titles borrowed from the French or any other nationality will be necessary and adequate. His own worth will forge his crown, and his worth will not be measured in tricks and stunts and puzzles and cleverness. His sole object will not be to spring effects upon his unwary reader. His will be sincere honest art—with due apologies for this obvious contradiction in terms, for art can be nothing but sincere!—a result of deep, genuine emotions and an overflowing imagination. His very soul will be imbued with the simple truth, so succinctly put by Mr. H. L. Mencken, that "the way to sure and tremendous effects is by the route of simplicity, naturalness, and ingenuousness."

Archibald Henderson

It is easy to see that O. Henry is a "contemporary classic." One good reason is because I say so. Other good reasons are because other good critics, scattered all about, say so. Still another reason is that his publishers, despite their natural objection to singling out certain stories as "best stories" and so cutting in on the "general works," have finally decided that they can no longer resist the clamorous demand, voiced now steadily and insistently ever since Will Porter died in 1910, for a single-volume collection of his best short-stories. They appear now under the title of *Selected Stories from O. Henry*—a volume which contains twenty-five stories. The editor, Professor C. Alphonso Smith, head of the Department of English in the United States Naval Academy, concludes his introduction with this sensible observation, which wholly disarms criticism:

> The twenty-five stories that follow are arranged chronologically and represent O. Henry's chief regional interests, his favorite themes, his varying technique, his humor and pathos, and the four distinctive stages of his career. That they are the best twenty-five stories that he wrote no two readers would probably agree. With the exception of perhaps six of these stories substitutes equally good but hardly better could probably be found. When it is remembered that the ten lists of O. Henry's best stories resulted in a vote of sixty-two best, it can hardly be expected that my own choice of twenty-five will escape the dissent of the critic. If censure be mingled with dissent, no harm will be done; a closer study of O. Henry's work will be ample recompense for both censor and censured. . . .

O. Henry is fortunate in having so enthusiastic a biographer, so encomiastic an interpreter. With an admiration for O. Henry that is almost unbounded, the editor presents to us only the most nearly impeccable of O. Henry's writings. If this consistent panegyrism gives

From "O. Henry—A Contemporary Classic," *South Atlantic Quarterly* 22 (July 1923): 270–78.

Professor Smith the air of the special pleader, if O. Henry's gravest faults are gloryed over by being ignored and so concealed, no grave damage is done. Delightful as is much of O. Henry's writing, unparalled [sic] as time-killers as are so many of his stories, not even his most ardent admirer would claim for a considerable part of his writing anything more than a brief, hectic life. Written for current "popular" magazines, dashed off frequently under high pressure while the editor with bull-dog tenacity waited the long hours in Porter's own room for the manuscript to be completed, many of these stories deserve to be classified as cheap, trivial, insignificant, ephemeral. After the tumult and shouting have passed, a careful critical commentary would greatly clarify the issues— and help us to assay the output of the Great O. Henry Mine, to separate the dross from the gold. . . .

Meantime, let us acknowledge with fitting gratitude that Professor Smith is O. Henry's best interpreter, if not his acutest critic. In addition to his *O. Henry Biography*, other important essays by Professor Smith on O. Henry have appeared. At my invitation, he delivered a notable address on O. Henry at Raleigh in 1914; an excellent survey of O. Henry's career appeared in the *World's Work*; a recent essay, published by the Martin Hoyt Company, and soon to appear in the Library of Southern Literature, is the astutest interpretation of O. Henry as literary artist which has come from Professor Smith's pen.

Van Wyck Brooks

. . . Meanwhile, the cheaper magazines and the literary syndicates, with which Norris and Dreiser themselves were connected in a way, produced an author of their own, the genius of the Sunday supplements, in the North Carolinian who called himself "O. Henry." With his neatness and brightness, his rapid effects, mechanical often, sometimes crude, with his settings in all-night restaurants and furnished rooms, with his characters, shop-girls, policemen, clerks, chorus girls and men from "home," he seemed perfectly suited for readers of the "all-fiction" press. *Describing himself as a "fictionist," addicted to the "writing game,"* as worried as a "retail butcher" about his bills, he worked like a night-copy writer, in shirt sleeves, at his desk, turning out stories on contract once a week. With a curiously colourless personality, he had something in common with both Kipling and Stevenson, the kings of the world of romance in 1900, and it pleased him also to think of the town in terms of a "new Arabian Nights,"—he presented himself as the Caliph of Bagdad-on-the-Subway. He pictured the glittering city as he knew the provinces wished to see it, as "inhabited by four million mysterious strangers" to whom almost anything might happen between sunrise and sunrise, and who had come from Topeka or Nome, from Jackson, Topaz or Cactus City, drawn by the love of money, by ambition or the stage. Some had come for the art schools there or because of the cheap excursion rates or the personal column advertisements or an annual convention, and O. Henry wrote about them for the "folks back home" who liked to share vicariously in their imagined adventures. He wrote for the "man who sits smoking," as he said, with his "slippered feet on another chair" and the woman who "snatches the paper . . . while boiling greens." He was intent on discovering for himself what he called the city's soul and meaning, and with all his banality he sometimes succeeded in this. For, with his unusual gift of invention, he conveyed a real feeling of the charm of New York, its romance and its multitudinous humanity and magic. . . .

From "New York: O. Henry," *The Confident Years* (New York: Dutton, 1952): 275–76.

172

A handful of O. Henry's stories dealing with Latin America and with Texas, where he had encountered desperados and witnessed a belated war with cattle-thieves, were among the best he was to write and by no means all trick stories of the artificial variety he produced so often. But, good as a few of these tales were, the "Westerns" inevitably recalled Bret Harte, as the stories of New Orleans suggested Cable and the Spanish-American stories Richard Harding Davis, while New York was really O. Henry's own,—it seemed to belong to him by right,—although it was the field of so many story-tellers. This was because of his attitude towards it, the fresh curiosity with which he approached it, his feeling of wonder about it, on certain levels, all of which made for a literary virtue transcending his occasional cheapness and coarseness, his sometimes unbearable jocularity and meretricious effects. He was like his own Raggles in *The Trimmed Lamp* who came to the city to study its note, to taste it and determine its place in the scale of cities, and who found himself baffled and bewildered at times by its ruthless, ironical, sphinx-like face, illegible, unnatural, glittering, serene and chill. O. Henry sought for its particular essence and flavour. His feeling of the mystery of the city and the will with which he probed it dignified some of the stories he wrote about New York. . . .

For O. Henry shared Dickens's vision of a happy domesticity, sharing as well his feeling for the city streets, for the crowds and the lights of the metropolis, the night-blooming cereus unfolding its dead-white heavy-odoured petals. With his brisk and often too obvious stories, too hard or too soft in the wrong way, O. Henry was occasionally an artist, nevertheless, who escaped from the mechanical formulas of the cheap magazines, the last to vindicate Howells's belief that the "more smiling aspects of life" were the most characteristic of America, as no doubt they had been.

Notes to Part 3

1. F. L. Pattee, *The Development of the American Short Story* (New York: Harper and Brothers, 1923), 360–63.
2. N. Bryllion Fagin, *Short Story Writing: An Art or a Trade?* (New York: Thomas Seltzer, Inc., 1923), 41.
3. Pattee, 364. Mrs. Gerrould's lecture was delivered in Princeton and reported in the Philadelphia *Public Ledger*, 23 July 1916, and also reprinted in the *New York Times Book Review* of the same date. She held up Hawthorne, Henry James, Bret Harte, and G. W. Cable as masters of American short fiction but saw nothing of value in the writings of either Porter or Poe. Pattee's essay,

"The Journalization of American Literature: the Work of O. Henry" first appeared in the *Unpopular Review* (April 1916): 374–94, and was later reprinted as a concluding chapter on O. Henry in his book on the short story cited above.

4. "The Amazing Genius of O. Henry": originally published in his *Essays and Literary Studies* (1916), this essay was reprinted the following year in *Waifs and Strays*, 171–95. Leacock's swipe at Pattee and Gerrould appeared in "O. Henry and his Critics," *New Republic* 9 (2 December 1916): 121. See also W. T. Larned, "Professor Leacock and the Other Professors," in *New Republic* 9, (13 January 1917): 299. Mr. Larned gently chided Leacock for his counterattack on the professors, reminding him that Americans had a tendency to "canonize too quickly, without the tempering aid of *advocatus diaboli*"; that they enthroned overnight idols with flashy tricks of style and then kicked them to pieces shortly afterward.

5. See A. H. Quinn et al., *The Literature of the American People* (New York, 1951), 838; and R. E. Spiller et al., *Literary History of the United States* (New York, 1953), 744, 1385.

6. See Austin M. Wright, *The American Short Story in the Twenties* (Chicago, 1961), 6; the other book was, of course, Langford's *Alias O. Henry* (1957).

7. "O. Henry's Short Stories," *Waifs and Strays*, 277–80. Forman's later essays in the *Reader's Digest* as late as the 1940s show how fond memorials to Porter kept his O. Henry image fresh.

8. "O. Henry," *The Sewanee Review* 22 (April 1914): 222. Having established this postulate, Rollins filled the ten remaining pages of his essay with further validating evidence to show that, as a technical artist, O. Henry repeatedly strove to achieve in his stories Poe's ideal of the "single effect" and that he generally succeeded by employing Poe's own rhetorical devices, occasionally even more skillfully than the master himself.

Chronology

1862   William Sydney Porter born, second son of Dr. Algernon and Mary Jane Porter, at Greensboro, North Carolina, on 11 September.

1865   At mother's death, moves with father and brother into home of Grandmother and Aunt "Lina" Porter.

1867–1876   Develops talent for writing, drawing, literary appreciation, and storytelling under Miss "Lina's" dedicated private schooling.

1879   Begins working in Uncle Clark's drugstore as pharmacist apprentice.

1881   Licensed to practice pharmacy by North Carolina Pharmaceutical Association, 30 August.

1882–1884   Leaves home as guest of Dr. and Mrs. James Hall on visit to their four sons in southwest Texas. Remains as houseguest of Mr. and Mrs. Richard Hall at their cattle ranch in La Salle County; gains detailed knowledge of cattle raising in raw frontier country and develops talents as cartoonist and writer of humorous anecdotal letters.

1884–1886   Moves to Austin, living as house-guest of the Joseph Harrell family; keeps up his interest in sketch-writing and drawing along with choir-singing and other youthful social activities and part-time employment.

1887–1889   Marries Athol Estes, step-daughter of P. G. Roach, prominent Austin grocer; begins steady employment as draftsman in Texas Land Office, headed by Mr. Richard Hall, now Land Commissioner of Texas. Son born (1888) but dies shortly after birth. Second child, Margaret born (1889); Athol's health declining alarmingly.

1891   Loses post in Land Office when Richard Hall fails to win gubernatorial nomination; secures job as teller in First National Bank of Austin.

1894   Still as bank teller, begins publishing, in March, his own humor weekly, *The Rolling Stone*, which survives exactly one year; loses bank job in December upon disclosure of shortages in his accounts; indicted to stand trial in following July.

1895   Grand Jury returns no-bill, apparently closing case; but orders from Washington secured to reopen it in following year; secures job as feature writer on Houston *Post*, now writing many anecdotal sketches during ensuing six months.

1896   Arrested in Houston (February); en route to stand trial in Austin, switches instead to New Orleans and shortly afterwards moves on to Honduras; secures in both environs abundant factual data for future development in later fiction.

1897   Returns to Austin in January. Athol, desperately ill, dies 25 July. Awaiting trial, moves with Margaret into her grandparents' home; continues writing and receives publication acceptance of first story, "Miracle of Lava Canyon," from McClure Company in December.

1898–1901   Tried and convicted, February; with motion for appeal rejected, begins serving, in April, five-year sentence at Federal Penitentiary in Columbus, Ohio. While serving as Prisoner No. 30664 launches professional career as short-story writer, producing more than a dozen stories published under various pen names in national magazines; released on good behavior after serving shortened term of three years.

1901–1902   Lives for short time with Roaches and daughter Margaret in Pittsburgh; writes features and stories for both the Pittsburgh *Dispatch* and for New York magazines. At urging of Gilman Hall, editor of *Ainslee's*, moves to New York; quickly gains fame in magazine world under new pseudonym O. Henry, though largely unknown to public.

1903   Signs contract with New York *Sunday World* for weekly feature story; produces more than one hundred of these during ensuing two years and achieves nationwide fame.

1904   Publishes first book, *Cabbages and Kings*, a loosely unified collection of stories based on his experiences in Central America.

1906   In April publishes *The Four Million*, a collection of twenty-five of his most famous New York stories, which bring him worldwide acclaim.

1907–1910   Marries childhood girl friend, Sara Lindsay Coleman; vainly attempts to combine normal family life (including Margaret) with frenzied writing activity. Despite flagging energy, publishes seven more volumes of collected short stories and, collaborating with F. P. Adams, tries unsuccessfully to write stage plays based on his stories.

1910   After serious illness of more than six months, dies at Polyclinic Hospital, New York, on 5 June; buried in Asheville, North Carolina.

1910–1920   Five more posthumous single-volume collections, plus complete edition of his *Works* and authorized biography written by C. Alphonso Smith (1916) published by Doubleday.

Selected Bibliography

Books

Cabbages and Kings. New York: McClure, Phillips, 1904; London: Hodder & Stoughton, 1916.

The Four Million. New York: McClure, Phillips, 1906; London: Nash, 1916.

The Trimmed Lamp. New York: McClure, Phillips, 1907; London: Hodder & Stoughton, 1916.

Heart of the West. New York: McClure, 1907; London: Nash, 1916.

The Voice of the City. New York: McClure, 1908; London: Nash, 1916.

The Gentle Grafter. New York: McClure, 1908; London: Nash, 1916.

Roads of Destiny. New York: Doubleday, Page, 1909; London: Nash, 1916.

Options. New York & London: Harper, 1909; London: Nash, 1916.

Strictly Business. New York: Doubleday, Page, 1910; London: Nash, 1916.

Whirligigs. New York: Doubleday, Page, 1910; London: Hodder & Stoughton, 1916.

Sixes and Sevens. Garden City: Doubleday, Page, 1911; London: Hodder & Stoughton, 1916.

Rolling Stones. Garden City: Doubleday, Page, 1912; London: Nash, 1916.

Waifs and Strays. Garden City: Doubleday, Page, 1917; London: Hodder & Stoughton, 1920.

O. Henryana. Garden City: Doubleday, Page, 1920.

Postscripts, edited by Florence Stratton. New York & London: Harper, 1923.

O. Henry Encore, edited by Mary S. Harrell. Dallas: Upshaw, 1936; New York: Doubleday, Doran, 1939; London: Hodder & Stoughton, 1939.

Collections

The Complete Writings of O. Henry, 14 volumes. Garden City: Doubleday, Page, 1917.

The Biographical Edition, 18 volumes. Garden City: Doubleday, Doran, 1929.

The Complete Works of O. Henry, 2 volumes. Garden City: Doubleday, 1953.

Letters

Letters to Lithopolis, from O. Henry to Mabel Wagnalls. Garden City; Doubleday, Page, 1922.

Clarence Ghodes, "Some Letters by O. Henry," *South Atlantic Quarterly,* 38 (January 1939): 31–39.

Bibliographies

Paul S. Clarkson, *A Bibliography of William Sydney Porter*. Caldwell, Idaho: Caxton, 1938.

Richard C. Harris, *William Sydney Porter.O. Henry): A Reference Guide*. Boston: G. K. Hall, 1980.

Biographies

C. F. Richardson, "O. Henry and New Orleans," *The Bookman*, 39 (May 1914): 281–287.

C. Alphonso Smith, *O. Henry Biography*. New York: Doubleday, Page, 1916.

Sara Lindsay Coleman, *Wind of Destiny*. New York: Doubleday, Page, 1916.

Al Jennings, *Through the Shadows With O. Henry*. London: Duckworth, 1923.

Frances G. Maltby, *The Dimity Sweetheart*. Richmond, Va: Dietz Printing Company, 1930.

Robert H. Davis and Arthur B. Maurice, *The Caliph of Bagdad*. New York: Appleton, 1931.

William Wash Williams, *The Quiet Lodger of Irving Place*. New York: Dutton, 1936.

J. A. Lomax, "Henry Steger and O. Henry," *Southwest Review*, 24 (April 1939): 299–316.

Trueman O'Quinn, "O. Henry in Austin," *Southwestern Historical Quarterly*, 43 (October 1939): 143–157.

E. Hudson Long, *O. Henry, The Man And His Work*. Philadelphia: University of Pennsylvania Press, 1949.

Gerald Langford, *Alias O. Henry: A Biography of William Sydney Porter*. New York: Macmillan, 1957.

Ethel Stephens Arnett, *O. Henry from Polecat Creek*. Greensboro, N.C.: Piedmont Press, 1962.

Eugene Current-Garcia, *O. Henry*. New York: Twayne, 1965.

Richard O'Connor, *O. Henry: The Legendary Life of William S. Porter*. Garden City: Doubleday, 1970.

David Stuart, *O. Henry: A Biography of William Sydney Porter*. Chelsey, Michigan: Scarborough House, 1990.

References

Deming Brown, "O. Henry in Russia," *Russian Review*, 12 (October 1953): 253–258.

Brown, *Soviet Attitudes Toward American Writing*. Princeton, N.J.: Princeton University Press, 1962, pp. 230–238.

Paul S. Clarkson, "A Decomposition of Cabbages and Kings," *American Literature*, 7 (May 1935): 195–202.

Selected Bibliography

L. W. Courtney, "O. Henry's Case Reconsidered," *American Literature*, 14 (January 1943): 361–371.

Edward C. Echols, "O. Henry and the Classics—II," *Classical Journal*, 44 (October 19–May 1949): 209– 210.

Echols, "O. Henry's 'Shaker of Attic Salt,'" *Classical Journal*, 43 (October 1947–May 1948): 488– 489.

B. M. Ejxenbaum, *O. Henry and the Theory of the Short Story*, translated, with notes and a postscript, by I. R. Titunik (Ann Arbor: University of Michigan Press, 1968).

N. Bryllion Fagin, *Short Story Writing: An Art or a Trade?* New York: Seltzer, 1923, 36–42.

H. J. Forman, "O. Henry's Short Stories," *North American Review*, 187 (May 1908): 781–783.

Joseph H. Gallegly, "Backgrounds and Patterns of O. Henry's Texas Bodman Stories," *Rice Institute Pamphlet*, 42 (October 1955): 1–32.

Gallegly, *From Alamo Plaza to Jack Harris's Saloon: O. Henry and the Southwest He knew* (The Hague: Mouton, 1970).

William B. Gates, "O. Henry and Shakespeare," *Shakespeare Association Bulletin*, 19 (January 1944): 20–25.

Archibald Henderson, "O. Henry—A Contemporary Classic," *South Atlantic Quarterly*, 22 (July 1923): 270–278.

F. M. Kerchville, "O. Henry and Don Alfonso: Spanish in the Work of an American Writer," *New Mexico Quarterly Review*, 1 (November 1931): 367–388.

Stephen Leacock, "O. Henry and his Critics," *New Republic*, 9 (2 December 1916): 120–122.

Dan McAllister, "Negligently, Perhaps; Criminally, Never," *South Atlantic Quarterly*, 51 (October 1952): 562–573.

Gilbert Millstein, "O. Henry's New Yorkers and Today's," *New York Times Magazine*, 9 September 1962, pp. 36–38, 132–138.

Raoul Narcy, "O. Henry Through French Eyes," *Littell's Living Age*, 303 (11 October 1919): 86–88.

F. L. Pattee, *The Development of the American Short Story*. New York & London: Harper, 1923, pp. 357–376.

Pattee, "The Journalization of American Literature," *Unpopular Review*, 7 (April-June 1917): 374–394.

L. W. Payne, Jr., "The Humor of O. Henry," *Texas Review*, 4 (October 1918): 18–37.

H. T. Peck, "The American Story Teller," *The Bookman*, 31 (April 1910): 131–137.

Hyder E. Rollins, "O. Henry," *Sewanee Review*, 22 (April 1914): 213–232.

William Saroyan, "O What a Man Was O. Henry," *Kenyon Review*, 24 (1967): 671–675.

Papers

Greensboro Public Library, Greensboro, North Carolina, contains the most complete collection of Porter's papers.

Index

About the Author

Eugene Current-García is Hargis Professor Emeritus of American Literature at Auburn University. He helped to found the *Southern Humanities Review* in 1967 and served as editor and co-editor until 1979. His book publications include *What is the Short Story?*, *O. Henry, Realism and Romanticism in Fiction*, *Short Stories of the Western World*, and *American Short Stories Before 1850*. Since the 1940s, his articles and reviews have appeared in such journals as *American Literature, American Quarterly, Studies in Short Fiction*, the *Southern Review*, and *Mississippi Quarterly*, among others.

The Editor

General Editor Gordon Weaver earned his B.A. in English at the University of Wisconsin-Milwaukee in 1961; his M.A. in English at the University of Illinois, where he studied as a Woodrow Wilson Fellow, in 1962; and his Ph.D. in English and creative writing at the University of Denver in 1970. He is author of several novels, including *Count a Lonely Cadence, Give Him a Stone, Circling Byzantium,* and most recently *The Eight Corners of the World* (1988). Many of his numerous short stories are collected in *The Entombed Man of Thule, Such Waltzing Was Not Easy, Getting Serious, Morality Play, A World Quite Round,* and *Men Who Would Be Good* (1991). Recognition of his fiction includes the St. Lawrence Award for Fiction (1973), two National Endowment for the Arts Fellowships (1974, 1989), and the O. Henry First Prize (1979). He edited *The American Short Story, 1945–1980: A Critical History,* and is currently editor of *Cimarron Review.* He is professor of English at Oklahoma State University. Married, and the father of three daughters, he lives in Stillwater, Oklahoma.

DATE DUE

DEMCO 38-296

André Messager

Drawing of André Messager, reproduced from Jean Huré, *Musiciens contemporains*. Paris: Editions Maurice Senart, 1923.

André Messager

A BIO-BIBLIOGRAPHY

John Wagstaff

Bio-Bibliographies in Music, Number 33
DONALD L. HIXON, Series Adviser

GREENWOOD PRESS
New York • Westport, Connecticut • London

...tion Data

Wagstaff, John
    André Messager : a bio-bibliography / John Wagstaff.
      p.   cm. – (Bio-bibliographies in music, ISSN 0742-6968 ; no.
33)
    Includes bibliographical references and index.
    ISBN 0-313-25736-1 (alk. paper)
    1. Messager, André, 1853-1929 – Bibliography. 2. Messager, André,
1853-1929 – Discography.   I. Title.   II. Series.
    ML134.M539W3   1991
    016.78'092 – dc20   90-22928

British Library Cataloguing in Publication Data is available.

Library of Congress Catalog Card Number: 90-22928
ISBN: 0-313-25736-1
ISSN: 0742-6968

First published in 1991

Greenwood Press, 88 Post Road West, Westport, CT 06881
An imprint of Greenwood Publishing Group, Inc.

Printed in the United States of America

The paper used in this book complies with the
Permanent Paper Standard issued by the National
Information Standards Organization (Z39.48-1984).

10 9 8 7 6 5 4 3 2 1

Copyright Acknowledgments

The author and publisher gratefully acknowledge the following sources for
permission to use excerpted materials:

Le Directeur Général des Archives de France, for a paper relating to the
ballet *Les deux pigeons* located in the archives of the Paris Opèra.

La Bibliothèque Nationale, for extracts from letters by André Messager.

Every reasonable effort has been made to trace the owners of copyright
materials in this book, but in some instances this has proven impossible.
The author and publisher will be glad to receive information leading to
more complete acknowledgments in subsequent printings of the book and in
the meantime extend their apologies for any omissions.

For my parents

Contents

Acknowledgments

Many individuals and institutions have helped in the making of
this book: in Paris the staff of the Bibliothèque Nationale
(including the Phonothèque Nationale) showed much interest in the
project, and were consistently helpful, as were the staff of the
Archives Nationales. I am particularly grateful to both these
institutions for permission to quote from their collections of
Messager's correspondence. The staff of the Bibliothèque de
l'Opéra granted me access to their collection of Messager's
manuscript scores, and a number of useful secondary sources were
supplied by the Bibliothèque de l'Arsenal (Paris). My thanks
also go to M. Jean Gominet of the Bibliothèque Municipale,
Montluçon, for alerting me to a number of useful references and
for providing copies of them. Mme Jacqueline Dumora-Messager,
the composer's grand-daughter, patiently answered questions
concerning her distinguished grandfather.

In the United Kingdom, the collections of the British
Library, London, and the Bodleian Library, Oxford, once more
proved invaluable, and I am indebted to Chappell and Company (now
part of International Music Publishers) for allowing me access to
their archives. The staff of the U.K. National Sound Archive
provided much assistance in connection with the discography, and
the book would have been much poorer without their help. Patrick
O'Connor very kindly provided extra discographical information.

Finally but no less importantly, I am grateful to Christina
Bashford for her constant help in bringing this project to
fruition; and to JoAnne Edwards for patiently typing it.

Abbreviations

The following abbreviations are used in this Bio-bibliography:

arr.	arranged
c.	circa
Co.	Company
comp.	compiler
dir.	directed by
ed.	edited by; edition
eds.	editors
Eng.	English
et al	and others
etc.	and other things
f.	folio
ibid.	in the same place
idem	the same
jnr	junior
M.(M.)	Monsieur (Messieurs)
Mlle	Mademoiselle
Mme	Madame
ms	manuscript
no.,nos	numbers
op.	opus
op.cit.	work cited
orch.	orchestra(l)
p.,pp.	page(s)
passim	in passing
pseud.	pseudonym
rev.	revised
s.l.	sine loco [no place]
s.d.	sine dato [no date]
St	Saint
trans.	translation; translator
U.K.	United Kingdom
U.S.(A.)	United States (of America)
vol(s).	volume(s)

Introduction

Why a Bio-bibliography of André Messager? Firstly, and most
obviously, because in spite of enjoying a great reputation in his
own day, he is a musician whose life and music have been largely
unexplored over the past four decades: such a decline in
fortunes is in itself worth some explanation. Secondly, the
bio-bibliographical medium is well-suited to a study of a rather
neglected figure, since it provides essential, comprehensive and
up-to-date information in a convenient format which, it is hoped,
will provide other researchers with a starting point from which
to begin their own studies without having to engage in the
time-consuming bibliographical and discographical work which
might otherwise tempt them to put the subject aside in favour of
more immediately "accessible" musicians. Such an approach is
particularly tempting in Messager's case since, on the surface at
least, he was writing uncontroversial music in a traditional
idiom at a time when great innovations were occurring in the
contemporary musical language: and, history being what it is, we
are (arguably) still inclined to see the music of that time in an
"evolutionary" way, and to concentrate more on the innovative
elements of it when in reality the more "mainstream" works being
produced at the same time are just as worthy of our attention.
     The two completed French biographies of Messager both have a
descriptive sub-title: Michel Augé-Laribé entitles his study
<u>André Messager: musicien de théâtre</u>, emphasising the importance
in Messager's output of the operetta and opéra-comique, while
Henry Février calls his work <u>André Messager: mon maître, mon ami</u>.
Messager could equally well be referred to as a true "homme de
son époque", so important a part did he play in the musical life
of Paris, particularly in the 20th century, as composer,
conductor and administrator. As such he was often mentioned in
the contemporary musical and national press, and some press
comment on his life and works is included in this
Bio-bibliography.

Messager was born soon after the emergence of the Second Empire, which he saw develop and finally collapse. He was 16 when Berlioz died in 1869. He saw the inauguration of the Société Nationale de Musique in 1871, the climax of French wagnérisme in the late 1880's (he himself visited Bayreuth several times), and the premières of Debussy's Prélude à l'après-midi d'un faune and Pelléas et Mélisande (which he conducted) and Stravinsky's Le sacré du printemps. So, of course, did his lifelong friend Gabriel Fauré, but whereas Fauré tended, in his attitudes if not always in his music, to follow his old teacher Saint-Saëns in a growing conservatism in the face of new trends in musical composition, Messager seems constantly to have kept abreast of the new music. He knew and was admired by Debussy, and enjoyed friendships with most of the leading musicians of his day. His death in 1929 was marked by newspapers in Europe, Russia and even South America, and the general sentiment is that of the loss of an internationally admired musician.

Here, then, we have the final justification for a Bio-bibliography: it is because of Messager's importance in the age in which he lived that he deserves a reassessment, since by bringing him out of the shadows we gain a new perspective on the whole period in which he was musically active. This short study is offered in the hope that it will stimulate others to look more closely at the life of a musician whose reappraisal is well overdue.

The book opens with a brief biographical sketch, followed by a comprehensive worklist, which provides details of first performances (including cast lists and librettists where appropriate) publication details, principal reviews and so on. Works not composed by Messager, but arranged by him, are listed in Section 7 (pp. 80-84). While a large part of the worklist is given over (as we might expect) to the stage works, it will also be noted that Messager's output of songs and instrumental works was comparatively large. Some items, of course, are little more than salon pieces; but others have suffered a much less-justifiable neglect. The bibliography that follows attempts not only to list works that deal specifically with Messager, but also to alert readers to a number of general works that they may find useful in their own studies of the period in which Messager lived. Details of some archival materials (including letters and newspaper articles) are provided together with information on more generally available printed sources. The final part of the book consists of a discography, three appendices and an index.

A reviewer of Henry Février's biography of Messager, writing
in December 1948, noted that "s'il [Février] a comblé une grave
lacune, le sujet n'est pas encore épuisé" [If Février has filled
a serious gap in our knowledge, the subject is not yet
exhausted]. This is still true, and in the short study presented
here, many interesting questions must remain undiscussed. Future
scholars might, for example, further investigate Messager's time
at Covent Garden, or his activities as a member of the Société
Nationale de Musique - his relations with Saint-Saëns, or his
conducting technique, regarding which we have some documentary
and much pictorial evidence. Turning to the music itself, we
await a professional performance of the Symphony outside France;
and few singers in that country or outside it can be familiar
with many of the songs.

    There is thus much research still to be done. I hope that
interested readers will find this book a useful starting-point
for their own work.

Biography

André-Charles-Prosper Messager was born on 30 December 1853 in
Montluçon, a provincial town in west-central France which at this
time was assuming all the paraphernalia of an increasingly
industrialised society, including its own middle class.[1] It was
not, however, the industrial revolution that had made the fortune
of the Messager family, and given it a "position" in Montluçon:
both parents came from distinguished families. André's mother,
Sophie-Cornélie, was the daughter of a former officer of the
Chambre du Roy; while his father, a tax inspector, came from a
military family.[2] Although the family was at that time living in
the Auvergne, it was of Parisian origin. None of Messager's
relatives or ancestors seems to have had any musical talent, as
he himself confessed, and it was only through a fortuitous
combination of circumstances that he received any musical
instruction at all. But although the Messagers themselves were
not musical, they were no doubt well aware of the usefulness to a
young lady of learning the piano, and so it was that André's
elder sister was set to work. His description of her efforts
could well have been applied to many other girls of upper- and
middle-class families of the period:

> Personne n'était musicien dans ma famille. Il y avait bien
> ma soeur. Mais je n'ai pas dit qu'elle fût musicienne; j'ai
> dit qu'elle apprenait le piano ... Ce n'est pas tout à fait
> la même chose ... Le seul avantage que j'aie retiré de ses
> études, c'est qu'il y avait un piano à la maison: et c'est
> sur ce piano que j'ai pu m'exercer un peu, tout seul, dès
> que j'aie été assez haut pour atteindre les touches du bout
> des doigts.

> [No-one in my family was a musician. There was my sister, of
> course ... but I did not say that she was a musician, I said
> that she had piano lessons, which is not at all the same
> thing. The only advantage I gained from her studies was
> that there was a piano at home - and it was on this piano
> that I was able to practise a little, all by myself, from
> the time when I became tall enough to reach the keys with my
> fingertips.][3]

At the age of seven André was enrolled at the Institution Saint-Joseph, run by the Pères Maristes of Montluçon and, since his father did not wish actively to discourage his son's musical efforts, was given piano lessons. Looking back on this period, Messager was again disparaging, noting that his so-called piano professor "n'était pas plus pianiste que je ne suis grand Turc", partly because his preferences seemed to be for the violin.[4] The fact that the boy continued his attempts to learn the piano in spite of this, and even began to compose, shows great determination and an instinctive musical ability which he was to use to good effect in his more mature compositions.[5] Even so, he was never very much at home playing the piano in public, unless among friends or at the Société Nationale de Musique, where he took part in the premières of Chausson's Piano Trio in G minor (8 April 1882) and Chabrier's Valses romantiques (15 December 1883).

Toward the end of his time at the college he was given a new teacher, a M. Albrecht, who had come from the École Niedermeyer and had been a contemporary of Gabriel Fauré there.[6] Messager seems to have respected him and felt that at last he was making some progress. He took part in other musical activities in the College, which had a choir and, according to Augé-Laribé, "une sorte de musique militaire pour accompagner les processions et solenniser les distributions de prix" [A sort of military band, which played on parades and brought some dignity to school prize-givings.] Messager played the triangle and bass drum in this group.[7]

Such activities, while certainly not undesirable, were probably regarded by Messager's parents as a pleasant diversion from the more important business of ensuring that their son gained a solid classical education: this was seen as the first step along the road to one of the "professions", such as civil servant or doctor, which at this period took years of study. No doubt Messager, like Berlioz before him, would eventually have had to dispute with his parents the merits of a musical career over a more "respectable" one. Perhaps fortunately (as it turned out), circumstances intervened: the family lost money heavily, and it became imperative for André to train for a profession that would bring him employment and financial stability in the shortest possible time. The authorities at the École des Pères Maristes had heard from Albrecht of Messager's musical progress, and recommended him to Monseigneur de Dreux-Brezé, Bishop of Moulins, with the result that Messager was awarded a half-bursary to the École Niedermeyer in Paris in September 1869. The École Niedermeyer was viewed as a more suitable place for Messager to study than the Paris Conservatoire: the school had a reputation for producing fine organists, and Messager's family may well have felt that, if the worst happened, their son would be able to make a decent living in this way.[8]

The École de Musique Classique et Religieuse had been
founded by Louis Niedermeyer with a subsidy from the French
Government in 1853.[9] It became Niedermeyer's only lasting
success, his early attempts to write stage works having ended in
failure.[10] In his preface to Maurice Galerne's book about the
school, Messager paid tribute to its founder, although he never
knew him personally (Gustave Lefèvre, Niedermeyer's
brother-in-law, having taken charge in 1865):

> Comme beaucoup de précurseurs et d'initiateurs, Niedermeyer
> est peu et mal connu. Et pourtant, ne devrait-il pas être
> placé au premier rang par sa réforme de l'accompagnement du
> Plain-Chant et la fondation de son École qui ont été les
> bases de la renaissance de la musique religieuse en France?
> Il faut se reporter à la première moitié du 19e siècle, à
> cette époque où la musique religieuse était représentée par
> les cantiques dont la fadeur n'était surpassé que par le
> mauvais goût, par des adaptions des pires cavatines aux
> paroles de l'office ou de l'accompagnement des thèmes
> liturgiques n'avait d'autres règles que le goût, plutôt
> douteux, d'organistes ignorants, pour se rendre compte de la
> révolution operée par Niedermeyer, en proscrivant toute
> harmonisation qui ne fût pas justifiée par l'emploi des
> intervalles qui caractérisent chaque mode du plain-chant.

> [Like many pioneers and innovators, Niedermeyer is very
> little known. Yet does he not deserve a place in the first
> rank for his reform of the accompaniment of plainchant, and
> for the foundation of his School, which have been the basis
> of the rebirth of religious music in France? We must go back
> to the first half of the 19th century, to the time when
> religious music was marked by melodies whose blandness was
> surpassed only by their bad taste, when the words of the
> Office were adapted to the worst cavatinas, and where the
> accompaniment of liturgical melodies was governed solely by
> the frequently dubious taste of unskilled organists, to
> understand Niedermeyer's revolution in forbidding the use of
> any harmonies not sanctioned by the use of chords common to
> the mode of the plainchant.][11]

Messager did not enter the school at a particularly happy moment
in its history. During the Franco-Prussian War the establishment
was moved to Lausanne, and Lefèvre wrote to his former pupils and
professors asking for their help in re-establishing it there:
Fauré was one of those who responded, and so commenced his
lifelong friendship with Messager.[12] Saint-Saëns, who became an
enthusiastic and influential supporter of both musicians, also
taught at the school. Messager's other teachers were Eugène

Gigout (harmony and counterpoint), Adam Laussel (piano) and
Clement Loret (organ). The school library had a large collection
of music dating from the 16th to 19th centuries, and Niedermeyer
is known to have had a particular interest in the choral works of
Palestrina and Lassus. Besides the three annual prizes for
composition, organ and plainchant accompaniment established by
the French Government in 1854, Niedermeyer also awarded a prize
for the best performance of Bach's organ works, and although
Messager never won it, we may well imagine him performing some of
these works in the churches of which he later became organist.[13]
He also had a subscription to the Bach Gesellschaft edition of
the complete works of Bach, and in 1908 conducted a complete
performance of the B minor Mass with the Société des Concerts du
Conservatoire.

Messager left the École Niedermeyer in 1874 and straightaway
succeeded Fauré as organist of Saint-Sulpice, Fauré having in the
meantime moved on to the Madeleine. This was the first of a
number of organists' posts Messager was to hold, and, had he
wished, he could probably have settled down to life as a fairly
undistinguished church musician.[14] From Saint-Sulpice he moved
later to the church of Saint-Paul--Saint-Louis (1881), and was
maître de chapelle at Sainte-Marie-des-Batignolles from 1882 to
1884.

Paris in the decade after the Franco-Prussian War and the
Commune (1870-1871) could boast a very wide range of musical
activities. Following the success of Jules Pasdeloup's Sunday
afternoon Concerts Populaires, founded in 1861, Edouard Colonne
had created his own series in 1873, and charged a lower admission
price.[15] Both societies had been established with the aim of
performing and promoting the works of a younger generation of
French composers, and were initially successful in doing so,
although the staple fare of each, as also at the performances of
the Société des Concerts du Conservatoire, soon turned out to be
the symphonies of Beethoven.[16] Charles Lamoureux founded his
Harmonie Sacrée in 1873, with the aim of performing large-scale
works for chorus and orchestra, and, in addition to conducting
the first complete performances in France of Bach's St Matthew
Passion, (March and April 1874), put on Handel's Messiah and
Judas Maccabeus.[17] The Société Nationale de Musique, founded in
1871, also aimed to bring a new French musical voice to the
attention of a wider audience but, although its concerts were
advertised and reviewed in Le ménestrel, it retained something of
the air of a rather exclusive club. Messager was a member of the
society and made contact there with many of his musical
contemporaries, who were themselves at the beginning of their
careers. He certainly knew Duparc through the society, and had
probably met d'Indy by the time he left the École Niedermeyer.
(Charles Langrand remembered playing the overture to Wagner's Die

Meistersinger in an 8-hand arrangement with d'Indy, Duparc and
Messager in about 1875.)[18]
     We may assume that Messager had himself tried his hand at
composition by the time he left the École Niedermeyer: perhaps
some music for the Mass, or a few songs. If so, none of these
pieces has yet come to light. In 1875 he entered a competition
organised by the Société des Compositeurs for the composition of
a symphony, his first attempt at a large-scale orchestral work.
Augé-Laribé cites a letter from Messager to his sister which
gives some idea of the amount of effort he had put into the
composition of his entry:

>   Depuis trois mois je suis très occupé d'une symphonie à
>   grand orchestre que je fais pour un concours ouvert à la
>   Société des Auteurs et Compositeurs de Musique ... Je
>   t'assure que j'ai joliment travaillé depuis ces trois mois;
>   c'est très long à faire et on ne peut malheureusement pas
>   s'en occuper continuellement; les idées musicales viennent
>   quand elles veulent et ne se commandent pas.
>
>   [For the past three months I have been very busy with a
>   symphony for large orchestra, which I am composing for a
>   competition open to the Société des Auteurs et Compositeurs
>   de Musique ... I assure you that I have worked very happily
>   over the last three months; it's a long job, and I
>   unfortunately cannot spend all my time on it; the musical
>   ideas come when they will, and not to order.][19]

Messager won the first prize of a gold medal, and his Symphony
[W94] received its first performance on 20 January 1878 at the
Concerts Colonne.[20] A reviewer in the Revue et gazette musicale
de Paris, 27 January 1878, noted that "De très sérieuses qualités
se montrent, en effet, dans la symphonie en question", but made
it clear that he did not regard the work as a complete
masterpiece. The Scherzo, although it made little impression on
the public at the première, he regarded as the best movement.
Interesting too, in view of Messager's later success as an
orchestrator, is the reviewer's remark that "son orchestration
... a d'élégance, mais n'est pas assez nourrie; les parties du
milieu y sont presque toujours trop faibles". [His orchestration
... is elegant, but is not substantial enough; the inner parts
are almost always too weak.] Augé-Laribé notes later performances
of the work at the Concerts Populaires, Angers, on 15 December
1878 and at the Concerts Straram in 1930. He does not mention a
further performance at the École Niedermeyer noted in Le
ménestrel of 11 December 1881 (p.16), where the reviewer notes
that "de remarquables compositions symphoniques de MM. Gigout, G.
Fauré [?the D minor Symphony] et Messager" were performed.

Messager followed the Symphony with two more competition
pieces, a cantata Promethée enchainé [W90], to a text by Georges
Clerc (1877), entered for a competition organised by the Ville de
Paris (it won second prize); and Don Juan et Haydée [W91], to a
text by Byron, which was Messager's entry for a contest in
Saint-Quentin in 1877.[21]   This work was awarded only a second
prize, being unfinished when submitted.   Both pieces remain
unpublished.

In addition to working for competitions and fulfilling his duties
as an organist, Messager naturally had to seek other sources of
income to make a decent living.   Like Debussy later on, he began
to earn some money by writing piano transcriptions of the
works of other contemporary composers for Durand, and continued
to undertake similar work until well into the 20th century.   All
the early transcriptions are of pieces by Saint-Saëns, but
Messager also made arrangements at a later date of works by
Augusta Holmès, Lalo and Chabrier (see WORKLIST, Section 7).
      Far more lucrative than transcription was work for the
theatre;   Antoine Banès claims that Messager made his début in
this field in collaboration with Gaston Serpette, Widor, Massenet
and Delibes, with Les païens [W1], to a text by Henri Meilhac, in
about 1876. The work was produced by the Cercle de l'Union
Artistique at the Place Vendôme.[22]   Messager followed up with
three pieces for the Folies-Bergère, of which he had become music
director, in 1878 and 1879.   The Folies did not then have the
reputation they subsequently came to enjoy, as Augé-Laribé is
quick to point out.[23]   The first of the three slight pieces was
Fleur d'oranger [W38], which had over 200 performances.   For
solo piano and very short, it consisted of a simple series of
dances performed by characters based on the mythological persons
of Damon and Clorinda; the corps de ballet played the parts of
the (almost) obligatory shepherds.
      The other two works were Les vins de France [W39] and
Mignons et vilains [W40], published by Minier in 1879.   Les vins
de France is dedicated to Eugène Augé. Both scores highlight
Messager's great inventiveness in the field of the dance, and the
mazurka and the valse, two dances for which Messager seems to
have had a particular liking, feature in both compositions.   The
music is lively, and even from a glance at the piano score we can
gain an idea of the energy and verve of the pieces in performance
by a theatre orchestra.   Mignons et vilains, in two tableaux,
includes a berceuse, various pieces in a pastoral idiom and, for

the opening of the second tableau, a pavane of great refinement
and grace.

Besides these slight theatrical works, whose main benefit
(other than financial) would have been to prepare Messager for
the larger-scale theatrical pieces he was to write later on, two
further works in manuscript in the Bibliothèque Nationale deserve
our attention. Each is a collaboration with Gabriel Fauré. The
first, the Messe des pêcheurs de Villerville [W92], was composed
during 1881. Villerville was the site of a summer residence of
the industrialist Camille Clerc; both Fauré and Messager, at
that time sharing a home in Paris, attended his Parisian soirées.
Jean-Michel Nectoux publishes a number of letters from Fauré to
the Clerc family written between 1875 and 1883 in his Gabriel
Fauré: his Life through his Letters, and from these and other
evidence concludes that the Mass had its première in Villerville
in 1881. Manuscript 20301 in the music department of the
Bibliothèque Nationale, Paris, consists of five movements for
3-part women's chorus, solo violin, and organ. The Kyrie and O
Salutaris are by Messager, and are written at least in part in
his hand, while the Gloria, Sanctus and Agnus Dei are the work of
Fauré. The Kyrie, in E flat major, takes up three pages of 24-
stave manuscript paper, while the O Salutaris, in A flat, takes
up a further three pages after the Sanctus.[24] Ms 20302 of the
Bibliothèque Nationale contains an orchestral version of the
work, and dates from c.1882. The scoring is for flute, oboe,
clarinet in B flat, harmonium, 3-part chorus, solo violin and
strings. All the movements except the Agnus Dei are in
Messager's hand.[25] Finally, manuscript Vma1191 consists of
orchestral parts to the latter version, and was professionally
copied on 14-stave paper. The movements by Messager remain
unpublished (but not unrecorded - see the DISCOGRAPHY), while
Fauré went on to write his own Kyrie, and published his work as
the Messe basse in 1907.
The other Messager-Fauré collaboration has given rise to
some controversy regarding its date, with estimates ranging from
1880 to 1888. A sketch of the piece, "Souvenirs de Bayreuth"
[W96], a "Quadrille sur les motifs favoris de l'Anneau du
Nibelung", was found among Fauré's papers at the time of the
latter's death in 1924: it was dated 1880, and when Costallat
published the work (in 1930; with a 2-hand arrangement by
Gustave Samazeuilh), they accepted this date. Augé-Laribé himself

proposes a date of c.1886, for two reasons: first of all, he
suggests that the skill of such a musical parody would not have
been appreciated, even in as highly cultivated a musical salon as
that of Mme Baugniès (later Mme de Saint-Marceaux), where it is
said to have been first improvised, as early as 1880; and
secondly, he cannot believe that Fauré and Messager would have
entitled a work "Souvenirs de Bayreuth" without first having
visited Bayreuth itself. On his first point, Augé-Laribé may
conceivably be correct; but his second point is erroneous for
the purposes of the argument, since Messager and Fauré did not
visit Bayreuth together until 1888, although Messager is recorded
as having heard Parsifal and Tristan there in 1886.[26] Jean-Michel
Nectoux and Robert Orledge, with their dating of 1888, seem to
accept the reasoning that the two musicians would not have
written the work before visiting Bayreuth in 1888 but (I would
suggest) may also be mistaken in their dating since it is
difficult to see why Messager and Fauré would have improvised a
piece on themes from The Ring when it was Parsifal and Die
Meistersinger that they had heard at Bayreuth in that year.
We are therefore forced once again to consider the date of
composition of the work, and, rather than discounting 1880 as a
possible date, we would do well to assess the likelihood of the
piece's origins being rooted in the early 1880's. Two questions
need to be answered, as before. First, would Fauré and Messager
have been sufficiently familiar with The Ring in the early 1880's
to improvise on themes from it? And second, would the company at
Mme Baugniès have been able to appreciate it? The answer to the
first question we have from Nectoux, in his excellent edition of
Fauré's correspondence. In a letter to Marie Clerc, written from
Munich, and dated 21 September 1879, Fauré describes how he,
Messager and Lascoux heard Das Rheingold and Die Walküre. Fauré
and Messager were already familiar with all parts of The Ring,
having heard them in Cologne five months earlier. Fauré adds "we
enter the unknown this evening with Siegfried, but no matter what
they say about it we are not afraid of the dark". Further on in
the letter a more mischievous note creeps in:

De ce qu'on représente ici la Tétralogie de Wagner ne
concluez pas que tous les Bavarois aiment exclusivement la
musique de haute volée: ils ont entendu vingt fois de suite,
tout récemment, et avec une joie délirante, Der Postillon
von Longjumeau!!!

[Just because Wagner's Ring cycle is being performed here,
you mustn't conclude that all Bavarians like exclusively
high-quality music; quite recently they listened twenty
times running, going wild with delight, to The Postillon of
Longjumeau!!!][27]

Possibly the incongruity of such a pairing of styles at the same
location stimulated Fauré and Messager's sense of the ridiculous,
and inspired them to improvise the Quadrille at a later date.
    We may be certain, then, that by 1880 Messager and Fauré
would have known The Ring. Would the company at Mme Baugniès'
have appreciated it? Saint-Saëns certainly would, having
introduced Fauré - and Messager also (see APPENDIX 3) - to
Wagner's music in their student days at the École Niedermeyer. He
had also been present, with Alphonse Duvernoy, Augusta Holmès and
Vincent d'Indy, at the original Bayreuth performances of The Ring
in 1876. Chabrier, another early Wagnerite, certainly frequented
the salon, as did Chausson and d'Indy.
    We are now left with the lesser problem of why the piece
should have been entitled Souvenirs de Bayreuth when in fact
neither Fauré nor Messager had been present at Bayreuth to hear
The Ring during the 1880's. We should first of all note that The
Ring was not performed at Bayreuth between 1876 and 1896.
Furthermore, the undated manuscript 17769 at the Bibliothèque
Nationale, Paris, which is in Messager's hand, is headed
"Quadrille sur les motifs favoris de l'Anneau du Nibelung - R.
Wagner", with no trace of the words "Souvenirs de Bayreuth".
None of the writers who mentions the work before its publication
by Costallat in 1930 in fact makes use of such a title. As late
as March 1929 Gustave Samazeuilh still referred to the
composition as "le Quadrille" and made the observation that, in
his opinion, the work had never been written down before that
time:

> Je tiens aussi à mentionner le Quadrille, de la plus
> amusante fantaisie, qu'il [Messager] composa avec Gabriel
> Fauré, pour piano à quatre mains, sur les thèmes favoris de
> la Tétralogie, et que les deux amis jouèrent bien souvent,
> pour notre régal, aus temps héroiques du wagnérisme, dans
> des maisons amies. Ce quadrille devenu célèbre n'avait, je
> crois, jamais été réalisé sur le papier.
>
> [I must also mention the imaginative and amusing Quadrille,
> which he composed with Gabriel Fauré for piano, four hands,
> on favourite themes from The Ring, and which the two friends
> often used to play for our delight, in the heady days of
> wagnérisme, at the houses of friends. This quadrille (which
> has become famous) has never to my knowledge been written
> down on paper.][28]

He agrees with Augé-Laribé's statement that there was a
manuscript version of the work made by Fauré, and declares that
Costallat's performing version was made partly from this
manuscript, and partly from that written by Messager shortly
before his death; the manuscript referred to is presumably that
now held in the Bibliothèque Nationale. Since Samazeuilh himself
was responsible for a 2-hand arrangement of the work, his
testimony should obviously be taken seriously. He gives the
following account of how Messager eventually came to write down
the work:

> On saura gré, sans doute, aux suggestions amicales qui ont
> obtenu de Messager, longtemps refractaire, qu'il en écrive,
> cet hiver même, les premières figures. C'est là même son
> dernier manuscrit, hélas! inachevé, mais qu'une esquisse
> retrouvée par M. Philippe Fauré dans la musique de son père
> permettra heureusement de completer.

> [We should be thankful that (doubtless because of requests
> from friends) Messager, who had long been reluctant, finally
> wrote down the opening motifs of the piece this winter. It
> was, in fact, his very last manuscript, unfinished alas, but
> fortunately capable of being completed by means of a sketch
> discovered by M. Philippe Fauré among his father's music.][29]

We may therefore propose that the title Souvenirs de Bayreuth was
formulated either by Samazeuilh himself, or by editors at
Costallat, quite possibly to distinguish it from Chabrier's
Souvenirs de Munich, published by Costallat in the same year. If
so, the word "Souvenirs" in the title gives an added poignancy to
what was Messager's last manuscript.
    To complete the list of Messager's compositions of
1880-1881, we should note an orchestral composition, Loreley
[W95], which remained unperformed until 2 March 1930, when
Gabriel Pierné conducted it at a concert in Messager's memory at
the Concerts Colonne. The piece, described as a "ballade pour
orchestre", is in the tradition of the symphonic poems of
Saint-Saëns and of Duparc's Lénore (1875). It remains
unpublished.

En 1880, je trouvai l'occasion, tout à fait par hasard, de
faire mes débuts comme chef d'orchestre, en acceptant un
engagement pour inaugurer l'Eden-Théâtre de Bruxelles, où je
restai un an, composant encore deux nouveaux ballets ...

[In 1880 I gained the opportunity (completely by chance) to
make my début as a conductor, by accepting an engagement to
open the Eden Théâtre in Brussels, where I stayed for a
year, composing two more ballets there ...]

claimed Messager in 1908.[30] Perhaps this opportunity came
through the influence of Saint-Saëns, but given Messager's
theatre experience at the Folies-Bergère he would not have been
entirely unsuited to the task of taking over the Eden-Théâtre,
which was, according to Février, "un simple music-hall" at the
time.[31] Of the two new ballets Messager mentions we have no
trace; we can only speculate, too, on the type of repertoire he
would have conducted in Brussels. Perhaps of greater
significance is what he might have heard, since there were more
opportunities to hear Wagner's music in Belgium at that time than
there were in France.

On his return to Paris in 1882 Messager became organist of
the church of Saint-Paul -- Saint-Louis, which had enjoyed a
distinguished musical tradition for some centuries.
Compositional activity seems almost to have ceased until 1883,
when he was commissioned by the publisher William Enoch (who from
this point until 1890 was his chief publisher) to complete the
operetta François les bas-bleus [W3], begun by the composer
Firmin Bernicat and left unfinished at his death. The work was
premièred with great success at the Folies-Dramatiques on 8
November 1883. Fauré reported to a friend that Messager was
making much money from the work; it was entirely orchestrated by
Messager, and according to Augé-Laribé, Messager wrote 15 of the
25 numbers.

1883 was also the year of Messager's first marriage, to a
girl from Le Havre named Edith Clouet; he met her while standing
in for Saint-Saëns as conductor of some concerts in the district.
Fauré, himself only recently married, played the organ at the
wedding, apparently incorporating into the concluding voluntary a
melody from one of Messager's works for the Folies-Bergère. It
was at the wedding that Henry Février first encountered Messager:
he described the bridegroom as "souriant et heureux, svelt et
distingué, l'oeil vif, menton volontaire, bouche moqueuse, la
moustache conquérante, les cheveux noirs déjà clairsemés: tel
nous le verrons plus tard au pupitre de l'Opéra". [... smiling
and happy, slim and distinguished, eye bright, strong chin, a
mocking mouth, imperious moustache, and black hair already
growing thin; just as we were later to see him on the conductor's

rostrum at the Opéra.][32]
      Messager produced a steady stream of works between 1883 and
1890, including songs and piano pieces. The songs include the
Chanson de ma mie [W56], to a text by Théodore de Banville,
Mimosa [W57], and Regret d'avril [W55], to a poem by Armand
Silvestre, who, judging by the number of his works set by
Messager, seems to have been the composer's favourite poet.
Whereas Fauré became more and more attracted to the works of
Verlaine in the late 1880's, and abandoned Silvestre's poems
after some early settings, Messager still found sufficient
interest and variety in Silvestre's works to continue setting
them. Other poets whose texts he used included Catulle Mendès
(Chanson mélancolique [W65]), and Victor Hugo. Messager's songs
range from works that are little more than drawing-room ballads,
such as the Arioso [W70], or La chanson des cerises [W64], in
which the composer makes a brave attempt to create something of
musical merit out of a banal text, to much more serious and
subtle pieces, expressive of deeper emotions, their texts set
much more carefully and thoughtfully: La chanson de ma mie
[W56], Mimosa [W57] and Neige rose [W66] are examples of this
latter style, in which the voice and piano accompaniment together
create an effective musical support for the poetry. The 2-hand
piano works [W101-106], Messager's only pieces for this medium,
were published in late 1888.[33]   They comprise the Impromptu in A
flat op.10, Habanera op.11, Menuet op.12 (dedicated "à Mme J.
Février") the Mazurka op.13 (dedicated to Jenny Clouet ?his
sister-in law), a Caprice-polka op.14 and the Valse op.15. In
the absence of any other piano works by Messager, and to judge by
their style, we may conclude that these were intended merely as
salon pieces, to make their composer a little extra money.
Nevertheless, they were sufficiently popular for Léon Lemoine to
republish them in 4-hand arrangements in 1904.
      No new theatrical works by Messager enjoyed first
performances in 1884, for reasons that will become clear later;
but in 1885 there were three: Le petit poucet [W4], at the Gaité
on 28 October; La fauvette du temple [W5], at the
Folies-Dramatiques on 17 November; and La Béarnaise [W7], at the
Bouffes-Parisiens on 12 December. Of Le petit poucet we know
little; Enoch published the "Chanson des loups" and a Quadrille
on the principal themes, but nothing else of this incidental
music for a fairy ballet remains. Augé-Laribé was dismissive of
La fauvette du temple, regarding it as rather a puerile sop
to the tastes of the period.[34] Nevertheless the work had six
performances in London in 1891 (in English), and the vocal score
and selections from the piece were published by Enoch's London
branch.[35] La Béarnaise, like Les p'tites Michu [W23] later on,
was based partly around a confusion of identical-looking
characters. The piece is dedicated to Jeanne Granier, who

created the title role after taking over as female lead at the last minute.[36] The berceuse achieved some popularity as a separate piece.

Although these projects were in themselves moderately successful, most of Messager's time during 1884 must have been spent on a potentially much more important venture. On the recommendation of Saint-Saëns, Vaucorbeil, now director of the Opéra in Paris, commissioned a ballet from Messager on the subject of Lafontaine's fable of Les deux pigeons [W41]. Both Février and Augé-Laribé are somewhat in error regarding the details of the commission. Février claims that Messager received a letter from Saint-Saëns in 1885 informing him that a commmission was likely; and Augé-Laribé is confused by Messager's own account of events as related in Musica of 1908, in which he, too, claimed that the letter from Saint-Saëns arrived in 1885.[37] To his credit, Augé-Laribé cites the text of what he assumed to be another letter, dated 5 March 1883, in which Saint-Saëns writes that he has recommended to Vaucorbeil that the ballet to succeed Théodore Dubois' Farandole at the Opéra should be written by Messager. In fact this was the only letter that Saint-Saëns wrote on the subject, since Vaucorbeil actually commissioned the ballet of Les deux pigeons from Messager and Henry de Régnier on 30 May 1884, according to a file of correspondence in the Archives Nationales, Paris. In view of the importance of this correspondence to the present argument, I quote it here in full:

30 mai 1884

Messieurs;
Je m'empresse de vous confirmer par écrit ce que j'ai déjà l'honneur de vous dire de vive voix; Je reçois le programme du ballet des Deux Pigeons composé par M. Henry Régnier, et je confie à M. André Messager la tâche d'en écrire la musique.

Je mets cependant à mon acceptation cette condition; que la partition de M. Messager, me sera remise entièrement orchestrée le 1er janvier 1885: mon intention étant de faire représenter les deux pigeons dans le courant de cette même année, 1885, et désirant, si les nécessités de mon répertoire l'exigaient, être en mesure de produire cet ouvrage soit aux printemps, soit à l'automne.
Veuillez Messieurs, m'accusez réception de cette lettre et me dire si vous acceptez la condition de l'engagement que je vous propose, et reçevez l'assurance de mes sentiments distingués.

Le directeur de l'Opéra
[signed] Vaucorbeil

[Messieurs: I am hastening to confirm in writing what I have already had the pleasure of informing you verbally; I have received the plan of the ballet Les deux pigeons from M. Henry Régnier, and am entrusting the task of writing the music for it to M. André Messager. I am, however, imposing the following condition of acceptance; that M. Messager's score, completely orchestrated, will be delivered to me on the 1st January 1885, since I want to produce Les deux pigeons in the course of the 1885 season and wish, if circumstances demand, to be in a position to produce the work either in spring or autumn. Be so good, messieurs, as to confirm receipt of this letter, and to inform me whether you accept the proposed condition. Yours etc.][38]

Not surprisingly, Messager and Régnier replied quickly, accepting the condition imposed. The final letter in the file, written by Messager and dated 30 December 1884, advises the directors that the score is complete; the composer also asks about the best method of delivering the work to them.[39]

Messager and Régnier must have been disappointed when their ballet failed to obtain a performance in either the spring or autumn of 1885. The première, in fact, was not until 18 October 1886, when it served to open the new season. Although the work had a successful first run in Paris, its first London performance did not take place until June 1906, at which time it enjoyed only three performances in all. Messager himself conducted the London première. A further disappointment was the almost complete lack of performances in Paris between 1886 and 1910, when Messager himself was responsible for reviving the work at the Opéra. Broussan, his co-director, was adamant that it was in fact at his insistence that Messager was eventually persuaded to revive the work, and a letter dated 1956 preserved as part of ms RésA647 at the Bibliothèque de l'Opéra confirms this.[40]

Messager's next première was Le bourgeois de Calais [W8]: but it was as much a failure as Les deux pigeons had been a success. Augé-Laribé judged the librettists and composer equally responsible for the work's lack of success. The plot was in line with the rather nationalistic thinking given currency in France at this period through the efforts of Paul Deroulède and his Ligue des Patriotes, and it is not surprising that the text of one number, "Il faut savoir mourir pour la patrie" was revived in the middle of World War I, and given the title Le credo de la victoire [W87].

Isoline [W10], to a libretto by Catulle Mendès, was no more successful than Le bourgeois de Calais, and came at the end of another rather lean year for Messager. Two other events from 1888 are far more noteworthy: firstly, Messager met Albert Carré for the first time, while working on an adaptation of another

work by Firmin Bernicat entitled Les beignets du roi; and
secondly, in the summer he managed to hear Parsifal at Bayreuth.
(Presumably the few songs and piano pieces he had written had
been selling well.) Carré gives details of his first meeting
with Messager in his memoirs, Souvenirs de théâtre (Paris:
Librairie Plon, 1950). Les beignets du roi had been premièred in
Brussels in 1882, at which time Bernicat's music had been
adequate. For the Parisian production Carré renamed the work Les
premières armes de Louis XV and decided that more music was
required. Carré takes up the story: Bernicat's widow

> ... me proposa de faire faire la musique additionnelle par
> un jeune compositeur de ses amis qui avait déjà achevé une
> autre partition de son mari, celle de François les
> bas-bleus. Je reverrai toujours l'entrée, dans le petit
> salon de Mme Bernicat, de ce jeune homme à la silhouette
> svelte, distinguée, à la figure fine, traversée d'une
> moustache d'officier. Notre hôtesse, nous présentant, unit
> pour la première fois ces deux noms qui, si souvent par la
> suite, devaient être liés: "M. Albert Carré ... M. André
> Messager".

> [... suggested to me that the additional music be
> commissioned from a young composer friend who had already
> completed another of her husband's scores, that of François
> les bas-bleus. I will always remember the entry into Mme
> Bernicat's salon of that slender, distinguished young man,
> his handsome face sporting an officer's moustache. Our
> hostess, introducing us, brought together for the first time
> two names that were so often to be linked in later times:
> M. Albert Carré ... M. André Messager.]

Two further premières took place in 1889, Colibri [W11], at the
Vaudeville, and Le mari de la reine [W12], at the
Bouffes-Parisiens. Colibri was a small-scale one-act show, to
words by Louis Legendre; of its success or failure we know
nothing. In the same way, only one extract from Le mari de la
reine achieved any lasting success - this was "Si j'avais vos
légères ailes", a "valse chantée" of the type that was popular at
that period. Otherwise the work was a complete flop, and Février
relates how Messager autographed his score with the words "En
souvenir du meilleur de mes fours". [As a souvenir of the best of
my failures.][41] Years later, in his memoirs (see APPENDIX III),
Messager could make no other comment about Le mari de la reine
than that it passed "inaperçu". Augé-Laribé attributes its
failure to the fact that it was rather hastily put together to

take advantage of the large number of tourists in Paris for the
Exposition Universelle of 1889. Unfortunately, by the time the
piece came to be staged in December, not only had most of the
tourists departed, but Paris was also in the grip of an influenza
epidemic.

Both Février and Augé-Laribé state that Messager made a
somewhat more positive contribution to the Exposition by
conducting a number of concerts of Russian music at the
Trocadéro. Both writers are incorrect: the concerts, which took
place in June, were in fact conducted by Rimsky-Korsakov, as he
relates in his memoirs.[42] Rimsky-Korsakov did however meet
Messager, whom he described as "rather colourless", at a
newspaper reception in June 1889:

> In the midst of rehearsals we visited the Exposition. There
> were also dinners in honour of the Russian musicians at
> Colonne's house and in the editorial offices of some paper
> where, after dinner, a loathsome, old, stout operetta diva
> sang, and my Capriccio and Glazunov's Styenka Razin were
> played four-hands on a grand piano by Pugno and Messager.[43]

The orchestral players were drawn from Colonne's orchestra and
were highly praised by Rimsky-Korsakov, who also mentions that
the concerts were an almost total failure, since Belaieff, who
had arranged them from Moscow, had failed to ensure adequate
publicity. Rimsky-Korsakov noted ruefully that the only
practical result of the concerts was to secure him an invitation
to go to Brussels the following year.[44]

By the end of 1889, then, the "rather colourless" Messager must
have felt somewhat pessimistic about the future; in spite of
having had many stage works performed, he could point to only one
undisputed success, Les deux pigeons. All his subsequent
enterprises had ended, to a greater or lesser extent, in failure,
and he was no longer so sought after by librettists. His only
solid conducting achievement had been the year in Brussels at the
beginning of the decade; and little of his work was being
published. At the beginning of the 1890's, however, the
long-awaited success did come. La Basoche [W13] (later known in
England as The King of the Students), to a libretto by Albert

Carré, received its first performance at the Opéra-Comique under
Jules Danbé in May 1890.[45] An immediate success, it was taken up
by many other European houses; the first English performances
were at the Royal English Opera House between November 1891 and
January 1892.[46] Février assigns a special place to the work in
the history of French musical theatre, hailing it as "le dernier
des grands opéras-comiques français du XIX siècle". [The last of
the great 19th century comic operas.][47] It marked a turning
point in Messager's compositional career, and set him back on the
road to success; in 1891 he was created a Chevalier de la Légion
d'Honneur.

Two stage works date from 1891; the first, Hélène
[W14], was "musique de scène" for a drama by Paul Delair. A
"Noël" from the piece was published separately and according to
Février, a suite from the work was later performed at the
Concerts Colonne (see WORKLIST).[48] The other work, Scaramouche
[W43], was a collaboration with Georges Street. For some reason
Augé-Laribé attempts to play down Street's part in the work,
claiming that Street was an illegitimate son of Liszt who died of
alcohol poisoning. Scaramouche seems to have been one of only a
few stage works by Street, although he is occasionally mentioned
in the Bibliographie musicale française as the composer of a few
songs. A Georges Street was also responsible for a small
pamphlet, Lohengrin à l'Eden, published in 1887, which formed a
part of the extensive pro- and anti-Wagner literature inspired in
that year by Lamoureux's abortive attempt to perform Lohengrin in
Paris. (Unfortunately the Bibliothèque Nationale has no copy of
this pamphlet, and the copy in the British Library is lost.)
Street was also for a time a critic on Le matin. His friendship
with Messager must have been of quite long standing, since
Messager dedicated a Passepied [W100], published in Le gaulois
in 1888, to him. It is impossible to tell from the printed score
which numbers in Scaramouche are by Messager, and which by
Street. The piece was not a great success, and has not been
revived.[49]

Messager now tried his hand at something a little less
lightweight, and during 1892 completed his Madame Chrysanthème
[W15] which uses the libretto later set by Puccini in Madame
Butterfly. The piece has some Wagnerian touches: the opening,
set on the foredeck of a French ship sailing into Japan, has
obvious reminiscences of The Flying Dutchman, although that work
had not at the time been staged in France. One of the sailors
sings a Breton folk song, longing for his native land. There are
also a number of recurring melodies, used to give some overall
musical structure to the piece. Perhaps because he set more
store by this work than by some of his previous efforts, Messager
conducted the première himself at the Théâtre de la Renaissance
in January 1893; it was not especially well received.

While on the subject of Wagner, it is perhaps appropriate at this
point to correct a further error in Augé-Laribé's narrative,
namely that Messager successfully conducted a performance of Die
Walküre at Marseilles during 1892, in which Lucienne Bréval sang.
If Augé-Laribé had been correct, this event would have pre-dated
the première of Die Walküre at the Paris Opéra by almost a year.
As it turns out, it was in fact Lohengrin that was performed at
the Grand Théâtre in Marseilles in 1892, with Die Walküre
presented there only in April 1897, according to a number of
sources; and, although Messager had a female performer from the
Paris Opéra in his production of Die Walküre, it was not Lucienne
Bréval but Thérèse Ganne who, according to Le ménestrel, enjoyed
"un succès éclatant en jouant d'une façon très brillante le rôle
de Brunehilde". [A resounding success in a brilliant performance
as Brunhilde.][50] André Gouirand, in his book La musique en
Provence et le Conservatoire de Marseille (Marseille: P. Ruat;
Paris: Fischbacher, 1908), 451, declares that Messager was
recommended by the Wagner family as a suitable conductor for Die
Walküre, and that "rien n'avait été negligé pour rendre dans son
integrité scrupuleuse l'oeuvre de Wagner". [No effort was spared
to render Wagner's work to perfection.] Victor Combarnous, in his
L'histoire du Grand-Théâtre de Marseille (Marseille: 1927,
reprinted Marseille: Lafitte, 1980), 228-229, concurs with this
statement.

Messager, like Fauré, had contacts in England. We have already
seen that La Basoche and La fauvette du temple had been staged
there; and William Enoch had a publishing house in London from
which Messager's other works could be distributed. In addition,
Chappell and Co. published much of his music (including La
Basoche) from 1891 onwards; their catalogue included excerpts
from various works, intended for domestic music-making. There
was still a taste for French operetta in London, and there are
stylistic similarities between the works of Gilbert and Sullivan
and the works of their French counterparts, although Messager's
works are not laced with, or in any way dependent on, political
satire in the same way as the English works. Richard d'Oyly
Carte, proprietor of the Savoy Theatre, had François Cellier as
his musical director, and it was Cellier who conducted the London
première of La Basoche. These, and no doubt many less obvious
connections, inspired Messager to attempt a work intended first
and foremost for the London stage.[51] The result was Mirette
[W18], premièred in 1894; Cellier conducted.[52]

Mirette in fact exists in two versions. The first, staged from 3 July to 11 August 1894, had lyrics by Frederick E. Weatherley and Harry Greenbank; the new version, with "new lyrics by Adrian Ross", ran from 6 October to 6 December of the same year. The Savoy Theatre had been closed in the intervening months while d'Oyly Carte desperately tried to find some way of reviving the fortunes of his enterprise, but, according to Cellier, things were already going badly.[53]

An Irish composer, Miss Dotie Davis, who at the time had a small reputation in London as a composer of romances, also had some responsibility for the music of Mirette, according to Messager himself (see APPENDIX 3).[54] If this was so, it is surprising that she was not acknowledged in the vocal score. Augé-Laribé claims that they met at a London publishers (?possibly Chappell's). Edith Clouet had by now divorced Messager and was terminally ill, and Messager, presumably taken by the charms of Miss Davis, married her in 1895. They lived at The Firs, Castle Hill, Maidenhead, where the only child of the marriage, Madeleine Hope Andrée (Miss Davis was known professionally by the name Hope Temple), was born on 30 December 1898, as Messager was celebrating his 45th birthday. Albert Carré was godfather.

In Paris, the Théâtre Sarah Bernhardt, a temporary home of the Opéra-Comique after the disastrous fire of May 1887, was the location for Messager's Le chevalier d'Harmental [W20]. This was another piece in Messager's more serious vein, and its failure was a great blow to the composer, who was apparently very tempted thereafter to retire to Maidenhead and to enjoy a quieter life. For some reason he and Léon Carvalho, now reappointed as director of the Opéra-Comique, were daggers drawn ("à couteaux tirés", says Février), and Carvalho continually interrupted rehearsals to annoy his enemy, even to the extent of trying to amend the orchestration of the work, by which the composer set great store.

Some writers have viewed all Messager's operettas as aberrations from his strong desire to write more serious works, and Albert Carré certainly felt that the composition of grand opera in a quasi-Wagnerian mould had been Messager's final aim. Indeed, the difficulties of staging serious opera in Paris, allied to financial constraints, may effectively have forced Messager into light opera. We should not forget that he began his career without money, and until the early 1890's was still not well-off. Albert Carré gave his interpretation of events in an article for Le matin in 1932:

Pourquoi n'a-t'il pas suivi les instincts de son génie? Pourquoi n'avons-nous pas de lui, quelque ouvrage comparable à Pelléas et à Pénélope? Parce que, tout jeune encore,

marié de bonne heure, Messager avait eu à gagner sa vie et
que l'opérette seule lui en offrait le moyen immédiat et
durable. Parce que le succès même de Véronique et des
p'tites Michu, ces merveilles d'un genre faussement relégué,
parmi les genres inférieurs, ne lui permet plus de se
dérober à ce que l'on attendait de lui. Parce qu'à Paris,
un artiste est étiqueté, classé, enfermé dans l'étroit
couloir d'une manière unique dont il ne peut se départir
sans danger pour sa renommée.

[Why did he not follow the instinct of his genius? Why do
we not have a work from his pen in the same vein as Pelléas
or Pénélope? Because, while still very young, and married
early in life, Messager had to earn his living, and only
operetta offered him a swift and sure way. Because even the
success of Véronique and Les p'tites Michu, those marvels of
a genre wrongly relegated to an inferior artistic position,
still did not allow him to give his attention to writing the
works we expected of him. Because in Paris, an artist is
pigeon-holed: locked into the narrow corridor of a "personal
style" from which he may not deviate without risk to his
reputation.][55]

A new libretto arrived in Maidenhead in 1896: Les p'tites Michu,
by Georges Duval and Albert Vanloo. Messager read and was
inspired by it, not discovering until later that the book had
already been rejected by three other composers. The première of
Les p'tites Michu [W23] was on 16 November 1897 at the
Bouffes-Parisiens, and the piece had an equally resounding
success in London at Daly's Theatre (then at the height of its
popularity) between April 1905 and June 1906, during which time
it received 400 performances. Following the success of the work
in Paris, Albert Carré, the newly-appointed director of the
Opéra-Comique, did not hesitate to choose Messager as his musical
director. This was an important turning point for the composer,
since for the first time it gave him the opportunity to conduct a
first class orchestra on a regular basis. He stayed with the
Opéra-Comique from 1898 to 1904, and spent a further fifteen
months as music director there from September 1919 to December
1920. Messager was well known for his wide knowledge of the
musical repertoire, and took the opportunity to introduce to the
Parisian public a number of new works, including Debussy's
Pelléas et Mélisande (April 1902), d'Indy's Fervaal (March 1898),
Gustave Charpentier's Louise (February 1900)[56] and Reynaldo
Hahn's L'île du rêve (March 1898).[57]
    1898 was also the year of the première of what has remained
Messager's most popular stage work, Véronique [W24]. Florestan,
the male lead, was played in the first production by Jean Périer,

who had earlier come to Messager's attention in 1896 when he
played Angelin in La fiancée en lotérie. We may assume that it
was Messager who later recommended to Debussy that Périer should
play Pelléas in his own opera. Véronique, like Les p'tites
Michu, was first performed at the Bouffes-Parisiens, and based on
a libretto by Duval and Vanloo. The English production in 1904
ran for 895 performances and became, according to Gänzl, "the
biggest foreign success in Britain since Audran's La poupée".[58]

Due to his new responsibilities as conductor and
administrator, Messager spent less time on composition during the
years 1899 to 1905. There is no evidence that he disliked his
new role, and he and Carré seem by-and-large to have enjoyed a
good working relationship. Only one of his works had a
performance at the Opéra-Comique during this period, the ballet
Une aventure de la Guimard [W45], to a scenario by Henri Cain.
There has been dispute over the dating of this work: Augé-Laribé
claims that Messager was commissioned to write it for an official
reception at the Opéra-Comique, and that it received its première
there in November 1900; while the Enciclopedio dello spettacolo
gives the date of the first performance as October, at
Versailles, with Messager conducting. However, the manuscript of
the ballet in the Bibliothèque de l'Opéra contains a note which
explains the work's origins: on the reverse of the fly-leaf
Messager has written in his own hand "Ce ballet a été composé
pour la fête donnée à l'occasion du congrès des Chemins de fer,
dans la Parc de Versailles Septembre 1900". [This ballet was
composed for festivities at the railway conference held in the
park at Versailles in September 1900.][59] The première must have
been in late September, as Messager has written at the end of the
manuscript "26 Sept. 1900 3h du matin".

The manuscript of another unpublished yet interesting work
is also located in the Bibliothèque de l'Opéra.[60] For the
Exposition Universelle of 1900, a number of books of autograph
scores by musicians from both France and abroad were compiled.
One of these volumes contains two Messager autographs. The second
of these, 198b, is of "Les harpes d'or qui chantent dans la
nuit", from Act 1, scene 4 of Madame Chrysanthème; the other,
no.198, is of Messager's setting of the poem "Arpège", by Albert
Samain. (The same text was set by Gabriel Fauré, in about 1897,
according to Orledge.) Messager's setting of the song, beginning
"L'âme d'une flûte soupire", is in a completely different style
to his salon pieces, and has something of the mysterious quality
of Debussy's Chansons de Bilitis about it. Messager continued to
compose songs well into the 20th century, and a new edition of
the best of them is well overdue.

Paul Taffanel resigned as conductor of the Société des
Concerts du Conservatoire in May 1900. Although the society had
a reputation for musical conservatism and élitism, the post of

conductor was one of the most prestigious in Paris. Messager was
therefore unwilling to allow the opportunity to secure the
position pass him by and accordingly sent his application to the
society. The two letters he sent in support of his application
are now preserved in the Bibliothèque Nationale, Paris,
Département de la Musique, as lettres autographes 31 and 32. The
second is in some ways more interesting than the first; writing
on the eve of the election, 11 June 1901, Messager assures the
selection committee that he will not use the society's concerts
as a "champ d'expériences pour les tentatives nouvelles"
[laboratory for new musical initiatives], and that the most
modern music will not have a place at the concerts unless
sanctioned by the Committee. He is more interested in drawing
the public's attention to the lesser-known symphonies of Mozart,
along with the works of Bach and Handel in more than fragmentary
form. In the event, it was Georges Marty, himself trained at the
Conservatoire, who obtained the post, and Messager had to wait
until Marty's death in 1908 before he could take up the position.
Debussy was one of those who regretted Messager's initial failure
to secure the appointment, and made his feelings clear in La
revue blanche (1 July 1901). However, Messager was compensated
for this lack of success by being appointed manager of the Grand
Opera Syndicate in London in 1901, and was responsible for
encouraging further performances of Wagner's works there. Harold
Rosenthal has pointed out that Messager's appointment seems
inexplicable, even given Messager's successes in London with La
Basoche and Mirette. Possibly his associations with d'Oyly Carte
also played a part.[61] Furthermore, Messager was musical director
at the Opéra-Comique, and the traditional English snobbery for
anything foreign may also have been a factor in his
appointment.[62] For the first few years of his employment
Messager seems to have been content to arrange contracts and
undertake routine administration, rather than conducting any
works himself. Before 1905 he conducted only two pieces - La
princesse Osra by Herbert Bunning on 14 July, 1902, with Mary
Garden as the Princess; and Saint-Saëns' Hélène, with Nellie
Melba, in March 1904. In 1905 he conducted Bizet's Carmen and
Gounod's Faust and Roméo et Juliette, together with Gluck's
Orphée and Mozart's Don Giovanni, with Caruso in the role of Don
Ottavio. The "first performance in England" of Gluck's Armide,
with Lucienne Bréval, was given on 6 July 1906, and Messager also
conducted the English première of Massenet's Le jongleur de
Notre-Dame in June of the same year.[63] Messager took advantage
of his position at Covent Garden to hear many singers of
international reputation; some, like Emma Calvé and Lucienne
Bréval, he was to use later at the Paris Opéra. Of Caruso he had
earlier written to Carré, in May 1902: "Nous avons eu la chance
de tomber sur un tenor italien extraordinaire, Caruso; quel

dommage qu'il ne chante pas en français; c'est certainment la
plus belle voix que j'ai jamais entendu". [We have had the good
fortune to discover an extraordinary Italian tenor, Caruso; what
a pity he does not sing in French; his is certainly the most
beautiful voice I have ever heard.][64]

"A la mémoire de Georges Hartmann, et en témoignage de profonde
affection à André Messager". [In memory of Georges Hartmann, and
as a sign of deep affection to André Messager.] So reads the
dedication to Debussy's Pelléas et Mélisande, of which Messager
conducted the première on 30 April 1902.[65] The roots of
Messager's friendship with Debussy went back to the beginning of
the 1890's, and both Messager and Hartmann (Debussy's friend and
publisher) would have experienced the genesis and development of
Debussy's opera through almost a decade. Debussy himself
referred to Messager affectionately as Pelléas and Mélisande's
"grand père". However, the first meeting between Debussy and
Messager was not particularly promising. Debussy wrote to
Chausson on 2 October 1893:

> J'ai rencontré Messager qui, en vertu de je ne sais quelle
> amitié, m'a invité à diner! Et il m'a parlé musique très
> bizarrement; il disait "Allons, encore quelques années de
> travail et puis je me retire à la campagne, et change mon
> habit contre un gilet de flanelle immuable".
>
> [I have met Messager, who, by virtue of I don't know what
> friendship, invited me to dinner! Moreover, he talked of
> music very strangely; he said "now, just a few more years'
> work, and then I shall retire to the country and change into
> an impermeable flannel jacket".][66]

We must assume that Messager was not being wholly serious, since
in spite of the only moderate success of Madame Chrysanthème in
1893, he had a number of projects that looked promising,
including a contract with Ricordi to have some of his works
published in Milan. There is no reason to suppose that an early
retirement interested him in the slightest.

As previously noted, Messager's administrative responsibilites
during the period 1900 to 1904 left him very little time for
composition. There is an unpublished song, Sur la mer [W54],
written while the Opéra-Comique company was on a visit to
Aix-les-Bains; a 4-hand arrangement of Lalo's Namouna [W130];
and a Morceau de concours [W111] for a piano competition at the
Conservatoire. For his next theatrical work, first performed in
1905, Messager again used the librettists Duval and Vanloo; his
setting of their Les dragons de l'impératrice [W25] included both
Charles Prince and Mariette Sully in its cast. Messager's name
on the score was enough to guarantee it a hearing (this time at
the Théâtre des Variétés), but the work did not enjoy the lasting
success of Véronique. Fortunio [W26], which followed in 1907,
has, however, enjoyed a number of revivals. Jean Périer and
Marguerite Carré created leading roles. Perhaps surprisingly,
none of Messager's operettas received performances at the
Opéra-Comique during the time that he was musical director there,
although he and Albert Carré did have plans to perform Madame
Chrysanthème in 1902.[67]
    While Messager was conducting the première of Fortunio, he
already knew that he was assured of a more prestigious conducting
position, having been elected as one of the directors of the
Paris Opéra. He took up this appointment in January 1908, and
almost certainly as a result was created Officier de la Légion
d'Honneur. In spite of Messager's experience as an administrator
at Covent Garden, the Ministre des Beaux Arts felt that it was
necessary to have a co-director who would concentrate purely on
administration, and chose Frederick Broussan. Broussan had
something of a reputation for rescuing ailing theatres, having
previously saved houses at Nancy and Brest from financial
collapse. He had then moved on to Lyons and had amazed the local
population by staging a full performance of Wagner's Ring, with
great success.[68] He does not, however, appear to have been a
particularly colourful character, and little more was heard of
him after he and Messager departed from the Opéra in 1914.
    Messager and Broussan's directorship of the Opéra was only
moderately successful, due to shortage of funds for new
productions, and constant disputes with staff. The emphasis as
far as repertoire was concerned was on Wagner, whose works the
Opéra now happily embraced, after stiff opposition in the
previous century. Fauré's Pénélope was also performed there in
1913, and other highlights included Rameau's Hippolyte et Aricie
(1908), Ravel's L'heure espagnole and Moussorgsky's Boris
Godunov.[69] Some measure of the costs involved in bringing a work
to the stage can be gained from a contract letter in the Archives
Nationales from Messager to Lucienne Bréval, a singer Messager
had known since the 1890's: Miss Bréval is to sing at the Opéra
from 1 February to 31 July 1908, and will be paid 8000F per month

on the understanding that she sings eight performances per month.
She is specifically contracted to sing Phèdre in Rameau's
Hippolyte et Aricie in March 1908.[70]
    If we are to believe Augé-Laribé, disputes between Messager
and Broussan came about because of basic personality clashes;
Augé-Laribé even portrays Broussan as a small-time theatre
director who nevertheless regarded himself as far superior to his
partner. According to Eugène Berteaux, Messager did not even
find Broussan as staunch a supporter of Wagner's music as he
might have wished - the Opéra's performances of Götterdämmerung
in 1907 caused something of a directorial storm.[71] Alfred
Bruneau, however, claimed that the reason that Messager and
Broussan eventually lost their privilège was the success of the
ballet L'Amoureuse leçon, composed by Bruneau, Ravel, Roussel and
d'Indy, and produced by Jacques Rouché (Messager's and Broussan's
eventual successor) at the Théâtre des Batignolles. He also
claimed that Messager later blamed him for the loss of the
directorship, but it is difficult to work out the truth of the
situation, given Bruneau's obvious hostility to Messager, as
noted in his "Souvenirs" in the Revue internationale de musique
française (see BIBLIOGRAPHY).
    It was on the strength of his experience as a Wagner
conductor that Messager was finally appointed chef d'orchestre of
the Société des Concerts du Conservatoire in 1908; his first
concert was on 18 November that year.[72] Included in a
wide-ranging repertoire were the following premières:

Humperdinck	Hansel and Gretel	
	Overture	7 March 1909
Haydn	Violin Concerto in C	6 December 1909
Paul Vidal	Ecce sacerdos magnus	9 January 1910
Liszt	"Faust" symphony	March 1910
R. Strauss	Don Juan	November 1911
J. S. Bach	Cantata for the Feast	
	of John the Baptist	14 January 1912
C. Tournemire	Psalm 57	18 February 1912
Chausson	Hymne Védique	November 1912

Conducting the society of course enabled Messager to work with
top-class musicians with international reputations, and there are
no signs of a slackening of standards during his time there.
Manuscript 17668 of the music department of the Bibliothèque
Nationale, Paris, contains a number of appreciative notices of
Messager from this time, including testimonies from Louis Diémer,
Arthur de Greef and Jacques Thibaut.[73]

On the outbreak of war in 1914, Messager may well have felt it
time to "retire to the country and change into an impermeable
flannel jacket", as he had remarked to Debussy so many years
earlier. Nevertheless, on completing his duties at the Opéra in
1914-1915, he immediately took on the responsibility of
conducting the Matinées Nationales de la Sorbonne, organised by
Alfred Cortot and Romain Coolus, using musicians from the
Conservatoire orchestra. Being too old for active war service
himself, Messager undertook a number of concert tours during the
war - to South America in 1916; to Switzerland; and, in late
1918, to the U.S.A. and Canada. His Argentine tour from June to
November 1916 was criticised by some writers back in France, as
he chose to conduct a number of Wagner's works there. In a
letter written to La renaissance, 5 February 1916, in reply to
the question "Doit-on jouer Wagner après la guerre?", he had made
his own position on the matter quite plain:

> Je trouve qu'au milieu des angoisses de l'heure actuelle,
> Wagner et la musique allemande présentent bien peu
> d'intérêt. La question de savoir si on pourra où non jouer
> plus tard les oeuvres wagnériennes me laisse pour le moment
> dans la plus complète indifférence. Anéantissons d'abord
> les Allemands: nous discuterons après.
>
> [I find that in the midst of the agonies of the present
> time, Wagner and German music are of very little interest.
> The question of whether one could perform Wagner's works at
> a later date, or not, is at this moment a matter of complete
> indifference to me. Let us annihilate the Germans first:
> we can talk afterwards.]

For the Swiss tour in March 1917, the programme was an all-French
affair, with the exception of a number of Beethoven's symphonies.
The orchestra visited Geneva, Lausanne, Neuchâtel, Berne, Zurich
and Basle.

In addition to his contribution to the war effort, Messager
had once more begun to compose, writing Béatrice [W28], a
"légende lyrique" in the same serious mould as Madame
Chrysanthème and Le chevalier d'Harmental. Although Béatrice
should have gone into rehearsal at the Paris Opéra in September
1914, the war intervened. The work was first performed at the
Monte Carlo Opera in that year, and it was not to be seen in
Paris until 1917, when Wolff conducted it at the Opéra-Comique.
Like Madame Chrysanthème, Béatrice was a work which Messager
hoped would receive more than a few isolated performances in his
own lifetime. Set in 16th-century Sicily, it is the story of a

nun who has entered a convent as the result of a vow she made while nursing back to life a young man, Lorenzo, during the war. He discovers her in the Convent, and asks her to leave the institution and come away with him, to which she eventually consents. To prevent her absence being discovered, the statue of the Virgin, to whom Béatrice has shown exceptional devotion, comes to life and takes her place. In Act 2 Béatrice samples the pleasures of secular life, but quickly grows tired of them. She spends the next few years in search of new sensations in a demi-monde of corruption and vice, and finally (Act 4), makes her way back to the Convent, where the Virgin tells her that she has been expecting her. The work was not popular, and had only a few performances.

Messager's next stage work, produced at the end of the war, had a long gestation period.[74] Monsieur Beaucaire [W30], based on the novel of the same name by Booth Tarkington, is concerned with high society in 18th-century Bath. It was commissioned by the English impresario and theatre manager Gilbert Miller in 1916 but, due to various delays, was not performed until April 1919 at the Prince of Wales' Theatre, Birmingham, with Maggie Teyte as Lady Mary. The London première took place a fortnight later. A number of pieces of material preserved in the archives of the English publishers Ascherberg, Hopwood and Crew shed light on Miller's efforts to obtain a performance of the work towards the end of the war. For a consideration of £400, plus royalties of 1s 4d (7p) for each vocal score, 6d (2 1/2p) for each piano score and a further 6d for each separate song from the operetta sold in the U.K., Miller agreed to produce Monsieur Beaucaire "at a first-class West End London Theatre" within 12 months of the date of the agreement. He further agreed to have the work produced in the U.S.A. and Canada for a consideration of £300 plus royalties. Since Miller was not, in the event, able to deliver his part of the bargain, he presumably forfeited his money. Ascherberg bought back the U.S. and Canadian copyrights in September 1919 for the sum of £300.[75] Messager was too ill to attend the premières in London or Birmingham, his illness probably due in no small part to the fact that, at the age of 65, he had just returned from an exhausting post-war "propaganda tour" with the orchestra of the Société des Concerts. The tour had in addition been as arduous in its preparation as in its execution. Once more the autograph letters in the Bibliothèque Nationale, Paris, provide an important record of this event which, but for Messager's skill as an administrator, might never have taken place. The society gave concerts in 50 cities between October and December 1918.[76] The idea of a tour was first suggested in Summer 1917 and was co-ordinated by a French Government body known as Action Artistique à l'Etranger. The concerts were intended to counter German wartime propaganda that French art was of poor quality. In a rough "balance sheet" of 19 February 1918, Messager attempted to calculate the costs of the tour: there were originally to be thirty concerts over a period of ten weeks. Travel from Paris to New York and back would cost 53000F. The Wurlitzer Company of Cincinnati offered to supply double basses, cellos, harps and percussion, to save transport costs.[77] In July Messager gave firmer details of the works to be played: about 30 pieces would be performed, representing the best of French music, including Debussy's La mer and, more controversially, Dukas' Symphonie, of which Messager stated "Nous avons le devoir de faire connaître la musique française et ne pouvons négliger une oeuvre de cette importance". [We have a duty to advertise French music, and cannot overlook such an important work.][78] Three problems now presented themselves: first of all, the army refused to release a number of musicians whom Messager regarded as indispensable soloists; second, Philippe Gaubert, deputy conductor of the Société des Concerts, demanded a fee of 3000F every time he was called upon to conduct; and finally, it was suggested that the departure date of the company be moved back from October to November. On the last point, Messager wrote to the authorities that he had already contracted with His Majesty's Theatre, London, for an opéra comique in three acts (presumably Monsieur Beaucaire) to be delivered to them on 1 November 1917, and to be performed on about 15 December - proof that Miller had at least tried to honour his agreement with Ascherberg. Messager's relationship with Gaubert continued to cause problems throughout the tour, and the unhappiness provoked by the whole affair caused Messager to resign his post in April 1919. In a letter to the Committee, he stated "Divers incidents survenus pendant cette tournée, l'attitude et l'état d'esprit d'un certain nombre des artistes de l'orchestre ne me permettaient plus de solliciter de l'Assemblée Générale le renouvellement de mon mandat expiré depuis la fin de 1915". [A number of events which have occurred during the tour, and the attitude and morale of a certain number of performers, prevent me from seeking a renewal of my contract (which expired at the end of 1915) from the General Assembly.][79]

That Messager's services were still in demand after this incident is amply proved by the fact that he was soon asked by the Isola brothers and Carré to direct the 1919-1920 season at the Opéra-Comique. His productions included the first complete performance in France of Mozart's Così fan tutte. He thus entered what was to be his final decade without any signs of giving up his musical activities, and was doing as much as ever, as music critic on Le gaulois and (from 1921 to 1926) on Le figaro, on which he was Fauré's successor. He did, however, begin to succumb to the kidney complaint that was finally to kill him, and at one point in 1921 was so ill that a number of French papers reported his death. Several stage works were, however, still to come, the first of which, La petite fonctionnaire [W32], a return to music in a light vein, was premièred at the Théâtre Marigny in May 1921. The "petite fonctionnaire" of the title works for the Post Office; she falls for a Viscount in her home town, but he is more interested in marrying a girl of his own class. The fonctionnaire therefore accepts the protection of an older man who offers her a life of luxury in Paris. As time goes by she becomes dissatisfied with the arrangement, and the Viscount becomes equally disillusioned with his lot. In the best operetta tradition, a complex chain of events leads finally to a marriage between the Viscount and his "petite fonctionnaire".

L'amour masqué [W33], which followed in 1923, was Messager's first collaboration with Sacha Guitry. It became one of Messager's most popular and most recorded works. Guitry had first of all asked the composer Ivan Caryll to write the music, but Caryll died before the work was completed. Scored for a small orchestra because of the size of the Théâtre Edouard VII (site of the première, 15 February 1923), the work was intended primarily as a vehicle for Guitry's wife, Yvonne Printemps, to whom the work is dedicated. She recorded the most popular numbers from the show on disc (see DISCOGRAPHY).

Around the same time Messager was asked by Marguerite Long to provide a re-orchestration of Chopin's 2nd Piano Concerto [W127]; Messager himself later conducted the work at two Concerts Colonne. His interest in Chopin's music was of long standing - he was a member of the Comité d'Honneur of the Société Chopin, established in 1910, and he orchestrated a number of Chopin's piano pieces (in collaboration with Paul Vidal) for a Suite de danses [W126] performed at the Opéra in 1913.[80] No doubt his interest in the composer was further kindled by a relationship with Marguerite Long, noted by Janine Weill in her book Marguerite Long: une vie fascinante (Paris: Julliard, 1969).[81]

In 1926 Messager received a further honour from the French musical establishment: election to the presidency of the Société des Auteurs et Compositeurs Dramatiques, the first composer ever to hold that office. He could, apparently, be an occasionally irascible chairman! In the same year he succeeded Paladilhe as a member of the Académie des Beaux Arts, and had two new works premièred in Paris - Passionnément [W34] at the Théâtre de la Michodière in January, and Deburau [W35], another collaboration with Guitry, at the Théâtre Sarah Bernhardt in October. The score, dedicated by Messager "à la mémoire de Gabriel Fauré", featured both Guitry and Yvonne Printemps. The music starts with a lively, deliberately studied fugato movement, but soon breaks into a minuet for the "entrée de la duchesse", followed by the apparently inevitable Messager waltz. Marie's romance, "On s'adore", moves easily and gracefully over a simple but effective accompaniment.

In September 1927, in recognition of his services to musical life, Messager was appointed Commandeur de la Légion d'Honneur, and began what was to be his final work, Coups de roulis [W36]. In spite of Messager's years, Augé-Laribé judged the work to show neither the traces of age nor of Messager's ill-health, which was by this time becoming ever more extreme. He lived to see the work premièred at the Théâtre Marigny on 29 September 1928, with Marcelle Denya, and in fact had himself conducted the répétition générale the day before. A letter of March 1928 indicates that Messager still entertained hopes of seeing his opera Béatrice performed again: he gave his permission for Robert Brussel to arrange for performances in Darmstadt.

When he died on 24 February 1929 Messager left one unfinished work, to a text by André Rivoire. The piece, entitled Sacha [W37], was premièred at Monte Carlo, having been completed by the composer Marc Berthomieu.

Messager was buried at the spot he desired, near to the graves of Fauré and Debussy in the Cimitière de Passy, not far from the Trocadéro, where he had first made contact with Russian musicians in 1889. At his funeral on 1 March, at the church of Saint-François-des-Sales, the oration was given by Charles Méré, president of the Société des Auteurs et Compositeurs Dramatiques.[82] The orchestra of the Société des Concerts du Conservatoire played at the funeral. According to Méré, the society had lost more than a great musician: it had lost one of its best presidents, a guide and a counsellor. Although Messager was by now something of the "grand old man" of French music, having outlived both Debussy and Fauré, his death was felt by musicians of the younger as well as the older generation, and was reported in papers all around the world, all of which give in their despatches a sense of the loss of an internationally important figure.

NOTES

1. See Pierre Bonnaud, "Montluçon", La grande encyclopédie,
Paris: Librairie Larousse, 1971-1978, 13: 7156-7158. Montluçon
developed as a mining town during the 1830's and 1840's, and by
1853 was experiencing a population explosion: from 8810
inhabitants in 1851, it grew to 15289 in 1856. The town also had
a Philharmonic Society, founded in 1851.

2. Further genealogical details of both sides of the family are
given in Michel Augé-Laribé, André Messager: musicien de théâtre,
Paris: Editions du Vieux Colombier, 1951, 17-19.

3. Messager to Jaboune, published in Jaboune's Les grands hommes
quand ils étaient petits, Paris: Flammarion, 1925. Quoted in
Augé-Laribé, André Messager, 19-20, and in Henry Février, André
Messager: mon maître, mon ami, Paris: Amiot-Dumont, 1948, 18-19.

4. Jaboune, Les grands hommes. Quoted in Augé-Laribé, André
Messager, 20, and Février, André Messager, 18-19.

5. See for example Louis Beydts, Charles Gounod et André
Messager: conférence dite par l'auteur à Paris le 29 avril 1941,
Nancy: imp. E. Spillmann, 1942, 28: "Messager, dès ses débuts,
possède cette indéniable originalité. Il y a chez lui un tour de
main, une aisance désinvolte, et avec celà une mélancolie
gracieuse qui n'appartiennent qu'à lui, et qui fait que l'on
reconnaît sa musique entre toutes". [Messager, from the
beginning, possessed an unquestionable originality. He had a
dexterity, a casual easiness of style, which, combined with a
gracious melancholy, belonged to him alone, and made his music
distinguishable from that of any other composer.]

6. Fauré attended the school from 1854 to 1865. A M. Albert
Albrecht and a Mme Albrecht are listed in The Universal Music and
Dramatic Directory of 1915 as piano teachers in Montluçon,
together with a J. Albrecht, who taught violin.

7. Augé-Laribé, André Messager, 21.

8. Augé-Laribé, André Messager, 22, notes that at the time
Messager joined the school, it had only about a dozen pupils, all
of whom were little more than children; it was at that time
situated near the Place Clichy.

9. The fullest accounts of the École Niedermeyer are to be found in Maurice Galerne, L'École Niedermeyer: sa création, son but, son développement, Paris: Editions Margueritat, 1928, and in Gustave Lefèvre and Mme veuve Henri Heugel, "L'École de Musique Classique Niedermeyer", in A. Lavignac and L. de la Laurencie, eds., Encyclopédie de la musique, Paris: Delagrave, 1931, 2: 3617-3621.

10. See his biography in F. J. Fétis, Biographie universelle des musiciens, 2nd ed., Paris: Librairie de Firmin-Didot, 1863, 5: 319-321, and in the Supplément et complément, ed. A. Pougin, Paris: Firmin-Didot, 1880, 2: 273. A further biography of Niedermeyer, entitled Vie d'un compositeur moderne (1802-1861), was published in Paris by Fischbacher in 1893. Saint-Saëns wrote the introduction to this work.

11. Galerne, L'École Niedermeyer, 5. Messager also acknowledges Niedermeyer's work in reviving the music of Palestrina, Lassus, Janequin and Victoria, work later taken up by Henry Expert.

12. See Fauré's account of his first meeting with Messager in Musica, September 1908. Fauré later dedicated his Madrigal, op. 35, to Messager.

13. See also Augé-Laribé, André Messager, 150; " ... quand il lisait de la musique, c'était le plus souvent du Bach, parfois le Liszt des Anneés de pèlerinage". [... when he played music it was most often that of Bach, or sometimes that of Liszt's Années de pèlerinage.]

14. Messager was in fact organiste du choeur, Widor being in charge of the grand orgue.

15. For an account of Pasdeloup's activities, see Elisabeth Bernard, "Jules Pasdeloup et les Concerts Populaires", Revue de musicologie 57 (1971), 150-178. Notes on the foundation of Colonne's "Concerts Nationales" are in the Revue et gazette musicale de Paris, 2 March, 9 March and 23 March 1873. Seat prices at the concerts ranged from 50 centimes to three francs.

16. It was almost impossible for the general public to obtain tickets for performances by the Société des Concerts du Conservatoire: subscriptions were jealously guarded and often passed down from father to son.

17. See Hugues Imbert, Portraits et études, Paris: Fischbacher, 1894, 67-101, for a contemporary view of Lamoureux's achievements and personality.

18. Cited in Léon Vallas, Vincent d'Indy, 2 vols., Paris: Albin Michel, 1946, 1: 194.

19. Augé-Laribé, André Messager, 38-39.

20. See the Revue et gazette musicale de Paris, 20 January 1878, 22, and the review of the work in the issue of 27 January, 30.

21. Details of the competition and the results were published in Mémoires de la Société Académique des Sciences, Arts, Belles-Lettres, Agriculture et Industrie, 4e série, vol.1 (1878), 58-68. The competition of 1877 was the first to be organised by the town of Saint-Quentin. According to the rules of the competition, the cantata was to be for three voices, and only French composers were allowed to enter. There were 14 entrants: the first prizewinner received a gold medal, 300 francs and a guaranteed performance of his work at the Théâtre de Saint-Quentin. Messager was awarded second prize, because "soit manque de temps, soit lassitude" [due either to lack of time, or laziness] he had not been able to finish his score satisfactorily. The winner was the Prince Edmond de Polignac, whose setting was accordingly performed on 26 November 1877. It is worthy of note that Vaucorbeil, who was later to commission Les deux pigeons [W41], and who was at that time President of the Société des Compositeurs de Musique, was head of the competition jury, and he must surely have met Messager either in the course of the competition itself, or at the concert of 26 November at which, according to a report in the Journal de Saint-Quentin (and reproduced in the Mémoires cited above), both he and Messager were present; the latter was listed as "organiste de Saint-Sulpice".

22. A. Banès, "Messager", in "L'Opéra nouveau", special number of La revue théâtrale (1908), 2. Banès also claims that Messager had a brief spell at the Théâtre des Variétés before passing on to the Folies-Bergère. I have been unable to confirm this statement.

23. Augé-Laribé, André Messager, 43, notes drily that "on aurait pu conduire aux Folies-Bergère M. Le maréchale de Mac-Mahon, et même Mme la maréchale, sans les faire rougir". [One could have taken M. le marechal Mac-Mahon to the Folies-Bergère, and even the marshall's wife, without causing them to blush.] The orange flower of the title is offered by Damon to his shepherdess.

24. The manuscript also contains sketches for Fauré's 1st Impromptu.

25. Robert Orledge claims that this movement was orchestrated by Fauré. Orledge, Gabriel Fauré, London: Eulenberg Books, 1979, rev. 1983, 269.

26. See Albert Lavignac, Le voyage artistique à Bayreuth, Paris: Delagrave, 1897.

27. Nectoux, Gabriel Fauré: his Life through his Letters, 95.

28. Gustave Samazeuilh, "Un serviteur de la musique: André Messager", Courrier musical 31 (15 March 1929), 199-200.

29. For further notes regarding Souvenirs de Bayreuth, see the WORKLIST, item [W96].

30. "André Messager par ... André Messager", Musica, September 1908. In fact, in his letter applying for the conductorship of the Société des Concerts du Conservatoire (Bibliothèque Nationale, Paris, Département de la Musique, lettre autographe 31), Messager claimed that he secured the post through the help and advice of Joseph Dupont, founder of the Brussels Concerts Populaires. There is a brief biography of Dupont (who had taken over the directorship of these concerts in 1873) in F. J. Fétis's Biographie universelle des musiciens, 2nd ed., Supplément et complément, 1: 290-291.

31. Février, André Messager, 29.

32. [... smiling and happy, slim and distinguished, eye bright, strong chin, a mocking mouth, imperious moustache, and black hair already growing thin; just as we were later to see him on the conductor's rostrum at the Opéra.] Février, André Messager, 12. We should bear in mind that Février would have only been about eight years of age at the time: his account may therefore be somewhat embroidered.

33. There are no copies of the original publication of these works in either the British Library, London, or the Bibliothèque Nationale, Paris; but the publication date of 1888 is confirmed by an entry in the Bibliographie musicale française for October-December 1888, 52.

34. Augé-Laribé, André Messager, 53.

35. The London performances were at the Royalty Theatre from 16
to 21 November 1891, and were reviewed in The Stage, 19 November,
The Times, 17 November, and The Saturday Review, 21 November
1891. The reviewer of The Times was not amused by the piece, and
commented: "Its attractions were not greatly increased by the
interpolated dances composed respectively by Mr. W. C. Levey and
Mr. Arthur E. Godfrey, who conducts the performance with some
skill". I have been unable to find these dances, either at
Chappell and Co. or at the British Library.

36. Février, André Messager, 33. The matter is also reported in
L. Rohozinski, ed. Cinquante ans de musique française, Paris:
Editions Librairie de la France, 1925, 1: 252.

37. Augé-Laribé, André Messager, 56-57. Louis Laloy, writing in
Cinquante ans de musique française, ed. L. Rohozinski, Paris:
Editions Librairie de la France, 1925, 1: 71-74, claims that
Messager gave the same story to him personally.

38. Archives Nationales, Paris, AJ13, 1197. There are in fact
two copies of this letter in the file, one Vaucorbeil's rough
draft, the other a fair copy. The valedictory sentence is
slightly different in each, and the text cited here is that of
the fair copy. In view of Vaucorbeil's previous experience of
Messager's work at the competition in Saint-Quentin, the imposed
condition does not seem surprising. I am grateful to the
administration of the Archives Nationales for permission to cite
this letter.

39. Vaucorbeil having died in the meantime, the letter is
addressed to Ritt and Gailhard, the new directors. There are two
manuscript sources for Les deux pigeons in the Bibliothèque de
l'Opéra in Paris. The first, ms Rés647, was donated by
Messager's grand-daughters on 4 June 1956, according to a note on
the inside cover: Mme Jacqueline Dumora-Messager has also
confirmed that the manuscript was given by the family. With
green mottled boards and a cream leather spine, it bears the
words "A. Messager. Les deux pigeons. Partition d'orchestre".
It contains 300 pages of 20-stave paper, and is clearly in
Messager's handwriting. Some blue pencil markings indicate that
it was used in performance. The other manuscript, A647a(I-II),
consists of two volumes bound in grey cloth. Volume 1 has 212
pages, and volume 2, 306 pages. On the opening page of volume 1
is the inscription "Partition d'orchestre. M. E. Altès, Chef
d'orchestre". While this manuscript also shows signs of use in
performance (there are markings in red and blue pencil), it is a
much smarter autograph than Rés647; on the last page of vol.2

Messager has written "Fin. Deo Gratias". I would suggest that it was this manuscript, rather than Rés647, that was presented to the Directors of the Opéra in January 1885.

40. Broussan, then 98 years old, writes "Ce fut sur mes instances réiterées que Messager se décida à faire monter à l'Opéra, son ballet des "Deux Pigeons", que je considérais musicalement comme l'égal du meilleur ballet". [It was at my repeated insistence that Messager decided to have his ballet Les deux pigeons produced at the Opéra: it is a ballet that I would consider equal to the best.] The performances of 1910 were preceded by a revival of the work in 1893, for which several choreographic sketches survive in the Bibliothèque de l'Opéra, Paris.

41. Février, André Messager, 45. Willy [Henry Gauthier-Villars] in La paix of 20 December 1889 began his review: "Je sors, enchanté, des Bouffes-Parisiens, où le Mari de la Reine vient de tomber à plat ..." [I depart, enraptured, from the Bouffes-Parisiens, where the Mari de la reine has just fallen flat ...]

42. Originally published in 1908. English translation, My Musical Life, published by Alfred A. Knopf in 1923, and in a revised edition in London by Eulenberg Books in 1974. Page numbers given here refer to the Eulenberg edition.

43. Rimsky-Korsakov, My Musical Life, 302-303. Rimsky-Korsakov noted that Pugno was a fine pianist, but says nothing of Messager's keyboard skills.

44. Ibid, 302.

45. According to a manuscript prompt copy of the libretto used in the original performances at the Opéra-Comique, Clément Marot was played by Gabriel Soulacroix, the Duc de Longueville by Lucien Fugère, and Marie by Lisa Landouzy. This manuscript copy, Bibliothèque de l'Opéra, Pièce B409, is a libretto in grey cloth headed "Théâtre National de l'Opéra-Comique: Souffleur". It includes the censor's authorisation and confirms the date of the première as 30 May, in a pencil note. There are 153 pages, numbered in pencil. Most of the text appears to have been used, with only a few small cuts indicated.

46. The Times of 4 November 1891 made the interesting observation that, in La Basoche, "the influence of Die Meistersinger is felt to an extent that is almost absurd, both in the bright overture and again in the procession of the guild, but elsewhere the music is as original as it is charming".

47. Février, _André Messager_, 49.

48. The scene "Mort d'Hélène" survives in manuscript at the Bibliothèque Nationale (ms Don Malherbe 7205), signed by Messager and dated November 1891.

49. A score of _Scaramouche_ in the Bibliothèque Nationale, Paris, Département de la Musique (Cons. L4692), bears the dedication "A l'ami Maton, souvenir d'ancienne et très sincère amitié. G. Street". It is possible that Messager and Street met through their mutual acquaintance, Albert Carré.

50. The work was also reviewed in _Le figaro_, _Le gaulois_ and _Le Voltaire_, as noted in the "dossier de l'oeuvre" relating to the piece in the Bibliothèque de l'Opéra.

51. Messager was certainly not unaware of the concessions he would have to make to English taste; in a letter to R. Blondel dated 27 November 1894, responding to a suggestion that _Mirette_ be performed on the Continent, he says of the work: "C'est tout à fait exportation, et les multiples concessions faites au goût anglais ne me rendent pas très désireux de propager cette partition". [It is intended for export only, and the many concessions I have had to make to the English taste do not make me very willing to disseminate this score.] Bibliothèque Nationale, Paris, Département de la Musique, _lettre autographe_ 5. For more details of Messager's activities in England, especially his work with the British Musical Defence League, see William Boosey, _Fifty Years of Music_, London: Ernest Benn, 1931.

52. J. P. Wearing, in _The London Stage, 1890-1899: a Calendar of Plays and Players_, 2 vols., Metuchen, NJ, and London: Scarecrow Press, 1976, claims that Messager conducted the first performance; but a note in the vocal score states that Cellier conducted, although the work was produced "under the personal supervision of the Author and Composer".

53. See the brief account in F. Cellier and Cunningham Bridgeman, _Gilbert, Sullivan and D'Oyly Carte_, London: I. Pitman, 1894, 332; Cellier's statement that _Mirette_ had already had great success in Paris is quite incorrect - the vocal score of the "new version" states that the work was written "expressly for the Savoy Theatre".

54. Little is known of Miss Davis. Her forenames were Alice Maude, although she seems to have been known to everyone as Dotie. William Boosey (who wrote the words of _Colin Deep_) notes that she studied first of all with André Wormser in Paris,

subsequently taking further lessons with Messager (William
Boosey, Fifty Years of Music, London: Ernest Benn, 1931, 29).
Isidore de Lara, in his autobiography Many Tales of Many Cities,
London: Hutchinson, 1938, states that he first met her in Paris
between 1892 and 1894, and at the same time made the
acquaintance, through Miss Davis, of Frederick Delius. She was,
according to de Lara, very beautiful, and "was universally
admired and appreciated by the musical world in Paris. Her box
at the dress rehearsals of the Opéra-Comique, and the Grand
Opera, was quite a salon, where came in turn all the great
artists, critics, and outstanding personalities of the beginning
of the 20th century" (op. cit., 99, 173-174). Concerning
Messager's acquaintance with Delius, see Lionel Carley, Delius:
the Paris Years, London: Triad Press, 1975, 15-16. An
advertisement for Chappell and Co.'s "new and popular songs" for
1894-1895 lists three songs by Miss "Temple" then in vogue: The
Lights of Home; Colin deep; and Airlie Bay. I think it most
unlikely that Miss Davis had any significant part in the creation
of Mirette, although one cannot ignore Messager's statement to
the contrary, stated in his memoirs (see APPENDIX 3). Some
further biographical details of Miss Davis are provided in Who
was Who, 3, London: A. & C. Black, 1947. Miss Davis was born in
Ireland of English parents, and was educated at a private college
in Ireland. She originally studied to become a pianist, but had
to give up this ambition due to sporting accidents. She began
composing at the age of 14, and although a list of her songs is
given, there is no mention of any part in the composition of
Mirette. She died in 1938 (op. cit., 1332). There is an
obituary in Etude [Philadelphia] 56 (July 1938), 422.

55. Albert Carré, "Entr'actes", Le matin, 23 February 1932.

56. For details of the cast of this production, press notices,
and details of Mary Garden's subsequent role in the opera, see
Marc Delmas, Gustave Charpentier et le lyrisme français, Paris:
Delagrave, 1931, 84-91.

57. Hahn was not over-impressed by Messager's conducting on this
occasion, and writing to a friend he stated "L'exécution a été
très bonne. Evidemment, Messager aurait pu diriger mieux: ce
n'est pas un chef de théâtre, il est trop exclusivement musical;
il s'attache trop aux details, il ne sent pas derrière lui l'âme
du public, il ignore ce flou variable, qui fait haleter,
soupirer, attendre." [It was performed very well. Obviously,
Messager could have conducted better; he is not a master of the
theatre, being too exclusively musical; he sets too much store by
detail without feeling the spirit of the public behind him, and
does not understand the variable musical flow which makes one

hold one's breath, sigh, and wait ...] Cited in Bernard Gavoty, Reynaldo Hahn: le musicien de la Belle Epoque, Paris: Editions Buchet/Chastel, 1976, 59.

58. Kurt Gänzl, The British Musical Theatre, 2 vols., Basingstoke: Macmillan, 1986, 1: 865. Gänzl also gives background to the English production.

59. Bibliothèque de l'Opéra, Paris, ms Rés2281. This is a grey cloth volume, with strengthening of green leather at the corners. It contains 134 pages, written in Messager's own hand. A further note in another hand states "Puis repris et représenté devant le Roi de Suède le 28 avril 1096 [i.e.1906]". This may explain why, among the honours conferred on Messager, we note the distinction Commandeur de l'Étoile Polaire de Suède. Other honours he enjoyed were Commandeur de Saint-Anne de Russie, Commandeur de Leopold II de Belgique, and Commandeur de Sainte-Alexandre de Bulgarie.

60. Bibliothèque de l'Opéra, Paris, ms 1900 𝄞 XII(198).

61. Harold Rosenthal, Two Centuries of Opera at Covent Garden, London: Putnam, 1958, 278.

62. James Harding, Folies de Paris, London: Chappell, 1979, 136, further points out that Messager knew Lady de Grey, sister-in-law of the Chairman of the Grand Opera Syndicate; she is known to have patronised French musicians. Orledge reminds us that Fauré was well connected in English social circles at this time, largely through his acquaintance with the painter John Singer Sargent; perhaps Sargent was able to exert some influence, as noted by Percy Grainger in a letter to Sargent's biographer Evan Charteris in 1926: "Remarkable as his [Sargent's] playing was, intense as his delight in active music-making was, I consider his greatest contribution to music, lay in the wondrously beneficent influence he exerted on musical life". E. Charteris, John Sargent, London: Heinemann, 1928, 149.

63. Fuller details of Messager's activities at Covent Garden may be found in J. P. Wearing, The London Stage, 1900-1909: a Calendar of Plays and Players, 2 vols., Metuchen, NJ, and London: Scarecrow Press, 1981. Wearing does not mention that Messager also conducted, on 12 July 1905, a "Grand operatic Benefit Matinée for Mlle Bauermeister's Farewell"; this concert included Acts 1 and 2 of Gounod's Roméo et Juliette and Act 3 of La bohème, with Caruso as Rodolfo.

64. Bibliothèque Nationale, Paris, Département de la Musique, lettre autographe 12.

65. Letters between the two men on the subject of Pelléas are in Jean [André-]Messager, comp., L'enfance de Pelléas: lettres de Claude Debussy à André Messager, Paris: Dorbon-Ainé, 1938. I do not therefore propose to treat the episode of Pelléas in detail, particularly as this work seems all too often to take up a disproportionate amount of space in the Messager literature. Messager himself wrote an article on the subject, entitled "Les premières représentations de Pelléas", printed in La revue musicale, special number (May 1926), 110-114; and Henri Büsser also gives some details of preparations for the première in his De Pelléas aux Indes Galantes, Paris: Fayard, 1955.

66. Cited in François Lesure, ed., Claude Debussy: lettres 1884-1918, Paris: Hermann, 1980, 56.

67. Bibliothèque Nationale, Paris, Département de la Musique, lettres autographes 14 and 16 (to Albert Carré). In the first, dated 29 August 1902, Messager states that the staging of Madame Chrysanthème at the Opéra-Comique is "une des choses que je désire le plus. Vous savez, la pièce n'est pas si mal que ça, et il faudrait peu de choses pour qu'elle soit tout à fait bien. J'ai l'intention de refaire ce qui m'a paru clocher et je voudrais bien avoir votre conseil à ce sujet". [One of the things I would like most. You know, the piece isn't all that bad, and would only need a little alteration to make it work completely. I intend to reshape what seems clumsy to me and would very much appreciate your advice on the matter.] Lettre autographe 16 was written from Milan, 17 February 1903 or 1904: Messager has met a singer in Milan named Friche, who (he states with all his usual candour) "n'est pas une femme pour l'Opéra-Comique". He concludes the letter: "Le travail que vous avez été assez gentil de faire pour Chrysanthème m'a paru excellent. Il y a peut-être un peu trop de vers, mais j'arrangerai celà en faisant la musique. Mille fois merci pour toute la peine que vous avez prise". [The work which you have had the goodness to do for Chrysanthème seems excellent to me. There is perhaps a little too much verse, but I will fix that when I write the music. A thousand thanks for all the trouble you have taken.] If Messager did set more spoken dialogue to music subsequently, we have no trace of it. Gabriel Fauré, reviewing the performance of Puccini's Madame Butterfly at the Opéra-Comique in December 1906, made another plea for a revival of Madame Chrysanthème, but noted that the political situation existing between France, Russia and Japan at that time would probably prevent it.

68. See Edouard Gauthier, "M. Broussan", in "L'Opéra nouveau", special number of La revue théâtrale, Paris 1908. There are two photographs of Broussan included in the article, and a further photograph in Février, André Messager, between pp.32 and 33.

69. Février gives details of many works performed at the Opéra between 1908 and 1914, as does Louis Laloy in Cinquante ans de musique française, 1: 90-91. Laloy also gives interesting details of receipts. Février's own Monna Vanna was staged at the Opéra in 1909, after some dispute with Maeterlinck concerning who should sing the female lead. Février's account of this episode, the details of which seem almost too similar to those of Debussy's own dispute with Maeterlinck over the role of Mélisande to be true, is nevertheless confirmed by correspondence in the Archives Nationales, Paris, file AJ13, 1195.

70. Archives Nationales, Paris, file AJ13, 1195, 48.

71. Eugène Berteaux, En ce temps-là, Paris: Editions du Bateau-Ivre, 1956, 182-191.

72. This was a benefit concert for George Marty's widow. A list of works conducted by Messager during his term as director of the society's orchestra may be found in Arthur Dandelot, La Société des Concerts du Conservatoire (1828-1923), Paris: Delagrave, 1923, 166-180.

73. This is an oblong manuscript with a medal of Habaneck (founder of the Society in 1828) and marked "Société des Concerts du Conservatoire". It includes letters to the Society from Chopin, Saint-Saëns, Gounod and others. Jacques Thibaut's message reads "Ma plus chère amitié et mon enthousiaste admiration à l'orchestre unique au monde et à son admirable chef Monsieur Messager. 4 et 5 avril 1912".

74. Stated by Messager himself in a newspaper interview with Gaston Lebel for La volonté, 20 October 1925.

75. Ascherberg, Hopwood and Crew, "Play File A and B". The file also contains other documents pertaining to Monsieur Beaucaire, dealing in part with the sale of the work to Salabert in 1925 on the occasion of the first French production at the Théâtre Marigny, Paris, and in part with English amateur productions. After Monsieur Beaucaire closed in London, it was transferred to Broadway's New Amsterdam Theatre, where it had 143 performances (see Gänzl, The British Musical Theatre, 2: 147). I am grateful to Chappell and Co. for allowing me to have access to material in their archives.

76. The cities visited are listed by Albert Vernaelde in "La Société des Concerts", Encyclopédie de la musique, ed. A. Lavignac and L. de la Laurencie, 2: 3702-3703.

77. Bibliothèque Nationale, Paris, Département de la Musique, lettre autographe 65.

78. Bibliothèque Nationale, Paris, Département de la Musique, lettre autographe 40. In another letter (no.70), Messager asks Cortot to perform Fauré's Ballade for piano and orchestra on the tour, since Fauré will otherwise be represented only by the "Nocturne" from Shylock and "La fileuse" from Pelléas et Mélisande.

79. Bibliothèque Nationale, Paris, Département de la Musique, lettre autographe 55.

80. The manuscript is in the Bibliothèque de l'Opéra, Paris, ms A716bis. It has mottled boards and a red cloth spine with the inscription "Chopin - Suite de danses" in gold. There is no attribution inside either to Messager or to Paul Vidal, who (Augé-Laribé suggested) was originally commissioned to write the work, and whom Messager helped out when Vidal ran into difficulties. The work is for full orchestra including three flutes, cor anglais, double bassoon and an alto saxophone in E flat; this last instrument is used sparingly, and only in combination with other wind instruments, never as a soloist.

81. See especially pp.94-95, in which Janine Weill quotes Marguerite Long herself: "A la veille de partir pour l'Amérique du Sud, il [Messager] m'avait fait parvenir une "Invitation au voyage" qui, pour tentante qu'il fût, ne s'accordait pas avec la raison souveraine ... Je lui dis qu'après tant de brillantes conquêtes il risquait d'être deçu! ... Que sais-je encore? Et devant ma résistance, comme il fit alors bon marché de celles qui lui avaient cédé ... O éternel masculin". [On the eve of his departure for South America, he sent me an "Invitation to travel", which, tempting though it was, was not in keeping with all-important rationality ... I told him that after so many magnificent conquests he was likely to be disappointed ... What more do I know? And in the face of my resistance, how lightly he spoke of those other women who had given in to him ... eternal masculine!]

82. Extracts from the oration are quoted in Février, André Messager, 235-239. Février also quotes from Widor's Notice sur la vie et les oeuvres d'André Messager, a paper delivered at the annual meeting of the Académie des Beaux Arts in November 1929.

Worklist

The list of works presented here forms the most comprehensive
catalogue of Messager's works published to date. Of the two
previously published lists, that given by Octave Seré in his
<u>Musiciens français d'aujourd'hui</u> does not progress beyond 1911,
and that of Augé-Laribé, while hitherto the most comprehensive
list, omits a number of works, including the <u>Messe des pêcheurs
de Villerville</u>, <u>Les beignets du roi</u> and some songs. In addition
to these sources, there is, in the Bibliothèque Nationale, Paris,
a handwritten <u>Catalogue des oeuvres d'André Messager</u>, which,
while undated and bearing no signature, agrees in most respects
with the details of works supplied by Seré and Augé-Laribé, and
in addition includes details of a few compositions they do not
mention.[1] Seré likewise includes a few works not documented
elsewhere, and not traceable in the catalogues of the Library of
Congress, British Library or Bibliothèque Nationale. Such works
are included in this worklist in Section 3(a) "Unpublished
songs", or Section 6, "Miscellaneous Works", with appropriate
comment as to the source of the information.

1. Bibliothèque Nationale, Paris, Département de la Musique,
<u>Pièce 643</u>.

This list is divided into seven sections:

Section 1:   Stage works, excluding ballets

Section 2:   Ballets

Section 3:   Songs

Section 4:   Other vocal music

Section 5:   Instrumental works

Section 6:   Miscellaneous works, including works
                projected but apparently not completed

Section 7:   Arrangements of works by other composers

As far as possible the works presented in each section are laid
out in chronological order. Except where otherwise stated, works
were published in Paris, and stage works premièred in Paris.

SECTION 1: Stage works, excluding ballets

[W1] Les païens

> According to Antoine Banès in his article "Messager" for
> "L'Opéra nouveau", a special number of La revue théâtrale,
> (1908), this piece was written by Messager in collaboration
> with Gaston Serpette, Charles-Marie Widor, Jules Massenet
> and Léo Delibes c.1876, to a libretto by Henri Meilhac, and
> was produced by the Cercle de l'Union Artistique at the
> Place Vendôme, Paris. In view of Messager's acquaintance
> with Widor at this time (through his functions at
> Saint-Sulpice), and later links with Serpette, the
> possibility that such a piece may at one time have existed
> should not be ruled out, although there is no copy in the
> Bibliothèque Nationale, Paris, and the work is not mentioned
> elsewhere.

[W2] Rondeau de l'opérette chanté par Madame Judic dans "La
Revue Pornographique" au Cercle de la Presse

Text: Émile Blavet
Première: At the premises of the Cercle de la Presse, 31
December 1880
First published: Supplement to Le figaro, 12 January 1881
Notes: A light song in honour of Offenbach, beginning
"Pardon, messieurs, de troubler votre fête". According
to a report in Le figaro of 1 January 1881, the revue
began at 1 a.m. in a packed theatre intended for only
250 people. The report continues: "A une heure du
matin, ont frappé les trois coups. Daubray, qui joue
le compère, vient d'arriver. On n'attendait plus que
lui. L'orchestre fait son entrée. Il est représentée
par MM. Salvayre, Messager et Antony Choudens qui, tour
à tour, tiennent le piano". [At 1 a.m. there were
three knocks. Daubray, who was playing compère, had
just arrived. No-one was expecting anyone else. The
"orchestra" entered, represented by Salvayre, Messager
and Antony Choudens, who, one by one, played the
piano.] Of the rondeau, the reporter states it was
"admirablement chanté et détaillé - paroles de Blavet,
musique de Messager, un jeune compositeur de beaucoup
d'avenir".

[W3] François les bas-bleus

Opéra comique, 3 acts
Text: Ernest Dubreuil, Eugène Humbert, Paul Burani
Première: Folies-Dramatiques, 8 November 1883
Cast: François - Max Bouvet; Le marquis - Montrouge; Jasmin
- Bartel; Fanchon - Jeanne André; La comtesse -
Dharville
Chef d'orchestre - Désiré Thibault
First published: Enoch frères et Costallat, 1883
Notes: Completed by Messager after the death of Firmin
Bernicat. According to Augé-Laribé, 15 of the 25
numbers are by Messager, who also orchestrated the
whole work. Messager himself, however, claimed
authorship of only 12 numbers in a letter written to
Johannes Weber of Le temps in March 1888, after the
latter had suggested in his column of 12 March that
Messager's role in François les bas-bleus had been much
smaller than generally supposed. (The vocal score
states merely "terminée par André Messager".) Referring
to a subsequent letter in Le temps of 19 March, Weber

accepted Messager's statement regarding his
contribution to François les bas-bleus but went on to
query why, if Messager had made any significant
contribution to Les premières armes de Louis XV [W9]
(another Bernicat score for which Messager had written
some music), his name did not appear on any of the
playbills. Published in London as François the Radical
(Enoch and Sons, 1885). The Bibliothèque Nationale,
Paris, also possesses a Menuet de François les
bas-bleus: transcription pour piano par André
Messager, published by Enoch frères et Costallat, 1883,
and a Fantaisie brillante pour violon et piano by Émile
Périer. The indefatigable Émile Tavan also made a
"Mosaique" of the work. The duo from Act 2, "Espérance
en d'heureux jours", was published as a musical
supplement to L'illustration, 19 October 1895. François
les bas-bleus was performed at the Boston Museum
[theatre] in 1884, under the title Fantine, in a
translation by Benjamin Woolf (who also added some
extra music) and R. M. Field, at that time the director
of the Museum theatre. George Purdy provided the
orchestration. The original work was later performed as
far afield as St. Petersburg.
Reviews: L'art musical, 15 November 1883, January 1884

[W4] Le petit poucet

Musique de scène for a "féerie"
Text: Arnold Mortier, Eugène Leterrier, Albert Vanloo
Première: Gaité Theatre, 28 October 1885
Cast: Le petit poucet - Biana Duhamel
Notes: Only the "Chanson des loups" (published by Enoch
    frères et Costallat, 1885), a Quadrille and a set of
    waltzes by Alfred Fock were published.
Reviews: Le ménestrel, 22 November 1885

[W5] La fauvette du temple

Opéra comique, 3 acts
Text: Eugène Humbert, Paul Burani
Première: Folies-Dramatiques, 17 November 1885
Cast: Pierre Aubertin - M. Jourdan; St. Angénor - Gobin;
    Thérèse - Aimée Simon-Girard; Zélie - Mme Vialda;
    Joseph Abrial - Simon-Max; Cransac - Mme Duhamel
    Chef d'orchestre - Désiré Thibault
First published: Enoch frères et Costallat, [1885]

Notes: Premièred in Britain as <u>La fauvette</u> at the Edinburgh
Lyceum, 18 May 1891; Arthur E. Godfrey conducted.
London première (in English) at the Royalty Theatre, 16
November 1891, to a libretto by Alfred Rae. The lead
was played by Florence Burns, Pierre by Harry Child,
and St. Angénor by W. H. Rawlins. Published in England
by Enoch, 1891. Emile Waldteufel arranged a <u>Suite de</u>
<u>valses</u> on themes from the work (published 1886), and C.
Godfrey also arranged a selection (published London,
1891). Selections were also arranged by Émile Tavan.

Reviews: (English production): <u>The Times</u>, 17
November 1891; (French production): <u>L'art musical</u>, 30
November 1885; <u>Le ménestrel</u>, 22 November 1885; <u>Le</u>
<u>temps</u>, 28 December 1885

[W6] Gisèle

The only mention of this piece I have been able to discover
is in the legal columns of <u>Le temps</u> of 15 August 1886. The
work, an operetta in three acts, was to a text by François
Oswald and Maxime Boucheron, and had already been accepted
for production at the Bouffes-Parisiens. Unfortunately,
before the piece could be staged, the theatre management
went bankrupt. Messager and his librettists then sued the
new management following its failure to stage the work. The
report in <u>Le temps</u> reads as follows:

> En septembre 1884, M. François Oswald et Maxime
> Boucheron pour les paroles, M. André Messager pour la
> musique, firent recevoir aux Bouffes-Parisiens, dirigés
> alors par M. Cantin, une opérette en 3 actes intitulée
> <u>Gisèle</u>. Peu après. M. Cantin vendit sa part des
> Bouffes à M. Gaspari, gérant d'une Société qui fut
> bientôt mise en liquidation. Mme Ugalde pris alors la
> direction. Les auteurs, se fondant sur la traité de la
> Société des auteurs dramatiques qui, seul, a force de
> loi en pareille occasion, reclamèrent de la directrice
> la représentation de leur ouvrage où, à défaut,
> l'indemnité due depuis le mois de décembre dernier,
> échéance réglementaire du dédit. L'affaire est venue en
> justice. Mme Ugalde a été condamnée à payer à MM.
> Oswald, Boucheron et Messager une somme de 2500 fr. à
> titre de dommages-interêts, sauf son recours contre la
> liquidation de la Société Gaspari, qui avait, dit-on.
> laissé ignorer la réception de <u>Gisèle</u> au théâtre des
> Bouffes-Parisiens.

[In September 1884, M. François Oswald and Maxime
Boucheron, authors, and M. André Messager, composer,
provided for the Bouffes-Parisiens (whose director at
that time was M. Cantin) an operetta in three acts
entitled Gisèle. Shortly afterwards, M. Cantin sold
his stake in the Bouffes to M. Gaspari, director of a
society which soon went into liquidation. Mme Ugalde
then took over as director. The authors, relying on
the treaty of the Société des Auteurs Dramatiques,
which alone has legal status in such a case, demanded
from the director either that their work be performed
or, failing this, that they were awarded compensation
from the previous December, this being the statutory
penalty. The matter came to court, and Mme Ugalde was
ordered to pay the sum of 2500 francs in damages to MM.
Oswald, Boucheron and Messager, unless she were to
appeal against the liquidation of the Société Gaspari,
which had, it was claimed, not informed her of the
receipt of Gisèle at the Théâtre des Bouffes-
Parisiens.]

The episode does not seem to have prevented Messager from
offering La Béarnaise [W7] to the Bouffes-Parisiens a year
later, at which time Mme Ugalde (the singer Delphine Beauce
Ugalde, 1829-1910) was still in charge.

[W7] La béarnaise

Opéra comique, 3 acts
Text: Eugène Leterrier, Albert Vanloo
Première: Bouffes-Parisiens, 12 December 1885
Cast: Jacquette - Jeanne Granier; Bianca - Mily-Meyer;
    Pomponio - M. Maugé; 1e Duc - Lucien Murator;
    Perpignac - Vauthier; Carlo - Paravacini
    Chef d'orchestre - Marius Baggers
First published: Enoch frères et Costallat, 1886
Notes: British première at the Grand Theatre, Birmingham,
    27 September 1886, to an English text by Alfred Murray.
    London première at the Prince of Wales' Theatre, 4
    October 1886. First published in London by Alfred Hays
    in 1886. The English version includes a song, "Silent
    Love" (Act 1, no.7), which does not appear in the
    French score. The work is dedicated to Jeanne Granier.
Reviews: Le ménestrel, 20 December 1885

[W8] Le bourgeois de Calais

    Opéra comique, 3 acts
    Text: Ernest Dubreuil, Paul Burani
    Première: Folies-Dramatiques, 6 April 1887
    Cast: Duc de Guise - Morlet; André - Duchèsne; Marthe - L.
        Borel; Comtesse de Civrac - Juliette Darcourt; Lord
        Trefford - Gobin
        Chef d'orchestre - Désiré Thibault
    First published: Enoch frères et Costallat, 1887
    Notes: The duet "Il faut savoir mourir pour la patrie" (Act
        3, no.19) was later published separately as Le credo de
        la victoire [W87]
    Reviews: L'art musical, 15 April 1887; Le temps, 11 April
        1887

[W9] Les premières armes de Louis XV

    Opéra comique, 3 acts
    Text: Albert Carré, after Benjamin Antier
    Première: Menus-Plaisirs, 16 February 1888
    Cast: Le Roi - Marie Nixau; Antoinette - Jeanne Pierny
    Unpublished
    Notes: Originally entitled Les beignets du roi, with music
        by Bernicat, and produced in Brussels in February 1882.
        Carré required extra music for the 1888 Paris
        production, and was introduced to Messager by
        Bernicat's widow.
    Reviews: L'art musical, 29 February 1888; Le temps, 12
        March, 19 March 1888

[W10] Isoline

    "Conte de fées", 3 acts and 10 scenes
    Text: Catulle Mendès
    Première: Théâtre de la Renaissance, 26 December 1888
    Cast: Eros/Oberon - M. Morlet; Isolin - Marie Nixau; Isoline
        - Antonia Aussourt; Titania - Berthe Thibault; La belle
        fille/Violente - Germaine Gallois; Daphnis - Wolff;
        Chloë - Précourt
        Chef d'orchestre - Gabriel-Marie
    First published: Enoch frères et Costallat, 1888
    Notes: The "Madrigal d'Isoline", in a transcription for
        violin and piano by Ingeborg Magnum, was published in
        Paris and London by Enoch in 1897, along with the

"Pavane des fées", the most popular piece from the
work. The vocal score was not published in London until
1900.
Reviews: L'art musical, 31 December 1888; Le temps, 31
December 1888

[W11] Colibri

Comédie, 1 act
Text: Louis Legendre
Première: Vaudeville, 12 June 1889
First published: Choudens fils, 1890 (Sérénade only)

[W12] Le mari de la reine

Opérette, 3 acts
Text: Ernest Grenet-Dancourt, O. Pradels
Première: Bouffes-Parisiens, 18 December 1889
Cast: Justine - Mily-Meyer; La reine - Aussourd; Florestan -
Albert Piccaluga; Yakoub - Tauffenberger; Patouillard
- Montrouge; Tomba-Kopo - Gailhard
First published: Choudens fils, 1890
Notes: Includes the "valse chantée", "Si j'avais vos
légères ailes" (Act 2, no.12), which was published
separately.
Reviews: L'art musical, 31 December 1889; La paix, 20
December 1889; Le temps, 23 December 1889

[W13] La Basoche

Opéra comique, 3 acts
Text: Albert Carré
Première: Opéra-Comique, 30 May 1890
Cast: Clément Marot - Gabriel Soulacroix; Duc de
Longueville - Lucien Fugère; Marie - Lisa
Landouzy; L'éveillé - Carbonne; Colette - Molé-
Truffier; Roland - Bernäert
Chef d'orchestre - Jules Danbé
First published: Choudens, 1890
Notes: Performed in Hamburg under the title Die zwei
Könige, 19 October 1891, and in London at the Royal
English Opera House, 3 November 1891, in an English
translation by Augustus Harris and Eugene Oudin. In
the latter production Clément Marot was played by Ben
Davies, the Duc de Longueville by David Bispham, and

Marie by Esther Palliser; François Cellier conducted.
The work was published in an Italian translation by
Leoncavallo and Ettore Gentili by Ricordi in Milan in
1892. The "Passe-pied" from Act 3 was published
separately. The English version, published by Chappell
in 1891, was used for broadcasts by the BBC (British
Broadcasting Corporation) on 26 and 28 May 1930.
Messager was awarded the Prix Monbinne of the Académie
des Beaux Arts for the work in 1892; he later won the
prize again, for Fortunio (see below, [W26]). The
first American performance of the work was at the
Chicago Auditorium on 2 January 1893 (in English).
Reviews: (Paris production): L'art musical, 15 and 30 June
1890; Le temps, 1 June 1890; (London production): L'art
musical, 31 December 1891; The Westminster Review 136
(December 1891), 700-703; (Chicago production): The
Critic [N.Y.], 22 (March 1893), 135; Harper's Weekly,
11 March 1893; (Other productions): L'art musical, 15
December 1890, 15 September 1891 (Brussels); 9 November
1893 (Lyons)

[W14] Hélène

Drame lyrique, 4 acts and 5 tableaux
Text: Paul Delair
Première: Vaudeville, 15 September 1891
Cast: Sylvie - Marie Leconte; Hélène - Marthe Brandès
Chef d'orchestre - Gabriel Marie
First published: Choudens fils, 1891
Notes: An orchestral Suite de concert, extracted from the
work and arranged by Messager himself, was published by
Choudens in 1891. This consisted of: Prélude; Hélène et
Sylvie; Orage; La cimitière; Aurore and La nuit de
Noël. Manuscript Don Malherbe 7205 at the Bibliothèque
Nationale, Paris, Département de la Musique, is an
autograph of the scene "Mort d'Hélène", dated November
1891. The "Nouveau noël chanté dans le drame Hélène"
was published separately by Choudens in 1891. Carré
gives some details of the work (which had only 16
performances), in his Souvenirs de théâtre, 162;
although he thought the piece unsuitable for the
Vaudeville, he accepted it to please Coquelin, who was
a friend of Delair. Dedicated by Messager "à mon ami
Albert Carré".
Reviews: L'art musical, 30 September 1891

[W15] Madame Chrysanthème

> Comédie lyrique, prologue, 4 acts, epilogue
> Text: Pierre Loti, adapted by Georges Hartmann
>   and André Alexandre
> Première: Théâtre de la Renaissance, 30 January
>   1893
> Cast: Mme Chrysanthème - Jane Guy; Pierre - Delaquerrière;
>   Yves - Jacquin; Kangourou - Charles Lamy; M. Sucre -
>   Declercq; Mme Prune - Caisso
>   Chef d'orchestre - Messager
> First published: Choudens fils, 1893
> Notes: Autograph ms of 11 bars of the air from Act 4, scene
>   1 ("Les harpes d'or qui chantent dans la nuit") is in
>   the Bibliothèque de l'Opéra, Paris, ms 1900 ♭ XII
>   (198b); signed "A. Messager, 9 septembre 1892". The
>   first American performance was at the Chicago
>   Auditorium, 19 January 1920. A ballet from the work,
>   "arrangé pour orchestra restreint par Charles Delsaux",
>   was published by E. F. Kalmus, c.1970.
> Reviews: (Paris production): Echo de Paris, 1 February 1893;
>   Gil blas, 1 February 1893; Le journal, 31 January 1893;
>   Journal des débats, 5 February 1893; Le ménestrel, 5
>   February 1893; Le temps, 6 February 1893; (Chicago
>   production): Drama [Chicago] 10 (June 1920), 294-295

[W16] Miss Dollar

> Opérette, 3 acts and 5 tableaux
> Text: Charles Clairville, A. Vallin
> Première: Nouveau-Théâtre, 22 December 1893
> Cast: Sam Trukson - Decori; Gaetan - M. le Gallo; Miss
>   Dollar - Mlle Blanche-Marie; Colombella - Augustine
>   Leriche; Durozoir - M. Barral; Turlure - Marthe Fugère
>   Chef d'orchestre - Henri José
> First published: Choudens fils, 1894
> Notes: There is a "dossier de l'oeuvre" in the Bibliothèque
>   de l'Opéra, Paris, containing some press notices of the
>   work.
> Reviews: L'art musical, 28 December 1893; Le matin, 27
>   December 1893; Le temps, 1 January 1894

[W17] Amants éternels

> Pantomime, 3 tableaux
> Text: Corneau, Gerbault
> Première: Théâtre Libre, 26 December 1893
> Unpublished
> Reviews: Le temps, 1 January 1894

[W18] Mirette

> Opera, 3 acts
> Text: Michel Carré, with English lyrics by Frederick E.
>   Weatherley, Harry Greenbank and (in revised version
>   only) Adrian Ross
> Première: (1st version): London, Savoy Theatre, 3 July
>   1894; (2nd version): Savoy Theatre, 6 October 1894
> Cast: Mirette - Maud Ellicott; Bobinet - Walter Passmore;
>   Picorin - Courtice Pounds; Bianca - Florence Perry; The
>   Marquise - Rosina Brandram; Baron von den Berg - John
>   Coates; Gerard - Scott Fishe
>   Chef d'orchestre - François Cellier
> First published: London: Chappell and Co., 1894
> Notes: Supposedly a collaboration with Hope Temple (i.e.
>   Alice Maude Davis, who became Messager's second wife in
>   1895), although her name does not appear either on the
>   title-page of the vocal score or in any of the
>   separately published numbers from the work. The
>   best-known song, "Long ago in Alcala", was republished
>   in London and Melbourne by Chappell in 1904 "with an
>   extra verse by B. B." - there is a copy of this version
>   in the British Library, London.
> Reviews: The Times, 4 July 1894

[W19] La fiancée en lotérie

> Opérette, 3 acts
> Text: Camille de Roddaz, Alfred Douane
> Première: Folies-Dramatiques, 13 February 1896
> Cast: Angelin - Jean Périer; Mercédès - Armande
>   Cassive; Carmen - Augustine Leriche; Zaparta -
>   Hittemans; Lopez - Vauthier
> First published: Choudens, 1896. Parts for the entr'acte to
>   Act 3, published by C. F. Schmidt, are in the music
>   library of the British Broadcasting Corporation.
> Notes: According to the Catalogue général des oeuvres
>   dramatiques et lyriques faisant partie du répertoire de

la Société des Auteurs et Compositeurs Dramatiques, the
piece was a collaboration with Paul Lacôme, a fact not
noted on the vocal score. The romance "Rappelez-vous
votre jeunesse" (Act 1, no.5) was published separately
as a supplement to L'illustration, 21 March 1896, where
it was noted as "chantée par M. J. Périer".
Reviews: Le ménestrel, 16 February 1896, 52-53; Le temps,
14 February 1896

[W20] Le chevalier d'Harmental

Opéra comique, 5 acts
Text: Paul Ferrier, after Alexandre Dumas and Auguste
    Maquet
Première: Théâtre Sarah Bernhardt (by the company of the
    Opéra-Comique), 5 May 1896
Cast: Buvat - Lucien Fugère; L'Abbé Brigaud - Carbonne;
    Roquefinette - Jacques Isnardon; Bathilde - Mlle
    Marignan; Philippe d'Orléans - Marc-Nohël; Laval -
    Rivière; Duchesse de Maine - Mlle Chevalier; Mme Denis
    - Evel
    Chef d'orchestre - Jules Danbé
First published: Choudens, 1896
Notes: An "air de danse" from Act 1 and a mélodie, "C'est
    que je t'aime" from Act 2 were published separately as
    a supplement to L'illustration, 25 April 1896.
Reviews: Le ménestrel, 10 March 1896, 146-148; Le temps, 6
    May 1896

[W21] La montagne enchantée

"Pièce fantastique", 5 acts, 12 tableaux
Text: Albert Carré, Emile Moreau
Première: Théâtre de la Porte St. Martin, 12 April 1897
Cast: Asitaré - Jane Hading; Fatima - Mme Desclauzas; Firoux
    - Desjardins; Le prophète - Gravier; Prince Melchior -
    Gauthier; Leila - Mlle Baboulène; Kadour - Harmand; Le
    lévite - Pierre d'Assy
    Chef d'orchestre: Xavier Leroux
First published: Alphonse Leduc, 1897
Notes: Includes spoken dialogue. A collaboration with Xavier
    Leroux. Each composer signed his own pieces in the
    collaboration, from which we learn that Messager had
    the minor role, providing the music for the whole of
    tableaux 3 and 14, and most of the music for tableaux 7

and 12. The serenade from Act 2 ("Tes yeux qui font
désastres") was published as a supplement to
L'illustration of 3 April 1897, more than a week before
the première.
Reviews: Le ménestrel, 18 April 1897, 124

[W22] Le procès des roses

Pantomime
Text: Catulle Mendès
Première: Théâtre Marigny, 1897
Unpublished. According to Augé-Laribé, the manuscript is
    lost. The archives of the Théâtre Marigny no longer
    exist.

[W23] Les p'tites Michu

Operétte, 3 acts
Text: Albert Vanloo, Georges Duval
Première: Bouffes-Parisiens, 16 November 1897
Cast: Marie-Blanche - Alice Bonheur; Blanche-Marie - Odette
    Dulac; Mlle Herpin - L. Laporte; Michu - Regnard; Mme
    Michu - Vigouroux; Général des Ifs - Barral; Gaston -
    Rigaud; Bagnolet - Brunais; Aristide - Maurice Lamy
    Chef d'orchestre - Désiré Thibault
First published: Choudens, 1897
Notes: Dedicated "A Monsieur A. M. Coudert En témoinage de
    gratitude et de vive sympathie" (Coudert was at that
    time director of the Bouffes-Parisiens). Adapted for
    the English stage in 1905 as The Little Michus, words
    by Henry Hamilton, lyrics by Percy Greenbank. English
    première in London, Daly's Theatre, 29 April 1905, with
    Mabel Green as Marie-Blanche and Adrienne Augarde as
    Blanche-Marie, Willie Edouin as the Général des Ifs,
    Robert Evett as Gaston, Ambrose Manning as Michu, Amu
    Augarde as Mme Michu, and Louis Bradfield as Aristide.
    The English version includes the following additional
    songs, all with words by Percy Greenbank: "The Song of
    the Regiment (Act 1, no.6); "The Regiment of Frocks
    and Frills" (Act 3, no.22); "Miss Nobody from Nowhere"
    (Act 2, no.13a); "This Little Girl and That" (Act 1,
    no.11); "I would like to be a Grand Lady" (all
    published London and Melbourne: Chappell and Co.,
    1905), and "My old Home", published by Chappell and
    Co. in 1906. These last two numbers were not published
    in the 1905 vocal score, and may have been added

during the course of the show. A <u>Little Michus Waltz</u> by
Ernest Bucalossi was published by Chappell in 1905,
according to notes in their archives - but there are no
extant copies in the British Library or in the
Bibliothèque Nationale, Paris. The work opened on
Broadway, New York, on 31 January 1907, with Amy
Augard, Adrienne Augarde, Louis Bradfield, Adeline
Genée and Denise Orme. The "Prière à St Nicolas" was
published as a supplement to <u>L'illustration</u>, 27
November 1897.
Reviews: (French production): <u>Le temps</u>, 22 November 1897;
(English production): <u>The Era</u>, 6 May 1905; <u>The
Illustrated London News</u>, 6 May 1905; <u>The Stage</u>, 4 May
1905; <u>The Times</u>, 1 May 1905; <u>The World</u>, 2 May 1905 (see
also BIBLIOGRAPHY, [B135]).

[W24] Véronique

Opéra comique, 3 acts
Text: Albert Vanloo, Georges Duval
Première: Bouffes-Parisiens, 10 December 1898
Cast: Florestan - Jean Périer; Véronique - Mariette Sully;
Agathe - Anna Tariol-Baugé; Estelle - Léonie Laporte;
Coquenard - M. Regnard; Loustot - Maurice Lamy
Chef d'orchestre; Désiré Thibault
First published: Choudens, 1898
Notes: First performance in England (in French) at the
Coronet Theatre, Notting Hill, London, 5 May 1903;
first West End performance at the Apollo Theatre, 18
May 1904, with English text by Henry Hamilton, lyrics
by Lilian Eldee, and alterations and additions by Percy
Greenbank; conducted by Arthur Wood. Cast: Florestan
- Lawrence Rea; Hélène - Ruth Vincent; Coquenard -
George Graves Agatha - Kitty Gordon; Ermerance - Rosina
Brandram; Loustot - Fred Emney. First American
performance at the Broadway Theatre, New York, 30
October 1905 (in English). The cast included Kitty
Gordon, Valli, and Ruth Vincent. "D'puis c'matin" (Act
1) was published as a supplement to <u>L'illustration</u> of 7
January 1899.
Reviews: (English production): <u>The Era</u>, 21 May 1904; <u>The
Illustrated London News</u>, 28 May 1904; <u>The Sketch</u>, 1
June 1904; <u>The Stage</u>, 19 May 1904; <u>The Times</u>, 19 May
1904; <u>The World</u>, 24 May 1904 (see BIBLIOGRAPHY,
[B135]).

[W25] Les dragons de l'impératrice

Opéra comique, 3 acts
Text: Albert Vanloo, Georges Duval
Première: Théâtre des Variétés, 13 February 1905
Cast: Cyprienne - Mariette Sully; Capitaine Agénor -
    Charles Prince; Capitaine St. Gildas - Alberthal;
    Lucrèce - Germaine Gallois; Marguerite - Marguerite
    Fournier
    Chef d'orchestre - O. de Lagoanère
First published: Enoch, 1905
Notes: English rights acquired by Chappell and Co., London,
    in March 1905. The "Romance de Cyprienne" ("Il
    m'aime", Act 3, no.24) was published separately as a
    supplement to L'illustration no.3237 (1905).

[W26] Fortunio

Comédie lyrique, 4 acts and 5 tableaux
Text: Gaston-Armen de Caillavet, Robert de Flers
Première: Opéra-Comique, 5 June 1907
Cast: Fortunio - Fernand Francell; Maître André - Lucien
    Fugère; Landry - Jean Périer; Jacqueline - Marguerite
    Carré
    Chef d'orchestre - Messager
First published: Choudens, 1907; "Nouvelle version",
    Choudens, 1910
Notes: Awarded the Prix Monbinne of the Académie des Beaux
    Arts in 1908.
Reviews: Gabriel Fauré: Le figaro, 6 June 1907

[W27] Le bon roi Dagobert

Listed in Seré as "en préparation". P. B. Gheusi, in his
Cinquante ans de Paris: mémoires d'un témoin 1889-1938,
sheds some light on the project, which was to be based on
André Rivoire's play of the same name, premièred on 7
October 1908 at the Comédie-Française, and later set to
music by Samuel Rousseau. It was apparently Messager
himself who made the initial request that Gheusi write the
libretto, but both men soon realised that the last act had
too little substance to make a satisfactory musical play.
Gheusi also mentions other requests from Messager regarding
other collaborations; these apparently came to nothing
because Messager broke agreements (op. cit., 177-178, 391).

[W28] Béatrice

Légende lyrique, 4 acts
Text: Gaston-A. de Caillavet, Robert de Flers,
      after Charles Nodier
Première: Monte Carlo, 21 March 1914; Paris
      première: Opéra-Comique, 21 November 1917
Cast (1914): Béatrice - Andrée Vally; Lorenzo -
      Charles Rousselière; Musidora - Alphonse Royer; La
      vierge - Raynal-Monti; La supérieure - Alex; Soeur
      Monique - Rossignol; L'evêque - Robert Marvin
      (1917): Béatrice - Yvonne Chazel; Lorenzo - M.
      Fontaine; La Vierge - Mlle Vaultier
      Chef d'orchestre - (1914): Léon Jehin; (1917): A. Wolff
First published: A. Fürstner, 1914
Notes: In the Paris production of 1917, Yvonne Gall of the
      Opéra was to have played Béatrice; in a letter now in
      the Bibliothèque Nationale, Paris, Département des
      Manuscrits (ms. nouv. acq. française 17590, f.97),
      Messager asks Jacques Rouché if he can "borrow" her to
      rehearse the role for the Opéra-Comique production.
      The work enjoyed only three performances in Monte
      Carlo, on 21 and 28 March, and 7 April , according to
      T. J. Walsh (see BIBLIOGRAPHY, [B134]). Walsh includes
      photographs of the sets for Béatrice on pp.157 and 158
      of his book.
Reviews: Le figaro, 20 March 1914; Le ménestrel, 28 March
      1914

[W29] Miousic

Louis Schneider, in his Les maîtres de l'opérette française:
Hervé; Charles Lecocq (Paris: Perrin, 1924), 239, notes that
Lecocq was commissioned in 1914 to write an operetta in
collaboration with Messager, Camille Erlanger, Xavier
Leroux, Reynaldo Hahn, Henri Hirschmann, Rodolphe Berger and
Paul Vidal. The work was apparently produced at the Olympia
Theatre, Paris, on 21 March 1914. It does not appear to
have been published.

[W30] Monsieur Beaucaire

Romantic opera, 3 acts
Text: Frederick Lonsdale, after the novel of the same title
      by Booth Tarkington. Lyrics by Adrian Ross.
Première: Prince of Wales' Theatre, Birmingham, England, 7
      April 1919; London première: Prince's Theatre, 19 April
      1919
Cast: Beaucaire - Marion Green; Philip Molyneux - John
      Clarke; Lady Mary Carlyle - Maggie Teyte; Duke of
      Winterset - Robert Parker; Beau Nash - Robert
      Cunningham
First published: London: Ascherberg, Hopwood and Crew; New
      York: Leo Feist, 1918
Notes: French première (in a translation by André Rivoire):
      Théâtre Marigny, 21 November 1925. The work is
      dedicated to Ivan Caryll. In the French production
      Lady Mary was played by Marcelle Denya and Beaucaire by
      André Baugé. Broadway première: 11 December 1919, with
      Marion Green and Blanche Tomlin.
Reviews: (English production): The Era, 23 April 1919;
      Illustrated London News, 3 May 1919; The Saturday
      Review, 10 May 1919; The Sketch, 21 May 1919; The
      Stage, 24 April 1919; The Times, 21 April 1919 (cited
      by Wearing - see BIBLIOGRAPHY [B135]); (French
      production): Comoedia, 21 November 1925; Le figaro, 23
      November 1925; Le gaulois, 22 November 1925; Journal
      des débats, 24 November 1925; Le petit journal, 22
      November 1925; Le soir, 22 November 1925

[W31] Cyprien, ôte ta main de là!

Fantaisie, 1 act
Text: Maurice Hennequin
Première: Concerts Mayol, 1920
Cast: Charles Prince (for whom it was written)
First published: Max Eschig, 1920

[W32] La petite fonctionnaire

Comédie musicale, 3 acts
Text: Alfred Capus, Xavier Roux
Première: Théâtre Mogador, 14 May 1921
Cast: Suzanne - Edmée Favart; 1e Vicomte - Henry Defreyn;
      Lebardin - Louis Maurel
First published: Choudens, 1921

Notes: Choudens also published a suite, arranged by L.
    Delsaux, consisting of One-step; Tango; and Shimmy
Reviews: Comoedia, 16 May 1921; Journal des débats, 29 May
    1921; Le matin, 16 May 1921; Le temps, 16 May 1921

[W33] L'amour masqué

Comédie musicale, 3 acts
Text: Sacha Guitry
Première: Théâtre Edouard VII, 15 February 1923
Cast: Elle - Yvonne Printemps; Lui - Sacha Guitry; Baron -
    Urban; Le Maharadjah - Pierre Darmant. The cast also
    included Suzanne Duplessis and Louis Maurel
    Chef d'orchestre - Joseph Szulc
First published: Salabert, 1923
Notes: Originally commissioned by Guitry from the composer
    Ivan Caryll, and completed by Messager after Caryll's
    sudden death. The somewhat unusual circumstances
    surrounding the commission are reported in William
    Boosey, Fifty Years of Music, London: Ernest Benn,
    1931, 193. A letter from Fauré to Messager concerning
    the work is reproduced in Augé-Laribé, André Messager,
    200-201. According to Ken Bloom, American Song: the
    Complete Musical Theatre Companion, (2 vols., New York:
    Facts on File, 1985), the song "J'ai deux amants" was
    performed in the show Naughty Cinderella, which opened
    on Broadway in November 1925, and included music by
    Irving Berlin and Henri Christiné.
Reviews: Comoedia, 16 February 1923; Le figaro, 16 February
    1923; Le gaulois, 16 February 1923; L'intransigeant, 16
    February 1923; Journal des débats, 19 February 1923; Le
    ménestral, 23 February 1923; Le petit parisien, 15
    February 1923

[W34] Passionnément

Comédie musicale, 3 acts
Text: Maurice Hennequin, Albert Willemetz
Première: Théâtre de la Michodière, 16 January 1926
Cast: William Stevenson - René Koval; Robert Perceval -
    Georges Bury; Julia - Denise Grey; Captain Harris -
    Lucien Baroux; Le Barrois - Charles Lorain; - John -
    Julien Carette; Kety - Jeanne Saint-Bonnet; Hélène -
    Renée Duler
    Chef d'orchestre - Géoris

First published: Salabert, 1926 [in full and vocal score]
Notes: The full score issued by Salabert in 1926 is a
      facsimile of what appears to be Messager's autograph,
      although there is no note to this effect in the score
      itself. The score has a number of crossings-out and
      insertions, implying that it was the one used in early
      (if not first) performances. The first American
      performance took place at the Jolson Theatre, New York,
      on 7 March 1929.
Reviews: Comoedia, 16 January 1926; Le figaro, 16 and 18
      January 1926; Journal des débats, 20 January 1926; Le
      ménestrel, 22 January 1926

[W35] Deburau

      Comédie, 4 acts, prologue
      Text: Sacha Guitry
      Première: Théâtre Sarah Bernhardt, 9 October 1926
      Cast: Marie Duplessis - Yvonne Printemps;
          Deburau - Sacha Guitry
      First published: Salabert, 1926
      Notes: Dedicated "à la mémoire de Gabriel Fauré"
      Reviews: Le ménestrel, 15 October 1926

[W35a] Suite funambulesque

      This work, listed as a separate item in Augé-Laribé's
      discography, consists of a suite of six pieces from Deburau,
      entitled Cassandre; Pantomine Valse; Clownerie; Scène
      d'amour; Solitude de Pierrot; and Parade-Finale.
      Published by Salabert, 1930.

[W36] Coups de roulis

      Opérette, 3 acts
      Text: Albert Willemetz, after the novel by
Maurice Larrouy
      Première: Théâtre Marigny, 29 September 1928
      Cast: Béatrice - Marcelle Denya; Puy-Pradel - Raimu;
          Kermao - Robert Burnier
          Chef d'orchestre - Paul Letombe
      First published: Salabert, 1928
      Reviews: Journal des débats, 26 October 1928, 689-691; Revue
          des deux mondes, 1 December 1928, 703-706

[W37] Sacha

> Opérette, 3 acts
> Text: André Rivoire, after Maurice Donnay
> Première: Monte Carlo, 1930
> Unpublished
> Notes: Completed by Marc Berthomieu after Messager's death.
>   Messager began writing the work in the early 1920's.
>   Further performance in Paris by the Association
>   Française d'Action Artistique, 1 July 1936; Jean
>   Messager was the speaker.

SECTION 2: Ballets

[W38] Fleur d'oranger

> Divertissement, 1 act
> Première: Folies-Bergère, 1878
> First published: Lemoine, 1881
> Notes: Dedicated to Mme H. Depret

[W39] Les vins de France

> Divertissement, 2 tableaux
> Première: Folies-Bergère, 1879
> First published: Minier, [s.d.]
> Notes: Dedicated to Eugène Augé

[W40] Mignons et vilains

> Divertissement, 2 tableaux
> Première: Folies-Bergère, 1879
> First published: Minier, [s.d.]
> Notes: Dedicated to Mme Marie Clerc (wife of the
>   industrialist Camille Clerc)

[W41] Les deux pigeons

Ballet, 2 acts.
Scenario: Henry de Régnier and Louis Mérante, after
    Lafontaine's fable
Première: Théatre National de l'Opéra, 18 October 1886
Cast: Gourouli - Rosita Mauri; Pepio - Marie Sanlaville
    Chef d'orchestre - Madeir de Montjau
First published: Enoch, 1886
Notes: Commissioned by Vaucorbeil in May 1884. Dedicated to
    Camille Saint-Saëns. Revived at the Opéra in 1893 and
    1910, and performed in London on 21 June 1906, with
    Messager conducting. Gourouli was played there by Aida
    Boni; Pepio by Irma Legrand. An annotated score used
    for the 1893 revival is in the Bibliothèque de l'Opéra,
    Paris, Pièce B.905, and includes eight choreographic
    sketches for the production.
Reviews: L'art musical, 31 October 1886; Le temps, 25
    October 1886; (revival): L'art musical, 8 February 1894

[W42] Les bleuets

Ballet, 1 act
Unpublished
Notes: According to Augé-Laribé, André Messager, 67, the
    manuscript is lost. He adds "personne n'en parle plus.
    Il avait été monté sur une petite scène du Quartier
    Latin". The piece was composed c.1889.

[W43] Scaramouche

Pantomime-Ballet, 2 acts and 4 tableaux
Text: Maurice Lefèvre, Henri Vuagneux
Première: Nouveau-Théâtre, 17 October 1891
Cast: Arlequin - Felicia Mallet; Colombine - Cornélia Riva;
    Scaramouche - Henry Krauss; Gilles - Paul Clerget
    Chef d'orchestre - Louis Ganne
First published: Choudens fils, 1891
Notes: A collaboration with the composer Georges Street. A
    valse from Act 2 was published separately by Choudens
    fils in 1891, and by G. Wittmann as no.2 of his
    Réunions musicales in 1892.
Reviews: L'art musical, 31 October 1891

[W44] Le chevalier aux fleurs

Ballet, 3 acts
Première: Théâtre Marigny, May 1897
Notes: A collaboration with Raoul Pugno, whom Messager had
    known from at least the late 1880's. There is a
    dispute over the date of the première: Augé-Laribé
    gives 25 May 1897, while Seré gives 15 May.
Reviews: Le temps, 31 May 1897

[W45] Une aventure de la Guimard

Ballet, 1 act
Première: Parc de Versailles, September 1900, at a
    railwaymen's conference. First Paris performance at
    the Opéra-Comique, 6 November 1900 (according to the
    vocal score published by Choudens).
Cast: La Guimard - Mlle Jeanne Chasles
First published: Choudens, 1901. The work was still in
    print in a 6-hand arrangement in 1923.
Notes: The autograph manuscript is in the Bibliothèque de
    l'Opéra, Paris, ms Rés2281. A note in Messager's hand
    states: "Ce ballet a été composé pour la fête donnée à
    l'occasion du Congres des chemins de fer, dans la Parc
    de Versailles Septembre 1900". Choudens published a
    four-movement suite from the work, consisting of
    Rigaudon; Aria; Sicilienne; and Tambouraine.

SECTION 3: Songs

A number of the songs listed here can be dated only
approximately. Those marked with an asterisk were included
in the collection Quinze mélodies d'André Messager published
by Enoch et Costallat in 1910. That collection includes in
addition the "Chanson de la fauvette" from La fauvette du
temple, plus "Charme, rêve, image" and the Valse du miroir
"Je suis jolie" from Isoline.

[This section is divided into two parts: (a) Unpublished
songs and (b) Published songs]

(a) Unpublished songs

[W46] Rêverie

Text: Armand Silvestre
Notes: According to Seré, this song was composed on 4 July
    1876.

[W47] Mélodie

Text: Henri Cazalis
Notes: Listed in Pièce 643 only

[W48] Rosyllian

Text: Tristan Klingsor
Notes: Performed by Roger Bourdin at the concert given in
    Messager's memory at the Salle Gaveau, Paris, February
    1930 (see APPENDIX II)

[W49] Aux pays bleu

Listed in Pièce 643 only; according to that list, the song
was composed on 13 November 1877.

[W50] Souvenir

Text: Unknown
Notes: Mentioned in a report in L'art musical, 28 February
    1878, p.69: "Un des régals de la soirée [at the Société
    Nationale] consistait dans l'audition de deux nouvelles
    mélodies de M. Messager, le jeune symphoniste applaudi
    tout dernièrement aux concerts du Châtelet. Ces deux
    mélodies sont exquises. La première, Souvenir, nous a
    particulièrement plu. L'harmonie est pleine de ces
    modulations, si fréquentes chez Schumann, qui charment
    l'oreille et ravissent le coeur. M. Mouliérat l'a dite
    avec un goût parfait ..." [One of the delights of the
    evening was the performance of two new songs by M.
    Messager, the young symphonist recently applauded at
    the Châtelet. These two mélodies are exquisite. The
    first, Souvenir, particularly pleased us. The harmony
    is full of those modulations (so common in Schumann)
    which charm the ear and delight the heart. M. Mouliérat

sang it with perfect taste.] The name of the second of
the two pieces performed is not given: perhaps it was
Aux pays bleu [W49], in view of its date.

[W51] Les baisers

   Text: Henri Cazalis
   Listed in Seré and Pièce 643

[W52] Le facteur rural

   Noted in Philippe Fauré-Fremiet's biography Gabriel Fauré
   (Paris: Editions Rieder, 1929), 39. The poem was by Fauré,
   and was set to music by Messager, possibly spontaneously,
   without ever being written down. There is now no trace of
   the piece.

[W53] Arpège

   Text: Albert Samain
   Notes: Autograph manuscript in the Bibliothèque de l'Opéra,
       Paris, ms 1900 198b. Performed by Yvonne Gall at the
       Messager memorial concert in 1930 (see APPENDIX II).

[W54] Sur la mer

   Composed at Aix-les-Bains, 5 August 1901, during a visit by
   the Opéra-Comique. Performed by Yvonne Gall at the Messager
   memorial concert in 1930 (see APPENDIX II).

(b) Published songs

[W55] Regret d'avril*

   Text: Armand Silvestre
   First published: Enoch frères et Costallat, 1882
   Notes: Dedicated to "Madame la Comtesse Emmanuelle Potocka".
       This may be the daughter of Countess Delfina Potocka,
       dedicatee of Chopin's 2nd Piano Concerto, op.21.

[W56] Chanson de ma mie*

Text: Théodore de Banville
First published: Enoch frères et Costallat, 1882
Notes: Dedicated to Mme Alice Castillon. Later published as
a supplement to L'illustration no.3372 (1907).

[W57] Mimosa*

Text: Armand Silvestre
First published: Enoch frères et Costallat, 1882
Notes: Dedicated to Mlle Amélie Duez

[W58-62] Nouveau Printemps*

A cycle of five songs entitled "Se peut-il qu'une larme";
"Mai vient"; "Une reseau d'ombres emprisonné"; "La lune
egrène en perles blonds"; and "Dans les arbres blancs de
givre".
Texts: Heinrich Heine, translated into French by Georges
Clerc
First published: Enoch frères et Costallat, 1885
Notes: Dedicated to Gabriel Fauré

[W63] Gavotte

"Danse chantée"
Text: Théodore de Banville
First published: According to Augé-Laribé, André Messager,
227, published in a musical supplement to Paris noël,
c.1887. The work is not mentioned in Seré or Pièce 643.

[W64] La chanson des cerises*

Text: Armand Silvestre
First published: Enoch frères et Costallat, 1889
Notes: Dedicated to Mme Fonade (although this dedication
does not appear in the collection of 1910).

[W65] Chanson mélancolique*

    Text: Catulle Mendès
    First published: Enoch frères et Costallat, 1889
    Notes: Dedicated to Mlle Emma Noël

[W66] Neige rose*

    Text: Armand Silvestre
    First published: Enoch frères et Costallat, 1889
    Notes: Dedicated to the Marquis d'Ivry

[W67] O canto do Paris n'America

    First published by Choudens fils, 1890, and described as a
    "Paraense composto especialmente para as suas amaveis
    freguezas" [Popular song composed especially for his dear
    customers.] The copy in the Bibliothèque Nationale, Paris,
    Département de la Musique, is a piano transcription of what
    was presumably originally a vocal piece. On the reverse of
    the copy is a drawing of a large square building with the
    words "Paris n'America" on it, which may eventually explain
    the origins of the work.

[W68] A une fiancée

    Text: Victor Hugo
    First published: Enoch frères et Costallat,
      1891; London: Metzler and Co., 1891
    Notes: Augé-Laribé, André Messager, 227, states that the
      song was composed c.1888

[W69] Fleurs d'hiver

    Text: Armand Silvestre
    First published: Société Anonyme d'Edition Mutuelle de
      Musique, 64 rue de la Victoire, 1889
    Notes: Dedicated "à mon ami Bouvet, de l'Opéra-Comique"

[W70] Arioso*

    Text: Paul Burani
    First published: Enoch frères et Costallat, 1891

[W71] Ritournelle

   Text: Henry Gauthier-Villars [Willy]
   First published: Tellier/Heugel, 1894

[W72] Chant d'amour

   Text: Armand Silvestre
   First published: Fromont, 1894
   Notes: Dedicated to the opera singer Jean de Reszke

[W73] Chanson d'automne

   Text: Paul Delair
   First published: Tellier/Heugel, 1894

[W74] Le bateau rose

   Text: Jean Richepin
   First published: Tellier/Heugel, 1894

[W75] Douce chanson [Heart of Mine]

   Text: Emile Blémont
   First published: As a supplement to L'illustration, 21 April
    1894, and by Fromont, 1894.
   Notes: English text "Heart of Mine", beginning "On the
    silence stealing, Cloister bells are pealing", by Paul
    England, published in London by Metzler and Co., c.1896.

[W76] Notre amour est chose légère [Love Eternal]

   Duet
   Text: Armand Silvestre
   First published: London: Metzler and Co., c.1896, to English
    text "Love eternal", beginning "Love with us is light as
    the breezes", by Paul England.

[W77] Aimons-nous

   Text: Emile Blémont
   First published: London: Chappell, 1897, with French text

[W78] Curly Locks

    Text: Frederick E. Weatherley
    First published: London: Metzler and Co., c.1897

[W79-84] Amour d'hiver

    A cycle of six songs entitled "Ce fut au temps du
    chrysanththème"; "Je porte sur moi ton image"; "Que l'heure
    est vite passée"; "Ne souffre plus"; "Quand tu passes, ma
    bien-aimée"; and "L'hiver de cet an est si doux".
    Texts: Armand Silvestre
    First published: Paris; Berlin: A. Fürstner, 1911
    Notes: Dedicated to Maria Kousnezoff. A German translation
      with parallel English text was published in Paris by
      Fürstner in 1912. "Quand tu passes" was re-published by
      Boosey and Hawkes in 1943.

[W85] Pour la patrie

    Text: Victor Hugo
    First published: London: Daily Telegraph Newspaper, 1914
    Notes: Messager's contribution to King Albert's Book: a
      Tribute to the Belgian King and People. His composition,
      beginning "Ceux qui pieusement sont morts pour la patrie"
      appears on pp.41 and 42 of the book.

[W86] La fête de la France

    Listed in Franz Pazdirek, Universal-handbuch der
    Musikliteratur aller Zeiten und Volker (Vienna: Verlag der
    Musikalischen Literature, [s.d.]), 21: 523, as being for
    voice and piano, and published by Labbé. No mention of a
    piece with this title appears in either Augé-Laribé, Février,
    Pièce 643 or Seré.

[W87] Le credo de la victoire

    Duet
    Text: Ernest Dubreuil, Paul Burani
    First published: Enoch, 1916
    Notes: Extract from Le bourgeois de Calais [W8]

[W88] La paix de blanc vêtue

    Text: L. Lahovary
    First published: Maurice Senart, 1922

[W89] Va chercher quelques fleurs

    Text: Louis Aufauvre
    First published: Maurice Senart, 1922

SECTION 4: Other vocal music

[W90] Promethée enchainé

    Cantata
    Text: Georges Clerc
    Notes: Composed in 1877 for a competition organised by the
      Ville de Paris. It is described in <u>Pièce 643</u> as a "scène
      dramatique pour solistes, choeur et orchestre".
    Unpublished

[W91] Don Juan et Haydée

    Cantata, 3 voices
    Text: Byron
    Notes: Messager's entry for a contest at Saint-Quentin in
      1877; it won second prize.
    Unpublished

[W92] Messe des pêcheurs de Villerville

    Composed in collaboration with Gabriel Fauré. Messager wrote
    the Kyrie and O Salutaris movements, and in 1882 conducted
    the first performance of the second, orchestrated version at
    Villerville; the first version had received its première at
    Villerville in September of the previous year. The work is
    to be found in three manuscripts at the Bibliothèque
    Nationale, Paris, Département de la Musique: ms 20301, which
    contains the original version for womens' voices, solo violin
    and organ; ms 20302, the orchestrated version of 1882; and
    Vma1191, which consists of written-out orchestral parts for
    the second version. Further information on the genesis of

the work may be found in Jean-Michel Nectoux, comp., Correspondence Gabriel Fauré (Paris: Flammarion, 1980), and in Robert Orledge, Gabriel Fauré (London: Eulenberg Books, 1979, rev. 1983).

[W93] Les chameliers

According to F. Mark Daugherty and Susan M. Simon's Secular Choral Music in Print (Philadelphia: Musicdata, 1987), this work, to a text by A. Lepitre, consists of a 4-part mixed chorus, with optional piano and was published by Enoch. The work is also referred to in Die Musik in Geschichte und Gegenwart; I have been unable to trace a copy. Given the subject matter, it may be an arrangement of a piece from L'amour masqué [W33].

SECTION 5: Instrumental works

[W94] Symphony in A major

Composed in 1875 for a competition organised by the Ville de Paris. La chronique musicale of 15 May 1876 (pp.193-194) carried a report of the results of the contest, and that of a quartet competition, run concurrently. 25 symphonies and 18 quartets had been entered in all (there is no evidence to suggest that Messager also entered the quartet competition). The jury included Ambroise Thomas, Reber, Vaucorbeil (at that time President of the Société des Compositeurs), Bourgault-Ducoudray, Colonne, Théodore Duboie, Guilmant and Wekerlin. The first public performance was at the Concerts Colonne, 20 January 1878, with further performances in Angers on 15 December 1878, and at the Concerts Straram on 1 May 1930. The work was thought for some time to be lost, and was "rediscovered" only after Messager's death, as reported by L'excelsior in its issue of 24 January 1930:

En classant les papiers laissés par André Messager, son fils, notre confrère Jean-André Messager a retrouvé l'orchestration complète de l'unique symphonie écrite par le célèbre compositeur, orchestration qu'on croyait perdue ...

[While sorting the papers left by André Messager, his son, our colleague Jean-André Messager, has found the complete orchestration of the single symphony written by the famous composer, an orchestration previously considered lost ...]

First published: Choudens, 1948
Review: L'art musical, 31 January 1878

[W95] Loreley

"Ballade pour orchestre", unpublished. According to Augé-Laribé, André Messager, 225, the work was probably composed in the early 1880's. It was performed at the Concerts Colonne on 2 March 1930.

[W96] "Souvenirs de Bayreuth"

Piano duet composed in collaboration with Gabriel Fauré, c.1880. Philippe Fauré-Fremiet, in his Gabriel Fauré (Paris: Editions Rieder, 1929), 39, noted "A Villerville, chez les Clerc, d'accord avec André Messager, il met toute la Tétralogie en quadrille, on ne peut plus respectueusement; Fafner se dandine et Siegmund a l'air de jouer du galoubet". [At the Clerc's in Villerville, he made a quadrille, with André Messager, of the whole Ring, with the greatest of respect. Fafner waddled about and Siegmund seemed to be playing the flageolet.] The work seems to have had a long gestation, and was not written down until some considerable time afterwards; thus Colette, in her essay "Un salon de musique en 1900" in Maurice Ravel par quelques-uns de ses familiers (Paris: Editions du Tambourinaire, 1939), 119, noted "Un quadrille parodique, à quatre mains, où se donnaient rendezvous les leitmotive de la Tétralogie, sonnait souvent le couvre feu". Finally Willy, in his book Garçon, l'audition! (Paris: H. Simonis Empis, 1901), 210, observed "Mais l'extasiante peroraison du Crépuscule des Dieux [performed by the Lamoureux orchestra], fit tout oublier ... jouée comme seuls savent jouer l'orchestre du patron, et chez Madame de Saint-Marceaux, les deux mains d'André Messager". [But the ecstatic peroration made up for everything ... played as only Lamoureux's orchestra can, or, at the house of Mme de Saint-Marceaux, the two hands of André Messager.] The work was first published in 1930 by Costallat, with a 2-hand arrangement by Gustave Samazeuilh. It is in five sections, and obviously not complete. Modulatory

passages would be required between sections, which are in B
minor, G sharp minor, B flat major, E major and E flat major.
Colettes's memories are again interesting in this matter, as
in her Journal à rebours (Paris: Fayard, 1941) she states:
"Souvent, côté à côté sur la banquette d'un des pianos.
Gabriel Fauré et Messager improvisaient à quatre mains, en
rivalisant de modulations brusquées, d'évasions hors du ton.
Tous deux aimaient ce jeu, pendant lequel ils échangaient des
apostrpohes de duellistes: "Pare celle-là! ... Et celle-là,
tu l'attendais? Va toujours, je te repincerai" ... Fauré,
emir bistré, hochait sa huppe d'argent, souriait aux embûches
et les redoublait ..." [Often, side by side on the piano
stool, Gabriel Fauré and Messager improvised, piano, four
hands, rivalling each other in their abrupt modulations and
moves away from the tonic. Both of them loved this game,
during which they exchanged insults like duellists: "Parry
that!" ... and that - were you expecting that? ...Keep going,
I'll get you ..." Fauré, the swarthy "emir", would shake his
silver mane, smiled at the traps set for him, and increased
them ..."]. Colette follows this quotation by suggesting that
it was Chabrier's parody that often preceded curfew, rather
than Fauré/Messager's; but I am inclined to trust her earlier
account in the work on Ravel cited above.

[W97-99] Trois valses pour piano à quatre mains

Composed c.1884 and first performed at a concert of the
Société Nationale de Musique, 13 December 1884. D'Indy, to
whom the work was dedicated, was one of the performers.
Messager was probably the other. The second of d'Indy's own
set of three waltzes (op.17) written in December 1882, is
dedicated to Messager, whose waltzes were first published by
Enoch frères et Costallat in 1884.

[W100] Passe-pied

For piano. Published as no.27 of a collection entitled "La
danse", issued by Le gaulois as a special subscribers'
supplement in 1888. The work, in two movements (B minor and
B major), is dedicated "à mon ami Georges Street".

[W101-106] Piano pieces

A set of six pieces entitled Impromptu (op.10), dedicated to
Léon Lemoine; Habanera (op.11), dedicated to G. Neymark;
Menuet (op.12), dedicated to Mme J. Février; Mazurka
(op.13), dedicated to Mlle Jenny Clouet; Caprice-polka
(op.14), dedicated to Mme L. Kahn; and Valse (op.15),
dedicated to Mme O. Diey. All first published by Lemoine in
Autumn 1888, and in 4-hand arrangements made by Lemoine
himself in 1901. Enoch frères et Costallat published a piano
arrangement of the "Pavane des fées" from Isoline as "op.13"
in 1888. Lemoine also published the pieces in his Panthéon
des pianistes in 1904.

[W107-109] Pieces for violin and piano

A Barcarolle, Mazurka and Serenade written for the Hungarian
violinist Tivador Nachez. First published London: Metzler
and Co., 1896-1897, and in Mainz: Schott, 1897.

[W110] Solo de concours for clarinet and piano

Composed for a competition at the Conservatoire in 1899, and
published by Evette and Schaeffer in the same year. Reissued
by Heugel in 1980.

[W111] Morceau de concours du Conservatoire pour piano (Classe
des femmes)

Published as a supplement to Musica 12 (1903), together with
a competition piece by Georges Marty. Also published by Le
monde musical (?1903). The work is an allegretto in G minor,
35 bars long.

[W112] Idylle for piano

A piece with this title is listed in the catalogue of the New
York Public Library. It may be a piano arrangement of a
vocal work, and is not listed elsewhere.

SECTION 6: Miscellaneous works, including works projected but apparently not completed

[W113] Impressions orientales

   Listed in Pièce 643 only; noted there as unpublished.

[W114-118] Morceaux de lecture à vue

   All unpublished, and listed in Pièce 643 only:

   Pour violon (1913)
   Pour trompette (1918)
   Pour cor en fa [s.d.]
   Pour flûte [s.d.]
   Pour alto [i.e. viola] [s.d.]

[W119] Un monsieur pressé

   A work with this title is included in the collection of the
   Bibliothèque Nationale, Paris, Département de la Musique, at
   shelf mark 4° Vm15 13103. It consists of one and a half
   minutes of Messager's stage music adapted and arranged by the
   composer Raoul Moreau, and was intended to accompany silent
   films in which music of a busy, bustling nature was required.
   Along with other titles such as Poursuite comique and Noce
   villageoise by Benjamin Godard, and En suivant la course by
   Henry Février, it formed part of an extensive literature of
   "genre music" of a sort required for silent films of the
   time. Published by Choudens in 1927, Messager's contribution
   to the series appeared towards the end of the "silent" era.
   The title page of the series in which Un monsieur pressé and
   Soir à Montmartre [W120] appeared explains its aims:

      GAIETYFILM. Nouvelle collection d'Oeuvres Caractéristiques
      POUR GRAND ET PETITS ORCHESTRES arrangées spécialement à
      l'usage des Cinemas pour: Poursuites et Scènes comiques,
      Vaudevilles, Quiproquos amusants, Courses et toutes scènes
      mouvementées d'un caractère gai.

   In addition to the Gaietyfilm collection, there was a

Tragicfilm series; none of Messager's music was included in the latter.

[W120] Soir à Montmartre

Described as a "One step de André Messager", this composition consists, like [W119], of selections of Messager's music arranged by Raoul Moreau for small orchestra and intended for use in the silent cinema. Published by Choudens in 1927, it is three minutes in length.

SECTION 7: Arrangements of works by other composers

EMMANUEL CHABRIER

[W121] España

Reduction for piano, 4 hands, by Messager; published c.1925

[W122] Gwendoline

Heugel published a "Partition piano et chant, texte français et allemand; nouvelle édition avec accompagnement simplifié par A. Messager" in 1889.

[W122a] Gwendoline. Selections

Messager arranged the following numbers from Chabrier's opera for piano, 4 hands, in 1893: Ouverture; Prélude (Act 1); and Choeur nuptial (Act 2). All published by Heugel.

[W123] Le Roi malgré lui. Selections

Messager arranged the Fête polonaise from this work for piano, 4 hands, in 1887. Published by Enoch in Paris.

[W124] CHANSONS POPULAIRES D'ALSACE

A collection of 12 folk-songs in Alsatian dialect compiled by
André Alexandre, for which Messager provided harmonisations.
Published Nancy: Berger-Levrault, c.1920.

GUSTAVE CHARPENTIER

[W125] Impressions d'Italie

2- and 4-hand arrangements of Charpentier's "Suite
symphonique" were published by Heugel in 1892.

[W125a] A separate arrangement for 2 pianos, 4 hands, was
published by Heugel, and is listed in Bibliographie musicale
française (January-March 1900), 28.

FRÉDÉRIC CHOPIN

[W126] Suite de Danses

Together with Paul Vidal, Messager orchestrated 14 piano
pieces by Chopin for a ballet entitled Suite de danses at the
Opéra. The work was first performed there on 23 June 1913,
under Alfred Bachelet. The manuscript of the work is in the
Bibliothèque de l'Opéra, Paris, ms A716bis.

The pieces are as follows:

1.	Polonaise in A major, op.40: full orchestra.
2.	Nocturne in C minor, op.48 no.1: marked "Pas de deux".
3.	Prelude in D flat, op.28 no.15: strings alone.
4.	Mazurka in C major, op.56 no.2: marked "coupé" in pencil in score.
5.	Valse brillante in A flat, op.34 no.1: full orchestra.
6.	Mazurka in G minor, op.24 no.1: headed "Variation homme". The oboe is prominent.
6bis	Mazurka in C major, op.67 no.3: marked "coupé" in score.
7.	Nocturne in A flat, op.32 no.2: marked "coupé" in score.
7bis	Nocturne in F major, op.15 no.1: "Pas de 6, pas de

8". Features four cellos.
8.   Valse in D flat, op.64 no.1: marked "Variation
       femme".
9.   Mazurka in D major, op.33 no.2 "Variation des
       élèves".
9bis   Valse op.64 no.2: "Coupé". Messager and Vidal set
       the piece in D minor, instead of the C sharp minor
       of the original piano piece.
10.   Valse brillante in F major, op.34 no.3.
11.   Polonaise-Final: return to the Polonaise in A
       major, op.40.

[W127] Piano Concerto no.2 in F minor, op. 21

Messager re-orchestrated this concerto at the request of
Marguerite Long, who performed it twice at the Concerts
Colonne. In a letter to a friend (Bibliothèque Nationale,
Paris, Département de la Musique, lettre autographe 99),
Messager wrote that no editor seemed interested in his
orchestration of the work. He mentions, however, that he has
orchestrated Chopin's Polonaise in E flat, and that Heugel is
to publish both works: but this seems never to have taken
place.

GABRIEL FAURÉ

[W128] Tarentelle op.10 no.2

Jean-Michel Nectoux and Robert Orledge note in their worklist
to Orledge's biography of Gabriel Fauré (London: Eulenberg
Books, 1979), 284, that Messager made an orchestral
arrangement of the above-mentioned work c.1880; this exists
as ms 17783 at the Bibliothèque Nationale, Paris.

AUGUSTA HOLMES

[W129] Au Pays Bleu

Tellier published a 4-hand arrangement by Messager of this
work in 1897.

EDOUARD LALO

[W130] Namouna. Selections

Messager transcribed the following movements from the ballet
for 2 pianos, 4 hands: Prélude; Thème varié; Parade de
foire; and Fête Foraine. Published by Hamelle in 1904.

RAOUL PUGNO

[W131] Pour le Drapeau!

According to Augé-Laribé, André Messager, 83, Messager
orchestrated this "mimodrame". This is not confirmed by the
vocal score, however (published Leduc, 1895).

CAMILLE SAINT-SAENS

[W132] Le Déluge. Selections

Messager made a 4-hand arrangement of the Prélude to this
work in 1879; published by Durand, Schoenewerk et Cie.

[W133] Etienne Marcel

The vocal score, made by Messager, was published by Durand
and Schoenewerk in 1879.

Messager also made the following arrangements of the piece:

[W133a] Arrangement for piano solo: Durand, Schoenewerk, 1884
[W133b] Selection of "airs de ballet" for piano: idem, 1879
[W133c] Pavane from the opera (piano, 4 hands, and piano, 2
        hands): idem, 1879
[W133d] Ronde de Nuit, piano: idem, 1879
[W133e] Valse (piano, 4 hands and piano, 2 hands): idem, 1879

[W134] Henry VIII

4-hand arrangement by Messager of the "Marche du Synod",
published by Durand, Schoenewerk et Cie, 1883.

[W135] Messe de Requiem op.54

Vocal score arranged by Messager and published by Durand, Schoenewerk et Cie, 1878.

[W136] Phryné

Saint-Saëns related (Musica, 1908), how he orchestrated Act 2 of this work, while Messager orchestrated Act 1. According to Saint-Saëns, this fact had not been known before he revealed it in that interview. However, when reviewing a production of the work at the Opéra-Comique in 1899, Willy stated "L'instrumentation (M. Messager y travailla, dit-on) est d'une désinvolture érudite" [The orchestration (M. Messager worked on it, they say) is casually erudite], indicating that Messager's role as orchestrator was in fact recognised even at that date. See Willy [Henry Gauthier-Villars], Garçon, l'audition! (Paris: H. Simonis Empis, 1901), 45. Messager also composed a number of recitatives for a performance of the work in Milan in November 1896: there is a copy of the vocal score, published by Durand in Paris in 1896, in the Bibliothèque Nationale, Paris.

[W137] Symphony no.2 in A minor op.55

Durand and Schoenewerk published an arrangement by Messager for piano, 4 hands, in 1879.

RICHARD WAGNER

[W138] Tannhäuser. March

Messager's arrangement (2 pianos, 4 hands) of this piece was published by Durand, Schoenewerk et Cie in 1893. It is in B major. Messager's name was not cited on the title-page, and appears only inside the score. His is one of a great many arrangements of the work in print at this period.

Bibliography

ARCHIVAL SOURCES

1. Letters

A large number of Messager's letters are available for
consultation in the Bibliothèque Nationale, Paris, both in the
Département de la Musique and in the Département des Manuscrits;
further letters may be found in the French Archives Nationales,
Paris. The Department of Manuscripts at the British Library,
London, possesses six letters, and doubtless much more of
Messager's correspondence is still in private hands. Letters to
Messager from other correspondants are noticeably absent from the
collections of both the British Library and the Bibliothèque
Nationale.[1]
    Messager's handwriting is neat, easily legible and
distinctive, as is his signature: he always signs himself "A.
Messager", rather than using his full first Christian name.

    Manuscripts containing letters are described below.

Bibliothèque Nationale, Paris, Département des Manuscrits

[A1] Ms Nouv. Acq. fr. 17590

A red folio volume marked "Correspondance Jacques Rouché, volume
12". There are seven autograph letters from Messager to Rouché
(who succeeded Messager and Broussan as director of the Opéra in
1914), numbered 90, 91, 92/3, 94, 95/6, 97 and 98, and dated as
follows:

                90:    4 novembre 1908
                91:   19 avril 1913
                92/3: 24 avril 1914
                94:   19 mai 1914
                95/6: 11 juillet 1914
                97:    8 septembre 1917
                98:   14 septembre 1917

All the letters relate to administrative matters at the Opéra: engagements of singers, use of electric light and so on. In letter 97, Messager asks Rouché if he will temporarily release Yvonne Gall from her commitments at the Opéra in order that she might sing the title role in Béatrice [W28] at the Opéra-Comique. Rouché granted the favour, and Messager expresses his thanks in letter 98. Yvonne Gall did not, in fact, sing the title role in Messager's opera on this occasion, as Messager changed his mind and selected Yvonne Chazel for the part instead, as related by P. B. Gheusi (Guerre et théâtre 1914-1918. Nancy: Berger-Levrault, 1919, 332-333).

[A2] Ms Nouv. Acq. fr. 24638

A folio volume with a brown leather spine and paper-covered boards, marked "Papiers Alexandre Dumas fils, Correspondance III: Fabre-Muller". The manuscript contains one letter from Messager (no.537), undated and without an address. It must, however, relate to Vaucorbeil's commission of Les deux pigeons in May 1884 (see WORKLIST, [W41]). Messager encloses a press cutting from Le gaulois which has obviously embarrassed him, and asks his friend to try to see Vaucorbeil that evening to inform him that he [Messager] has had nothing to do with the press report. The cutting reads as follows:

> A propos de ballet, on a cité bien des compositeurs - depuis M. Paladilhe jusqu'à M. Planquette - comme devant écrire la musique des Deux Pigeons. Nous sommes en mesure de donner le nom véritable du musicien auquel s'est définitivement adressé M. Vaucorbeil; c'est M. André Messager. Le directeur de l'Opéra pouvait certes plus mal choisir.
>
> [On the subject of ballet, the names of a number of composers - from M. Paladilhe to M. Planquette - have been mentioned in connection with the composition of the music for Les deux pigeons. We are in a position to reveal the name of the musician whom M. Vaucorbeil has definitely commissioned for this task: it is M. André Messager. The director of the Opéra could certainly have chosen worse.]

[A3] Ms Nouv. Acq. fr. 24966

A folio volume with a red leather spine and paper boards, marked "Georges de Porto-Riche - Correspondance XV: Martial - Mugnier". The manuscript includes two letters from Messager, and one from his wife, numbered 251, 252 and 253/4.   In letter 251, a "carte pneumatique" of 27 January [year not given], Messager requests M. and Mme Porto-Riche to alter the date of their visit for dinner, as Messager is conducting <u>Fidelio</u> on that day.   In letter 252 (on notepaper of the Société des Auteurs et Compositeurs Dramatiques), dated 29 May 1923, Messager congratulates Porto-Riche on his election to the Académie Française, "où votre place était depuis si longtemps marquée".[" ... where a seat has been reserved for you for so long".][2]   The letter from Mme Messager, undated, is an invitation to dinner.

[A4] Ms Nouv. Acq. fr. 24278

A folio volume with dark marbled boards and a leather spine, marked "Autographes Felix et Paul Nadar - XIX: Megnin - Mols". It contains three items from Messager: the first is a "carte pneumatique" dated 26 July [year not given], and relates to a competition at the Conservatoire; the other items are visiting cards, both from around 1927.

Bibliothèque Nationale, Paris, Département de la Musique

[A5] The file of 100 autograph letters in the music library of the Bibliothèque Nationale forms by far the largest single, available collection of Messager's correspondence. The letters, as presently numbered in the files at the Bibliothèque Nationale, are in a random order. A large number of them (nos. 36-55, 57 and 65-73) deal with the American tour undertaken by the Société des Concerts du Conservatoire in 1918, ending with Messager's resignation from the conductorship of the society in April 1919. A smaller number, mainly addressed to Carré, date from 1902; extracts from nos. 11-14, 16 and 18-20 of this correspondence were published by Henri Borgeaud in his article "Lettres d'André Messager à Albert Carré: extraits relatifs à Pelléas et Mélisande", <u>Revue de musicologie</u> 48 (1962), 101-104. The remainder of the letters cover miscellaneous topics; in no. 22, for example, Messager thanks Chabrier for his good wishes on his [Messager's] appointment to the Legion d'Honneur; and in a letter of 21 November 1924, Messager writes to support an attempt to have a Parisian street named after Chabrier.

In order to aid researchers consulting this interesting
collection, letters bearing dates are listed here in
chronological order; the numbers given are those assigned by the
Bibliothèque Nationale. Two of the letters are numbered 99, with
no number 95; they are listed here as 99a and 99b according to
their order in the file.

```
1891:   22, 26
1894:   5
1898:   27
1901:   31, 32
1902:   11, 12, 13, 14
1903:   15
1904:   16, 61
1908:   17
1910:   96
1911:   97, 33, 91
1912:   34, 98
1913:   18, 92
1914:   35
1917:   64, 36, 37, 63, 62, 6
1918:   65, 66, 71, 72, 67, 68, 69, 39, 40, 70, 42, 46,
        47, 73, 48, 49, 50, 51, 41, 44, 52, 53, 45, 7
1919:   20, 19, 54, 55, 56, 57, 58, 59
1920:   60
1922:   93, 94
1924:   24, 76, 77, 78, 79, 8, 9, 74, 23, 75, 99b, 80
1925:   99a
1926:   10, 81
1927:   82, 25, 83, 1, 84
1928:   2, 85, 88
```

In addition to file [A5], the Bibliothèque Nationale, Paris, also
possesses three letters (similarly preserved in the Département
de la Musique) from Messager to Paul Dukas, dating from November
1909 to February 1910. Two of the letters concern Dukas'
symphony, while the other relates to Ariane et barbe-bleu. The
letters are at shelf-mark W48 (406-408). Finally, letter W46
(34) in the Département de la Musique, addressed to Martenot,
requests him to play the 1st harp part in Pelléas et Mélisande,
since M. Lundin has missed most of the rehearsals. The letter is
dated 15 April 1902.

Archives Nationales, Paris

[A6] Dossier AJ13, 1195

Two volumes of official correspondence from the Opéra, labelled "25 juillet 1908; 7 decembre 1907" [sic], and "12 juillet 1912; 29 octobre 1914", with decorated cloth boards and a green spine. Volume 1 contains 496 items, all carbon copies, volume 2, 372 pages, almost all typed.

A large number of the letters are addressed to Dujardin-Beaumetz, Under-Secretary of State for the Arts; but a number of lettres autographes in volume 1 also relate to Henry Février's opera Monna Vanna, which Messager undertook to stage at the Opéra, but which never reached production because of difficulties with Maeterlinck of the same sort that beset Debussy in relation to Pelléas et Mélisande. These letters are on pp. 24, 59 (to Maeterlinck), 141, 296, 386 and 430. Included in volume 2 are letters to Mary Garden (194), Philippe Gaubert (233-235; from which we learn that Gaubert's relations with Messager were not good as early as 1913); and to Heugel (236).[3]

[A7] Dossier AJ13, 1197

Three letters (one of which exists in two versions), relating to Les deux pigeons [W41]. Only one of these is a Messager autograph, the others being written by Henry de Régnier and Vaucorbeil. In his own letter, Messager informs Ritt and Gailhard (who had in the meantime succeeded Vaucorbeil as directors of the Opéra) that his score is ready, and asks about the best method of delivering it.

British Library, London, Department of Manuscripts

[A8] Ms Egerton 3305

A folio manuscript bound in black, with gold tooling and a coat of arms on the front cover. On the spine are the words "Percy Pitt Papers Vol. V". The manuscript contains five autograph letters from Messager to Pitt (Messager's successor at Covent Garden); they are numbered 155, 156/7, 158, 159 and 160, and are dated as follows:

155:	7 December 1905
156/7:	19 December 1905
158:	14 January 1906
159:	13 March 1909
160:	26 October 1911

As in the case of the letters in [A1], the majority of the letters deal with administrative matters regarding singers and contracts. All are written in French. In letter 158, Messager complains to Pitt that Richter has engaged a new cor anglais player, although Messager himself has virtually completed contractual arrangements with another player named Grundstoett. Messager complains that Richter has not always chosen new orchestral personnel well, and cites problems with a violin player in the previous year.

Author's collection

[A9]

I cite here the texts of two Messager autograph letters in my possession, in order to give as complete a picture as possible of the surviving Messager correspondence. The text of a further letter is cited in the introduction to the DISCOGRAPHY. In the first, dated 6 December 1901 and addressed to "Mon cher maître" (probably Gustave Lefèvre, head of the École Niedermeyer), Messager writes "Me voici déjà empeché d'aller demain matin à l'Ecole! Monsieur Carré m'a convoqué à 10h pour l'audition d'une oeuvre nouvelle et je n'y puis manquer. Voulez-vous que je fasse mon cours Lundi ou Mardi à la même heure? Un mot, je vous prie, et croyez que je suis désolé de ce contre-temps. Mes plus affectueux sentiments de dévouement [Signed] A. Messager". [Already I am prevented from attending the School tomorrow morning! M. Carré has summoned me at 10 o'clock to hear a new work, and I cannot be absent. Would you like me to teach my course on Monday or Tuesday at the same time? A brief word, I beg of you; and please believe that I am sorry about this problem".] It is written on notepaper of the Opéra-Comique.

The other letter, written from the Opéra on 25 April 1911, is of much more interest. Messager writes to Mlle G. Peron that he is unable to assign her a role in either of the two Ring cycles taking place at the Opéra that year, as he himself will not be conducting (he did not conduct the work again until 1913). He agrees to mention her to Mottl and Nikisch, who will both be

conducting, but regrets that he can do no more: "Mademoiselle,
Je suis extrèmement touché de votre aimable lettre,
malheureusement je ne puis vous donner satisfaction que très
relativement. Tout d'abord nous ne donnons que deux cycles, mais
vous ne perdrez rien à la suppression de celui que je devais
diriger, puisque vous aurez Mottl et Nikisch pour les deux
autres. Ensuite je ne puis que vous inscrire avec une mention
toute spéciale pour celui qui vous conviendrait le mieux, sans
pouvoir vous garantir absolument le 1er rang. Croyez que je
ferai tout mon possible pour vous donner satisfaction et veuillez
agréer l'assurance de mes sentiments très distingués [Signed] A.
Messager".

["Mademoiselle, I am extremely touched by your friendly letter,
but unfortunately I can give you very little satisfaction in the
matter. First of all, we are only giving two [Ring] cycles, but
you should not lose out through the cancellation of the cycle I
was to conduct, as you still have those of Mottl and Nikisch
remaining. Consequently I can only put in a special word for you
for whichever of the two cycles you prefer, without being at all
able to guarantee you a place in the first rank. Believe that I
will do all I can to satisfy you, and be assured of my very best
regards".]

Mlle Peron was not, in the end, chosen for either of the Ring
cycles of 1911. An article by René Delange on these productions
(including photographs) appears in Musica, June 1911, 102-103.

NOTES

1.   Thus Antoine Bloch-Michel, in his Bibliothèque Nationale:
lettres autographes conservées au Département de la Musique:
catalogue sommaire, Paris: Bibliothèque Nationale, 1984, notes
only the few letters from Debussy, which have since been
published by François Lesure in his edition of Debussy's
correspondence.

2.   Messager does not otherwise seem to have known Porto-Riche;
for a biography of this writer, see Hendrik Brugmans, Georges de
Porto-Riche: sa vie, son oeuvre, Paris: E. Droz, 1934.

3.   The problem on this occasion concerned Gaubert's ballet
Philotis; Enoch was demanding a performance fee for the work,
which was to be staged at the Opéra. Messager, however, advises
Gaubert that he understands that Enoch had only agreed to publish
the piece after the Opéra had accepted it.

2. Newspapers and journals [A10]

Because of his popularity as a composer (at least of light music)
and his status in the French and English musical establishments
after 1898, Messager and his stage works were the subject of many
journal articles in the international press. Premières were
widely reported, as much in the national papers as in journals
intended specifically for musical matters. The musical press in
France during Messager's lifetime was very prolific: all the
national papers (Le figaro, Le temps, Le gaulois, etc.) had their
own music and theatre critics, as did "quality" periodicals, such
as the Journal des débats and the Revue des deux mondes.
Furthermore, the post of critic on such periodicals was
frequently held by established composers - Messager's own work
for La grande revue, Le figaro and Le gaulois confirms this. In
the British press, reviews may be found in The Times, The Stage,
The Musical Times and many more. For a comprehensive list of
English and French musical periodicals of the period, the reader
should consult Imogen Fellinger's article "Periodicals" in The
New Grove.
    Fortunately for the researcher in France, the newspaper
archives of the Fonds Montpensier at the Bibliothèque Nationale,
Paris, Département de la Musique, include a large selection of
press cuttings relating to Messager's life and works [A10],
including files on his work as a chef d'orchestre and as a
director of the Opéra; there are also two files of obituaries.
It is not my intention to list here every press cutting
concerning Messager and his work to be found in the Fonds
Montpensier, and there would be little point in doing so, since
only a few give fresh insights into the life and work of the
composer. The majority of cuttings listed in the "Printed
Sources" section of the bibliography below are articles by
established contemporary writers (such as Henri de Curzon or
Henry Malherbe) or writers who had a particular knowledge of
Messager's work, such as Robert Brussel or Georges Pioch; but
where a lesser-known writer provides a particularly interesting
or perceptive view of an aspect of Messager's life and work, his
contribution is also listed.

3. Other archival sources

[A11] Bibliothèque de l'Opéra, Paris

In addition to the files on Messager's stage works held in the
Fonds Montpensier (see [A10] above), there are a number of
"dossiers d'oeuvre" at the Bibliothèque de l'Opéra, relating to

La Basoche [W13], Béatrice [W28], Le chevalier d'Harmental [W20],
Les dragons de l'impératrice [W25], Fortunio [W26], Isoline
[W10], Miss Dollar [W16], Monsieur Beaucaire [W30] and Véronique
[W24]. Together with press cuttings, these dossiers contain many
choreographic or scenic sketches for productions at the Opéra or
Opéra-Comique, along with details of finance and other
administrative items; there are, for example, a number of
sketches for Madame Chrysanthème, dating from the time of the
first production in January 1893, as well as documents concerning
a revival of Les deux pigeons in the same year.

[A12] Chappell and Co., London

The archives of Chappell and Co. contain a small amount of
material pertaining to contracts, including a number signed by
Jean Messager, in which he signs over his copyrights to Véronique
and Les p'tites Michu [W23]. The most extensive correspondence
(none of which bears Messager's signature) relates to Monsieur
Beaucaire, as mentioned in the BIOGRAPHY.

[A13] Royal Opera House, Covent Garden, London

Although Messager spent nearly seven years at the present Royal
Opera House as director of the Grand Opera Syndicate, the
archives of the opera house are unfortunately very scanty for the
period 1901-1908. As noted by other scholars, Messager's
contribution to the house as a conductor was negligible before
about 1906, during which time he was occupied primarily with
administration.

PRINTED SOURCES

1. Messager's own writings (including press interviews)

As previously noted, Messager's works and activities were well
documented in the French and foreign press. Like many other
composers of the period, such as Gabriel Fauré (whom he succeeded
as music critic of Le figaro), Saint-Saëns and Debussy, Messager
contributed to the ever-growing corpus of serious writing,
criticism and, on occasions, trivia, by writing articles for and
letters to contemporary journals, and occasionally giving
interviews. He contributed regularly to Le figaro from 1921 to
1926, and in the final years of the 19th century and early years
of the 20th wrote for Musica and La grande revue. The selection
of writings presented here will give an idea of the scope of
Messager's literary work, and, it is hoped, encourage other
researchers to take up the topic.

Items are listed in chronological order.

[M1]   Contribution to "Hommage à Chabrier", a collection of
tributes in a limited edition of Chabrier's Briséis, published in
1897 by Enoch.   Messager's article is also reproduced in Francis
Poulenc's Emmanuel Chabrier (see item [B109]).

[M2] Reply to the "Enquête sur l'orientation musicale" in Musica
(October 1902), together with responses from Debussy, Alfred
Bruneau, Camille Erlanger, André Gédalge, Xavier Leroux and
Vincent d'Indy.

[M3] "La Tosca; le Théâtre Lyrique; Le roi Arthus; L'étranger",
La grande revue, 15 December 1903.

[M4] "Le centenaire de Berlioz", La grande revue, 15 January
1904.

[M5] "Hélène; la symphonie en si bemol de V. d'Indy", La grande
revue, 15 March 1904.

[M6] "La fille de Roland; le fils de l'étoile", La grande revue, 15 June 1904.

[M7] "L'oeuvre dramatique de Saint-Saëns", Musica, June 1907.

[M8] "André Messager par ... André Messager", Musica, September 1908.

[M9] Reply to the question "Doit-on jouer Wagner après la guerre?", La renaissance, 5 February 1916.

[M10] "Il faudrait créer à Paris un nouveau Théâtre-Lyrique", Comoedia, 31 October 1921.

[This article is about an operetta competition organised by Comoedia; 28 composers have entered, and Messager highlights the difficulties such composers experience in obtaining performances of their works in Paris.]

[M11] Interview with Le petit journal, 16 May 1922, under   the title "Croyez-vous à une crise de l'opérette?".

[M12] "Lettre ouverte à Antoine", Comoedia, 1 March 1923.

[Messager's reply to a letter from a M. Antoine, entitled "Trop de musique".]

[M13] "Souvenirs", Cinquante ans de musique française, de 1874 à 1925, ed. L. Rohozinski. Paris: Editions Librairie de la France, 1925 [see APPENDIX 3].

[M14] "Une lettre de M. André Messager", Comoedia, 23 April 1925.

[The letter in question concerns the performance of Belgian works on the French stage.]

[M15] Interview with Gaston Lebel for La volonté, 20 October 1925.

[The interview covers the genesis of Monsieur Beaucaire, which, Messager tells his interviewer, he has wished to set to music for a long time; it has simply been a matter of finding a suitable librettist.]

[M16] "Les premières représentations de Pelléas", La revue musicale, special number (May 1926), 110-114.

[M17] Reply to the question "Où va la musique moderne?" for an article by Pierre Maudru in Comoedia, 28 March 1928.

[M18] Preface to Maurice Galerne: L'École Niedermeyer: sa création, son but, son développement. Paris: Editions Margueritat, 1928.

2. Other writings on Messager's life and works

Books and articles cited in this section are included either because (a) they give a useful background to the period in which Messager lived and worked; or (b) they include at least a paragraph specifically concerning the composer. Newspaper articles have been included where they give significant new insights into the composer and/or his work, or where they present new biographical information. (Reviews of specific works will be found in the WORKLIST). All items listed here were published in Paris, unless otherwise stated.

[B1] AUGÉ-LARIBÉ, MICHEL. André Messager: musicien de théâtre. Editions du Vieux Colombier, 1951.

[Augé-Laribé was Messager's son-in-law, and took advantage of his contacts with the family to discover details of the composer's family tree. Unlike Février [B53], he includes a worklist and a discography. Unfortunately Augé-Laribé's book contains occasional errors of fact, and there are frequent discrepancies between première dates as given in the worklist and those cited in the main body of the book. Augé-Laribé does, however, attempt to place Messager's life

and music in the context of the period in which the
composer lived and worked, and frequently interrupts his
narrative to present a picture of contemporary musical
life, for example as Messager would have experienced it in
Paris just after the Franco-Prussian War]

[B2] BANES, A. "Messager", La revue théâtrale, special number:
"L'Opéra nouveau" (1908), 2

[B3] BARRICELLI, J.-P. and LEO WEINSTEIN. Ernest Chausson: the
Composer's Life and Works.
Norman, OK: Oklahoma University Press, 1955

[B4] BELLAIGUE, CAMILLE. "André Messager", Revue des deux mondes
50 (15 March 1929), 459-462

[B5] BERTEAUX, EUGENE. "Avec le père de Véronique", En ce
temps-là. Editions du Bateau Ivre, 1946, 182-191

[In spite of its title, the chapter concerning Messager is
actually given over to an account of performances of
Wagner's Le crépuscule des dieux at the Opéra in 1907]

[B6] BEYDTS, LOUIS. "André Messager", Le théâtre lyrique en
France depuis les origines jusqu'à nos jours, 3 vols. Radio
Paris, 1938-1939, 3: 82-90

[B7] --------. Charles Gounod et André Messager: conférence
dite par l'auteur à Paris le 29 avril 1941. Nancy: imp. E.
Spillmann, 1942

[B8] --------. "L'opérette: André Messager", Le théâtre lyrique
en France depuis les origines jusqu'à nos jours, 3 vols. Radio
Paris, 1938-1939, 2: 304-315

[B9] BORGEAUD, H. "Lettres d'André Messager à Albert Carré:
extraits rélatifs à Pelléas et Mélisande", Revue de musicologie
48 (1962), 101-104.

[Borgeaud's "extraits" are unfortunately just that, and he

never cites a complete letter. See also section [A5] above]

[B10] BORGEX, L. "André Messager et l'opinion anglaise", Comoedia, 27 February 1929

[Borgex claims that Messager spoke English perfectly, which seems surprising, given that the letters to Pitt preserved in the British Library [see A8] are in French. Perhaps Messager preferred to conduct business correspondence in his own language]

[B11] BOSCHOT, ADOLPHE. "André Messager est mort", Echo de Paris, 25 February 1929

[An obituary, later printed in Boschot's Le mystère musical, Plon, 1929, and in Les maîtres d'histoire: portraits de musiciens, Plon, 1946.]

[B12] --------. Chez les musiciens (du 18e siècle à nos jours), 1st series. Plon, 1922

[B13] BRUNEAU, ALFRED. "Les concerts", Le figaro, 25 April 1901

[A review of a concert conducted by Messager at the Vaudeville on 25 April 1901; the programme included Debussy's Prélude à l'après-midi d'un faune. See Messager's account of the performance in APPENDIX III. Emile Vuillermoz also remarked on the performance of this work in his preface to Jean Messager's L'enfance de Pelléas [B96]]

[B14] --------. La musique française: rapport sur la musique en France du XIIIe au XXe siècle: la musique à Paris en 1900 au théâtre, au concert, à l'Exposition. Bibliothèque Charpentier, 1901

[B15] --------. "Souvenirs inédits", introduction et notes par Danièle Pistone, Revue internationale de la musique française [RIMF] 7 (1982), 9-82

[B16] BRUSSEL, Robert. "L'oeuvre d'André Messager", Musica, September 1908, 133-135

[B17] BRUYAS, FLORIAN. Histoire de l'opérette en France 1855-1965. Lyon: Emmanuel Vite, 1974

[The most complete survey of Messager's operetta output. Bruyas stays strictly within the confines of his subject, omitting any mention of Béatrice and of other works that are not strictly operettas]

[B18] BÜSSER, HENRI. De Pelléas aux Indes Galantes. Fayard, 1955

[Büsser was one of Messager's deputies at the Opéra, but had first met him at the École Niedermeyer. In addition to a chapter on this aspect of his life, Büsser also includes a section on "L'Opéra-Comique d'Albert Carré (1901-1905)", which provides details of the preparations for the première of Pelléas et Mélisande, and an essay on Messager and Broussan's directorship of the Opéra]

[B19] CARRAUD, GASTON. "André Messager", La liberté, 7 June 1907

[B20] CARRÉ, ALBERT. "Entr'actes", Le matin, 23 February 1932

[B21] --------. Souvenirs de theâtre, réunis, présentés et annotés par Robert Favart. Plon, 1950

[With Büsser's book [B18], this is one of the few contemporary sets of memoirs to give any insight into Messager's character]

[B22] --------. "Souvenirs sur André Messager", Comoedia, 1 March 1929

[B23] CHAMPLIN, JOHN D., jnr. "André Messager", Cyclopedia of Music and Musicians, 3 vols. New York: Charles Scribner's Sons, 1893, 2: 565

[One of the earliest appearances of Messager's name in a musical dictionary. Scribner states erroneously that Messager was still organist at Saint-Paul--Saint-Louis at the time of the book's publication]

[B24] CHARPENTIER, RAYMOND. "André Messager", Chantecler, 2 March
1929

[B25] CLÉMENT, F. and P. LAROUSSE. Dictionnaire des operas, rev.
ed. Librairie Larousse, [?1905]; reprinted New York: Dâ Capo,
1969

   [A useful source for première information, etc. The first
   edition was published in 1880]

[B26] COEUROY, ANDRÉ. "André Messager", Paris-midi, 25 February
1929

[B27] --------. La musique française moderne. Delagrave, 1921

[B28] COMBARIEU, JULES. Histoire de la musique, 3 vols.
Armand-Colin, 1919, 3: passim.

[B29] --------. "L'influence de la musique allemande sur la
musique française", Jahrbuch der Musikbibliothek Peters 2 (1895),
22-32

   [Messager is mentioned only briefly towards the end of the
   article]

[B30] CORDEY, J. La Société des Concerts du Conservatoire. [La
Société], 1941

[B31] CURZON, HENRI DE. "André Messager", Journal des débats, 26
February 1929, 362-363

   [An obituary notice]

[B32] --------. "Les interprètes d'André Messager", Musica,
September 1908, 139-140

   [Includes notes on Jacques Isnardon, Lucien Fugère, Odette
   Dulac, Alice Bonheur, Henry Krauss and Max Bouvet]

[B33] --------. L'oeuvre de Richard Wagner à Paris et ses interprètes (1850-1914). Maurice Senart, [s.d.]

[B34] --------. "L'opérette française entre Charles Lecocq et Claude Terrasse", L'opérette: figaro artistique illustré, April 1931, 25-28

[B35] DANDELOT, ARTHUR. La Société des Concerts du Conservatoire (1828-1923). Delagrave, 1923

    [The most detailed work on its subject]

[B36] DESAYMARD, JOSEPH. Emmanuel Chabrier d'après ses lettres: l'homme et l'oeuvre. Fernand Roches, 1934

    [Included is a letter from Chabrier to Van Dyck, in
    which the composer notes that a complete performance of
    Gwendoline took place on 8 and 15 May "chez une grande
    dame très riche". Fauré played the harmonium and
    Messager and d'Indy percussion]

[B37] DUFRESNE, CLAUDE. Histoire de l'opérette. [s.l.]: Fernand Nathan, 1981

    [Rather slight coverage, far inferior to Bruyas [B17]]

[B38] DUKAS, PAUL. "André Messager", Les écrits de Paul Dukas sur la musique. Société d'éditions françaises et internationales, 1948, 674-676

    [An obituary, even though the editors of Dukas' book
    claimed it was written in 1924. There are also passing
    references to Messager conducting at the Opéra-Comique]

[B39] DUMESNIL, RENÉ. "André Messager", Dictionnaire de la musique, ed. Marc Honegger. Bordas, 1970, 2/1986, 2: 819

[B40] --------. "André Messager", Les maîtres d'histoire: portraits de musiciens français. Plon, 1938, 111-119

[B41] --------. Histoire illustré du théâtre lyrique. Editions d'histoire et d'art, 1953.

[B42] DUMESNIL, RENÉ. La musique contemporaine en France, 2 vols.
A. Colin, 1930

[B43] --------. La musique en France entre les deux guerres.
Geneva: Editions du Milieu du Monde, 1946

[B44] --------. Portraits de musiciens français: vingt-cinq
portraits de musiciens contemporains. Plon, 1937

[B45] EMMANUEL, MAURICE. "Maurice Emmanuel et son temps
(1862-1938): lettres inédites", Revue Internationale de la
musique Française [RIMF] 11 (June 1983), 7-92

    ERNST, ALFRED see [B60]

[B46] ESTALENX, J.-F. d' "Lacôme, Chabrier, Messager",
Littératures: annales de l'Université de Toulouse-le-Mirail 10
no.2 (1974), 27-55

[B47] FAURÉ, GABRIEL. "André Messager", Musica, September 1908,
131-132

[B48] --------. Opinions musicales. Editions Rieder, 1930

    [Includes reviews of Rameau's Hippolyte et Aricie and
    Wagner's Parsifal from Le figaro, 14 May 1908 and 2 January
    1914]

[B49] FAURÉ-FRÉMIET, PHILIPPE. Gabriel Fauré. Editions Rieder,
1929

    [Includes information on the Quadrille [W96], and on
    Messager's and Fauré's visits to the Clerc family at
    Villerville]

    FAVART, ROBERT see [B21]

[B50] FAVRE, GEORGES. "Les romans de Pierre Loti et le théâtre lyrique", Cahiers Pierre Loti 55 (June 1970), 37-42

[Includes a brief discussion of Madame Chrysanthème]

[B51] FERCHAULT, GUY. "André Messager", Larousse de la musique, ed. N. Dufourcq. Librairie Larousse, 1957, 2: 41-42

[B52] --------. "André Messager", Die Musik in Geschichte und Gegenwart, ed. F. Blume. Kassel; Basel: Bärenreiter, 1949-1986, 9: 143-146

[B53] FÉVRIER, HENRY. André Messager: mon maître, mon ami. Amiot-Dumont, 1948

[Février is much more selective than Augé-Laribé [B1] about the works he discusses, and confines most of his discussion to the stage music. He did, however, know Messager for longer than Augé-Laribé, having caught sight of the composer at his [Messager's] first wedding in 1883. Février occasionally takes advantage of his position to express his own views in a rather more forthright manner than a purely objective biographer would have done (especially with regard to his own opera Monna Vanna, produced at the Opéra in 1909), but gives vivid sketches of the composer which, while making his own work much less "scholarly" than Augé-Laribé's, gives it an immediacy which is attractive. It also, unfortunately, admits some factual errors into the text]

[B54] GALERNE, MAURICE. L'École Niedermeyer, sa création, son but, son développement. Editions Margueritat, 1928

[Preface by Messager]

[B55] GÄNZL, KURT. The British Musical Theatre, 2 vols. Basingstoke: Macmillan, 1986

[B56] GAUTHIER-VILLARS, HENRY. Entre deux airs. Flammarion, 1895

[B57] --------. Garçon, l'audition!. H. Simonis Empis, 1901

[B58] GAUTHIER-VILLARS, HENRY. Notes sans portées.
Flammarion, 1896

[B59] --------. Soirées perdues.
Tresse et Stock, 1894

[B60] GAUTHIER-VILLARS, HENRY, with ALFRED ERNST. Lettres de
l'ouvreuse: voyage autour de la musique. Léon Vanier, 1890

[B61] GAVOTY, BERNARD. Reynaldo Hahn: le musicien de la Belle
Époque. Éditions Buchet/Chastel, 1976

[B62] GENEST, EMILE. L'Opéra-Comique connu et inconnu ... depuis
l'origine jusqu'à nos jours. Fischbacher, 1925

[B63] GHEUSI, P. B. "André Messager: sa vie et son oeuvre", Le
figaro, 25 February 1929

[B64] --------. Cinquante ans de Paris: mémoires d'un témoin
1889-1938. Plon, 1939

     [Gheusi knew Messager well, especially during the latter
     part of the composer's career, and although he apparently
     did not particularly like Messager, gives a vivid character
     sketch on p.391 of the book]

[B65] --------. Guerre et théâtre 1914-1918: mémoires d'un
officier du Général Gallien, et journal parisien du directeur de
l'Opéra-Comique pendant la guerre. Berger-Levrault, 1919

     [Includes details of plans to stage Béatrice at the
     Opéra-Comique]

[B66] --------. L'Opéra-Comique pendant la guerre. Éditions de
"La Nouvelle Revue", [c.1919]

[B67] GOUBAULT, CHRISTIAN. La critique musicale dans la presse française de 1870 à 1914. Geneva; Paris: Slatkine, 1984

[Goubault supplies some details of Messager's work as a music critic, and also includes a section concerning the Paris performances of Parsifal in 1914]

[B68] GOURRET, JEAN. Histoire de l'Opéra-Comique. Publications Universitaires de Paris, 1978

[B69] GROVER, RALPH SCOTT. Ernest Chausson: the Man and his Music. London: Athlone Press, 1980

[B70] HAHN, REYNALDO. "André Messager: chef d'orchestre", Musica, September 1908, 136

[B71] --------. Notes: journal d'un musicien. Plon, 1933

[B72] --------. "Notes sur André Messager", Le figaro, 22 January 1936;   19 February 1936

[Reproduced in Hahn's L'oreille au guêt. Gallimard, 1937, 107-113]

[B73] --------. Thèmes variés. Janin, 1946.

[Hahn gives details of a soirée in Fauré's honour in 1910 at which Messager was present, and provides an anecdote regarding Messager's time at the Opéra]

[B74] HARDING, JAMES. Folies de Paris: the Rise and Fall of French Operetta. London: Chappell, 1979, 121-150

[An excellent general survey of the subject. Unfortunately much of the material concerning Messager is taken directly from Augé-Laribé and Février]

[B75] HIRCHMAÑN, HENRI. "Un hommage à André Messager", Le petit journal, 9 June 1923

[B76] HUGHES, GERVASE. "André Messager", Composers of Operetta.
London: Macmillan, 1962, 91-99

[Like Bruyas [B17], covers the operettas only]

[B77] HURÉ, JEAN. "André Messager", Musiciens contemporains, 1st
album. Maurice Senart, 1923

[B78] JABOUNE, pseud. Les grands hommes quand ils étaient petits.
Flammarion, 1925

[B79] JEAN-AUBRY, GEORGES. La musique française d'aujourd'hui.
Paris, 1916. Eng. trans. by Edwin Evans published London: Kegan
Paul, 1919; reprinted New York: Books for Libraries Press, 1976.

[A useful general survey of the period, with a preface by
Gabriel Fauré]

JOLLY, CYNTHIA see [B109]

[B80] JONES, J.BARRIE, trans. Gabriel Fauré: a Life in Letters.
London: Batsford, 1989

[The majority of the letters cited by Jones are not in
either the French or English editions of NECTOUX (see
[B100]). A small number include references to Messager]

[B81] KEMP, ROBERT. "Nos compositeurs: André Messager", Petit
parisien, 22 February 1923

[B82] KLEIN, HERMANN. "André Messager", Grove's Dictionary of
Music and Musicians, 2nd ed., ed. J. A. Fuller-Maitland. London:
Macmillan, 1907, 3: 183

[There is no entry under "Messager" in the first edition of
Grove's Dictionary. Klein's article was reproduced, with
some revisions, right up to the 5th edition of 1954; the
entry in The New Grove (1980) is by Andrew Lamb [B86]]

[B83] KOLB, JEAN. "Collaborateurs et interprètes pleurent le charmant maître disparu", Paris soir, 26 February 1929

[Includes tributes from Albert Willemetz, Mariette Sully, Marcelle Denya and Raimu]

[B84] LALO, PIERRE. "André Messager", De Rameau à Ravel: portraits et souvenirs. Albin Michel, 1947, 143-150

[A reprint of an article originally published in Le temps, 14 April 1941. A typescript of the original is in the Bibliothèque Nationale, Paris, Département de la Musique, 4° Vm Pièce 368]

[B85] LALOY, LOUIS. La musique retrouvée 1902-1927. Plon, 1928

[Most of the book is given over to Debussy's music, with Messager mentioned only in passing for his role in the production of Pelléas et Mélisande]

[B86] LAMB, ANDREW. "André Messager", The New Grove Dictionary of Music and Musicians, ed. Stanley Sadie. London: Macmillan, 1980, 12: 202-203

[B87] LANDORMY, P. La musique française après Debussy. Gallimard, 1948

[B88] LAVIGNAC, ALBERT. Le voyage artistique à Bayreuth. Delagrave, 1897

[B89] LEFEVRE, GUSTAVE and Mme veuve HENRI HEUGEL. "L'École de Musique Classique Niedermeyer", Encyclopédie de la musique, ed. A. Lavignac and L. de la Laurencie. Delagrave, 1931, 2: 3617-3621

[B90] LESURE, FRANCOIS, ed. Claude Debussy: lettres 1884-1918. Hermann, 1980. Eng. trans. by Roger Nichols published London: Faber, 1987

[B91] LUBBOCK, MARK and DAVID EWEN. The Complete Book of Light Opera. London: Putnam, 1962

[B92] MALHERBE, HENRY. "André Messager", Le temps, 26 February
1929

[B93] MATTFIELD, JULIUS. A Handbook of American Operatic
Premières 1731-1962. (Detroit Studies in Music Bibliography; 5).
Detroit: Detroit Information Service, 1963

[B94] MAUCLAIR, CAMILLE. Histoire de la musique européenne
1850-1914. Fischbacher, 1914

     [A useful general survey of the period, although there is no
     material specifically concerning Messager]

[B95] [ANDRÉ-]MESSAGER, JEAN. "Mon père: André Messager",
Comoedia, 7 November 1942

     [Jean Messager states among other things that his father
     continued to write Masses even after his appointment to the
     Folies-Bergère]

[B96] --------, comp. L'enfance de Pelléas: lettres de Claude
Debussy à André Messager. Dorbon-Ainé, [1938]

[B97] MICHEL, FRANCOIS. "André Messager", Encyclopédie de la
musique, ed. F. Michel. Fasquelle, 1961, 3: 188-189

[B98] MUSICIENS CÉLEBRES. Les musiciens célèbres. Geneva:
Editions d'Art Lucien Mazenod, 1946, 272-273

[B99] MYERS, ROLLO. Emmanuel Chabrier and his Circle.   London:
J. M. Dent, 1969

[B100] NECTOUX, JEAN-MICHEL, comp. Correspondance Gabriel Fauré.
Flammarion, 1980. Eng. trans., Gabriel Fauré; his Life through
his Letters, published London: Marion Boyars, 1984.

[B101] --------. Gabriel Fauré.
Editions du Seuil, 1972

NOEL, EDOUARD <u>see</u> [B125]

[B102] NORTHCOTT, RICHARD. <u>Records of the Royal Opera,</u>
<u>Covent Garden, 1888-1921</u>. London: Press Printers, 1921

[B103] ORLEDGE, ROBERT. <u>Gabriel Fauré</u>. London: Eulenberg
Books, 1979, rev. 1983

OUVREUSE DE LA CIRQUE D'ÉTÉ, L', <u>pseud</u>. <u>see</u> GAUTHIER-
VILLARS, HENRY [B56-B60]

[B104] PIOCH, GEORGES. "André Messager", <u>Le soir</u>, 18 August 1927

[B105] --------. "Le <u>Crépuscule des dieux</u> à l'Opéra", <u>Musica</u>,
December 1908, 192-193

[B106] --------."L'esprit français dans l'oeuvre d'André
Messager", <u>Musica</u>, September 1908, 141

[B107] PIZON, P."André Messager", <u>Bulletin de la Société</u>
<u>d'Émulation du Bourbonnais</u> (1954-1955), 19-43

[Includes much useful biographical material]

[B108] POUGIN, ARTHUR. "André Messager", <u>Biographie universelle</u>
<u>des musiciens et bibliographie générale de la musique</u>, comp.
F.-J. Fétis, supplementary vols., Firmin-Didot, 1881, 1: 214

[B109] POULENC, FRANCIS. <u>Emmanuel Chabrier</u>. Paris; Geneva: La
Palatine, 1961. Eng. trans. by Cynthia Jolly published London:
Denis Dobson, 1981

[B110] PRADEL, PIERRE. "André Messager", <u>Bulletin des amis de</u>
<u>Montluçon</u>, 2nd series, 10 (1929), 20-23

[B111] PUGNO, RAOUL. "Nos chefs d'orchestre: la trinité dominicale", Musica, November 1910, 166

[B112] RAPHANEL, JEAN. Histoire au jour le jour de l'Opéra-Comique; 1st series (1 January-30 June 1898). Bibliothèque de La Vie Théâtrale, 1898

   [Includes material concerning Messager's appointment as musical director of the Opéra-Comique, and the Paris première of d'Indy's Fervaal]

[B113] ROBERT, GUSTAVE. La musique à Paris, 1896-1897. Fischbacher, 1898.

   [This series of yearbooks provides a review of the musical highlights of the years under discussion. The volume cited here includes comments on a performance of Messager's Nouveau printemps at a concert given by the Société Nationale de Musique in December 1896. There is, unfortunately, no mention of Messager in the other volumes published during the 1890's]

[B114] ROHOZINSKI, L., ed. Cinquante ans de musique française, de 1874 à 1925, 2 vols. Editions Librairie de la France, 1925

   [See especially the sections dealing with opera and operetta, and Messager's memoirs (this book, APPENDIX 3)]

[B115] ROSENTHAL, HAROLD. Opera at Covent Garden: a Short History. London: Gollancz, 1967

[B116] --------. Two Centuries of Opera at Covent Garden. London: Putnam, 1958

[B117] SAINT-SAENS, CAMILLE. Au courant de la vie. Dorbon-Ainé, 1914

[B118] --------. École buissonnière: notes et souvenirs. Lafitte, 1913

[B119] SAMAZEUILH, GUSTAVE. Musiciens de mon temps. Renaissance du Livre, 1947

[B120] --------. "Un serviteur de la musique: André Messager", Courrier musical 31 (15 March 1929), 199-200

[B121] SCHNEIDER, LOUIS. Les maîtres de l'opérette française. Perrin, 1924

[B122] --------. "Trois grands compositeurs: Offenbach, Hervé, Lecocq", L'opérette: figaro artistique illustré, April 1931, 14-24

[B123] SERÉ, OCTAVE. "André Messager", Musiciens français d'aujourd'hui, new ed. Mercure de France, 1911, 307-319

   [There is an extensive worklist and a short bibliography
   included with this article, a copy of which may also be
   found in the Fonds Montpensier, Bibliothèque Nationale,
   Paris, Département de la Musique]

[B124] SOUBIES, ALBERT, ed. Almanach des spectacles. Flammarion, 1874-1918

   [A useful source of general information concerning
   theatrical premières, cast lists, etc.]

[B125] STOULLIG, EDMOND. Les annales du théâtre et de la musique. Ollendorff, 1875-1916

   [Like [B124], a useful theatrical almanach. Early issues
   written in collaboration with Edouard Noël]

[B126] TIERSOT, JULLIEN. Un demi-siècle de musique française: entre les deux guerres (1870-1917). Alcan, 1918

[B127] TOYE, FRANCIS. "André Messager", The Morning Post, 27 February 1929

[B128] TRAUBNER, RICHARD. Operetta: a Theatrical History.
London: Gollancz, 1984

[B129] VERNAELDE, ALBERT. "La Société des Concerts", Encyclopédie
de la musique, ed. A. Lavignac and L. de la Laurencie. Delagrave,
1931, 2: 3702-3703

[B130] VUILLERMOZ, ÉMILE. "A la mémoire d'André Messager",
Epoque, 10 February 1949

     [Includes a drawing of Messager by Sacha Guitry]

[B131] --------. "André Messager", L'illustration, 2 March 1929,
207

[B132] --------., under pseudonym of G. DARCY. "André Messager",
Musica, August 1912

[B133] W., H. "Portraits contemporains: André Messager", La vie
populaire, 15 October 1891

[B134] WALSH, T. J. Monte Carlo Opera, 1910-1951. Kilkenny:
Boethius Press, 1986

[B135] WEARING, J. P. The London Stage, 1890-1899: a Calendar of
Plays and Players, 2 vols. Metuchen, NJ, and London: Scarecrow
Press, 1976

     [Further vols. covering the periods 1900-1909 and 1910-1919
     were published in 1981 and 1982; both contain useful
     information about Messager productions]

[B136] WEILL, JANINE. Marguerite Long: une vie fascinante.
Julliard, 1969

[B137] WIDOR, Charles-Marie. Notice sur la vie et des oeuvres
d'André Messager. [For the Académie des Beaux Arts, 1929]

    [Reprinted in Henry Février, André Messager, 240-248]

    WILLY, pseud. see GAUTHIER-VILLARS, HENRY [B56-B60]

[B138] WOLFF, Stéphane. Un demi-siècle d'Opéra-Comique
(1900-1950). A. Bonne, 1953

[B139] --------. L'Opéra au Palais Garnier (1875-1961).
Paris; Genève: Slatkine, 1983 [1st published: Paris:
"L'Entr'acte", 1962]

Discography

INTRODUCTION

The small number of sound recordings of Messager's music
commercially available at the present time is symptomatic of a
noticeable decline in the popularity of Messager's works since
the early 1960's. Many of the recordings produced since then
have been anthologies of tracks originally recorded between 1925
and 1950, although Mackerras and J-P. Jacquillat's recordings of
Les deux pigeons are notable exceptions. Furthermore, the
anthologies thus created are often intended (or so it would seem)
more to highlight the talents and triumphs of a particular singer
than to provide any sort of representative selection of
Messager's oeuvre.
        In spite of the comparatively large number of recordings
listed here, it is disappointing that so many of Messager's works
remain unrecorded: what a pity, for example, that the artists
who took part in the Messager memorial concert in 1930 (see
APPENDIX II), did not record the many rarely performed pieces
presented on that occasion. There is no complete recording of
Madame Chrysanthème, of the Symphony, or of Béatrice, the work by
which Messager set so much store.
        A further matter of regret is that we have no recordings of
Messager himself, either as pianist, organist or (most
regrettable of all) as conductor. Recordings of his performances
of Pelléas, Così fan tutte or Parsifal, the three works for which
he was most acclaimed in his own day, would doubtless be very
revealing.[1] Augé-Laribé (among others) tells us of Messager's
attention to detail, and of his quick grasp of the essential
qualities of a work, and it is obvious from many of Messager's
letters to Albert Carré that he had an excellent understanding of
the strengths and shortcomings of the singers who worked for him.
Whether Messager actually distrusted the recording medium is not
clear, although such an attitude would have been surprising,
given the success on disc of many of the artists who worked with
him. One of the lettres autographes at the Bibliothèque
Nationale, Paris, mentions that an American company wished to
make recordings of a number of works during the tour of the
U.S.A. by the Société des Concerts du Conservatoire at the end of

the First World War: the French were to be offered 15% royalties
on these recordings.[2] The arrangement is not mentioned again in
the numerous letters relating to the tour at the Bibliothèque
Nationale, and it would be tempting to assume that the idea was
dropped, were it not for a further reference to the matter by
Albert Vernaelde, who, having listed the cities visited by the
French orchestra, adds:

> Ajoutons enfin que, sur les vives sollicitations d'une
> grande firme américaine, la Société des Concerts a consenti
> à consacrer plusieurs matinées pour enregistrer des disques
> qui sont conserves à l'égal de réliques particulièrement
> précieuses.
>
> [We should add finally that, at the earnest request of a
> large American company, the Société des Concerts agreed to
> devote a few mornings to making discs, which are now
> preserved as if they were particularly precious relics]

In spite of this, it has not yet been possible to trace these
"precious" recordings.

A final piece of evidence indicates that Messager was
afforded at least one other opportunity to record on disc, this
time by the Gramophone Company. In an autograph letter presently
in my possession and dated 5 April 1923, he writes to a company
representative as follows:

> Cher Monsieur:
>   Je serais très heureux que la Cie du
> Gramophone enregistre des fragments de "l'Amour Masqué" et
> je vous remercie de votre aimable proposition de diriger
> l'orchestre qui les executera. Mais, en toute conscience,
> je ne crois pas que ma présence ajoute grand chose à
> l'intérêt de l'enregistrement. Chaque morceau est marqué
> au metronome dans la partition piano et chant. Il suffira
> donc que la personne qui dirigera veuille bien se conformer
> à ces indications. Croyez, je vous prie, à l'expression de
> mes sentiments les meilleures.
>
>   [Signed] A. Messager

[Dear Sir: I would be very happy for the Gramophone Company
to record extracts from L'amour masqué, and thank you for
your kind invitation to conduct the orchestra that will
perform them. But in all conscience I do not believe that
my presence will add much interest to the recordings: each
piece has a metronome mark in the vocal score, so all will
proceed quite satisfactorily if the person who is to
conduct will be kind enough to conform to those markings.
Yours etc. A. Messager]

There is no reason to suppose that Messager was being
deliberately self-effacing, and we may therefore propose that
(surprising as it may seem) he may not have sufficiently
understood the importance of the recording medium as a means of
preserving personal interpretations of music for posterity.

The discography comprises all commercially produced recordings,
whether still commercially available or not. By far the largest
library collection of recordings of Messager's compositions is in
the Phonothèque Nationale, 2 rue Louvois, Paris 75002; items
included in that collection are here marked with an asterisk.
Dates of recordings are given where known; in the case of items
in the Phonothèque Nationale, the dates given are those of their
deposit there, unless otherwise stated. The only previously
published discography of Messager's music is in Augé-Laribé's
André Messager: musicien de théâtre [B1]. Perhaps surprisingly,
I have been unable to find copies of a number of the recordings
he cites, although the details he gives are often confirmed by
entries in the World's Encyclopedia of Recorded Music (WERM).
Items cited by Augé-Laribé are indicated by the letters AL and,
if confirmed by the World's Encyclopedia, by the letters WERM.
Since Augé-Laribé's book was published in 1951, it follows that
all recordings cited by him must precede that date. In addition
to the sources cited above, details of other recordings have been
extracted from Robert Bauer's New Catalogue of Historical Records
1898-1908/9, 2nd ed., London: Sidgwick and Jackson, 1947;
Diapason and Gramophone magazines; R. G. Darrell's The
Gramophone Shop Encyclopedia of Recorded Music, New York: Crown
Publishers, 1936, 3/1948; F. F. Clough and G. J. Cuming's
indispensable World's Encyclopedia of Recorded Music, London:
Sidgwick and Jackson; Decca, 1952, with supplements; and a

number of more specialised discographies, including V. Liff,
"Yvonne Printemps: a Discography", Recorded Sound 31 (July
1968), 311-313; Patrick O'Connor, Yvonne Printemps 1894-1977,
Richmond: Dimbleby and Sons, 1978 [limited edition of 300 copies]
], 14-17; Victor Girard, "Lucien Fugère", Record Collector 8
no.5 (May 1953), 101-109; Rodolfo Celletti's Le grande voci,
Rome: Istituto per la collaborazione culturale, 1964; and Roland
Mancini, Fanély Revoil, Paris: Opéra, 1969. Opern auf
Schallplatten 1900-1962: ein historischer Katalog, Vienna:
Universal Edition, 1974; John R. Bennett's Dischi Fonotipia,
[s.l.]: Oakwood Press, 1964 [first published by the Record
Collector Shop, 1953]; and Frank Andrews' Columbia 10" Records
1904-1930, London: City of London Phonograph and Gramophone
Society, 1985, also provided useful information, as did the
catalogue of discs in the Rogers and Hammerstein Archive of
Recorded Sound in the New York Public Library and, of course, the
catalogue of the Library of Congress. I was also fortunate to be
allowed access to catalogue cards prepared by the National Sound
Archive in London which have been created as their contribution
to the next edition of WERM: these entries are noted in the
discography by the letters "NSA WERM". Finally, the collection
of record companies' catalogues held on microfilm at the National
Sound Archive provided details of a number of records that have
probably long since disappeared.

In spite of having access to all these sources, it has
nevertheless been impossible in all cases to find extant examples
of all the recordings noted here: frustratingly, a disc will
often be described in a catalogue as consisting of "Selections",
without further details of what the "selections" are, and with
little hope of finding a library copy of the disc to check them.
Thus it has not always been possible to provide full details of
items; where this is the case, a general category of
"Selections" follows the work or works in question, giving as
much information regarding the performers as can be gained
without having actual sight of (or the opportunity to listen to)
the item. A further problem for the discographer is that, in
some early discographies at least, works in a light vein were not
always considered sufficiently "serious" to merit inclusion. I
have attempted to overcome this problem by consulting dealers'
catalogues wherever possible. Moreover, it has not always been
possible to give full details of performers where a large number
of different artists appear in a compilation album; as a result,
there are a few places in the discography where performers' names
have not been included.
Entries are laid out alphabetically by title of composition and
excerpt. Each entry has a unique number, followed by record
numbers, performers, and date of issue where known.

NOTES

1. Pierre Lalo, in a five-page typescript <u>Grandes
artistes d'autrefois et d'aujourd'hui</u> (Bibliothèque
Nationale, Paris, Département de la Musique, <u>4°Vm Pièce 368</u>),
later included in his book <u>De Rameau à Ravel: portraits et
souvenirs</u>, says of Messager's performance of <u>Parsifal</u> that

> Sous sa direction, Parsifal, sans rien perdre de sa
> grandeur, prit une clarté française, une sobriété, une
> noblesse, un ordre, en accord avec le caractère par lequel
> il se distingue de tous les drames wagnériens, et que les
> plus célèbres chefs de Bayreuth ne lui ont toujours donné.

> [Under his direction, <u>Parsifal</u>, without losing any of its
> grandeur, assumed a French clarity, and a sobriety,
> nobility and order that are in accordance with the
> character of the piece, and distinguish it from all
> Wagner's other music dramas. Even the most famous Bayreuth
> conductors have not always been able to do this.]

2. Bibliothèque Nationale, Paris, Département de la Musique,
<u>lettre autographe</u> 49 (14 August 1918).

L'AMOUR MASQUÉ

Air du Maharadjah ("Chant Birman"; Lalla vabim ostogenine) (Act 2, no.11)

[D1] IDEAL 13436 Louis Lynel; orch. dir. G. Briez   AL

Couplets du charme (Il est un pouvoir dont le temps) (Act 2, no.13)

[D2] DOMINION B20 Rose Carday   1929
[D3] GRAMOPHONE DB5114 Yvonne Printemps Recorded 7 March 1941
[D4] VEGA V30M791 Jany Sylvaire; orch. dir. R. Cariven   1958
[D5] VSM FDLP1088 Yvonne Printemps   1959
[D6] VEGA 30BM15010   1962
[D7] VEGA MT10186 Jany Sylvaire; orch. dir. R. Cariven 1965
[D8] VSM C-064-12869 Yvonne Printemps   1975
[D9] EMI C154-14343/5*(3 discs) Yvonne Printemps
                (Issued 1976)   Recorded 1929

Depuis l'histoire de la pomme (Act 2, no.7)

[D10] GRAMOPHONE DB5114 Yvonne Printemps Recorded 7 March 1941
[D11] VSM FDLP1088 Yvonne Printemps   1959
[D12] VSM C-064-12869 Yvonne Printemps   1975
[D13] EMI C154-14343/5*(3 discs)Yvonne Printemps
                (Issued 1976)   Recorded 1929

J'ai deux amants (Act 1, no.2)

[D14] GRAMOPHONE E543/P826 Yvonne Printemps   1929
[D15] GRAMOPHONE DB5114 Yvonne Printemps Recorded 7 March 1941
[D16] VEGA V30M791* Jany Sylvaire; orch. dir. R. Cariven 1958
[D17] VEGA V30P0889* Jany Sylvaire; orch. dir. R. Cariven 1962
[D18] VSM 17096* (also issued as GRAMOPHONE 7ERF-17096)
                Yvonne Printemps   1962
[D19] VEGA 13002 Jany Sylvaire   1966
[D20] PLAISIR MUSICAL 30320 Yvonne Printemps   1966
[D21] PATHÉ OP3320 Yvonne Printemps   1972
[D22] DECCA 7108 Régine Crespin   1972
[D23] DECCA 99028 Jany Sylvaire; orch. dir. R. Cariven   1972
[D24] VSM C-051-12092 Yvonne Printemps   1975
[D25] VSM C-064-12869 Yvonne Printemps   1975
[D26] EMI C154-14343/5*(3 discs) Yvonne Printemps   1976
[D27] DECCA 417 337-4DA (tape) Régine Crespin   1987

[D28] VICTOR 4182 Yvonne Printemps   [s.d.]

Je m'étais juré qu'à vingt ans

[D29] GRAMOPHONE DB5114 Yvonne Printemps   Recorded March 1941
[D30] VSM FDLP 1088 Yvonne Printemps   1959
[D31] VSM C-064-12869 Yvonne Printemps   1975
[D32] EMI C154-14343/5*(3 discs)Yvonne Printemps
                (Issued 1976)   Recorded 1929

Viens s'il est vrai

[D33] GRAMOPHONE 7ERF-17096* Yvonne Printemps, Sacha
                Guitry   1962
[D34] PLAISIR MUSICAL 30320 Yvonne Printemps, Sacha
                Guitry   1966
[D35] EMI C154-14343/5*(3 discs)Yvonne Printemps
                (Issued 1976)   Recorded 1929

Vingt ans

[D36] VEGA V30M791* Jany Sylvaire; orch. dir. R. Cariven   1958

[D37] VSM 30BM15010* Jany Sylvaire; orch. dir. R. Cariven 1962
[D38] VEGA MT10186 Jany Sylvaire; orch. dir. R. Cariven   1965

Selections

[D39] VEGA V30M706* Aimé Doniat, Jany Sylvaire; orch.
                and chorus dir. M. Cariven   1957
[D40] VEGA V45P1908 Aimé Doniat, Jany Sylvaire; orch.
                and chorus dir. M. Cariven   1958
[D41] PATHÉ STX120* Marthe Altéry; orch. dir. J. Metehen   1958
[D42] VEGA 13001   Aimé Doniat, Jany Sylvaire; orch. dir.
                M. Cariven   1968
[D43] DECCA 115016 Recorded by artists at the Palais Royal
                on the occasion of a revival of
                L'amour masqué in 1970. Extracts
                issued on DECCA 461204A and
                461205A (1971)   1970
[D44] DECCA 115320/1 (2 discs) Jany Sylvaire, Régine
                Crespin, et al.   1977

ARIOSO

[D45] PATHÉ SAPHIR 381* Albert Vaguet   [s.d.]

LA BASOCHE

A ton amour simple et sincère (Act 3, no.18)

[D46] GRAMOPHONE G and T32656 Gabriel Soulacroix   1902
[D47] GRAMOPHONE GC4*   "M. Tirmont, ténor de
                    l'Opéra-Comique"
                    [The copy of this disc in the
                    Phonothèque Nationale is claimed
                    to be the only surviving example:
                    matrices 32268/9]   [s.d.]
[D48] ODEON 188844 Roger Bourdin; orch. dir. G. Cloez   AL
[D49] POLYDOR 524040 André Gaudin; orch. dir. A. Wolff   AL
[D50] POLYDOR 561016 André Gaudin; orch. dir. A. Wolff   AL
[D51] COLUMBIA DF1188 Pierre Deldi; orch. dir. E. Bigot   AL
[D52] ODÉON 188702 Miguel Villabella; orch. dir. G. Cloez   AL,
                                                            WERM
[D53] ODÉON XOC134 Miguel Villabella; orch. dir. G. Cloez   1959

Air de Marie (Mon escorte? Mes gens?) (Act 1, no.5)

[D54] COLUMBIA D19066   Georgette Simon; orch. dir.
                    Clemandh   AL

Eh, que ne parliez vous (Act 2, no.12)

[D55] PATHÉ DTX341 Michel Dens (stereo version numbered
                    ASTX341)   1967
[D56] VSMC-181-12544/5 (2 discs) Michel Dens   1985

Elle m'aime (Act 3, no.16)

[D57] BLACK ZONOPHONE 2011   Lucien Fugère   1902
[D58] ODÉON 188588 Etienne Billot; orch. dir. G. Cloez   AL
[D59] GRAMOPHONE P757 Emile Rousseau   [s.d.]
[D60] COLUMBIA D13045 Lucien Fugère; orch. dir. Élie
                    Cohen   AL,
                                                            WERM

[D61] DECCA FAT173819 Louis Musy   NSA
                                                               WERM
[D62] DECCA 215819 Louis Musy   NSA
                                                               WERM
[D63] ODÉON ORX504* Fernand Francell; Orchestre de
                    l'Opéra-Comique   1962
[D64] DECCA 99041 Louis Musy   1972
[D65] DECCA 115320/1 (2 discs) Louis Musy   1977

En l'honneur de notre hymenée (Act 3, no.15)

  [D66] ODÉON 188659 Marie-Thérèse Gauley; orch. dir. G.
                     Cloez   AL

Jamais j'aurais dû le comprendre (Act 3, no.17)

  [D67] COLUMBIA D19066 Georgette Simon; orch. dir.
                       Clemandh   AL

Je suis aimé (Act 1, no.1)

  [D68] GRAMOPHONE GC4* "M. Tirmont, ténor de
                    l'Opéra-Comique" [The copy of
                    this disc in the Phonothèque
                    Nationale is claimed to be the
                    only surviving example: matrices
                    32268/9]   [s.d.]
  [D69] PATHÉ SAPHIR 571* Gabriel Soulacroix   [s.d.]
  [D70] POLYDOR 524040 André Gaudin; orch. dir. A. Wolff   AL
  [D71] POLYDOR 561016 André Gaudin; orch. dir. A. Wolff   AL
  [D72] COLUMBIA 17827D R. Bonelli; T. Paxson, piano   WERM

J'irai chez les oiseaux (Act 3, no.18)

  [D73] PATHÉ SAPHIR 571* Gabriel Soulacroix   [s.d.]
  [D74] ODÉON 188526 David Devriès   [s.d.]

Oui, de rimes je fais moisson (Act 1, no.1)

  [D75] ODÉON 188844 Roger Bourdin; orch. dir. G. Cloez   AL

Overture (Prélude)

[D76] ODÉON 165693 Odéon Orchestra   AL,
WERM

Passe-Pied (Entr'acte to Acts 2 and 3)

[D77] PATHÉ 8010* Orchestre Pathé-Frères
[With the "Rigodon" [sic] from
Rameau's Dardanus: matrix 6913]   [s.d.]
[D78] ODÉON 165693 Odéon Orchestra   AL,
WERM

Pourrais-je aimer une autre femme? (Act 2, no.10)

[D79] PATHÉ X91035 André Baugé, Lucienne Gros;
orch. dir. G. Andolfi   AL

Prière à St. Nicolas (Act 1, no.3)

[D80] ODÉON 188659 Marie-Thérèse Gauley; orch. dir. G.
Cloez   AL

Quand tu connaitras Colette (Act 1, no.2)

[D81] GRAMOPHONE P757   Emile Rousseau   [s.d.]
[D82] ODÉON 188702 Miguel Villabella; orch. dir. G.
Cloez   AL, WERM
[D83] ODÉON XOC134* Miguel Villabella; orch. dir. G.
Cloez   1959
[D84] ODÉON AOE 1037 Miguel Villabella; orch. dir. G.
Cloez   1959
[D85] ODÉON ORX503* Fernand Francell; Orchestre de
l'Opéra-Comique   1962

Si de la souveraineté (Act 1, no.7)

[D86] BLACK G. AND T. 34010 Jeanne Daffeyte,
Delvoye et al.   1903-4
[D87] COLUMBIA D14253 Louise Dhamarys, Georgette
Simon, et al.; orch. dir. Clemandh   AL

Trop lourd est le poids (Act 1, no.6)

    [D88] COLUMBIA D13045 Lucien Fugère; orch. dir.
                    Élie Cohen
                    [The copy of this disc in the
                    Phonothèque Nationale is claimed
                    to be the only surviving example]   AL,
                                                        WERM

Selections

    [D89] DECCA TW91125 Louis Musy; orch. dir. R. Benedetti   1956
    [D90] DECCA 173819 Louis Musy; orch. dir. R. Benedetti   1958
    [D91] PATHÉ DTX30199* Liliane Berton, Michel Dens,
                    et al.; Orchestre de l'Association
                    des Concerts Colonne, dir. J. Pernoo
                    [Stereo version issued as ASTX130001.
                    Also issued as PLAISIR MUSICAL 30199,
                    (stereo 130001)]   1962
    [D92] DECCA 99014 Orch. dir. R. Benedetti   1971

LE CHEVALIER D'HARMENTAL

Je suis la reine de la nuit (Act 1, scene 5)

    [D93] DECCA TW91125 Moizan   1956
    [D94] DECCA 115320/1 (2 discs) Moizan   1977

Selections

    [D95] DECCA 99014 Orch. dir. R. Benedetti   1971

COUPS DE ROULIS

Ce n'est pas la première fois

    [D96] GRAMOPHONE DA4952* Roger Bourdin; orch.
                        dir. L. Beydts   1943
    [D97] ODÉON 166533 Roger Bourdin; orch. dir. P. Minssart AL
    [D98] GRAMOPHONE L690 Robert Burnier   AL
    [D99] VEGA V30M791* Aimé Doniat; orch. dir. R. Cariven 1958
   [D100] BARCLAY 80066 Orch. dir. R. Lefèvre   1958
   [D101] VEGA V30P0875* Aimé Doniat; orch. dir. R. Cariven 1962
   [D102] VEGA MT10192 Aimé Doniat   1967
   [D103] VEGA 13015 Aimé Doniat; orch. dir. R. Cariven   1967

[D104] DECCA 99027 Aimé Doniat; orch. dir. R. Cariven   1972
[D105] DECCA 115320/1 (2 discs) Aimé Doniat;
                       orch. dir. R. Cariven   1977

C'est charmant, très parisien

[D106] POLYDOR 522337 Edmée Favart; orch. dir. F. Weiss   AL

Complets de Béatrice (Je suis le sécretaire)

[D107] GRAMOPHONE DA4951/3* (3 discs) orch.
                       dir. L. Beydts   Recorded 1943
[D108] ODÉON 166352 Edith Manet; orch. dir. P. Minssart   AL

Couplets de Sola Mirrhys

[D109] VEGA V30M791* Jany Sylvaire; orch. dir. R. Cariven 1958
[D110] VEGA 13002 Jany Sylvaire; orch. dir. R. Cariven   1966

Duo (C'est un coup du roulis)

[D111] GRAMOPHONE DA4953* Jacqueline Francell,
                       Roger Bourdin; orch. dir. L.
                       Beydts   Recorded 1943
[D112] ODÉON 166352 Edith Manet, Roger Bourdin;
                       orch. dir. P. Minssart   AL
[D113] COLUMBIA RF60 Germaine Feraldy, Le Clezio;
                       orch. dir. J. Jacquin   AL
[D114] CBS 62338 Paulette Merval, Marcel Merkès   1965

En amour il n'est pas de grade

[D115] ODÉON 166533 Roger Bourdin; orch. dir. P. Minssart AL
[D116] VEGA V30M751* A. Dassary; orch. dir. R. Cariven   1957
[D117] DECCA 6057 A. Dassary; orch. dir. R. Cariven   [s.d.]
[D118] BARCLAY 80066* orch. dir. R. Lefèvre   1958
[D119] BARCLAY 80096* Luc Barney   1959
[D120] VEGA 30BM15010*   1962
[D121] VEGA MT10186 [Reissued 1968 as VEGA LT13020]   1965
[D122] DECCA 115320/1 (2 discs) A. Dassary;
                       orch. dir. R. Cariven   1977

Les hommes sont bien tous les mêmes

[D123] COLUMBIA D19138 Marcelle Denya   WERM
[D124] POLYDOR 522337 Edmée Favart; orch. dir. F. Weiss   AL
[D125] GRAMOPHONE DA4951* Jacqueline Francell; orch. dir.
                        L. Beydts   AL
[D126] BARCLAY 80066* Dominique Tirmont; orch. dir. R.
                        Lefèvre   1958

Marche (Act 1)

[D127] GRAMOPHONE L690 Robert Burnier   AL
[D128] CBS 62338 Marcel Merkès   1965
[D129] DECCA 99031   1972

Pardonnez un moment d'emoi

[D130] CLUB NATIONALE DU DISQUE CND 1049/1052* (4 discs)
                        Robert Massard   [s.d.]

Qu'ai je donc?

[D131] CLUB NATIONALE DU DISQUE CND 1049/1052* (4 discs)
                        Liliane Berton, Robert Massard   [s.d.]

Quand on fait ça

[D132] GRAMOPHONE DA4953* Jacqueline Francell,
                        Arlette Guttinger; orch.
                        dir. L. Beydts   1943

Quand on n'a pas le pied marin

[D133] COLUMBIA D19140 Marcelle Denya, Nelson   WERM

La quarantaine

[D134] GRAMOPHONE DA4952* Roger Bourdin;
                        orch. dir. L. Beydts   1943

Rondeau

[D135] GRAMOPHONE DA4951/3* (3 discs)
             Orch. dir. L. Beydts   1943

Tous les deux me plaisent

[D136] GRAMOPHONE DA4951/3* (3 discs) Jacqueline
             Francell; orch. dir. L. Beydts   1943

Selections

[D137] ODÉON 166352 Orch. dir. V. Alix
             [An orchestral "Fantaisie";
             also listed in WERM as
             PARLOPHONE P85157]   AL
[D138] VEGA V45P1908 Aimé Doniat, Jany Sylvaire;
             orch. and chorus dir. M. Cariven   1958
[D139] PACIFIC LDP A234* Lena Dachary, Camille Maurane;
             orch. dir. A. Bernard   1959
[D140] VEGA V30P0894 Aimé Doniat, Jany Sylvaire;
             orch. dir. M. Cariven   1962
[D141] VEGA 30BM15015* Aimé Doniat, Jany Sylvaire, et al.   1962
[D142] CBS BR155010 Marcel Merkès, Paulette Merval   1963
[D143] VEGA 13001 Aimé Doniat, Jany Sylvaire;
             orch. dir. M. Cariven   1968
[D144] VEGA LT13026 A. Dassary   1969

DEBURAU

L'aboyeur marseillais des funambules

[D145] EMI C154-14343/5* (3 discs) Sacha Guitry

                                                         Issued 1976

Air ("On s'adore")

[D146] PATHÉ X0606 Yvonne Printemps

Conseils de Deburau à son fils

[D147] PHILIPS Réalités V19* Sacha Guitry   1959
[D148] EMI C154-14343/5* (3 discs) Sacha Guitry   Issued 1976

J'ai fuit pendant vingt ans les femmes

[D149] EMI C154-14343/5* Sacha Guitry   Issued 1976

Scène de l'interview

[D150] HMV D1705 Sacha Guitry   Recorded 1 July 1929
[D151] VSM FKLP7008 Yvonne Printemps, Sacha Guitry   1955
[D152] VSM "Les voix illustres" Yvonne Printemps,
              Sacha Guitry   1967
[D153] VSM FALP50040 Yvonne Printemps, Sacha Guitry   [s.d.]
[D154] PATHÉ X0606 Yvonne Printemps, Sacha Guitry   [s.d.]
[D155] EMI C154-14343/5* (3 discs) Yvonne Printemps,
              Sacha Guitry   1976

Suite funambulesque

[D156] POLYDOR 522028/9 (2 discs) Orch. dir. P. Godwin   AL,
                                                             WERM

LES DEUX PIGEONS

Danse hongroise

[D157] BARCLAY 80131* "Walberg et son grand orchestre"   1960

Suite

[D158] VOCALION K05107, K05114 Band of His Majesty's
              Life Guards   1923
[D159] PATHÉ 5162, 5175/6 Bande de la Garde Républicaine   1927
[D160] ACTUELLE 15131, 15155, 15159 Bande de la Garde
              Républicaine   1927
[D161] COLUMBIA 9647/8 (2 discs) Bande de la Garde
              Républicaine   1929
[D162] HMV L938/9 (2 discs) Orch. dir. E. Bervily   1933
[D163] PATHÉ PAT-PDT 135/8* (4 discs) Orchestre de
              l'Association des Concerts Colonne,
              dir. J. Fournet   1947
[D164] HMV C3778/9 (2 discs) Orchestra of the
              Royal Opera House, Covent Garden,
              dir. H. Rignold   1948
[D165] COLOMBIA D11020/1 (2 discs) Bande de la Garde
              Républicaine   AL
[D166] ODÉON 250001/2 (2 discs) Orch. dir. P. Minssart   AL,
                                                            WERM

[D167] PATHÉ SAPHIR 7113/5* (3 discs) [Artists not
named on records]   [s.d.]
[D168] DECCA LX3093* Orch. de l'Opéra-Comique,
dir. L. Blareau   1952
[D169] HMV Stereophonic Tape 1509 Orchestra of
the Royal Opera House, Covent
Garden, dir. C. Mackerras   1957
[D170] HMV CLP1195 Orchestra of the Royal Opera
House, Covent Garden, dir. C.
Mackerras   1958
[D171] HMV SXLP30022 Orchestra of the Royal Opera
House, Covent Garden, dir. C.
Mackerras   1958
[D172] PATHÉ DT25005 Orchestre du Théâtre National
de l'Opéra, dir. L. Fourestier   1958
[D173] DUCRETET-THOMSON 255C087* Orchestre du
Théâtre des Champs-Elysées, dir.
L. Fourestier   1959
[D174] PATHÉ ED17078 Orchestre du Théâtre National
de l'Opéra, dir. L. Fourestier   1959
[D175] TRIANON 4105 Orchestra of the Royal Opera
House, Covent Garden, dir. C.
Mackerras   1961
[D176] TRIANON TRX6167 Orchestra of the Royal Opera
House, Covent Garden, dir. C.
Mackerras   1967
[D177] VSMC-053-10017* Orchestre de Paris, dir. J-P.
Jacquillat   1970
[D178] ANGEL S36769 Orchestre de Paris, dir. J-P.
Jacquillat   1971
[D179] VSM C-151-12580/4 (5 discs) Orchestre de Paris,
dir. J-P. Jacquillat   1974
[D180] TRIANON CTRE6167 Orchestra of the Royal Opera
House, Covent Garden, dir. C.
Mackerras   1975
[D181] EMI/HMV ESD7048 Orchestre de Paris, dir. J-P.
Jacquillat   1977
[D182] DECCA CFP40298 Orchestra of the Royal Opera
House, Covent Garden, dir. C.
Mackerras   1979
[D183] EMI/HMV ESDW713 Orchestra of the Royal Opera
House, Covent Garden, dir. C.
Mackerras   1981
[D184] DECCA ASD 270038-1 Bournemouth Symphony Orchestra,
dir. J. Lanchbery [in his own
arrangement, and incorporating
some music from Véronique]   1984

[D185] CYBELIA CY815 Orchestre du Théâtre National
de l'Opéra, dir. Michel Quéval
[Compact disc]   1987

Valse

[D186] ULTRAPHON AP802 Association Symphonique
de Paris, dir. T. Mathieu   AL

Selections

[D187] PATHÉ 33DTX150 Orchestre du Théâtre National
de l'Opéra, dir. L. Fourestier   [s.d.]

LES DRAGONS DE L'IMPÉRATRICE

Selections

[D188] BLACK G. AND T. 33328/9 Juliette Simon-Girard   1903
[D189] GRAMOPHONE L841 Arr. and dir. E. Bervily   AL

LA FAUVETTE DU TEMPLE

Duo des chameliers (A travers le désert) (Act 3, no.22)

[D190] ODÉON ORX505 Ninon Vallin, Roger Bourdin   [s.d.]
[D191] PATHÉ X92002 Emma Luart, André Balbon; orch.
dir. G. Andolfi   AL,
WERM
[D192] DISCOPHILIA DIS 293 R. Heilbronner, P. Parzan   NSA
WERM
[D193] PACIFIC LDP A234* Lena Dachary, Camille Maurane   1959

Hélas! je ne dois pas entendre (Act 3, no.19)

[D194] BLACK G. AND T. 61077 Albert Piccaluga   1902

Le joli songe (Act 2, no.14)

[D195] PACIFIC LDP A234* Lena Dachary, Camille Maurane   1959
[D196] MODE CMD INT9361 Lena Dachary, Camille Maurane   1970

Selections

[D197] BLACK G. AND T. 33328/9 Juliette Simon-Girard   1903
[D198] ENOCH 8 Assoc. Symphonique de Paris, dir. F.
                Casadesus [Playing the "Fantaisie"
                on the work by Émile Tavan]   AL
[D199] ULTRAPHON AP805 Association Symphonique de
                Paris, dir. F. Casadesus [Playing
                the "Fantaisie" on the work by
                Émile Tavan]   AL
[D200] GRAMOPHONE L841 Orch. selection arr. and dir. E.
                Bervily   AL

LA FIANCEE EN LOTERIE

Boléro (Il est dans les nuits espagnoles) (Act 2, no.12)

[D201] DECCA TW91125 Colette Riedinger; orch.
                dir. R. Benedetti   1956
[D202] DECCA 115320/1 (2 discs) Colette Riedinger;
                orch. dir. R. Benedetti   1977

Selections

[D203] DECCA 99014 Orch. dir. R. Benedetti   1971

FORTUNIO

Complete recording

[D204] ERATO ECD 75390 (2 compact discs) Colette
                Alliot-Lugaz; Gilles Cachemaille,
                Francis Dudziak; Michel Trempont;
                Chorus and orchestra of the Opéra
                de Lyon, dir. John Eliot Gardiner   1988

"Air de Jacqueline"

[D205] ODÉON ORX113* Ninon Vallin; orch. dir. G. Cloez   1959

Air du chandelier (Ah, la singulière aventure) (Act 2, scene 2)

```
[D206] ODÉON 188541* Ninon Vallin, Roger Bourdin;
                     orch. dir. G. Cloez                   AL
[D207] ODÉON ORX503/5* (3 discs)                           1962
```

C'est un garçon de bonne mine (Act 2, scene 2)

```
[D208] GRAMOPHONE K6009 Emile Rousseau                     AL
[D209] ODÉON 188541* Ninon Vallin; orch. dir. G. Cloez     AL
```

J'aimais la vieille maison grise (Act 2, scene 5)

```
[D210] VOCALION (AEOLIAN COMPANY) L5021F* Henry Dangès;
                     Noel Gallon, piano
                     [The copy of this 80 rpm disc
                     in the Phonothèque Nationale is
                     claimed to be the only surviving
                     example. Recorded in London]         [s.d.]
[D211] GRAMOPHONE U45* "M. Marcelin, de
                     l'Opéra-Comique" [The copy of
                     this disc in the Phonothèque
                     Nationale is claimed to be the
                     only surviving example]              [s.d.]
[D212] PATHÉ 0456* Jean Marny [The copy of this
                     disc in the Phonothèque Nationale
                     is claimed to be the only
                     surviving example]                   [s.d.]
[D213] HMV B3154 Joseph Hislop [Sung in English as
                     "The Grey House"]                    1929
[D214] HMV DA946 John MacCormack; Edwin Schneider,
                     piano [Sung in French; re-issued
                     on VICTOR 1660, RUBINI GV523 and
                     PEARL/GEM M155/60 and GEM M274/5]    1929
[D215] COLUMBIA LF104* Georges Thill; orch. dir.
                     P. Chagnan [The copy of this disc
                     in the Phonothèque Nationale is
                     claimed to be the only surviving
                     example]                             1933
[D216] COLUMBIA LB10 Georges Thill; orch. dir. P. Chagnan 1933
[D217] GRAMOPHONE K7230 R. Buguet; orch. dir. E. Bervily  WERM
```

[D218] GRAMOPHONE P436* "M. Cazette, de l'Opéra-Comique"
      [Piano accompaniment. The copy of
      this disc in the Phonothèque
      Nationale is claimed to be the
      only surviving example. Reissued
      on RUBINI GV556/7 and CANTILENA
      6229]   [s.d.]
[D219] ODÉON 166804 Ninon Vallin; P. Darck, piano WERM
[D220] ODÉON 188521* Ninon Vallin; orch. dir. G. Cloez 1948
[D221] GRAMOPHONE K5945 Marcel Claudel AL,
      WERM
[D222] COLUMBIA D13056 Marcelle Denya; orch.dir. G. Truc AL
[D223] POLYDOR 561006 Raoul Gilles; orch. dir. A. Wolff AL
[D224] ODÉON 188603 Miguel Villabella; orch. dir.
      G. Cloez AL, WERM
[D225] ODÉON 188525 David Devriès; orch. dir. G. Cloez AL
[D226] COLUMBIA 33FH503* Georges Thill; orch. dir. P.
      Chagnan [1955?]
[D227] DECCA TW91125 Marcel Huylbrock; orch. dir. R.
      Benedetti 1956
[D228] DECCA 173819 Marcel Huylbrock 1958
[D229] PATHÉ DTX30159 Michel Dens; orch. dir. G. Tzipine 1958
[D230] COLUMBIA FC25039 Georges Thill; orch. dir. G. Cloez 1959
[D231] LUMEN 1-435 Irma Kolassi; Jacqueline Bonneau, piano 1959
[D232] DISCOPHILIA DIS303 L. Beyle [s.d.]
[D233] ODÉON ORX148* Ninon Vallin 1960
[D234] ODÉON AOE1039* Miguel Villabella; orch.
      dir. G. Cloez [s.d.]
[D235] VEGA 13015 Aimé Doniat 1967
[D236] VEGA V30D875 Aimé Doniat 1967
[D237] VEGA MT10192 Aimé Doniat 1967
[D238] VSM "Les voix illustres" 50041 Georges Thill 1968
[D239] PLAISIR MUSICAL 25039 Georges Thill 1968
[D240] CBS 62386 Marcel Merkès 1968
[D241] DECCA 99014 Marcel Huylbrock 1971
[D242] VSM C-053-12540 Michel Dens; orch. dir. G. Tzipine 1975
[D243] DECCA 115320/1 (2 discs) Marcel Huylbrock 1977
[D244] HMV HLM7183 Fernand Francell (Reissue of LYROPHON
      mx F3088) 1979
[D245] VSM C-061-12079M Georges Thill (Reissue of VSM
      50041) 1985

Je suis très tendre et très farouche (Act 1, scene 3)

[D246] ODÉON 188598 Miguel Villabella (Reissued on RUBINI
      GV547) AL

[D247] ODÉON ORX136* Miguel Villabella   (Reissued on RUBINI
             GV547)   1956
[D248] ODÉON ORX134 Miguel Villabella (Reissued on RUBINI
             GV547)   1959
[D249] RUBINI GV554 Albert Vaguet   [s.d.]
[D250] RUBINI GV556/7 De Creus
             [Originally issued by La Voix
             de Son Maître c.1910]   1981

Monsieur, je suis toute confuse (Act 1, scene 6)

[D251] PATHÉ DTX341 Liliane Berton (Issued in stereo
             on ASTX341)   1967
[D252] VSM C-181-12544/5 (2 discs) Liliane Berton   1985

Si vous croyez que je vais dire (Chanson de Fortunio) (Act 3,
scene 4)

[D253] COLUMBIA D13056 Marcelle Denya; orch. dir. G. Truc AL
[D254] ODÉON 188525 David Devriès; orch. dir. G. Cloez   AL,
                                                           WERM
[D255] POLYDOR 561006 Raoul Gilles; orch. dir. A. Wolff   AL
[D256] ODÉON 166444 Lucienne Radisse, cello; Nathalie
             Radisse, piano   AL
[D257] ULTRAPHON BP1565 Leila Ben Sedira; orch. dir. P.
             Devred   AL
[D258] GRAMOPHONE K5945 Marcel Claudel   AL,
                                                           WERM
[D259] ODÉON 188638 Miguel Villabella; orch. dir. G. Cloez AL
[D260] ODÉON ORX136* Miguel Villabella; orch. dir.G. Cloez 1956
[D261] VEGA V30M791* Aimé Doniat; orch. dir. R. Cariven   1958
[D262] ORPHEE 21050 Leila Ben Sedira   1964
[D263] VEGA 13015 Aimé Domiat   1967
[D264] VEGA MT10192 Aimé Doniat   1967
[D265] CLUB NATIONALE DU DISQUE CND 1049/1052* (4 discs)
             Michel Cadiou   [s.d.]
[D266] DECCA 115320/1 (2 discs) Aimé Doniat   1977
[D267] HMV HLM7183 Fernand Francell (Reissue of ODÉON
             mx XP4754)   1979
[D268] RUBINI GV556/7 De Creus [Originally issued by
             La Voix de Son Maître c.1910]   1981

Selections

[D269] VEGA V30M791 Lena Dachary, Jany Sylvaire,
          Willy Clément, et al.; orch.
          dir. R. Cariven   1958
[D270] ODÉON ORX503/5 (3 discs)   1960
[D271] PATHÉ DTX30197 Liliane Berton, Michel Dens,
          et al.; orch. dir. P. Dervaux
          [Issued in stereo as ASTX126:
          probably the first stereo issue of
          any of Messager's works]   1962
[D272] VEGA V30S875 Aimé Doniat; orch. dir. M. Cariven,
          J. Gressier   1962
[D273] EMI 2C 151 53332/6 (5 discs)   [197?]

FRANCOIS LES BAS-BLEUS

Il faut laisser toute espérance (Act 2, no.11)

[D274] RUBINI LV4 Gabriel Soulacroix   [s.d.]

Ronde (C'est François les bas-bleus) (Act 1, no.2)

[D275] GREEN ZONOPHONE X82692* Alexis Boyer
          [The copy of this disc in the
          Phonothèque Nationale is claimed
          to be the only surviving example]
          [c.1907]
[D276] PATHÉ X0713 René Gerbert   AL
[D277] COLUMBIA RF42 Georges Villier; orch. dir. A.
          Bernard   AL,WERM
[D278] DECCA TW91125 Massard; orch. dir. R. Benedetti   1956
[D279] DECCA 99014 Orch. dir. R. Benedetti   1971
[D280] DECCA 99025 Orch. dir. R. Benedetti   1972
[D281] DECCA 113520/1 (2 discs) Massard; orch. dir. R.
          Benedetti [Also issued on DECCA
          EFM455584]   1977

Selections

[D282] BLACK G. AND T. 3-32018 Gabriel Soulacroix
          [Title of recording not given]   1903-4
[D283] ENOCH 8 Association Symphonique de Paris, dir.
          F. Casadesus [Playing a "Fantaisie"
          on the work by Émile Tavan.]   AL

[D284] ULTRAPHON AP805   [s.d.]
[D285] ODÉON 238097 Orch. dir. P. Minssart   AL,
                                                              WERM

ISOLINE

Ah, ah, je suis jolie (Tableau 5, no.3)

[D286] GRAMOPHONE DA4830 Yvonne Brothier; orch.
                    dir. J. E. Szyfer   1933

Ballet (Tableau 8)

[D287] PATHÉ X96206/7 (2 discs) Orch. dir. Ruhlmann   WERM
[D288] GRAMOPHONE K5979/5980 (2 discs) Orch. dir.
                    Lauweryns   WERM
[D289] ODÉON 165961/2 (2 discs) Orch. dir. G. Cloez   WERM
[D290] DECCA 20103/4 (2 discs) Orch. dir. G. Cloez   WERM
[D291] COLUMBIA D11083/4 (2 discs) Musique de la Garde
                    Républicaine, dir. P. Dupont   AL
[D292] COLUMBIA DFX177 Orch. dir. J. E. Szyfer   AL
[D293] PATHÉ 45ED6* Orchestre de l'Association
                    des Concerts Lamoureux, dir.
                    L. Fourestier   1954
[D294] PATHÉ 33DTX150* Orchestre de l'Association
                    des Concerts Lamoureux, dir.
                    L. Fourestier   1954
[D295] PATHÉ DT25005 Orchestre de l'Association
                    des Concerts Lamoureux, dir.
                    L. Fourestier   1958
[D296] PATHÉ 33DTX150 Orchestre du Théâtre National
                    de l'Opéra, dir. L. Fourestier   [s.d.]
[D297] VSM C-053-10017* Orchestre de Paris, dir.
                    J-P. Jacquillat   1970
[D298] ANGEL S36789 Orchestre de Paris, dir
                    J-P. Jacquillat   1971
[D299] VSM C-151-12580/4 (5 discs) Orchestre de Paris,
                    dir. J-P. Jacquillat   1974

MADAME CHRYSANTHEME

Allons séparons-nous (Act 4, scene 7)

[D300] GRAMOPHONE U45* "M. Marcelin, de l'Opéra-Comique"
      [The copy of this disc in the
      Phonothèque Nationale is claimed
      to be the only surviving example]   [s.d.]

Ecoutez, c'est le chant des cigales (Act 3, scene 8)

[D301] BLACK G. AND T. 33529 Aino Ackté   1904-5
[D302] EMI 2C-069-73036 Mady Mesplé; Monte Carlo
      Philharmonic Orchestra, dir. P.
      Dervaux [Recorded 1980]   1983

Le jour sous le soleil béni (Act 3, scene 8)

[D303] COLUMBIA LFX167 Yoshito Miyakawa; orch. dir. Élie
      Cohen   AL

LE MARI DE LA REINE

Si j'avais vos légères ailes (Act 2, no.12)

[D304] ODÉON 36869/FONOTIPIA 39059 Aino Ackté   1905
[D305] ODÉON 56191 Lise Landouzy   1905-7
[D306] INTERNATIONAL RECORD COLLECTORS' CLUB IRCC 3104
      Aino Ackté   1953
[D307] COLUMBIA FCX727* Janine Micheau; orch. dir. P.
      Bonneau   1958
[D308] HMV HLM 7118/7129 (12 discs) Aino Ackté
      [Reissue of FONOTOPIA mx XPRI of 1905] 1977
[D309] HMV HLM 7252/7 (6 discs) Aino Ackté
      [Further reissue of FONOTOPIA mx XPRI] 1982

MESSE DES PECHEURS DE VILLERVILLE

[D310] HARMONIA MUNDI HMC 901292 Chapelle Royale,
           Petits Chanteurs de Saint Luois:
           Ensemble Musique Oblique; dir.
           Philippe Herreweghe [Compact disc]   1988

MIRETTE

Long ago in Alcala (Act 1, no.5)

[D311] BLACK G. AND T. 02050 Henry Lane Wilson   1904
[D312] COLUMBIA D213 George Platt   Recorded 1908
[D313] HOMOCHORD D1469 Franklin Kelsey; with piano   1930
[D314] HMV B8426 Roman Navarro   1936

MONSIEUR BEAUCAIRE

Air du rossignol (Act 2, no.13)

[D315] DECCA TW91125 Colette Riedinger   1956
[D316] VEGA MT10186   1965
[D317] VEGA LT13013   1967
[D318] PHILIPS 837473*   1970
[D319] DECCA 99014 Orch. dir. R. Benedetti   1971
[D320] PHILIPS 6747.064 (2 discs)   1975
[D321] DECCA 115320/1 (2 discs) Colette Riedinger   1977

Couplets de la rose

[D322] VEGA MT10186   1965
[D323] VEGA LT13013 Aimé Doniat   1967

Duo de la rose (Act 1, no.9)

[D324] SATURNE D601* Géori-Boué, Roger Bourdin;
                  Orch. Pasdeloup, dir. A. Wolff   1950
[D325] DECCA 99026   1972

English Maids

[D326] COLUMBIA DB695 Raymond Newell   1932
[D327] OPAL 817 Marion Green [Recorded 1919]   1983

Faut-il perdre tout espoir? (Act 2, no.14)

[D328] ODÉON MOE2141 Marcel Merkès   1958

Going to the ball

[D329] OPAL 817 [Recorded 1919]   1983

Honour and Love

[D330] PEARL/GEM 245 John MacCormack
                [Reissue of VICTOR mx B23756-1]   1982
[D331] OPAL 817 Marion Green [Recorded 1919]   1983

I do not know

[D332] EMI/HLM 7092 Maggie Teyte   Recorded 1919
[D333] OPAL 817 [Recorded 1919]   1983

I love you a little

[D334] OPAL 817 [Recorded 1919]   1983

Je ne le connais pas (Act 1, no.6)

[D335] EMI Selection du Reader's Digest*   1978

Lightly, lightly

[D336] EMI/HLM 7092 Maggie Teyte   Recorded 1919
[D337] HMV E182 Rosina Buckman, Fraser Gorge   [s.d.]
[D338] HMV B3430 A. Moxon, S. Robertson   WERM
[D339] OPAL 817 Maggie Teyte [Recorded 1919]   1983

Overture

[D340] PATHÉ PD89   Orchestre de l'Association
                    des Concerts Lamoureux,
                    dir. M. Cariven   AL

Philomel (Act 2, no.13)

[D341] EMI/HLM 7092 Maggie Teyte   Recorded 1919
[D342] PATHÉ PDT80 Fanély Revoil   WERM
[D343] HMVO3654 Rosina Buckman   [s.d.]
[D344] COLUMBIA DB633 Licette   [s.d.]
[D345] OPAL 817 Maggie Teyte [Recorded 1919]   1983

Pour faire une prisonnière (Act 1, no.5)

[D346] EMI Selection du Reader's Digest*   1978

Qu'est-ce qu'un nom? (Act 3, no.20)

[D347] ODÉON MOE2141* Marcel Merkès, Paulette Merval   1958
[D348] OPAL 817 Marion Green, Maggie Teyte, Princes
               Theatre Orchestra, dir. K. Russell
               [Recorded 1919]   1983

La rose rouge (Act 1, no.2)

[D349] PATHÉ X91016* André Baugé; orch. dir. G. Andolfi,
               [The copy of this disc in the
               Phonothèque Nationale is claimed
               to be the only surviving example]   c.1935
[D350] PATHÉ PG66 André Baugé   AL,
                                                               WERM
[D351] HMV SK104 Willy Clément   AL,
                                                               WERM
[D352] ODÉON 282557 Marcel Merkès   c.1953
[D353] PATHÉ ED3/4 (2 discs) Michel Dens; Orchestre
               de 1'Association des Concerts
               Lamoureux, dir. J. Gressier   1954
[D354] DECCA TW91125 Massard; orch. dir. R. Benedetti   1956
[D355] RCA 430125 André Baugé   1965
[D356] PATHÉ DTX341 Michel Dens(stereo version on ASTX341) 1967
[D357] PATHÉ OPTD50026 André Baugé; orch. dir.
               G. Andolfi   c.1968
[D358] VSM "Les voix illustres" 50026 André Baugé;
               orch. dir. G. Andolfi   1968
[D359] CBS S63520 Marcel Merkès   1970
[D360] DECCA 99014 Orch. dir. R. Benedetti   1971
[D361] DECCA 115320/1 (2 discs) Felix Clément   1977
[D362] OPAL 817 Marion Green [recorded 1919]   1983
[D363] VSM C-181-12544/5 (2 discs) Michel Dens   1985

Say no more

[D364] OPAL 817 [Recorded 1919]   1983

We are not speaking now

[D365] OPAL 817 [Recorded 1919]   1983

Selections

[D366] HMV C2443 The Light Opera Company (Sung in English) WERM
[D367] GRAMOPHONE L841 Selections arr. and dir. E. Bervily WERM
[D368] PATHÉ 33DTX150 Marthe Angelici, Liliane Berton,
              Michel Dens, et al.; Orchestre de
              l'Association des Concerts Lamoureux,
              dir. J. Gressier   [s.d.]
[D369] VEGA V30M791 Lena Dachary, Jany Sylvaire, Willy
              Clément, et al.; orch. dir. R. Cariven   1958
[D370] ODÉON FOC1019 Marcel Merkès   1960
[D371] VEGA V30Po894 Jany Sylvaire, Aimé Doniat; orch. dir.
              R. Cariven   1962
[D372] VEGA 30BM15010 Lena Dachary, Jany Sylvaire, Willy
              Clément, et al.; orch. dir. R. Cariven   1962
[D373] PLAISIR MUSICAL 30301 Liliane Berton, Camille
              Maurane; orch. dir. J. Gressier   1965
[D374] VEGA 13001 Jany Sylvaire, Aimé Doniat; orch.
              dir. R. Cariven   1968
[D375] PATHÉ OPTG3301 Liliane Berton, Camille Maurane;
              orch. dir. J. Gressier   1970
[D376] DECCA 99025   1972
[D377] EMI 2C 151 53332/6 (5 discs)   [197?]

PASSIONNÉMENT

Valse (Act 2, no.14)

[D378] RCA 430034 Bernard Alvi   1958
[D379] VEGA V30M791 Aimé Doniat   1958
[D380] VEGA 13015 Aimé Doniat   1967
[D381] VEGA MT10192 Aimé Doniat   1967
[D382] CBS 62396 Marcel Merkès   1968
[D383] DECCA 99014   1971

Vous avez comblé ma patronne (Act 3, no.16)

[D384] VEGA 13002 Jany Sylvaire   1966

Selections

[D385] COLUMBIA BF8/9 G. Feraldy   WERM
[D386] ULTRAPHON AP820/2 M. Berzia   WERM
[D387] VEGA V45P1901 Orch. dir. R. Cariven   1958
[D388] VEGA V451908 Orch. dir. R. Cariven   1958
[D389] PACIFIC LDP D234 Lena Dachary, Camille Maurane;
                          orch. dir. A. Bernard   1959
[D390] VEGA V30Po894 Jany Sylvaire, Aimé Doniat; orch.
                          dir. R. Cariven   1962
[D391] VEGA V30S875 Aimé Doniat; orch. dir. R. Cariven   1962
[D392] VEGA 13001 Orch. dir. R. Cariven   1968

LA PETITE FONCTIONNAIRE

Je regrette mon Pressigny

[D393] PATHÉ PP31 Fanély Revoil   1934-43
[D394] VSM C-053-10544M Fanély Revoil
                  [An anthology of recordings made
                  1934-1943]   1970

LES P'TITES MICHU

Blanche-Marie et Marie-Blanche (Act 1, no.2)

[D395] HMV 6059 Yvonne Brothier, G. Galland   WERM

This Little Girl and That (Act 1, no.11)

[D396] GRAMOPHONE GC3 Louis Bradfield
                  [Recorded in London, in English]   [s.d.]

Selections

[D397] GRAMOPHONE L841 [Orchestral selections arr.
                  and dir. E. Bervily.]   AL

[D398] PLAISIR MUSICAL 30301 Liliane Berton, Camille
              Maurane; orch. dir. J. Gressier
              [Also issued 1970 as PATHÉ OPTG3301]   1965
[D399] DECCA 99014 Orch. dir. R. Benedetti   1971
[D400] DECCA 99025   1972
[D401] EMI 2C 151 53332/6 (5 discs)   [197?]

SACHA

Air de Cercleux - la lettre

[D402] DECCA 115320/1 (2 discs) Louis Musy, Marcel
              Huylbrock; orch. dir. R. Benedetti
              [Previously issued as DECCA TW91125]   1977

SOLO DE CONCOURS POUR CLARINETTE ET PIANO

[D403] DECCA LX3129* Jacques Delecluse, clarinet;
                  Ulysse Delecluse, piano   1954
[D404] GRAMOPHONE C065-64959 W. Boeykens, clarinet; R.
                  Groslot, piano   [s.d.]
[D405] SIGNUM 008-00 W. Boeykens, clarinet; R. Groslot,
                  piano   [s.d.]
[D406] HMV 1A 065 64959 W. Boeykens, clarinet; R.
                  Groslot, piano   1982
[D407] PRO CIVITATE 010012 M. Mergny, clarinet   [s.d.]
[D408] FORLANE UM3539 Dangain, clarinet; Lerouge, piano 1985

SOUVENIRS DE BAYREUTH

[D409] GRAMOPHONE K5906 D. Herbrecht, L. Petitjean   AL,
                                                         WERM
[D410] FIORI MUSICALI STE60039 Geneviève Robin-Bonneau,
                  Jacqueline Joy   1967
[D411] WORLD RECORD CLUB ST999/1000 Geneviève
                  Robin-Bonneau, Jacqueline Joy   [s.d.]
[D412] ERATO STE60039* Geneviève Robin-Bonneau,
                  Jacqueline Joy (mono version
                  EFM42109)   [s.d.]
[D413] CASSIOPEE 369190 E. and. T. Heidsieck   1974
[D414] CONIFER/ARION ARN336025 Christian Ivaldi, Noël Lee 1980

[D415] CENTRE MUSICAL BöSENDORFER MAG2005 Danielle and
                      Marie Renault   1983
[D416] CONCERTO BAYREUTH CB13001 Bayreuth Festival
                      Orchestra (in orchestral arrangement) [s.d.]

VÉRONIQUE

Complete recordings

[D417] DECCA 163639/41 (3 discs) Géori-Boué, Marquet,
                      G. Moizan, Roger Bourdin,
                      de Rieux, Carpentier; orch. dir. P.
                      Dervaux [A recording made in 1953
                      by the Société Française du Son
                      to celebrate the centenary of
                      Messager's birth. Originally issued
                      under the number DECCA TW91093/4.
                      This recording was reissued later,
                      in whole or in part, under the
                      following numbers: DECCA 163630/1
                      (1968); DECCA ACL905 (1968); DECCA
                      SSL40225/6 (1971);   DECCA 115194/5
                      (1975); and DECCA 100109 (1975)
                      and IPG 115.194/5.]
[D418] EMI/PATHÉ 2-C-061-10176/7 (2 discs) Mady Mesplé,
                      Michel Dens, Guiot, D. Benoit,
                      J-C. Benoit; Orchestre de
                      l'Association des Concerts Lamoureux,
                      dir. J-C. Hartemann   1970

Separate numbers

Adieu je pars (Air de la lettre) (Act 2, no.16)

[D419] POLYDOR 521510* Robert Burnier; orch. dir.
                      J. Lenoir   c.1940
[D420] GRAMOPHONE SK104* Willy Clément; Orchestre de
                      l'Association des Concerts
                      Lamoureux, dir. M. Cariven   1949
[D421] ODÉON 188518 Roger Bourdin   WERM
[D422] GRAMOPHONE P685 Emile Rousseau   AL
[D423] GRAMOPHONE K7320 Robert Buguet; orch. dir. E.
                      Bervily   AL
[D424] PARLOPHONE 28541 Jean Vieuille; orch. dir. Frigara AL
[D425] COLUMBIA DF1188 Pierre Deldi; orch. dir. E. Bigot AL

[D426] DECCA FMT163716*   1957
[D427] VEGA V30S791* Orch. dir. R. Cariven   1958
[D428] ODÉON OS1175* Marcel Merkès   1958
[D429] VEGA 30BM15010   1962
[D430] VSM FDLP1088 Yvonne Printemps   1964
[D431] VEGA MT10186   1965
[D432] CLUB NATIONALE DU DISQUE CND1049/52* (4 discs)
                             Gabriel Bacquier   [s.d.]
[D433] TRIANON CTRY7136   1970
[D434] VSM C-064-10811-M Yvonne Printemps   1971
[D435] DECCA 99014 Orch. dir. R. Benedetti   1971
[D436] VSM C-064-12869 Yvonne Printemps   1975
[D437] DECCA 115320/1 (2 discs)   1977
[D438] HMV HLM7118/29 Jean Périer [with piano
                      accompaniment; originally
                      issued in 1905]   1977
[D439] EMI Selection du Reader's Digest* Michel Dens;
                      orch. dir. J.-C. Hartemann   1978
[D440] VEGA V30M791 Willy Clément; Orchestre
                      de l'Association des Concerts
                      Lamoureux, dir. M. Cariven   [s.d.]
[D441] VEGA 30Po388* Lucien Huberty; Orchestre
                      Pasdeloup, dir. J. Allain   [s.d.]
[D442] HMV HLM7252/7 Jean Périer [with piano
                      accompaniment; originally
                      issued in 1905]   1982
[D443] VSM C-057-12086 Michel Dens; Orchestre de
                      l'Association des Concerts
                      Lamoureux, dir. J. Gressier   1985

Air de la grisette

[D444] PATHÉ X2258 André Baugé   WERM
[D445] POLYDOR 521511 Robert Burnier; orch. dir. J. Lenoir AL

Allons à Romainville (Act 1, finale)

[D446] VEGA V30M791* Orch. dir. R. Cariven
                                                                     1958

C'est Estelle et Véronique (Act 1, finale)

[D447] GRAMOPHONE P343   [s.d.]
[D448] ODÉON 165531 Sim-Viva; orch. dir. A. Cadou   AL

[D449] DECCA M153 Danielle Brégis; L. Amato, piano   AL,
                                                       WERM
[D450] GRAMOPHONE DB5114 Yvonne Printemps   AL
[D451] GRAMOPHONE K7364 Fanély Revoil; orch. dir. E.
                  Bervily   AL
[D452] POLYDOR 521510* Lemichel du Roy; orch. dir. J.
                  Lenoir   AL
[D453] VSM FDLP1088 Yvonne Printemps   1964
[D454] VSM C-064-10811M Yvonne Printemps   1971
[D455] VSM C-064-12869 Yvonne Printemps   1975
[D456] EMI Selection du Reader's Digest* Mady Mesplé;
                  Orchestre de l'Association des
                  Concerts Lamoureux, dir. J-C.
                  Hartemann   1978
[D457] GRAMOPHONE C053-105104 Fanély Revoil; orch. dir.
                  E. Bervily   [s.d.]
[D458] GRAMOPHONE 2C-053-10151* Fanély Revoil; orch.
                  dir E. Bervily   [s.d.]
[D459] DECCA FMT163716*   [s.d.]

Chanson du Tourne-Bride

[D460] ZONOPHONE 83123* Tariol-Baugé
                  [The copy of this disc in the
                  Phonothèque Nationale is claimed to
                  be the only surviving example]   [s.d.]

La charmante promenade (Act 1, no.2)

[D461] DECCA FMT163716*   Géori-Boué, Mary Marquet   [s.d.]

Couplets d'entrée

[D462] COLUMBIA D12024 Louise Dhamarys; orch.
                  dir. M. Heurteur   AL,
                                                       WERM

Duetto de l'âne (De ci, de là: "Donkey Duet") (Act 2, no.11)

[D463] BLACK ZONOPHONE 1917   Streit, Melgaty   1902
[D464] PATHÉ 2557* Edmée Favart, Ponzio   [s.d.]

[D465] GRAMOPHONE P440* Yvonne Brothier, André Baugé;
       piano accompaniment
       [The copy of this disc in the
       Phonothèque Nationale is claimed
       to be the only surviving example]   [s.d.]
[D466] GRAMOPHONE L870 Marthe Coiffier, Emile Rousseau;
       orch. dir. G. Diot   [s.d.]
[D467] HMV B9870 Anne Ziegler, Webster Booth
       (sung in English)   WERM
[D468] PATHÉ PG67 Suzanne Laydeker, André Baugé;
       orch. dir. G. Andolfi   AL,
                                                  WERM
[D469] HMV B2939 W. Melville, D. Oldham (sung in English) WERM
[D470] DECCA M153 Danielle Brégis, Nicolas Amato AL,
                                                  WERM
[D471] ODÉON 188711* Emma Luart, Roger Bourdin; orch.
       dir. G. Cloez   AL
[D472] POLYDOR 521509 Lemichel du Roy, Robert Burnier;
       orch. dir. J. Lenoir   AL
[D473] SATURNE D603* Géori-Boué, Roger Bourdin   [s.d.]
[D474] DECCA EFM455593* Géori-Boué, Roger Bourdin [s.d.]
[D475] PATHÉ OPTD50026 Suzanne Laydeker, André Baugé;
       orch. dir. G. Andolfi   [s.d.]
[D476] DECCA TW91125 Géori-Boué, Roger Bourdin   1956
[D477] VEGA V30M791* Orch. dir. R. Cariven   1958
[D478] VSM FDLP1088 Yvonne Printemps, Jacques Jansen;
       orch. dir. M. Cariven   1959
[D479] VEGA V30Po873* Orch. dir. R. Cariven   1961
[D480] BARCLAY 80182* A.Grandjean, Luc Barney   1962
[D481] ODÉON OCE1034* Paulette Merval, Marcel Merkès 1963
[D482] CBS OCE1034   1965
[D483] RCA 430125 Ninon Vallin, André Baugé,   1965
[D484] BARCLAY 80205* Janine Hervé, Luc Barney   1966
[D485] VEGA 30Po388* Ninon Vallin, Lucien Huberty;
       Orchestre Pasdeloup, dir. J. Allain   [s.d.]
[D486] VEGA MT10187 [Later reissued as VEGA LT13019,
       and with extracts on SAP LDP5549]   1967
[D487] PATHÉ DTX341 Liliane Berton, Michel Dens
       [Also on stereo ASTX341]   1967
[D488] BARCLAY 80270 Orch. dir. M. Cariven [Stereo version
       BARCLAY BB91]   1969
[D489] CBS S63520 Paulette Merval, Marcel Merkès 1970
[D490] CLUB NATIONAL DU DISQUE CND1049/52* Micheline
       Dumas, Gabriel Bacquier   [s.d.]
[D491] PHILIPS 837473* Orch. dir. P. Bonneau   1970
[D492] TRIANON CTRY7136 Orch. dir. M. Cariven   1970
[D493] DECCA 99014 Orch. dir. R. Benedetti   1971

[D494] VSM C-064-10811M Yvonne Printemps, Jacques Jansen;
       orch. dir. M. Cariven   1971
[D495] DECCA 99026   1972
[D496] PHILIPS 6747.064 (2 discs)   1975
[D497] VSM C-064-12869 Yvonne Printemps, Jacques Jansen;
       orch. dir. M. Cariven   1975
[D498] DECCA 115320/1 (2 discs) Géori-Boué, Roger Bourdin 1977
[D499] PEARL SHE550 Sylvia Eaves, Robert Carpenter
       Turner; Kenneth Barclay, piano
       [sung in English]   Recorded May 1978
[D500] EMI Selection du Reader's Digest* Mady Mesplé,
       Michel Dens; orch. dir. J.-C.
       Hartemann   1978
[D501] FORUM 1008 Florence Raynal, Michel Trempont   1979
[D502] DECCA 99014* Géori-Boué, Roger Bourdin   [s.d.]
[D503] CHANDOS LBRD013 Madeleine Hill-Smith, P.
       Morrison; Chandos Concert Orchestra,
       dir. S. Barry [Sung in English. Also
       on Compact Disc CHANDOS CHAN8362]   1986

Duo de l'escarpolette (Swing Song) (Act 2, no.12)

[D504] BLACK ZONOPHONE 11392* Streit, Melgaty   1902
[D505] PATHÉ 2557* Edmée Favart, Ponzio   [s.d.]
[D506] GRAMOPHONE L870 Marthe Coiffier, Emile Rousseau;
       orch. dir. G. Diot   [s.d.]
[D507] RED VICTOR 89063 Emma Eames, de Gogorza   1911
[D508] HMV B9870 Anne Ziegler, Webster Booth
       [sung in English]   WERM
[D509] PATHÉ PG67 Suzanne Laydeker, André Baugé;
       orch. dir. G. Andolfi   AL,
                               WERM
[D510] HMV B2939 W. Melville, D. Oldham [sung in English] WERM
[D511] POLYDOR 516503 Lemichel du Roy, Robert Burnier;
       orch. dir. J. Lenoir   AL
[D512] COLUMBIA DF104/DF2491 Charpini, Brancato
       [piano accompaniment]   AL,
                               WERM
[D513] PARLOPHONE 28540 Flore George, Jean Vieuille;
       orch. dir. Frigara   AL
[D514] ODÉON 166386 Hélène Regelle, A. Roque;
       orch. dir. G. Cloez   AL
[D515] DECCA EFM455593* Géori-Boué, Roger Bourdin;
       orch. dir. P. Dervaux   [s.d.]
[D516] PATHÉ OPTD50026 Suzanne Laydeker, André Baugé;
       orch. dir. G. Andolfi   Recorded 1935
[D517] VEGA V30M791* Orch. dir. R. Cariven   1958

[D518] VSM FDLP1088 Yvonne Printemps, Jacques Jansen;
    orch. dir. M. Cariven   1959
[D519] GRAMOPHONE DB5114 Yvonne Printemps, Jacques
    Jansen; orch. dir. M. Cariven   [s.d.]
[D520] ODÉON 188710* Emma Luart, Roger Bourdin;
    orch. dir. G. Cloez   [s.d.]
[D521] VEGA V30Po873* Orch. dir. R. Cariven   1961
[D522] VEGA 30BM15015 Orch. dir. R. Cariven   1962
[D523] BARCLAY 80182* A. Grandjean, Luc Barney 1962
[D524] ODÉON OCE1034* Paulette Merval, Marcel Merkès 1963
[D525] RCA 430125 Ninon Vallin, André Baugé   1965
[D526] CBS OCE1034   1965
[D527] BARCLAY 80205* Janine Hervé, Luc Barney 1966
[D528] VEGA V30Po388* Ninon Vallin, Lucien Huberty;
    Orchestre Pasdeloup, dir. J. Allain [s.d.]
[D529] PATHÉ DTX341 Liliane Berton, Michel Dens
    [stereo version ASTX341]   1967
[D530] VEGA MT10187 [Later reissued as VEGA LT13019, and
    with extracts on SAP LDP5549]   1967
[D531] CLUB NATIONAL DU DISQUE CND1059/52* (4 discs)
    Micheline Dumas, Gabriel Bacquier [s.d.]
[D532] BARCLAY 80270 Orch. dir. M. Cariven [stereo
    version BARCLAY BB91]   1969
[D533] TRIANON CTRY7136   1970
[D534] PHILIPS 837473* Orch. dir. P. Bonneau   1970
[D535] VSM C-064-10811M Yvonne Printemps, Jacques Jansen 1971
[D536] DECCA 99014 Orch. dir. R. Benedetti   1971
[D537] DECCA 99026   1972
[D538] PHILIPS 6747.064 (2 discs)   1975
[D539] VSM C-064-12869 Yvonne Printemps, Jacques Jansen;
    orch. dir. M. Cariven   1975
[D540] DECCA 115320/2 (2 discs) Géori-Boué, Roger
    Bourdin; orch. dir. P. Dervaux   1977
[D541] EMI Selection du Reader's Digest* Mady Mesplé,
    Michel Dens   1978
[D542] FORUM 1008 Florence Raynal, Michel Trempont 1979
[D543] DECCA 99014* Géori-Boué, Roger Bourdin [s.d.]

Duo des Tuilleries

[D544] VEGA V30Po388* Ninon Vallin, Lucien Huberty;
    Orchestre Pasdeloup, dir. J. Allain [s.d.]

Eh bien, par ordre procédons

[D545] PARLOPHONE 28542 Flore George, Jean Vieuille;
                orch. dir. Frigara   AL
[D546] POLYDOR 521509 Lemichel du Roy, Robert Burnier;
                orch. dir. J. Lenoir   AL
[D547] DECCA 115320/1 (2 discs)   1977
[D548] EMI Selection du Reader's Digest* Mady Mesplé,
                Michel Dens; Orchestre de
                l'Association des Concerts
                Lamoureux, dir. J-C. Hartemann   1978

The Garden of Love (Like the bee to the garden of roses) (Act 3,
     no.17a)

[D549] GRAMOPHONE GC3551 Mabel Medrow [with piano
                accompaniment; Recorded in London]   [s.d.]

Une grisette mignonne

[D550] GRAMOPHONE P865 Emile Rousseau   AL
[D551] EMI Selection du Reader's Digest* Michel Dens;
                orch. dir. J.-C. Hartemann   1978

Ma foi, pour venir de province

[D552] DECCA LXT6126 Maggie Teyte   Recorded 1933
[D553] DECCA K993 Maggie Teyte   WERM
[D554] HMV K7364 Fanély Revoil   WERM
[D555] POLYDOR 521515 Lemichel du Roy; orch. dir. J.
                Lenoir   AL
[D556] DECCA ECLIPSE 830 Maggie Teyte   1979

Ouverture

[D557] PATHÉ PD89* Orchestre de l'Association des
                Concerts Lamoureux, dir. M. Cariven   WERM
[D558] PATHÉ X8706 Orch. dir. G. Andolfi   AL
[D559] ODÉON 165183 Odéon Orchestra   AL
[D560] DECCA 113757*   c.1957
[D561] DUCRETET-THOMSON 255C087* Orchestre des
                Champs-Elysées, dir. P. Bonneau   1958
[D562] DECCA 115767   1964
[D563] DECCA 99008   1971

[D564] PLEIADE P45158   [s.d.]

Partons pour Romainville (Act 1, finale)

[D565] EMI Selection du Reader's Digest*   1978

Petite dinde

[D566] DECCA LXT6126 Maggie Teyte   1947
[D567] DECCA K993 Maggie Teyte   Pre-1948
[D568] GRAMOPHONE K7364 Fanély Revoil; orch. dir. E.
                Bervily   AL
[D569] ODÉON 165510 Sim-Viva; orch. dir. M. Cariven   AL
[D570] DECCA FMT163716* Géori-Boué   1957
[D571] BARCLAY 80182* A. Grandjean   1962
[D572] DECCA ECLIPSE 830 Maggie Teyte   1979

Quand j'étais baron des merlettes

[D573] PATHÉ X91012 André Noel   WERM

Ronde

[D574] ZONOPHONE X83087* Tariol-Baugé
                [The copy of this disc in the
                Phonothèque Nationale is claimed to
                be the only surviving example]   [s.d.]

Voyons ma tante

[D575] ODÉON 165531 Sim-Viva; orch. dir. A. Cadou   AL
[D576] POLYDOR 521515 Lemichel du Roy; orch. dir. J.
                Lenoir   AL
[D577] DECCA FMT163716*   1957
[D578] ODÉON OCE1034* Paulette Merval   1963
[D579] EMI Selection du Reader's Digest* Mady Mesplé;
                Orchestre de l'Association
                des Concerts Lamoureux, dir.
                J-C. Hartemann   1978

Vrai dieu, mes bons amis (Act 1, no.4)

[D580] ODÉON 188552 Roger Bourdin; orch. dir. G. Cloez   AL,
                                                    WERM
[D581] POLYDOR 521511 Robert Burnier; orch. dir. J.
               Lenoir   AL
[D582] ODÉON OCE1034* Marcel Merkès   1963

Selections

[D583] VOCALION K05204 Band of His Majesty's Life Guards   1926
[D584] PARLOPHONE 22134 Orch. dir. V. Alix   AL,
                                                    WERM
[D585] DECCA K1770 Orch. dir. B. Howell   AL,
                                                    WERM
[D586] HMV C1684 Light Opera Company [Sung in English]   WERM
[D587] COLUMBIA DX303 Light Opera Company [Sung in
               English]   WERM
[D588] PARLOPHONE PR1344 Light Opera Company [Sung in
               English]   WERM
[D589] POLYDOR 27113 Orch. dir. Snaga   AL
[D590] GRAMOPHONE L841 Orch. selections arr. and
               dir. E. Bervily   AL
[D591] IDÉAL 12902 Marie-Louise Azema, Renée Legendre,
               Emile Rousseau; orch. dir. R.
               Guttinguer   AL
[D592] PLEAIDE P3075 Ninon Vallin, Lucien Huberty;
               Orchestre des Concerts Pasdeloup,
               dir. J. Allain   [s.d.]
[D593] PLEAIDE P45162 Ninon Vallin, Lucien Huberty;
               Orchestre des Concerts Pasdeloup,
               dir. J. Allain   [s.d.]
[D594] PATHÉ DTX125* Martha Angelici, Nadine Renaux,
               Camille Maurane, et al.; Orchestre
               de l'Association des Concerts
               Lamoureux, dir. J. Gressier
               [The copy of this disc in the
               Phonothèque Nationale is claimed to
               be the only surviving example]   [s.d.]
[D595] PATHÉ DTX138* Martha Angelici, Nadine Renaux,
               Camille Maurane, et al.; Orchestre
               de l'Association des Concerts
               Lamoureux, dir. J. Gressier   1958
[D596] BARCLAY 80066 Dominique Tirmont, Claude Hamyl,
               Michel Hamel; orch. dir. R. Lefèvre   1958

[D597] VEGA V30M791 Lena Dachary, Jany Sylvaire, Willy
             Clément, et al.; orch. dir. R. Cariven   1958
[D598] PATHÉ STX120 Marthe Altéry   1958
[D599] DECCA 153887* Géori-Boué, Roger Bourdin, de Rieux;
             orch. dir. P. Dervaux   1959
[D600] ODÉON OCE1010 Marcel Merkès, Roland Riffaud   1959
[D601] ODÉON FOC1019 Marcel Merkès   1960
[D602] PATHÉ 33DTX150 Marthe Angelici, Nadine Renaux,
             Camille Maurane, et. al.; Orchestre
             de l'Association des Concerts
             Lamoureux, dir. J. Gressier   [s.d.]
[D603] VEGA 30BM15015   1962
[D604] VEGA 30BM15010   1962
[D605] PLAISIR MUSICAL 30138 Orchestre de
             l'Association des Concerts
             Lamoureux, dir. J. Gressier   1964
[D606] DECCA 215716 Géori-Boué, G. Moizan, Roger Bourdin,
             et al.; orch. dir. P. Dervaux   1964
[D607] CBS XOC185* Paulette Merval, Marcel Merkès;
             orch. dir. J. Metehen [Stereo version
             issued on CBS63646 in 1971]   1965
[D608] DECCA 164167 Géori-Boué, G. Moizan, Roger Bourdin;
             orch. dir. P. Dervaux   1967
[D609] DECCA 99025 GUILDE INTERNATIONALE DU
             DISQUE SMS2228 Liliane Berton,
             Suzanne Auret, Remy Corazza;
             Orchestre des Concerts de Paris, dir.
             A. Gallois [Also issued in mono as
             MMS2228* in 1961]   1972
[D610] DECCA 99030   1972
[D611] EMI 2C 151 53332/6 (5 discs)   [197?]
[D612] VSM C-057-10841 Marthe Angelici, Camille Maurane;
             Orchestre de l'Association
             des Concerts Lamoureux, dir.
             J. Gressier   c.1980

Appendix I:
Alphabetical List of Works

A une fiancée [W68]
Aimons-nous [W77]
Amants éternels [W17]
Amour d'hiver [W79-84]
Amour masqué, L' [W33]
Arioso [W70]
Arpège [W53]
Aux pays bleu [W49]
Aventure de la Guimard, Une [W45]

Baisers, Les [W51]
Barcarolle [W107]
Basoche, La [W13]
Bateau rose, Le [W74]
Béarnaise, La [W7]
Béatrice [W28]
Bleuets, Les [W42]
Bon roi Dagobert, Le [W27]
Bourgeois de Calais, Le [W8]
Brigitte. See Véronique [W24]

Canto do Paris n'America, O [W67]
Caprice-polka, op.14 [W105]
Ce fut au temps du chrysanthème [W79]
Chameliers, Les [W93]
Chanson d'automne [W73]
Chanson de ma mie [W56]
Chanson des cerises [W64]
Chanson mélancolique [W65]
Chant d'amour [W72]
Chevalier aux fleurs, Le [W44]
Chevalier d'Harmental, Le [W20]
Colibri [W11]
Coups de roulis [W36]
Credo de la victoire, Le [W87]
Curly Locks [W78]
Cyprien, ôte ta main de là! [W31]

Dans les arbres blancs de givre [W62]
Deburau [W35]
Deux pigeons, Les [W41]

Don Juan et Haydée [W91]
Douce chanson [W75]
Dragons de l'impératrice, Les [W25]

Facteur rural, Le [W52]
Fantine. See François les bas-bleus [W3]
Fauvette du temple, La [W5]
Fête de la France, La [W86]
Fiancée en lotérie, La [W19]
Fleur d'oranger [W38]
Fleurs d'hiver [W69]
Fortunio [W26]
François les bas-bleus [W3]

Gavotte [W63]
Gisèle [W6]

Habanera, op.11 [W102]
Heart of Mine. See Douce chanson [W75]
Hélène [W14]
Hiver de cet an est si doux, L' [W84]

Idylle [W112]
Impressions orientales [W113]
Impromptu, op.10 [W101]
Isoline [W10]

Je porte sur moi ton image [W80]

Loreley [W95]
Love Eternal. See Notre amour est chose légère [W76]
Lune egrène en perles blondes, La [W61]

Madame Chrysanthème [W15]
Mai vient [W59]
Mari de la reine, Le [W12]
Mazurka (piano), op.13 [W104]
Mazurka (violin) [W108]
Mélodie [W47]
Menuet, op.12 [W103]
Messe des pêcheurs de Villerville [W92]
Mignons et vilains [W40]
Mimosa [W57]
Miousic [W29]
Mirette [W18]
Miss Dollar [W16]
Monsieur Beaucaire [W30]
Monsieur pressé, Un [W119]

Montagne enchantée, La [W21]
Morceau de concours...pour piano [W111]
Morceaux de lecture à vue [W114-118]

Neige rose [W66]
Ne souffre plus [W82]
Notre amour est chose légère [W76]
Nouveau printemps [W58-62]

Païens, Les [W1]
Paix de blanc vêtue, La [W88]
Pardon, messieurs, de troubler votre fête. See Rondeau [W2]
Passe-pied [W100]
Passionnément [W34]
Petit poucet, Le [W4]
Petite fonctionnaire, La [W32]
Piano pieces [W101-106]
Pieces for violin and piano [W107-109]
Pour la patrie [W85]
Premières armes de Louis XV, Les [W9]
Procès des roses, Le [W22]
Promethée enchainé [W90]
P'tites Michu, Les [W23]

Quand tu passes, ma bien-aimée [W83]
Que l'heure est vite passée [W81]

Regret d'avril [W55]
Reseau d'ombres emprisonné, Une [W60]
Rêverie [W46]
Ritournelle [W71]
Rondeau...chanté...dans "La Revue Pornographique" [W2]
Rosyllian [W48]

Sacha [W37]
Scaramouche [W43]
Se peut-il qu'une larme [W58]
Serenade [W109]
Soir à Montmartre [W120]
Solo de concours for clarinet and piano [W110]
Souvenir [W50]
Souvenirs de Bayreuth [W96]
Suite funambulesque [W35a]
Sur la mer [W54]
Symphony in A major [W94]

Trois valses pour piano à quatre mains [W97-99]

Va chercher quelques fleurs [W89]
Valse, op.15 [W106]
Véronique [W24]
Vins de France, Les [W39]

Zwei Könige, Die <u>See</u> La Basoche [W13]

Appendix II:
Programme of the Concert Given in
Messager's Memory at the Salle Gaveau,
24 February 1930

Première Partie

1. Trois Valses originales, 4 mains.
                Maurice Faure et Georges Truc

2. (a) Sérénade (Montjoyeux) (inédit)
   (b) Rosyllian (Tristan Klingsor)
   (c) Neige Rose (Armand Silvestre) (Enoch)
        Roger Bourdin

3. (a) Mimosa (A. Silvestre) (Enoch)
   (b) Arpège (A. Samain) (inédit)
   (c) Le bateau rose (J. Richepin) (Heugel)
        Yvonne Gall

4. Trois pièces pour violon (Eschig)
   (1) Serenade (2) Barcarolle (3) Mazurka
        Pierre Lepetit

5. Nouveau Printemps (G. Clerc) (Enoch)
        Roger Bourdin

Deuxième Partie

1. (a) La paix de blanc vêtue (Lahovary) (Senart)
   (b) Sur la mer (Cantilo) (inédit)
   (c) Viens cueillir quelques fleurs (Senart)
        Yvonne Gall

2. (a) Ritournelle (H. Gauthier-Villars) (Heugel)
   (b) Pour la patrie (V. Hugo) (Inédit)
   (c) Chant d'amour (A. Silvestre) (Jobert)
        Roger Bourdin

3. Fantaisie en forme de quadrille à 4 mains sur les
   motifs de la Tétralogie (en collaboration avec
   Gabriel Fauré)
                Maurice Faure et Georges Truc

4. Amours d'hiver (A. Silvestre) (Eschig)
        Yvonne Gall

5. Notre amour est chose legère (A. Silvestre) (Metzler,
    Londres)
        Yvonne Gall, Roger Bourdin

Appendix III:
Messager's Memoirs
(with English translation)

The following text is taken from L. Rohozinski, ed. <u>Cinquante ans de musique française: de 1874 à 1925</u>, Paris: Editions musicales de la librairie de France, 1925, 2: 395-398. A footnote explains that they have been edited by André Schaeffner, mainly from conversations with Messager himself; other details were drawn from Messager's autobiographical article in <u>Musica</u> of September 1908. The text here is given first in French, then in English translation (pp.161-164).

On ne relèverait parmi mes ascendants aucun musicien. J'appris, très jeune, le piano. Mais, plus tard, mon désir de devenir compositeur se heurta à bien des oppositions de la part de mon père. Enfin, par suite d'un revers de fortune, je pus réaliser ce désir et j'entrai à l'École Niedermeyer, où je fis toutes mes études musicales. Eugène Gigout y fut mon professeur de piano et Clément Loret mon professeur d'orgue. Je quittai l'école en 1874 pour remplir successivement les fonctions d'organiste du choeur à Saint-Sulpice, puis celles d'organiste du grand orgue à Saint-Paul-Saint-Louis (1881), enfin celles de maître de chapelle à Sainte-Marie des Batignolles, jusqu'en 1884. A ma sortie de l'école Niedermeyer je perfectionnai mon instruction musicale en travaillant la fugue, la composition et l'orchestration avec Camille Saint-Saëns - qui, contrairement à ce qu'on a maintes fois prétendu - ne fit à cette école qu'une très courte apparition. C'est d'ailleurs par l'entremise généreuse de Saint-Saëns que j'eus en 1885, la commande pour l'Opéra d'un ballet, les <u>Deux Pigeons</u>.
　　Mais déjà j'avais fait mes débuts comme compositeur, avec une <u>Symphonie</u>, très classique, en quatre parties, couronnée en 1876 par la Société des compositeurs et applaudie chez Colonne en 1878, la même année qu'un ballet aux Folies-Bergères, la <u>Fleur d'Oranger</u>, qui eut un très gros succès et qui fut suivi, sur la même scène, par deux autres ballets, les <u>Vins de France</u> et <u>Mignons et Vilains</u> (1879). Puis viennent différents opéras-comiques <u>François les Bas-Bleus</u> que Bernicat avait laissé inachevé (1883), la <u>Fauvette du Temple</u> et la <u>Béarnaise</u> (1885).
　　Outre Saint-Saëns, je connaissais à cette époque César Franck, tout le groupe de ses élèves et de mes confrères à la Société Nationale de musique, Chabrier, (alors expéditionnaire au Ministère de l'Intérieur) Vincent d'Indy, Duparc, Camille Benoît, Gabriel Fauré (avec qui je vivais comme un véritable frère), etc.
　　Beaucoup plus tôt j'avais connu Charles Gounod, qui fut la

camarade de collège de mon père. Il m'en imposait beaucoup.
J'eus d'ailleurs l'occasion de diriger le <u>Médecin malgré lui</u>,
qu'il avait écrit d'après l'arrangement assez lourd de la pièce
de Molière par Barbier et Carré. Gounod était très cultivé,
aussi bien musicalement que littérairement. Il ne faut pas
oublier à cet égard qu'il avait commencé par entrer au séminaire.
Alors que j'étais organiste à Saint-Sulpice, je me souviens
parfaitement d'avoir entendu diverses oeuvres religieuses (un <u>O
Salutaris</u>, un <u>Ave Maria</u>, etc.) attribuées à un <u>Abbé Gounod, des
Missions étrangères</u>. Il avait du reste toujours conservé un
certain fond de religiosité.

Quant à l'Abbé Liszt, je n'eus l'occasion de le rencontrer
qu'une seule fois, à Bruxelles, lors d'une grande réception en
son honneur. Franz Servais (qui passait à juste titre pour son
fils) venait d'organiser un festival Liszt à Anvers et une
exécution de la <u>Faust-Symphonie</u> à Bruxelles. Au cours de cette
réception Liszt joua avec Joseph Servais la <u>Sonate</u> pour
violoncelle de Chopin, puis tint l'un des deux pianos dans une
transcription de la <u>Danse macabre</u> de Saint-Saëns et finit par une
improvisation fort longue et ennuyeuse. - Liszt mourut l'été
suivant. C'est en arrivant à Bayreuth que j'appris sa mort
survenue la vieille [sic] même.

Je connus beaucoup César Franck. Nous étions du même comité
de la Société Nationale, et, à ce titre déjà, nous nous y
rencontrions toutes les semaines. Sa musique était alors fort peu
jouée ou très froidement accueillie. Mais il avait tellement
pris l'habitude de se retirer en lui-même qu'il ne s'apercevait
absolument de rien. Et pourtant ce fut une grosse blessure pour
lui lorsque Lamoureux, aux concerts de la Porte-Saint-Martin
(dont les programmes ne changeaient que tous les quinze jours)
crut devoir ne pas afficher une seconde fois les <u>Eolides</u>.

Je rencontrais Chabrier presque tous les jours, vers cinq
heures, chez Enoch (le père). Vincent d'Indy y venait aussi
quelquefois. Chabrier était d'une drôlerie impayable. Ce qui ne
l'empêcha pourtant pas de demander expressivement à Mendès le
livret de <u>Gwendoline</u>! Il avait le travail très longue et fort
difficile. Je pus m'en rendre compte en assistant à la
composition du <u>Roi malgré lui</u> qui avait d'abord été écrit en
opérette pour les Folies-Dramatiques, puis transformé en opéra-
comique - mais d'ailleurs sans beaucoup de changement dans le
livret (tiré d'une vieille pièce de M. et Mme Ancelot d'après les
indications de Victorin Joncières). Au bout de la 3^e
représentation, cette oeuvre faillit disparaître dans l'incendie
du 25 mai 1887. - Le gros succès était pour Chabrier quelques
années auparavant, avec <u>España</u>. Je ne sais quel fut le sort des
autres thèmes espagnols recueillis par lui lors de son voyage de
1882 et qu'il n'avait pas utilisés dans <u>España</u>: tout cela a-t-il
été détruit?

Comme élève de Saint-Saëns, et par suite de l'inimitié qui existait entre lui et Massenet, j'eus d'abord peu de contact avec ce dernier; pourtant l'échec de son Bacchus nous rapprocha. Massenet était un professeur admirable: chacun l'a déjà dit. Très érudit, en même temps que fort éclectique, il se tenait au courant des moindres nouveautés musicales. Il pouvait agacer par une certaine amabilité de convention, par une certaine flagornerie même; mais on s'apercevait assez vite que cela était tout de surface. Il avait tellement peur d'être oublié! Comme Saint-Saëns d'ailleurs, qui souffrait exactement de la même maladie! La colère de Saint-Saëns contre Massenet venait de ce qu'il retrouvait toujours ce "sacré bougre" dans ses jambes. Sur le tard, le caractère de Saint-Saëns était devenu des plus difficiles. Dans sa ridicule campagne contre Wagner l'artiste parlait contre sa conscience: ne m'avait-il pas fait lui-même initié à la musique de Wagner?...

Je ne connus Claude Debussy que quelques années avant Pelléas. La première oeuvre que j'entendis de lui fut la Demoiselle élue, alors que je n'avais pas encore eu l'occasion de le rencontrer. C'est grâce à l'éditeur Hartmann, l'un des librettistes de Madame Chrysanthème, que nous pûmes nous connaître. Hartmann avait ouvert en 1871 une boutique où se vendait du Paladilhe, du Massenet, etc.; même lorsqu'il ferma sa boutique, il continua de s'intéresser à certains jeunes musiciens - dont Debussy, qu'il soutint généreusement.

Du reste il ne faudrait pas croire que Debussy dût languir longtemps après le succès. Lorsque j'eus l'occasion de participer aux concerts symphoniques organisés au théâtre du Vaudeville par un Allemand (peut-être naturalisé Français), mari d'Yvette Guilbert, je dirigeai le Prélude à l'après-midi d'un faune, et le succès y fut tel que je dus bisser l'oeuvre.

Mais longtemps j'ignorai que Debussy fit la musique de Pelléas. A peine le sus-je que j'allai en entendre d'importants fragments chez lui, rue Gustave Doré. Lorsque l'époque des répétitions fut arrivée, Debussy donna chez lui une audition inoubliable de son oeuvre. Il avait une voix de basse, un peu rocailleuse, et chantait presque tout à l'octave inférieure, mais avec une telle émotion et un tel feu que tous les interprètes, même s'ils n'y comprenaient pas grand'chose, furent profondement saisis. Les études d'orchestre furent les plus difficiles de toutes: il y eut vingt-deux répétitions - longues, laborieuses, d'autant plus que le matériel d'orchestre, copié par un camarade de Debussy (comme lui dans la misère), était bourré de fautes. Quoique divisé en deux campes (les debussystes et les anti-debussystes), l'orchestre fit toujours preuve d'excellent volonté. Jamais peut-être on n'a rejoué Pelléas depuis dans d'aussi bonnes conditions.

Quant à Ravel, la première oeuvre que j'entendis de lui fut

le premier mouvement de son <u>Quatuor</u> présenté comme exercice
d'examen semestrial au Conservatoire.

Après les <u>Deux Pigeons</u> qui remportèrent un gros succès
(1886) je donnai successivement le <u>Bourgeois de Calais</u> (1887),
<u>Isoline</u> (1888), le <u>Mari de la reine</u> (1889) qui passa inaperçu aux
Bouffes, puis quelques mois plus tard (1890) à l'Opéra-Comique,
la <u>Basoche</u>. Puis suivirent un ballet-pantomime, <u>Scaramouche</u>,
représenté pour l'inauguration du Nouveau-Théâtre (1891), <u>Miss
Dollar</u> (1893) sur la même scène, <u>Madame Chrysanthème</u> (1893) à
l'Opéra-Comique, la <u>Fiancée en lotérie</u> aux Folies-Dramatiques
(1896) et presque en même temps, le <u>Chevalier d'Harmental</u> qui
tomba lamentablement à l'Opéra-Comique. Je fus tellement
découragé par cet insuccès que je ne voulus plus écrire du tout
et je tentai de me retirer en Angleterre, où j'avais d'ailleurs
fait représenter, en 1894, <u>Mirette</u>, opéra-comique écrit pour le
Savoy-Théâtre de Londres, en collaboration avec ma femme, alors
au sommet de sa réputation comme compositeur de lieder (sous le
nom de <u>Hope Temple</u>). C'est là que je reçus, un beau jour, un
rouleau flairant le manuscrit et que je mis de côté sans vouloir
l'ouvrir tout d'abord. C'était le livret des <u>P'tites Michu</u>. La
gaîté du sujet me séduisit et, renonçant à mes idées noires, je
me mis à écrire avec un tel entrain qu'en trois mois l'ouvrage
était terminé et joué la même années [sic] (1877) [i.e. 1897] aux
Bouffes avec un énorme succès. J'ai su depuis que ce livret
avait été refusé par deux ou trois compositeurs! <u>Véronique</u> lui
succéda au même théâtre en 1898.

Je n'ai jamais songé à écrire ce qu'on entend de nos jours
par <u>opérette</u>. Ce terme - qui contient trop souvent quelque chose
de péjoratif - semble s'être répandu à partir de Lecocq.
Beaucoup de mes oeuvres - et encore tout dernièrement <u>Monsieur
Beaucaire</u> - ne se sont intitulées opérettes que sur la demande
des directeurs de théâtre qui y voyaient je ne sais quelle chance
supplémentaire de succès. Je n'ai pas voulu non plus composer
des opéras-bouffes dont le meilleur type est fourni par les
oeuvres d'Offenbach où l'élément parodique reste très
prépondérant. Mon idée fut toujours de poursuivre la tradition
de l'opéra-comique français (avec dialogues), telle qu'elle se
continue à travers Dalayrac, Boieldieu, Auber. Malheureusement
je connus des conditions beaucoup moins favorables que celles où
se trouvèrent ces musiciens. Nous disposions de moins bons
chanteurs, d'orchestres de qualité beaucoup moindre et de fort
mauvais choeurs. Quand il s'agissait de demander à un alto
d'aller au-dessus du <u>ré</u>, à un violoncelle de jouer en <u>solo</u>, il
semblait qu'on exigeât des choses imposible [sic]. Quant aux
contrebassistes, c'étaient de purs ménétriers. Mais ce qui
devait beaucoup nous servir par la suite, ce fut la propagation
des sociétés de concerts symphoniques.

You would not find any musicians among my ancestors. When very young I learnt the piano; but later on, my intentions to become a composer met with much opposition from my father. Finally, because of a change in our fortunes, I was able to realise my ambition, and entered the École Niedermeyer, where I had all my musical studies. Eugène Gigout was my piano professor there, and Clément Loret my organ teacher. I left the school in 1874 to take up the post of organiste du choeur at Saint-Sulpice, went on to be organist at Saint-Paul--Saint-Louis (1881) and finally became maître de chapelle at Sainte-Marie des Batignolles (until 1884). On my departure from the École Niedermeyer I rounded off my musical studies by working at fugue, composition and orchestration with Camille Saint-Saëns, who, contrary to what has many times been suggested, spent only a very short time at the school. It was, furthermore, by the generous intervention of Saint-Saëns that I received the commission for the ballet Les deux pigeons from the Opéra in 1885.

However, I had already made my début as a composer with a symphony in four movements, very classical in style, which was awarded a prize by the Société des Compositeurs in 1876. It was applauded at one of Colonne's concerts in 1878, the same year as my ballet Fleur d'oranger, which had a great success at the Folies-Bergère and was followed on the same stage by two other ballets, Vins de France and Mignons et vilains (1879). Then came various opéras-comiques: François les bas-bleus, which Bernicat had left unfinished (1883), La fauvette du temple and La béarnaise (1885).

Besides Saint-Saëns, I also knew César Franck at this time, and all of his pupils, also my colleagues at the Société Nationale de Musique: Chabrier (then in the administration of the Ministry of the Interior), Vincent d'Indy, Duparc, Camille Benoît, Gabriel Fauré (with whom I lived as with a brother) etc.

Much earlier I had known Charles Gounod, who had been a contemporary of my father at college. He impressed me very much. I also had the chance to conduct Le médecin malgré lui, which he had written to the rather stodgy libretto by Barbier and Carré, from Molière's libretto. Gounod was very cultivated, both in music and literature. In this connection we should not forget that he had begun his career by entering a seminary. When I was organist at Saint-Sulpice, I well remember having heard various sacred pieces (an O salutaris, an Ave Maria, etc.) attributed to Abbé Gounod, foreign missionary. He always retained a certain air of religiosity.

As for the Abbé Liszt, I had the opportunity to meet him only once, in Brussels, during a grand reception in his honour. Franz Servais (who passed, with just cause, for his son) had organised a Liszt Festival in Antwerp, and a performance of the Faust-Symphony in Brussels. During the course of the reception

Liszt accompanied Joseph Servais in Chopin's cello sonata, then
played one of two pianos in a transcription of Saint-Saëns' Danse
macabre; he finished with a very long and tedious improvisation.
Liszt died the next Summer; it was on arrival at Bayreuth that I
heard of his death the evening before.

I knew César Franck well. We were on the same committee at
the Société Nationale, and in this capacity met every week. His
music was at that time little played, or coldly received; but he
had got so used to withdrawing into himself that he really
noticed nothing of this. Even so, he was very wounded when
Lamoureux, at the Porte-Saint-Martin concerts (where the
programmes changed only once a fortnight) saw fit not to perform
Les Éolides a second time.

I met Chabrier almost every day around 5 p.m. at Enoch's
(senior). Vincent d'Indy also came there sometimes. Chabrier
was really priceless. This did not, however, prevent him from
asking Mendès for the libretto of Gwendoline! He worked long and
hard: I can testify to that, having been present during the
composition of Le roi malgré lui, which was originally written as
an operetta for the Folies-Dramatiques, and was then transformed
into an opéra-comique, though without much change in the libretto
(drawn from an old piece of M. and Mme Ancelot, according to
Victorin Joncières). After its third performance the work was to
disappear in the fire of 25 May 1887. Chabrier's great success
had been with España some years before. I don't know what
happened to the other Spanish melodies he collected during his
trip there in 1882 which were not used in España: have they all
been destroyed?...

As a pupil of Saint-Saëns, and because of the enmity which
existed between him and Massenet, I initially had little contact
with the latter; however, the failure of his Bacchus brought us
together. Massenet was an excellent teacher: everyone has always
said so. Very learned, but at the same time very eclectic, he
kept abreast of the slightest musical novelties. His stiff
politeness, which one could almost have called fawning, could be
irritating; but one soon saw that this was all on the surface ...
He was so frightened of being forgotten, like Saint-Saëns, who
suffered exactly the same fear! Saint-Saëns' enmity towards
Massenet resulted from what he always called the "holy fellow" in
his legs. Later on, Saint-Saëns' character became more and more
difficult. In his ridiculous campaign against Wagner, the artist
spoke contrary to his own instincts: was it not he who had
introduced me to Wagner's music?

I only got to know Claude Debussy a few years before
Pelléas. The first of his compositions I heard was La demoiselle
élue, at which time I did not have the opportunity to meet him.
It was thanks to Hartmann, the publisher and one of the
librettists of Madame Chrysanthème, that we were able to get

acquainted. Hartmann had opened a music shop in 1871, and sold
the works of Paladilhe, Massenet, etc. there; even when he had
closed the shop down, he continued to take an interest in some
young musicians, including Debussy, to whom he gave generous
support.

But you must not think that Debussy had to wait long for
success. When I took part in some symphonic concerts at the
Vaudeville, organised by a German (or perhaps a naturalised
Frenchman) the husband of Yvette Guilbert, I conducted the
Prélude à l'après-midi d'un faune, which was so successful that I
had to conduct an encore.

Even so, for a long time I did not know that Debussy was
writing the music for Pelléas. I had only just found this out
when I went to hear significant portions of it at his home on the
rue Gustave Doré. When the time for rehearsals came, Debussy
gave an unforgettable performance of the work at his home. He
had a bass voice, a little harsh, and sang almost everything at
the lower octave, but with such emotion and verve that all the
performers, even if they understood little of it, were profoundly
moved. The orchestral rehearsals were the most difficult of all:
there were 22 rehearsals - long and laborious, the more so
because the orchestral parts, copied by one of Debussy's friends
(and, like him, poverty-stricken), were crammed with errors.
Although divided into two camps (the Debussy-ists and non-
Debussy-ists) the orchestra did everything with great goodwill.
Pelléas has, perhaps, never been performed since under such
excellent conditions.

As for Ravel, the first work of his that I heard was the
first movement of his Quartet, which he offered as an end of term
examination exercise at the Conservatoire.

After Les deux pigeons (1886), which had a great success, I
produced in succession Le bourgeois de Calais (1887), Isoline
(1888), Le mari de la reine (1889), which passed unnoticed at the
Bouffes[-Parisiens], then several months later (1890) La Basoche
at the Opéra-Comique. There followed a ballet-pantomine,
Scaramouche, produced for the opening of the Nouveau-Théâtre
(1891), Miss Dollar (1893) on the same stage, Madame Chrysanthème
(1893) at the Opéra-Comique, La fiancée en lotérie at the Folies-
Dramatiques (1896) and, almost at the same time, Le chevalier
d'Harmental, which was a disastrous flop at the Opéra-Comique. I
was so discouraged by this failure that I no longer wished to
write at all, and tried to retire to England, where I had already
presented, in 1894, Mirette, an opéra comique written for the
Savoy Theatre in London in collaboration with my wife, at that
time at the peak of her fame as a composer of lieder (under the
pseudonym Hope Temple). It was there that I received, one fine
day, a cylinder smelling of manuscript, which I put to one side
without at first wishing to open it. It was the libretto of Les

p'tites Michu. I was attracted by the gaiety of its subject, and putting aside my dark thoughts, I set to work with such enthusiasm that the work was completed in three months, and performed the same year (1877) [i.e. 1897] at the Bouffes, with great success. I have since found out that the libretto had been turned down by two or three composers! Véronique followed at the same theatre in 1898.

I have never intended to write what is nowadays called operetta. This designation - which all too often has pejorative overtones - seems to have become common since the work of Lecocq. Many of my works - including the latest of them, Monsieur Beaucaire - were only called operettas at the request of theatre directors who saw in that term some extra chance of success. Neither did I wish to compose opéra-bouffes, the best examples of which were provided by the works of Offenbach, where the element of parody is very dominant. My idea was always to continue the tradition of the French opéra-comique (with dialogue) as established by Dalayrac, Boieldieu and Auber. Unfortunately I came up against less favourable conditions than were enjoyed by those musicians. We had worse singers, orchestras of a much inferior quality and some very bad choruses. When it was a question of asking an alto to sing above D, or a cello to play a solo, it would seem that one was asking the impossible. As for double-bass players, they were like amateur fiddlers. What was to be of great service to us later, however, was the growth of concert societies offering symphonic repertoire.

André Messager

Index

Clemandh, M., [D54], [D67], [D87]
Clément, Felix, [D361]
Clément, Willy, [D269], [D351], [D369], [D372], [D420],
    [D440], [D597]
Clerc, Camille, 7, [W96], [B49]
Clerc, Georges, 6, [W58-62], [W90], 155
Clerc, Marie, 8, [W40]
Clerget, Paul, [W43]
Cloez, Gustave, [D48], [D52], [D53], [D58], [D66], [D75], [D80],
    [D82], [D83], [D84], [D205], [D206], [D209], [D220], [D224],
    [D225], [D230], [D234], [D254], [D259], [D260], [D289],
    [D290], [D471], [D514], [D520]
Clouet, Edith, 11, 19
Clouet, Jenny, 12, [W104]
Clough, F.F., 113
Coates, John, [W18]
Cohen, Élie, [D60], [D88], [D303]
Coiffier, Marthe, [D466], [D506]
Colette, pseud., [W96]
Cologne, 8
Colonne, Edouard, 4, 16, [W94]
Combarnous, Victor, 18
Comoedia, [W30], [W32], [W33], [W34], [M10], [M12], [M14], [M17]
Coolus, Romain, 26
Coquelin, M., [W14]
Corazza, Remy, [D609]
Corneau, M., [W17]
Cortot, Alfred, 26, 42
Costallat, publisher, 7, 9, 10, [W96]
Coudert, A.M., [W23]
Crespin, Régine, [D22], [D27], [D44]
Cuming, G.J., 113
Cunningham, Robert, [W30]
Curzon, Henri de, 89

Dachary, Lena, [D139], [D193], [D195], [D196], [D269],
    [D369], [D372], [D389], [D597]
Daffeyte, Jeanne, [D86]
Daily Telegraph, The, [W85]
Dalayrac, Nicolas-Marie, 160, 164
Danbé, Jules, 17, [W13], [W20]
Dandelot, Arthur, 41
Dangain, M., [D408]
Dangès, Henry, [D210]
Darck, P., [D219]
Darcourt, Juliette, [W8]
Darmant, Pierre, [W33]

Gabriel-Marie, M., [W10], [W14]
Gailhard, M., performer, [W12]
Gailhard, Pierre G. ("Pedro"), 35, [A7]
Galerne, Maurice, 3, 32, [M18]
Gall, Yvonne, [W28], [W53], [W54], [A1], 155, 156
Galland, G., [D395]
Gallois, A., [D609]
Gallois, Germaine, [W10], [W25]
Gallon, Noel, [D210]
Ganne, Louis, [W43]
Ganne, Thérèse, 18
Gänzl, Kurt, 21, 39, 41
Garden, Mary, 22, 38, [A6]
Gardiner, John Eliot, [D204]
Gaspari, M., [W6]
Gaubert, Philippe, 28, [A6], 88
Gaudin, André, [D49], [D50], [D70], [D71]
Gauley, Marie-Thérèse, [D66], [D80]
Gaulois, Le, 17, 28, 37, [W30], [W33], [W100], [A2], 89
Gauthier, Edouard, 41
Gauthier, M., [W21]
Gauthier-Villars, Henry [pseud. Willy], 36, [W71],
        [W96], [W136], 155
Gavoty, Bernard, 39
Gédalge, André, [M2]
Genée, Adeline, [W23]
Geneva, 26
Gentili, Ettore, [W13]
George, Flore, [D513], [D545]
Géori-Boué, Mlle, [D324], [D417], [D461], [D473], [D474], [D476],
        [D498], [D502], [D515], [D540], [D543], [D570], [D599],
        [D606], [D608]
Géoris, M., [W34]
Gerbault, M., [W17]
Gerbert, René, [D276]
Gheusi, P.B., [W27], [A1]
Gigout, Eugène, 4, 5, 157, 161
Gil Blas, [W15]
Gilbert, W. S., 18
Gilles, Raoul, [D223], [D255]
Girard, Victor, 114
Glazunov, Alexandre, 16
Gluck, Christoph Willibald, 22
Gobin, M., [W5], [W8]
Godard, Benjamin, [W119]
Godfrey, Arthur E., 35, [W5]
Godfrey, C., [W5]
Gordon, Kitty, [W24]

About the Author

JOHN WAGSTAFF is Music Librarian of the Oxford University Music Faculty Library, Oxford University. A specialist in French music, he is presently working on matters of musical historiography.